D1706276

The Agony of Spanish Liberalism

Also by Francisco J. Romero Salvadó:

TWENTIETH CENTURY SPAIN: Politics and Society, 1898–1998

SPAIN 1914–1918: Between War and Revolution

THE SPANISH CIVIL WAR: Origins, Course and Outcomes

THE FOUNDATIONS OF CIVIL WAR: Revolution, Social Conflict and Reaction in Liberal Spain, 1916–1923

Books by Angel Smith:

ANARCHISM, REVOLUTION AND REACTION: Catalan Labour and the Crisis of the Spanish State, 1898–1923

HISTORICAL DICTIONARY OF SPAIN

(ed. with Clare Mar-Molinero), NATIONALISM AND THE NATION IN THE IBERIAN PENINSULA: Competing and Conflicting Identities

(ed. with Emma Dávila-Cox), THE CRISIS OF 1898: Colonial

Redistribution and Nationalist Mobilisation

(ed. with Stefan Berger), NATIONALISM, LABOUR AND ETHNICITY, 1870–1939

(ed.), RED BARCELONA. SOCIAL PROTEST AND LABOUR MOBILIZATION IN THE TWENTIETH CENTURY

The Agony of Spanish Liberalism

From Revolution to Dictatorship 1913–23

Edited by

Francisco J. Romero Salvadó
Senior Lecturer, Department of Hispanic,
Portuguese and Latin American Studies,
University of Bristol, UK

and

Angel Smith
Reader in Modern Spanish History,
Department of Spanish, Portuguese and
Latin American Studies
University of Leeds, UK

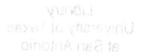

First published 2010 by
PALGRAVE MACMILLAN

Palgrave Macmillan in the UK is an imprint of Macmillan Publishers Limited,
registered in England, company number 785998, of Houndmills, Basingstoke,
Hampshire RG21 6XS.

Palgrave Macmillan in the US is a division of St Martin's Press LLC,
175 Fifth Avenue, New York, NY 10010.

Palgrave Macmillan is the global academic imprint of the above companies
and has companies and representatives throughout the world.

Palgrave® and Macmillan® are registered trademarks in the United States,
the United Kingdom, Europe and other countries.

ISBN: 978-0-230-55424-5 hardback

This book is printed on paper suitable for recycling and made from fully
managed and sustained forest sources. Logging, pulping and manufacturing
processes are expected to conform to the environmental regulations of the
country of origin.

A catalogue record for this book is available from the British Library.

Library of Congress Cataloging-in-Publication Data

The agony of Spanish liberalism : from revolution to dictatorship
1913–23 / edited by Francisco Jos Romero Salvado, Angel Smith.
p. cm.
Summary: "An exploration of the causes of the growing schism within
Spanish society between 1914–1923, and the political polarisation and social
violence that culminated in the Spanish Civil War. Essays analyse the crisis
and eventual downfall of Spain's elitist liberal order and its replacement by
an authoritarian dictatorship" – Provided by publisher.
ISBN 978-0-230-55424-5 (hardback)
1. Spain – Politics and government – 1886–1931. 2. Liberalism – Spain –
History – 20th century. I. Romero Salvadó, Francisco J., 1960– II. Smith,
Angel, 1958–

DP247.A576 2010
946'.074—dc22   2010002712

10 9 8 7 6 5 4 3 2 1
19 18 17 16 15 14 13 12 11 10

Printed and bound in Great Britain by
CPI Antony Rowe, Chippenham and Eastbourne

Contents

Figures and Tables

Figures

Tables

Contributors

Sebastian Balfour is Emeritus Professor of Contemporary Spanish Studies in the Department of Government of the London School of Economics and Political Science. He has published extensively on contemporary Spain. His books include *Dictatorship, Workers and the City. Labour in Greater Barcelona since 1939* (1989); *The End of the Spanish Empire 1898–1923* (1997); *Deadly Embrace. Morocco and the Road to the Spanish Civil War* (2002); (with Alejandro Quiroga), *The Reinvention of Spain. Nation and Identity since Democracy* (2007) – all of which were published in editions in Spanish. He has edited two books: (with Paul Preston), *Spain and the Great Powers in the Twentieth Century* (1999) and *The Politics of Contemporary Spain* (2005). He has also published numerous chapters and articles on contemporary Spain in edited books, academic journals and newspapers in both Britain and Spain. His latest book is an extensively revised and expanded third edition of his *Castro: A Profile in Power* (2009).

Francisco Cobo Romero is a Professor in Contemporary Spanish History at the Universidad of Granada. He is an expert on the field of agrarian politics in Spain and Europe during the first three decades of the 20th century. Recently, his research has focused on the social basis of early Francoism. His publications include: *Conflicto rural y violencia política* (1998); *De Campesinos a Electores* (2003); *Revolución campesina y contrarrevolución franquista en Andalucía* (2004); (co-authored with Teresa María Ortega López), *Franquismo y posguerra en Andalucía Oriental* (2005); and *Por la Reforma Agraria hacia la Revolución. El sindicalismo agrario socialista durante la II República y la Guerra Civil* (2007).

Chris Ealham teaches History at Saint Louis University in Madrid and is Honorary Research Fellow at Lancaster University. He is a specialist in the Spanish workers' movement, and his publications include *Class, Conflict and Culture in Barcelona, 1898–1937* (2004) and (edited with Mike Richards), *The Splintering of Spain: Cultural History and the Spanish Civil War* (2005). He is currently writing a book on the role of intellectuals within the Spanish anarchist and anarcho-syndicalist movements.

Pablo La Porte obtained his PhD from the University Complutense of Madrid in 1997. Following a period as visiting fellow at the London

School of Economics, he is currently lecturing in Spanish history at Heriot Watt University (Edinburgh). His research focuses on problems of perception and misperception in international politics. An expert on Spain's colonial war in Morocco, his recent publications include 'Marruecos y la crisis de la Restauración, 1917–1923', *Ayer Revista de Historia Contemporánea*, and 'Civil-Military Relations in the Spanish Protectorate in Morocco: The Road to the Spanish Civil War, 1912–1936', *Armed Forces and Society*.

Javier Moreno Luzón is Professor in Contemporary Spanish History at the Universidad Complutense de Madrid. He has been a visiting scholar at the London School of Economics and Political Science, the École des Hautes Études en Sciences Sociales, Tufts University, and the Minda de Gunzburg Center for European Studies of Harvard University. He is the author of several articles, numerous chapters, and books on political clientelism, monarchy, liberalism, parliamentarian elites, and parties in Restoration Spain (1875–1923). His current research involves Spanish nationalism and the nation-building process in the early 20th century.

Alejandro Quiroga is Reader in Spanish History at the University of Newcastle. His research interests include nationalism, conservative political thought, and ethnic conflict. He is the author of *Los orígenes del Nacionalcatolicismo* (2006), *Making Spaniards: Primo the Rivera and the Nationalization of the Masses, 1923–1930* (2007) and (with Sebastian Balfour), *The Reinvention of Spain* (2007).

Francisco J. Romero Salvadó is Senior Lecturer in Modern Spanish History at the University of Bristol. He has written extensively on the transition from elite to mass politics, the post-First World War crisis of the Liberal Monarchy, popular protest and praetorian intervention in political society. His recent publications include *The Spanish Civil War: Origins, Course and Outcomes* (2005) and *Foundations of the Civil War. Revolution, Social Conflict and Reaction in Spain, 1916–1923* (2008).

Angel Smith is Reader in Modern Spanish History at the University of Leeds. He works above all in areas of Spanish labour and social history and national identities and nationalisms in Spain. His most recent works are *Anarchism, Revolution and Reaction: Catalan Labour and the Crisis of the Spanish State, 1898–1923* (2007), and *A Historical Dictionary of Spain*, 2nd edition (2009). At present he is writing a book on the origins and rise of Catalan nationalism.

1
The Agony of Spanish Liberalism and the Origins of Dictatorship: A European Framework

Francisco J. Romero Salvadó and Angel Smith

Introduction

This book analyses the organic crisis of Spain's liberal order that culminated with the establishment of a military dictatorship headed by General Miguel Primo de Rivera in September 1923.[1] The decay of liberal politics in Spain is approached as a regional variant of the general crisis that engulfed most traditional (*fin de siècle*) European regimes in the aftermath of the First World War. At the root of this crisis was the fact that these regimes had taken only limited steps towards democratization. Before 1914, all ruling orders, even autocratic Russia, had introduced a modicum of civil liberties, embraced parliamentarian practices and replaced the feudal system with capitalist forms of production. In some, relatively free elections took place and ministers were to an important degree accountable to parliament. However, elements of the *ancien régime* still permeated Europe's political societies. At their apex, the heads of state (in most cases crowned sovereigns) ruled over extended courts and at the very least retained significant constitutional powers. In fact, armies were still the monarch's Praetorian Guard rather than a national institution. The upper houses of parliament were bulwarks of vested interests while a series of devices – ranging from limits to the franchise to giving disproportionate weight to rural areas, and, in southern Europe above all, sheer ballot-rigging – limited the power of lower chambers. This encouraged demands for democratic and even revolutionary change.[2]

The outbreak of the First World War proved a watershed. Its awesome socio-economic and human impact saw the rise of mass politics and the accelerated breakdown of hierarchical and clientelist-based governments.

Thus the armistice of November 1918 put an end to the armed conflict but gave way to a period of unprecedented social strife and political radicalism that umbilically tied the two world wars in what some scholars have named 'the Thirty Years' War of the twentieth century'; a European civil war that included the dawning era of Fascism and Communism and whose last and fiercest battle before the outbreak of the Second World War was the fratricidal conflict that broke out in Spain in July 1936.[3]

Growing social and political polarization produced revolutionary upheaval followed by the retreat of liberal-constitutional regimes throughout Europe and their replacement by various forms of dictatorial rule. In 1920, 26 out of Europe's 28 states were liberal parliamentary regimes, but by 1938 16 of them had succumbed to dictatorships. Only four remained by 1940.[4]

The fall of liberal regimes came in two distinct waves; the first in the aftermath of the First World War, hastened by the economic and social strains of war and social and national conflict; the second followed on from the 1929 Great Depression, which played a significant role in the rise to power of Germany's Nazi Party in 1933. It is on the origins of the Primo de Rivera coup during the 'first wave' of authoritarian takeovers that the chapters in this volume focus. In this introduction we will provide background information on the roots of the polarization of culture and society and the wellsprings of reactionary ideology in Spain. Furthermore, we aim to put events in Spain into their broader European context. When analyzing the failure of Spain's own revolution of 1917 particular attention will be paid to events in Russia, both in order to understand the greatly differing outcomes and also to chart the impact of the February and October revolutions in Russia on the social and political climate in Spain. Comparisons with other Western European countries also help explain why, while much of the continent faced a number of common problems, Spain was particularly vulnerable to an authoritarian takeover, despite not having entered the First World War. Furthermore, by contrasting events with those of Italy, a country which, both socially and politically, was quite similar to Spain, the reasons behind the differing paths taken by the counter-revolutionary assault on liberalism (with Benito Mussolini coming to power in Italy in 1922 and General Miguel Primo de Rivera in Spain in 1923) becomes clearer.

Liberalism and the Restoration regime, 1875–98

In Spain, the transition from the *ancien régime* to liberalism was accomplished in the 1830s. In a fierce civil war, urban liberal elites, backed by sectors of the army, crushed the absolutists or Carlists and laid the framework for the final dismantlement of the old order, including the disentailment of the land and the expropriation of ecclesiastical property.[5] Nevertheless, in a number of respects, compared to the more robust parliamentary regimes in Great Britain, France and even to late-comers such as Germany and Italy, serious shortcomings could be discerned in the construction of the new liberal nation-state.

Spain introduced universal manhood suffrage relatively early, in 1890. Only France, Germany, Switzerland and Denmark had previously taken this step (though, as noted, these states retained 'safeguards' which put a break on democratic politics).[6] Yet universal male suffrage in Spain made little difference to the political system. The meagre number of anti-dynastic MPs returned to parliament was an anomaly in the European context.[7] This was largely due to the fact that despite significant economic progress, by the turn of the century, it was still a relatively backward country in which two-thirds of its population continued to be engaged in the primary sector and with rates of illiteracy at 56 per cent.[8] This helps explain why, as Javier Moreno Luzón shows (Chapter 2, this volume), the façade of electoral politics hid a process of horse-trading between local bigwigs or *caciques* and the political elite. Two dynastic parties, the Conservatives and Liberals, monopolized power and rotated in office (the so-called *turno pacífico*), with the results of the elections decided in advance in a process of negotiation between the minister of the interior and the *caciques*. Variants of this system remained in place in other parts of southern Europe, most notably in Portugal (where it was known as *rotativismo*), Italy (*trasformismo*) and in the Balkan Peninsula.[9]

The result was that the classical liberal ideals of meritocracy and effective public administration permeated Spanish political life only imperfectly, to say the least.[10] The entrenched governing oligarchy, closely tied to the local *caciques*, overlooked citizens' real needs and oversaw the operation of costly and inefficient public services that served the interests of the influential and not of the collective.[11] In part because of the links established with local elites, the Spanish state was also reluctant, from the late 19th century, to raise the taxes required in order to adopt the more interventionist role in society which was becoming increasingly common in Western and Central Europe. Thus, in 1900–2 its public expenditure made up 9.4 per cent of national income, compared to an average of 15 per cent in France, Great Britain and Germany. Furthermore, Spain's finances had been overstretched, first by the Napoleonic invasion (1808–13), the subsequent attempts to reconquer her mainland American colonies, and then by the Carlist civil wars, while the officer corps were privileged. As a result, between 1850 and 1890, 27 per cent of its expenditure comprised interest on the public debt and another 25 per cent went on the military.[12] All attempts at budgetary reform were destined to failure given the structural constraints on which the regime rested. In these circumstances it would find it difficult to develop an effective state machine. The state bureaucracy was small and underpaid, and an elementary education system was rolled out only slowly.

This tendency to pact with powerful interests rather than confronting the need for their modernization and subordination to civil authority can be seen in other areas. In early 19th-century Europe, the Church supported the *ancien régime* and so collided with the liberal state. The Vatican would remain opposed to liberal institutions and rationalist thought through to the 20th century. This frequently provoked severe tensions between Church and state. The French Third Republic was anticlerical, separating Church and state in 1905. The Italian Risorgimento or unification of the country led to an open clash with the Vatican, with its logical conclusion being the seizure of Rome in 1870, thereby ending the papacy's temporal power. Pope Pius IX declared himself a prisoner and it 'inexpedient' (*non expedit*) for Catholics to collaborate with the new state. In Spain – the heart of the 16th-century Counter-Reformation – the Church's revolt against modernity was particularly widely supported, especially in rural areas. The Church-backed Carlist uprising against the new liberal order was finally defeated, but it thereafter soon recovered economic and political influence. From the 1840s, in order to defuse opposition, the dominant conservative-liberal tradition felt the need to re-establish the link between Church and state. Furthermore, it came to see the Church as a guarantor of moral order and a bulwark again dangerous, subversive left-wing doctrines.

A first step was taken down this path in 1851 with the signing of a new concordat, by which Catholicism was confirmed as the country's official religion and the state also assumed the obligation to pay the salaries of the lay clergy. Tacit support for the liberal system was made possible by the ascension of Pope Leo XIII (1878–1903), who, fearing the spread of socialism, began slowly to open the door for collaboration with Europe's liberal regimes (though Italian Catholics were still formally forbidden from participating in the politics of their country). Henceforth, despite its anti-liberal ideas the Catholic hierarchy worked with Spain's ruling order and the 'moderate' Catholic Party, the Unión Católica (Catholic Union), integrated into the Conservative Party in

1883. This allowed the Church to recapture the urban upper-middle classes, most especially through the rapid expansion of the religious orders and of their network of private schools (while religious education was obligatory in state elementary schools). This contrasted with the situation in the major Western European states, where from the late 19th century, state education – in which the religious component was limited – developed rapidly.[13] Importantly, therefore, at the turn of the century, Spanish bourgeois milieux were closely linked to the Church both culturally and, in many respects, ideologically.[14]

The Church remained a reservoir of anti-liberal thought. Its hierarchy may have compromised with the Restoration regime, but there were also more radical strands spurred on by the fear of secularization. Much of rank and file continued to sympathize with the Carlist movement, which combined the call for a return to an idealized theocratic monarchy with a populist anti-oligarchic rhetoric, contrasting an idyllic rural life with the moral perils of the urban world. And though the Unión Católica entered the Conservative Party, a Catholic Integrist movement took off, which would have no truck with liberalism. Under pressure from Leo XIII it broke up in the 1900s, but its ideas remained influential. Simultaneously, the leading Carlist intellectual, Juan Vázquez de Mella, offered a detailed Catholic-corporatist blueprint for the new society which proved attractive to the Right. Yet it would be those Catholics close to the Unión Católica who would ultimately be the greatest threat to liberalism, for it was within their ranks that an effort was made to mobilize support behind a new right-wing nationalism, which equated the Spanish national essence with Catholicism, and baptized dissidents as an anti-Spanish internal enemy.[15]

There were similarities in the position acquired by the Spanish army. Throughout Europe, the officer corps remained one of the key bulwarks of entrenched conservatism. By the turn of the century, a significant percentage of the military upper echelons came from the landowning aristocracy whose political and cultural values they obviously shared. Still, the officer class, even in Russia and Germany, did provide an avenue for upward mobility and increasingly co-opted strata from humble origins. Of course, they were indoctrinated in the military academies with the 'right principles' of hierarchy, duty and discipline – *esprit de corps*. This meant that they embodied 'the national idea' and so their task was not just to protect the motherland against foreign threats but also against the internal enemy. Indeed, in the last resort, they were to act as a police force against those threatening the social order.[16]

Nowhere was this 'praetorian sense of manifest destiny'[17] more clearly manifested than in Spain. Having delivered victory during the Carlist wars, the officer corps attained a paramount position as guarantor of the new state against insurrection from below and potential new absolutist challenges. In 1844, the Civil Guard was created to police the countryside and was put under military control. Simultaneously, the army became the ultimate arbiter of politics as the narrowly based liberal regime broke down into small bickering factions led by rival generals. For nearly three decades, *pronunciamientos* or military coups were the only valid means of political change.[18]

Tellingly, the Bourbon Restoration was the product of a *pronunciamiento* in December 1874. The architect of the regime, Antonio Cánovas del Castillo, managed, temporarily as it turned out, to return the army to its barracks. However, fear of the masses meant that the Restoration authorities never attempted to reform the army and subordinate it to civilian sovereignty. Both dynastic parties frequently responded to any sign of unrest with the suspension of constitutional guarantees and the declaration of martial law, which left the army in charge of public order.[19] In return, as Sebastian Balfour notes (Chapter 10, this volume), the armed forces acquired almost total institutional autonomy; an autonomy that was exceptional in comparison with other Western states. Officers were rewarded with promotions and aristocratic titles, and governments did little to tackle inefficiency in the armed forces, symbolized above all by its bloated officer corps, the payment of whose salaries left little for new equipment.[20]

Challenges to the Restoration regime, 1898–1914

Europe's liberal regimes faced significant challenges from the 1890s. In the first place there was the threat from below, embodied by the rising consciousness and organization of the lower classes. Increasingly powerful labour movements grew up, accompanied by escalating strike action. Even though before 1914 the percentage of workers affiliated to labour organizations was relatively small, protest and strike activity began to reach unprecedented heights. In Germany, the Social-Democratic Party had nearly 1 million members and its dependent Free Trade Unions about 2.6 million. In France and Italy, significant sections of the labour movement espoused the doctrine of revolutionary Anarcho-Syndicalism, which combined a radical rejection of 'bourgeois politics' with the argument that proletarian emancipation could only come through the result of workers' direct action rooted in grass-roots activism at the level of the factory and community. Such ideas were dominant in both the Confédération Générale du Travail (hegemonic in French labour) and the Italian Unione Sindacale Italiana (a rival to the dominant Socialist Confederazione Generale del Lavoro).[21]

In July 1889, Socialist parties established the Second International. In theory at least this pursued a Marxist programme of class struggle and revolution to establish the dictatorship of the proletariat. In practice, however, the growth of a large paid bureaucracy, the easy recourse to economic determinism, and the stress on the preservation of the organization meant that Socialist leaderships often showed reluctance to back revolutionary adventures.[22]

In the second place, a New or Radical Right emerged which moved beyond the conservatism of established elites, rejected any reasoned debate and adopted an extreme 'blood and land' xenophobic nationalism, wild imperialist rhetoric, racism, anti-leftism and anti-liberal corporatism. This was most visible in France, Italy and Germany. In France and Germany the groups which respectively coalesced to form Action Française and which made up the *völkish* nationalist leagues combined suspicion of big business and an idealization of the rural world with fierce anti-Semitism. The doctrinal bases of Italy's Radical Right, represented between 1910 and 1918, above all by the Associazione Nazionale Italiana (Italian Nationalist Association – ANI), had a more 'modern' feel. According to one of its leaders, Alfredo Rocco, 'Modern technology demanded an organic system whose highest expression was the professional syndicate, the organization in which owners and workers would meet.'[23] Particular stress was laid on the condemnation of the 'parasitic' Italian political class. Furthermore, its ideology, while based on reactionary anti-liberal Catholic corporatism, juxtaposed the 'productive' classes, above all the industrial bourgeoisie, to the 'unproductive' and corrupt liberal elites as the potential saviours of the nation, with the result that it was attuned to the world of industrial capitalism. For this reason, while the more backward-looking French and German movements comprised, above all, distressed farmers, retired officers, clerical employees, small businessmen and shopkeepers, the Italian Radical Right was able to reach out and attract the Futurist artistic movement and some sectors of Italian big business. Moreover, as we shall see in the next section, where the challenge by the working-class Left became particularly acute, wider liberal-conservative circles would, at least tacitly, back the far right as a (literal) club with which to beat socialism.[24]

Italian radical nationalists shared with their German counterparts a frustration at the lack of significant imperialist aggrandizement and the belief that they had been unfairly excluded from the race for colonial spoils by the Western 'plutocracies'. This occurred in a context in which, from the 1890s, imperial rivalries escalated and Europe began to divide into two power blocs. Europe's ruling and governing classes adopted a more aggressive nationalist discourse. Social Darwinism, with its claims that humanity was divided into a hierarchy of races, was widely adopted, and 'Social Imperialism' was increasingly viewed as a valid formula to buttress governments' domestic positions by transferring strife from the national to the international sphere in order to draw middle and even lower strata into an imperialist consensus.[25] From the turn of the century heightened imperialist rivalries were accompanied by a massive redistribution in colonial and international hegemony. Portugal had its ambitions in Africa checked by the concerted actions of Britain and Germany. Italy's dream of an Abyssinian Empire collapsed with the defeat at Adowa (1896). France was bitterly divided by the Dreyfus Affair while her colonial expansion foundered against the British at Fashoda (Sudan) in 1898. After suffering a comprehensive defeat in Manchuria and Korea against Japan, Russian tsarism was rocked by the revolutionary wave of 1905.[26]

The United States was the other non-European state to lay down its claim to great power status. This was partly achieved at the expense of Spain, which in a short war lost its last overseas territories in the Pacific and the Caribbean. The colonial defeat of 1898 (often referred to in contemporary circles as, simply, 'the Disaster') proved a catalyst to growing opposition. In an era of Social Darwinism, when the health of nations appeared to be marked by imperial expansion, Spain – until recent times the world's largest colonial power – seemed sick. As the dream of empire vanished, 'the Disaster' brought into question the capacity of the dynastic politicians to rule the country.[27] Blame was above all directed at the distant political 'oligarchy' and the *caciquista* networks it utilized in order to remain in power. As in the case of Italy, therefore, the regime came widely to be seen as an impediment to modernization. The new formula was called *Regeneración*, by which was meant the major institutional changes that were needed to rebuild the country and restore its prestige. Three opposing proposals were developed: a left-wing path predicated upon popular mobilization 'from below' against the Restoration regime, a liberal road based on reform of the regime 'from above', and an authoritarian route embodied by a strong leader or 'iron surgeon'. The picture was further complicated by the growth of regionalist/nationalist movements in the Basque Country and Catalonia, the latter in particular developing its own brand of Regenerationism. From

1917 the social and political climate would become increasingly polar-ized, and the left-wing and authoritarian routes came to the fore. Their final and bitter clash would take place in 1936.[28]

Left-wing Regeneration 'from below' began to gain ground after 1898 as in the larger cities an increasing number of Republicans were elected. In an urban environment, and in the rural south, Spanish politics was to an important degree built on the clash between the anti-liberal, theo-cratic world view of the Catholic Church and the materialist perspec-tive of the liberal-left, based on the Enlightenment cannon of progress and reason. Indeed, the growing influence of the Church meant that from the 1900s anticlericalism became a central element of political life. This helps explain why in Spain the urban-based 'little men' tended to remain on the Left, linked above all to Republicanism.[29] The most important exception in these years was in the Basque Country, where faced with breakneck industrialization and rapid migration, a virulently racist and populist movement, based on the petty bourgeoisie of Bilbao and its surrounds, appeared in the 1890s. However, it adopted a Basque nationalist rather than a Spanish nationalist ascription.

Both the Basque and especially the Catalan regionalist/nationalist movements were also strengthened by 'the Disaster'. In Catalonia in 1901, the grip of the *caciques* was loosened by the electoral success of both Republicans and the newly established Lliga Regionalista. The lat-ter, a social-conservative party with strong links to industrial interests,[30] followed a policy of Catalan nation-building at home while simultan-eously advocating the construction of a new decentralized but pro-busi-ness and interventionist Spanish state. The fact that sectors of business had distanced themselves from the regime would, over the subsequent two decades, prove particularly important, making it easier for Catalan business leaders to attack its policies and, eventually, play a leading role in undermining it.

The 'national problem' in Spain cannot be compared to that of the Habsburg Empire, which was torn apart at the end of the First World War by a host of competing 'micro nationalisms'. In most of Spain there was no serious challenge to Spanish national identity, and pro-Spanish currents contested the nascent alternative Catalan and Basque nationalisms in their own territories. Indeed, as Angel Smith points out (Chapter 6, this volume), there was ambiguity as to whether the Catalan movement should be referred to as 'regionalist' or 'national-ist' (conveniently covered over by its leaders through recourse to the term 'Catalanist'). Nevertheless, the challenge from these movements produced serious strains. In the 19th century, Spanish Liberalism had (with a brief radical interlude between 1868 and 1874) adopted a variant of the French nation-state-building model, which emphasized the centralization of political power in the capital. Hence, for most of the political elite, Catalan and Basque nationalist demands were seen as an affront, which called into question the liberal Spanish nationalist historical narrative, developed from the 18th century, which argued that since pre-Roman times Spain had formed a single cultural entity, and that down the centuries Spaniards had valiantly struggled against foreign invaders to secure their freedom and independence.[31] Conservative elements like Antonio Maura could aim for some compromise (because the Conservative Right had inherited elements of the Church's anti-Jacobin decentralizing discourse), but the Liberal Party in particular was extremely hostile and from 1901 even supported the anticlerical and populist rabble-rouser Alejandro Lerroux and his Radical Republican movement in order to stem the rising tide of Catalanism.[32]

As Alejandro Quiroga (Chapter 8, this volume) and Javier Moreno Luzón explain, faced with new challenges, in the 1900s for the first time the Restoration regime began to seriously pursue the 'nationalization of the masses', above all by both improving the education system and the erection of a nationalist toponymic landscape. This was combined with efforts to modernize the state apparatus.[33] However, as Quiroga stresses, because of the key ideological and cultural role assigned to the Church by conservative liberalism it took on board much of the new Catholic nationalist discourse, with the result that the dominant rendition of this 'official' or 'state nationalism' was suffused in Catholic imagery and gave the Church a primary role in the historical narrative of nation-building. And while this discourse could attract the conservative upper classes and make an impact in small towns and rural areas in the north and centre, it alienated broad sections of the population. This should be contrasted with the situation in France, and even to a degree in Italy, where a more liberal state nationalist discourse helped gain the loyalty of broader sectors of the urban populace.

Within the dynastic class, the main statesman associated with the idea of Regeneration was Antonio Maura. The idea was, at least in theory, to democratize the regime, mobilize a potentially dominant middle-class Catholic electorate and so put into practice the 'revolution from above' which would trump any left-wing 'revolution from below'.[34] There are disagreements amongst historians (including the contributors to this volume) on the extent to which the regime reformed and extended its social base between 1900 and 1923. As noted above, the regime did begin a serious programme of nation-building. However, substantial political reforms were not forthcoming. Despite democratizing rhetoric, Maura and other dynastic politicians continued to use *caciquista* networks to maintain power. They found it difficult to swim in the sea of mass politics.[35]

Some scholars have argued that the Liberal Prime Minister José Canalejas represented the liberal-left response to Maura's conservative Regeneration by offering a programme of social reform and mild anticlericalism. Killed in office by an anarchist gunman in November 1912, Canalejas never saw the accomplishment of his work. He enacted some significant measures (for example, forcing the middle and upper classes to undertake a period of military service), but his hopes of finding a modus vivendi with sectors of the Left imploded amidst a wave of strikes and repression.[36]

Maura's 1907 government had itself collapsed in October 1909 amidst a combination of popular outcry, dynastic intrigue and royal intervention. Not particularly keen on colonial ventures, he saw himself forced to intervene in the Moroccan Riff – a coastal strip of land in the north allotted to Spain in 1906 at an international conference – when a rebellion broke out there in 1909. However, with the bitter memories of 1898 still fresh, Spain could no longer use Social Imperialism to rally popular energies.[37] The call-up of working-class reservists – who could not pay the 1,500-peseta fee necessary for exemption from conscription – led to a week of rioting and church-burning in Barcelona, known as Tragic Week.

Unlike Italy's Red Week of June 1914, let alone the Russian Revolution of 1905, Spain's Tragic Week was not a concerted attack on the regime but a spontaneous explosion of anticlerical and anti-military feelings. Its consequences were, nevertheless, very significant. The Partido Socialista Obrero Español (Spanish Socialist Workers' Party – PSOE) formed an electoral alliance with the middle-class Republican groups. Subsequently, the domestic and international protest at the repression was the pretext used by the Liberals, in collusion with King Alfonso XIII, to oust Maura from office. When, four years later, Maura refused to rotate in office with the Liberals, the bulk of his party, desperate to regain the spoils of office, deserted him in favour of the more orthodox Eduardo Dato.[38]

The ousting of the regime's most charismatic statesman had parallels with the assassination, in September 1911, of Prince Petr Arkadievich Stolypin, the tsarist strongman since Russia's 1905 Revolution, and the fall of Italy's Liberal leader, Giovanni Giolitti, in March 1914. As Moreno Luzón notes, this proved a key moment in the break-up of the *turno pacífico*. The establishment of a Dato administration in 1913 triggered a genuine grass-roots mobilization that heralded the birth of right-wing mass politics in Spain and the irrevocable split of the Conservative Party. Mostly young middle-class students and white-collar workers rallied around the vilified Maura, and its movement even adopted the name of their admired leader (Maurismo). As Alejandro Quiroga notes, the Mauristas tried to construct a mass base, going so far as to set up workers' centres. However, Maurismo never constituted a coherent party, but was a broad church united in its devotion to Maura, monarchism and its bitter criticism of dynastic corruption. It embodied two currents, a Christian Democratic faction and a dominant nationalist and anti-liberal tendency that, like its French counterparts of Action Française or the Italians of the ANI, moved from traditional conservative positions to the far Right. Young Mauristas also showed also the determination to 'take to the street'.[39]

In other quarters anti-liberal ideological tendencies were already visible prior to Tragic Week. The Church remained a reservoir of anti-liberal sentiment. The colonial trauma gave anti-liberal Catholics additional ammunition as they could now give their critique of the political class a regenerationist flavour. And the events of Tragic Week provoked laments that excessive liberty had allowed subversive ideas to take hold.[40]

In some business circles, already in the late 19th century, especially in Catalonia, as in Italy a 'productivist' language developed, combining calls for corporatist representation in parliament and for joint employer and workers unions (*sindicatos mixtos*), which would make possible the reconstruction of the medieval guilds in a modern setting, thereby eliminating social conflict. This perspective further cemented the reconciliation between anti-liberal Catholicism and the world of capitalist industrialization. Significantly, calls for joint unions received enthusiastic backing in some sectors of the Catholic Church, with the extraordinarily powerful businessman-cum-Catholic evangelist Claudio López Bru, the Second Marquis of Comillas, a major backer.

The crisis of 1898 led to intense criticism of the regime within Catalan business circles (which had lost lucrative markets in the Caribbean). The Tragic Week then provoked a conservative reaction and heightened anti-liberal sentiment. Business leaders, with Catalan industrialists at the forefront, complained that the regime was not defending their interests with sufficient vigour and called for an exemplary repression, a stance echoed in broader bourgeois circles.[41] More diffusely, as mass mobilization intensified from the turn of the century, in some intellectual circles an elitist tone could increasingly be discerned, which evinced a pronounced distain for the eruption of 'the mob' on to the political stage.[42]

In the aftermath of 1898 discontent with the regime also grew within the military. As Sebastian Balfour explains, there was a sense within the officer corps that they were taking the blame for the defeat, but that the politicians had not given them the wherewithal to fight the war effectively. They were particularly chastened by public demonstrations against the military. This hastened a drift to the Right amongst the officers and precipitated threats of intervention. Embittered by the resounding defeat, they found a new role, that of defenders of national unity and of social order. In the context of the growth of peripheral nationalism and labour agitation, sectors of the army began to consider the existing liberal order as inadequate to crush the 'pernicious effects' of class conflict and separatism.[43] Many officers were particularly angered by the fall of Antonio Maura, with whose policies they had identified, in the aftermath of Tragic Week.[44] To worsen matters for the governing elites, the army found a ready ally in the new king. Alfonso XIII, on the throne since 1902, not only identified with his army officers but also often used his executive prerogatives to appoint and dismiss cabinets. Political crises were known as *'orientales'*, as they were produced and resolved at the Palacio de Oriente, Alfonso's residence.[45]

To sum up, the 'Disaster' provoked an intensified critique of the political class. Most critics envisaged this as opening the way to a more democratic political system, but within Catholic circles, amongst elements of the officer corps and within business circles, issues such as the corporative restructuring of the political system and a takeover of power by the military were on the agenda. The fear engendered by Tragic Week that the Restoration regime was having increasing difficult in maintaining social control served to intensify such sentiments. Then, the defenestration of Antonio Maura in 1913 encouraged the emergence of a far Right movement (Maurismo) which while still conserving links with the regime it was also highly critical of it.

The impact of the First World War and the revolutionary attraction

Spain did not enter the First World War but was greatly affected by it. Indeed, the war proved a catalyst for rapid socio-economic transformation and mass mobilization; a process that undermined – often fatally – the foundations of traditional liberal states.

In Spain, after an initial economic downturn, the opportunities to supply the warring powers and export to markets that they had vacated laid the basis for a boom. Unfortunately, a number of factors, most notably undersupply of the less lucrative home market and rising prices, also provoked huge shortages of staple products and an inflationary spiral. These factors encouraged, from 1916, a significant growth of labour organization, which was further radicalized by the battle to maintain real wages, leading to the historic labour pact of July 1916 between the Socialist trade union, the Unión General de Trabajadores (General Workers' Union – UGT), and the Anarcho-Syndicalist Confederación Nacional del Trabajo (National Labour Confederation – CNT). The war also produced political polarization around the neutrality question. As Moreno Luzón and Romero Salvadó (Chapter 3, this volume) explain, Spain was divided between liberals and leftist francophiles, who backed the Allies, and right-wing germanophiles, who sympathized with the Central Powers. In addition, the Allies became identified with the cause of the 'small nations' of Central and Eastern Europe, especially after the United States' president, Woodrow Wilson, issued his 14 Points on 8 January 1918. This stimulated the radicalization of the Catalanist movement, as indicated by the increasingly unruly nature of the demonstrations on the Catalan(ist) national day of 11 September. From the autumn of 1914 the Lliga Regionalista and the Catalan business associations also pressed the state for economic concessions, which they saw as essential in order to lay the foundations of the new industrial Spain.

Mirroring the pressures from below elsewhere on the continent, Spain experienced a revolutionary drama in 1917, a three-pronged offensive against the regime: first, the movement of army officers organized into military trade unions (*Juntas Militares de Defensa*) in June; second, in July, the summoning by the Lliga of an Assembly of dissident parliamentarians to initiate a process of constitutional reform and Catalan home rule; and third, the launching of a revolutionary strike in August by the PSOE-UGT, backed by the CNT, in order to secure the triumph of the Assembly programme.

As Romero Salvadó (Chapter 3, this volume) shows, the regime was able to face down the revolutionary challenge. Crucial in this respect was the failure of Maura to act as the vital link between army officers and parliamentarians. Despite the insistence by the Lliga leader, Francesc Cambó, that the Assembly represented the 'revolution from above', which he claimed to desire, Maura refused to endorse any extra-constitutional initiative that could endanger the throne. His attitude was a major political error; his last opportunity to play a leading part in the renovation of the regime.[46] Furthermore, the self-elimination of Maura provided the Conservative government headed by Eduardo Dato with the chance to pursue a reckless gamble: to bolster its prestige as saviour of the social order by luring the labour movement into an ill-timed general strike and consequently forcing the army to quell the disturbances. This initiative paid off in the short term. The Spanish troops obeyed the instructions of their officers, who forgot the regenerationist rhetoric espoused by the *Juntas* and put down the revolutionary strike with stunning brutality. This attitude was not surprising. At a European level, the period between 1917 and 1920 demonstrated that while disbanded peasant and worker soldiers would be a revolutionary force (playing a significant role in the Russian Revolutions of 1917, in the fall of the German monarchy and break-up of the Austro-Hungarian Empire in 1918), following the Armistice officers adopted their traditional conservative-authoritarian stance and headed the crushing of leftist revolts.[47]

The opportunity for democratic reform was lost with the failure of the assembly movement. As Smith shows for Catalonia (Chapter 6), the shock of army intervention shifted bourgeois opinion further to the Right. The business associations totally backed government repression. Crucially, praetorian intervention had ended hopes of ushering in democracy in Spain via reform from above or revolution from below. Nevertheless, it soon emerged how reckless Dato's gamble had been. The liberal regime owed its survival to mere military expediency. From now on, its existence rested inextricably on the attitude of the armed forces.[48]

It was not, however, immediately apparent that the revolutionary road in Spain was blocked. As charted by Chris Ealham (Chapter 4, this volume), Spain was caught in the red tide that swept over Europe following the Bolshevik Revolution of October 1917. In order to justify his party's takeover, Lenin had argued that Russia was the 'weakest link' in the capitalist-imperialist chain. Therefore, the successful example of Soviet power would act as the spark to ignite a socialist revolution throughout Europe.[49] Once in power, the Bolsheviks affirmed that their raison d'être was to export world revolution and so in March 1919 they founded a 'truly' revolutionary Third International (Comintern). Initially, events appeared to bear out their hopes. By making plausible, for the first time, the idea of a workers' state, Bolshevism had a mesmerizing effect across the continent, causing as much panic amongst the ruling elites as raising expectations amongst revolutionaries. Soviet states briefly sprang up in Bavaria, Slovakia and Hungary in 1919. An all-socialist administration in Germany had to fight off armed insurrections staged by the Spartacus League, soon re-named the German

Communist Party. The Habsburg Austro-Hungarian Empire imploded and its capital was dubbed 'Red Vienna'. Italy experienced a period of rural insurrections and factory occupations.[50]

It was during this time that both Right and Left started to draw parallels between Russia and Spain. Both were relatively undeveloped countries on the periphery of capitalist Europe, and it was either hoped or feared that Spain might be the next domino to fall. And in both labour agitation was often raw and violent. The Bolshevik example, the shortages of basic products and galloping inflation, led to a massive increase in the number of strikes, together with social upheaval, food riots and street protest. In Barcelona, and probably in other urban centres, this resulted, between late 1918 and early 1920, in a major redistribution of national income from capital to labour, which more than made up for the decline in real wages during the war years.[51]

Despite this escalation of social conflict, traumatized by the repression of August 1917, the Socialists returned to their traditional cautious stance. They experienced two splits – one by sections of the Socialist Youth in April 1920 and another the following year by a minority of the party. However, the subsequent Communist Party, unified in November 1921, failed to lure any significant number of workers from the two established traditions of socialism and anarcho-syndicalism.[52] It was the CNT that profited from acute class struggle to become Spain's dominant labour force. Francisco Cobo Romero (Chapter 5, this volume) analyses the case of Andalusia, one of the focal points of violent social conflict. Historically a land of insurrection, spearheaded by the CNT from the summer of 1918, the rural south experienced three years of upheaval, largely triggered by the influence of Russian events, known as the *Trienio Bolchevique*. By early 1919 the CNT was also totally dominant in the Catalan labour movement. This territory, as the studies by Ealham, Romero Salvadó and Smith reveal, constituted the Spanish version of Italy's Po Valley in that it was at the heart of both revolutionary agitation and the subsequent reaction. As Spain's economic powerhouse, Barcelona presented, as no other city, the critical combination of a large proletariat with an unequalled tradition of social struggle, an intransigent employer class, nationalist feelings amongst sections of its middle classes, and a restless officer corps, while all of them shared a widespread mistrust of the central administration.[53]

A vociferous campaign for political autonomy began in the Catalan capital, sparked by the conclusion of the Armistice in November 1918. The issue of Catalan autonomy was at the centre of Spain's political stage until it was suddenly eclipsed by the mobilization of the proletariat under the leadership of the CNT. The Catalan labour movement had been transformed radically in the summer of 1918 when the old craft trade unions had been replaced by local industrial unions (*Sindicatos Únicos*). The turning-point took place in February 1919 when a dispute broke out at the Anglo-Canadian hydroelectric concern known as La Canadiense. After 44 days, the workers obtained a stunning victory that was described in the sober centre-left newspaper *El Sol* as the victory of the only well-organized force in Spain.[54]

The slow death of the Spanish liberal regime and the origins of dictatorship, 1919–23

One of the most surprising paradoxes of the Bolshevik Revolution was that many European liberal states did not succumb to the feared 'Red Spectre' but fell victim to the triumphal march of a brutal 'black', authoritarian and nationalist reaction of which Fascism was the most glaring exponent. Soviet overconfidence combined with contempt towards national peculiarities and dogmatism split the labour movement and undermined the cause of revolution. The defeat of the Red Army at the gates of Warsaw saw Bolshevism's physical retreat from Central Europe. In March 1921, the crushing of a Communist uprising in Germany represented the swansong of the revolutionary offensive. By then, even the Bolshevik leaders had discarded their dreams of world revolution – confirmed by the conclusions of the Third (22 June–12 July 1921) and Fourth (5 November–5 December 1922) Comintern Congresses. The priority was now to break international isolation and consolidate the Soviet state.[55]

Nevertheless, the existence of Bolshevik Russia added to the recent industrial strife and revolutionary bluster caused widespread panic amongst broad social sectors. In Western Europe, outside Spain it was in Italy that such fears were most pronounced. The populist Fascist movement grew rapidly, mobilizing above all sectors of the lower middle and middle classes, along with decommissioned officers, and launching, from late 1920, a violent assault on labour unions in central Italy. It was backed up by the more elitist far Right organization, the ANI, which was more in tune with the wealthier middle classes. Fearing that their world was imperilled, landowners, sectors of industry, and even local liberal elites, bankrolled the Fascists' assaults on the Left. In much of Europe, business also realized that new structures would need to be put in place to stabilize labour relations, championing closer co-operation between government and business and the integration of the labour movement into a corporatist bargaining system supervised by a strong state. As Charles S. Maier argues, in Germany they viewed this as compatible with parliamentary liberalism, but in Italy there was more sympathy for reactionary Catholic-corporatist ideas of the ANI, which envisaged the subordination of labour to capital within an authoritarian regime.[56]

In Spain, as Ealham explains, some of the country's most sophisticated revolutionaries, Andreu Nin and Joaquín Maurín, who had leading positions within the CNT, set about trying to marry the country's syndicalist traditions with the construction of a more effective revolutionary force. No one could but admire that audacity with which the Bolsheviks had taken power. Yet between 1917 and 1923 it was the differences rather than the similarities with Russia that came to the fore. In Russia the army had disintegrated, leaving a power vacuum. Furthermore, Spain did not comprise small industrial islands in a vast peasant sea. On the contrary, from 1919 it would become clear that Spain had a large, vociferous bourgeoisie, able and willing to defend its interests.

Spain's reaction was triggered by both labour unrest and (to a lesser degree) the intensification of Catalan nationalist agitation. Alejandro Quiroga and Javier Moreno Luzón analyse the increasingly belligerent attitude taken by sectors of the Church who embraced (a highly conservative reading of) Social Catholicism and by the Maurista movement. In the aftermath of the First World War, they demanded a strong centralist state, which would outlaw radical Catalanism (thereby breaking with Antonio Maura's pro-decentralizing stance) and adopted a vociferous anti-liberal rhetoric. In small town and rural central Spain above all, the lay Catholic associations – Acción Católica (Catholic Action) and the Asociación Católica Nacional de Propagandistas (National Catholic Association of Propagandists) – developed a Catholic co-operative movement and regional Catholic leagues. The corporatist vision of the strongest nucleus of Social Catholics was, rather like Action Française, backwards-looking, extolling the virtues of the uncorrupted Castilian peasantry. As Moreno Luzón points out, these events emphasized the Church's ability to mobilize against secularization and the threat of the Left. It would be fully realized during the Second Republic.

However, in comparison with the Radical Right in Italy, France and Germany, Maurismo and the Social Catholics lacked a populist cutting edge in urban Spain. This probably had much to do with Spain's strong Republican tradition, which mobilized important sectors of the lower middle and working class. Despite efforts to reach out to the workers, Maurismo had an established middle-class feel to it, and the Catholic associations were under the control of the elite (as epitomized by the

Second Marquis of Comillas) and picked up little urban popular support. In addition, unlike Italian Fascism, the anti-liberal Catholic and Maurista Right was not able to forge any over-arching ideology or operate as a separate party. Important in this respect was the fact that its various components owned allegiance to other bodies. Many Mauristas retained their links to Antonio Maura, though some formed a separate Partido Social Popular (Popular Social Party) in 1922 (which, however, had a Christian-democrat wing). Given the centrality of Catholicism for these groups, the Vatican and Spanish episcopal hierarchy remained important sources of power and legitimacy. There was also a lack of clarity in right-wing thought, with some Mauristas, for example, seemingly favouring a hybrid system, combining universal suffrage and corporatism.[57]

On the contrary, Italy's Fasci di Combattimento offered a modernizing model for anti-liberal forces in Europe.[58] There was no equivalent in Spain to the former syndicalists, who initially constituted the 'revolutionary' elite that led the movement. Nor was there anything like the thousands of post-war ex-combatants and officers to organize its cadres. The Mauristas were the closest street phenomenon to the *Squadristi*, but, as noted, they were too middle class and lacked the ruthless violence that marked the black-shirts' expeditionary missions to instil fear amongst their enemies.[59]

Nevertheless, if unable to generate a counterpart to Italian Fascism, Spain did have an unequalled tradition of praetorian intervention. Indeed, whereas Italian's political elites – the Piedmont's Liberal class – led the Risorgimento without recourse to mass mobilization,[60] the military, as we have seen, had been from the 1830s the guarantor and often the arbiter of Spain's liberal politics. Under the pretext of 'national regeneration', it merely resumed its interventionist tradition in the aftermath of the First World War and led the overthrow of parliamentary liberalism.[61]

Praetorian counter-revolution had its capital in Barcelona.[62] As the CNT's stronghold, the apparent revolutionary threat was greatest there. Hence an alliance between industrialists and the army in Barcelona not only began to operate independently of the central government but also to behave as a veritable 'anti-state', bypassing and often even forcing the downfall of cabinets in Madrid. In this context, La Canadiense dispute proved a watershed. Bourgeois and also wider established middle-class circles, in Catalonia in particular, emerged from the dispute not only deeply anxious given the strength of the unions that they equated with Bolshevism, but they also felt indignant at what they considered the capitulation of the authorities in Madrid. Hence Catalan business launched incessant attacks on the political elite, which was seen as soft on CNT terrorism (if not actually in cahoots with the terrorists) and anti-industry, combined with outright demands for military intervention. Business was particularly upset that governments frequently attempted to use a carrot and stick approach with the CNT and integrate it into a system of state-sponsored collective bargaining. They developed a corporatist alternative, whereby workers would have to join state-sponsored unions (*sindicalización forzosa*).[63]

As Romero Salvadó notes (Chapter 7, this volume), significant numbers of Catalonia's industrial barons concluded in the spring of 1919 that to defend their corporate interests they had to close ranks and prepare for war: *Si Vis Pacem Para Bellum*.[64] They therefore resuscitated a Barcelona (subsequently Catalan) Employers' Confederation to co-ordinate action and a crucial alliance was sealed with the local garrison then headed by Captain General Joaquín Milans del Bosch.[65] Equally concerned with the escalation of labour protest, the army was willing to take drastic measures to curb the CNT and, in the process, undermine the Catalanist movement. Under ultimate army control, a bourgeois paramilitary force (Somatén) was organized to take on labour. Similar militias were subsequently set up in other parts of Spain.[66] Gangs were also hired to act as an employers' police force and a new right-wing labour union, the Sindicatos Libres, which recruited amongst Catholic and Carlist workers, was given strong support.

Other sectors of Catalan society and of the Catalan political elite were drawn into this counter-revolutionary coalition. As Quiroga notes, many Catalan Monarchists formed an association called the Unión Monárquica Nacional (National Monarchist Union), which shared business's belief that the Restoration parties were not dealing with the leftist threat severely enough. A more populist albeit ephemeral protest movement, the Liga Patriótica Española, was also founded principally as a reaction to Catalanist agitation. It enjoyed support in the Barcelona garrison, and attracted state functionaries, radical Carlists and even, it seems, some anti-Catalanist Republicans, who in early 1919 fought running street battles with radical Catalanists.[67]

There was no ideological unanimity within these groups. There were many 'old rightists' who would have been happy with a more authoritarian parliamentary settlement. However, the leadership of the Catalan Employers' Confederation (and its offshoot, the Spanish Employers' Confederation) adopted as its goal an authoritarian corporatist revolution led by the industrial elite. After the March on Rome in October

1922 it sympathized with Benito Mussolini, whom it viewed as having imposed order and effectively dealt with labour agitation through his Fascist unions. In this respect there were similarities with the ANI, which would integrate into the Italian Fascist Party in 1923 and ensure that Mussolini's dictatorship was reconciled with the Church and social elites.[68] This gave the anti-liberal agenda of the Catalan Employers' Confederation a more forward-looking feel to it than that of the Social Catholics discussed previously. The Catalan Right, operating in the eye of the labour storm were, like their Italian counterparts, aware that the clock could not be turned back and that in future their social pre-eminence could not be assured through the operation of clientelist politics in the context of a largely de-politicized population. Hence business's demand for the formation of statist unions. In addition, once the Italian Fascist Squads had been turned into an arm of the state in 1923, the idea was developed in Catalan right-wing circles that the Somatén might play an analogous role in Spain.

While these forces came increasingly to reject the Restoration settlement, Francesc Cambó and the Lliga Regionalista took a more ambiguous stance. As Angel Smith shows, the Lliga found itself in a difficult position, caught between the radicalism of its Catalanist activists and the conservatism of its more bourgeois backers. From 1919 it clearly backed the latter and left demands for democratization and Catalan autonomy on the back-burner. As a result it was briefly, to a degree at least, reconciled with the Restoration regime, and in tandem with Maura entered government both in 1918 and 1921. Cambó backed the repression of labour protest (justified as a necessary parenthesis while labour relations were institutionalized) while trying to build his interventionist pro-business state. But as this programme unravelled the Lliga threw in its lot with business and other critics of the Restoration, tacitly backing a coup. There were similarities in this respect with the position of Maura who, though more cautious, saw this solution as inevitable by the summer of 1923. In many respects their attitude can be compared to the Liberals led by Giolitti in Italy, who, from the winter of 1920–1, assumed that Fascism was a 'passing-storm' that could actually be brought into the governing system. The veteran Italian statesman, in a final attempt at *trasformismo*, made the error of including Fascists in his electoral coalition of May 1921. Having returned 25 MPs, the Fascists acquired a degree of legality, but this did not lead them to abandon the violent road to power.[69]

Such was the ferocity of the reaction that began in Spain in the spring of 1919 that Antonio Gramsci described it as the precursor of Italian Fascism.[70] Many Spanish capitals, but especially Barcelona, sank into a cycle of terror. As in Italy, faced with social warfare on this scale, impotent governments had to choose between being an accomplice to the reactionary backlash or enduring its subversive might. Between November 1920 and October 1922, General Severiano Martínez Anido, acting as civil governor of Barcelona, operated a virtually autonomous satrapy. Anarchist groups carried out some spectacular *atentados* such as the murder, on 8 March 1921, of Prime Minister Dato, but in general *cenetistas* were at the receiving end of an army-led dirty war. Gunmen within the ranks of the Sindicatos Libres were armed by the military and police to assassinate CNT activists. The violent and plebeian character of this union, combined with its virulent anti-liberalism, anti-socialism, and increasingly anti-business stance, showed some similarities to the Fascist syndicalist 'Left' in Italy. During 1922–3 a group of officers in Barcelona garrison, who formed a Fascist-inspired organization called La Traza, argued that it could play the same role in Spain as Mussolini's Fascist unions.[71] However, the Libres differed greatly from Italian Fascists. They were practically only active in Catalonia, established international connections with Catholic organizations and their activities were confined to labour affairs and not politics. Furthermore, their close links with the civil government under Martínez Anido resembled those Russian trade unions sponsored by Sergei Vasilevich Zubatov, the chief of the tsarist secret police (the Okhrana) in Moscow.[72]

It was not only officers in mainland Spain who derided the liberal regime. Those in the front line in Morocco, known as *africanistas*, were hardly likely to take a more emollient attitude. Sebastian Balfour shows how amongst front-line colonial officers, in the face of stiff resistance from the Berber clans of the Riff Mountains, a specific colonial mentality was forged, marked by a reckless disregard for human life and a disdain for what were seen as the feather-bedded Spanish civilian population. This would account for the savagery of the Army of Africa when it was transferred to Spain after the military rebellion against the Second Republic in July 1936. There was nothing on this scale in our period, but glimpses of this future could be discerned. General Martínez Anido, who was a veteran of the late 19th-century colonial wars, affirmed on being appointed Barcelona civil governor that 'I will act as though I were on active service'.[73]

The dramatic events of July 1921 at Annual, in which some 8,000 Spanish troops were massacred after over-extending their lines, increased military frustration with the regime. As Pablo La Porte shows (Chapter 9, this volume), as in 1898 there was a belief in army circles, also shared by the wider public, that the politicians were trying to wriggle out of their responsibilities. Furthermore, amongst the *africanistas* there was anger that subsequent governments tried to rein in spending and assert greater civilian control over military operations.

It was amidst this climate of political deadlock, social warfare and colonial defeat that Spain's praetorian-led reaction made its bid for power. As in Italy, the revolutionary threat, if it had ever existed, had all but vanished. Instead, it was the fear of return to 'normal conditions' and hence the reorganization of union power which concerned the Catalan Right. Furthermore, as Francisco Cobo Romero indicates for the case of Andalusia, sympathy for a military takeover extended to bourgeois milieux in other parts of Spain, in which links between local *caciques* and the Monarchist parties remained stronger. In order to understand how, despite the *caciquista* foundations of the regime, it became increasingly distanced from economic elites and the conservative middle classes, one has to remember that while many eminent political figures hailed from powerful families who held sway over large territories, they were professional politicians who operated within a liberal mental framework.

There were attempts by central governments – in Italy and in Spain – to regain social and political control, as exemplified by the 'Pacification Plan' and demobilization of the squads of summer 1921 in Italy, and by the restoration of constitutional guarantees (30 March) and the dismissal of General Martínez Anido (24 October) by the Conservative cabinet of Sánchez Guerra in Spain during 1922. The 1923 Liberal administration then tried to widen its social base by bringing on board the moderate liberal-left Reformist Party, promising significant political reforms, and taking a neutral stance on labour affairs.

Yet it was too little too late. Busting a general strike launched in July–August 1922 by a Socialist-led 'Alliance of Labour' catapulted Mussolini to power. Similarly, the outbreak of a massive transport dispute in Barcelona in May 1923 proved decisive. Lasting until July, the strike paralysed the city, confirmed the reconstruction of CNT power and brought back memories of the dreaded La Canadiense dispute. While the civil authorities sought a negotiated formula, Barcelona's Captain General, Miguel Primo de Rivera, enhanced his reputation by ensuring the unions' defeat with his forceful intervention.[74]

By this time, Primo de Rivera had already begun to conspire with a group of *africanista* generals based in Madrid. Bringing these figures on board was of key important because, though he had not previously been identified with the *africanista* cause, his coup was now assured widespread military support, both in the peninsula and in Morocco.[75] With the open complicity of leading sectors of the Catalan bourgeoisie,

Primo de Rivera staged a coup in September 1923. Like many other con-stitutional regimes in inter-war Europe, Spain's ruling order crumbled. Lacking a genuine popular mandate, the government could not resort to grass-roots mobilization. Faced with military sedition, the liberal regime's only (and, ultimately, vain) hope rested on the intervention of the king, the army's commander-in-chief.

Yet, crucially, the conspiracy enjoyed the sympathy of Alfonso XIII. The war had not been a happy one for what Eric Hobsbawm refers to as the 'international princes' trade union'.[76] The tsar had been forced to abdicate in February 1917, and the monarchs of Bulgaria and the German, Austro-Hungarian and Ottoman empires followed at the end of 1918. Alfonso feared that he would be next in line. He had been thought of as something of a liberal in the first 15 years of his reign, but, as Javier Moreno Luzón notes, the revolutionary events of 1917–18 drove him to the Right. In subsequent years he also grew weary of con-stant ministerial crises and was well attuned to military sentiment. From the start of his reign he had mixed in military circles and saw himself as a 'soldier-king'. And, as Pablo La Porte indicates, he was particularly identified with the Moroccan campaign and outraged by what he saw as the political elites' indecisiveness after Annual. Furthermore, both officers and monarch were exasperated by the fact that since 1922 the dynastic governments had willingly placed the question of responsibil-ities for the colonial disaster – in which the role of king and army was constantly debated and denigrated – on the parliamentary agenda.[77]

When faced with the Fascist 'March on Rome' in October 1922, a hesitant King Vittorio Emanuele III refused the petition of the cabinet, then led by Luigi Facta, to sign a decree establishing martial law and instead summoned Mussolini to form a new government. Alfonso mir-rored that attitude one year later, without the agonizing doubts that had troubled the Italian monarch. Seduced by the connotations of Fascism, a buoyant Spanish sovereign in his first visit abroad after the coup to Italy introduced Primo de Rivera as 'my Mussolini'.[78]

Alfonso's boast was telling. Spain's praetorian takeover in 1923 meant a departure from the army interventionism of the previous century. In line with the anti-liberal tendencies of the era, the army no longer attempted to seize power as the representative of a political faction but claimed to be acting as defender of the sacred values of the nation endangered by the mismanagement of the political class. The fact that Spain's liberal elite had never been able to subordinate the military to civilian rule gave Primo de Rivera the space to plan his coup without hindrance. Hence (as in 1936) the army became the lynchpin of a broader counter-revolutionary coalition. Primo de Rivera's initiative stopped short of the revolutionary mobilization of Fascism, and yet also constituted the local solution to the crisis of oligarchic liberalism in the new age of mass politics; a solution that pursued the creation of a strong and centralized state that would lead to economic modernization from above while destroying both the inefficient liberal system and the threat of the organized labour movement and separatism.

Notes

1. We use the Gramscian term of 'organic crisis' to argue that the crisis of Spanish liberalism was not conjunctural but involved the whole system. One of its glaring signs was that the regime was not only challenged from below but was also increasingly rejected (particularly from 1919) by significant sectors of the bourgeoisie and middle classes who no longer believed it to be able to deliver social containment. Quintin Hoare and Geoffrey Nowell-Smith (eds and trans.), *Selections from the Prison Notebooks of Antonio Gramsci* (London: Lawrence and Wishart, 1986), p. 212.
2. Arno J. Mayer, *The Persistence of the Old Regime: Europe to the Great War* (London: Croom Helm, 1981), pp. 4–7. It is obvious that Europe was not a single entity. It contained vastly different regional and national economies, traditions, political structures, etc. For example, for a brief analysis of the greater power of the British parliament vis-à-vis its Spanish counterpart see Javier Moreno Luzón in this volume, pp. 40–1. Despite these differences, however, in general, the forces of inertia and conservatism were still dominant in the key areas of government, the bureaucracy, armed forces and diplomacy.
3. Mayer, *The Persistence of the Old Regime*, p. 3; Paul Preston and Helen Graham (eds), *The Popular Front in Europe* (London: Macmillan, 1987), p. 1.
4. Stephen J. Lee, *European Dictatorships, 1918–1945*, 2nd edn (London: Routledge, 2000), pp. xi–xii. For 1920 we have preferred to use the term liberal constitutional regime rather than democracy because, as noted, these regimes still contained undemocratic features.
5. The first and decisive civil war lasted from 1833 to 1840, the second Carlist war lasted from 1846 to 1849 and was confined to Catalonia, while the third Carlist war (1872–6) was largely limited to the Basque Country and Navarra.
6. Eric J. Hobsbawm, *The Age of Empire, 1875–1914* (London: Abacus, 1994 [1987]), p. 85. These 'safeguards' were particular pronounced in the case of Germany where a Federal Parliament (Reichstag) was elected by a universal male franchise from 1871 but could not overthrow the government that was directly responsible only to the emperor (Kaiser). Finally, the Reichstag had the same power as the Upper House (Bundesrat), an unelected chamber formed by appointees of every state and where Prussia, the largest of all, was supreme. Furthermore, the hapless Reichstag was by-passed for domestic politics by the local parliaments. See David Blackbourn, *History of Germany, 1780–1918*, 2nd

edn (Oxford: Blackwell, 2003), pp. 173, 193–4, 200–1; Hans-Ulrich Wehler, *The German Empire, 1871–1918* (Oxford: Berg, 1991), pp. 52–4.

7. Teresa Carnero, 'Elite gobernante dinástica e igualdad política en España, 1898–1914', *Historia Contemporánea*, 8 (1992), pp. 35–73; Mercedes Cabrera and Fernando del Rey, 'De la Oligarquía y el caciquismo a la política de intereses. Por una relectura de la Restauración', in Manuel Suárez Cortina (ed.), *Las máscaras de la libertad. El Liberalismo Español, 1808–1950* (Madrid: Marcial Pons, 2003), p. 323.

8. Gabriel Tortella, 'La economía española a fines del siglo XIX', in José Luis García Delgado (ed.), *La España de la Restauración* (Madrid: Siglo XXI, 1985), p. 135. See also José María Jover and Guadalupe Gómez-Ferrer, 'La difícil modernización de la economía', in José María Jover, Guadalupe Gómez-Ferrer and Juan Pablo Fusi (eds), *España: Sociedad, Política y Civilización, Siglos XIX-XX* (Madrid: Debate, 2001), pp. 135–40.

9. As in Spain, a Liberal governing class monopolized political power in Italy. In the absence of party coherence, political barons on behalf of interest groups negotiated the establishment of parliamentary majorities by absorbing or 'transforming' rivals into broad governing coalitions through the promises of favours and administrative spoils. This manoeuvre was known as *trasformismo* and one of its most skilful representatives was Giovanni Giolitti (the regime's strong man between 1901 and 1914). The ruling order failed to 'transform' Italy's new emerging political forces; the right-wing Nationalists of the Associazione Nazionalista Italiana founded in 1910 and on the Left, the Italian Socialist Party after the Maximalist faction led by Constantino Lazzari and Benito Mussolini seized control at the Congress of Reggio Emilia in 1912. The Maximalists pursued the maximum programme – including revolution and the establishment of the dictatorship of the proletariat – and thus opposed those moderates, mostly strong in the parliamentary faction and in the trade union (Confederazione Generale del Lavoro), who were prepared to negotiate with the regime in order to obtain a 'minimum' number of reforms. See Denis Mack Smith, *Modern Italy* (London: Yale University Press, 1997), pp. 103, 249–54. For comparative studies of southern European states, see, for instance, Salvador Forner (ed.), *Democracia, elecciones y modernización en Europa, Siglos XIX-XX* (Madrid: Cátedra, 1997); Fernando García Sanz (ed.), *Españoles e italianos en el mundo contemporáneo* (Madrid: Consejo Superior de Investigaciones Científicas, 1990); and Silvana Casmirri and Manuel Suárez Cortina (eds), *La Europa del Sur en la época Liberal. España, Italia y Portugal. Una perspectiva comparada* (Santander: Publicaciones de la Universidad de Cantabria y Università di Cassino, 1998). Particularly suggestive are the articles by Manuel Suárez Cortina, 'Trasformismo y Turno: dos versiones Latinas de la Belle Epoque', in the aforementioned *La Europa del Sur,* pp. 227–49; and 'Demócratas sin democracia. Republicanos sin república. Los demócratas españoles e italianos en el apogeo y crisis del estado liberal, 1870–1923', in M. Suárez Cortina (ed.), *La Restauración entre el liberalismo y la democracia* (Madrid: Alianza, 1997), pp. 317–67.

10. On these liberal ideals see Norman Stone, *Europe Transformed, 1878–1918* (London: Fontana Press, 1983), pp. 15–20.

11. Mercedes Cabrera, Francisco Comín and Jose Luis García Delgado, *Santiago Alba. Un programa de reforma económica en la España del primer tercio del Siglo XX* (Madrid: Instituto de Estudios Fiscales, 1989), pp. 136–9.
12. Gabriel Tortella, *El desarrollo de la España contemporánea: historia económica de los siglos XIX y XX* (Madrid: Alianza, 1994), pp. 350–9. An overview of the 19th-century Spanish state can be found in Adrian Shubert, *A Social History of Modern Spain* (London: Unwin Hyman, 1990), pp. 168–90.
13. Stone, *Europe Transformed*, pp. 133–4.
14. There are two excellent surveys of the Spanish Church in English, Frances Lannon, *Privilege, Persecution and Prophecy: The Catholic Church in Spain, 1875–1975* (Oxford: Clarendon Press, 1987), and William J. Callahan, *The Catholic Church in Spain, 1875–1998* (Washington DC: The Catholic University of America Press, 2000). For a broader European perspective see Michael Burleigh, *Earthly Powers: The Clash of Religion and Politics in Europe from the French Revolution to the Great War* (New York: HarperCollins, 2005).
15. John N. Schumacher, 'Integrism: A Study of Nineteenth-Century Spanish Politico-Religious Thought', *The Catholic Historical Review*, 47 (1962–3), pp. 343–64; Martin Blinkhorn, 'Ideology and Schism in Spanish Traditionalism, 1876–1931', *Iberian Studies*, 1/1 (1972), pp. 16–24; José Alvarez Junco, *Mater Dolorosa. La idea de España en el siglo XIX* (Madrid: Taurus, 2001), pp. 433–64.
16. Samuel E. Finer, *The Man on Horseback: The Role of the Military in Politics* (London: Pall Mall Press, 1967), pp. 8–9; Mayer, *The Persistence of the Old Regime*, pp. 178–83. The mobilization of the army to quell street disturbances took place not only in Russia (i.e., the crushing of the revolution of 1905) and in Italy (i.e., quelling popular riots in the 1890s and during the Red Week of 1914) but also in the more 'progressive' French Third Republic. For instance, as both minister of the interior and prime minister, the centre-left Radical Georges Clemenceau (1906–9) often used the army to suppress strikes organized by the Anarcho-Syndicalist trade union, the Confédération Générale du Travail. See Roger Magraw, *France 1815–1914: The Bourgeois Century* (London: Fontana Press, 1993), pp. 308–9.
17. Finer, *The Man on Horseback*, p. 32.
18. Raymond Carr, *Spain, 1808–1975*, 2nd edn (Oxford: Oxford University Press, 1993), pp. 214–15. As Alvarez Junco (*Mater Dolorosa*, p. 277) points out, for parallels with the 19th-century Spanish modernizing army one would need to look to Kemal Atatürk in post-First World War Turkey, or, more generally, military regimes in 19th-century Latin America and 20th-century Africa.
19. Manuel Ballbé, *Orden público y militarismo en la España constitucional, 1812–1983* (Madrid: Alianza, 1985), pp. 247–8.
20. For additional information see Balfour in this volume, pp. 255–74.
21. Dick Geary, *European Labour Protest, 1848–1939* (London: Croom Helm, 1981), pp. 112–13.
22. Ibid., pp. 15, 90–3, 98–103.
23. Alexander J. De Grand, *The Italian Nationalist Association and the Rise of Fascism in Italy* (Lincoln: University of Nebraska Press, 1978), p. 99.
24. For these movements' social base see Charles Maier, *Recasting Bourgeois Europe: Stabilization in France, Germany and Italy in the Decade after World*

War I (Princeton, NJ: Princeton University Press, 1988), pp. 8, 26–7. Italian Nationalism is discussed in De Grand, *The Italian Nationalist Association*, pp. 2–5, 11, 49–51, for the German case see Michael Hughes, *Nationalism and Society: Germany, 1800–1945* (London: Arnold, 1988), pp. 130–63. There is a brief overview of the European Radical Right during this period in Martin Blinkhorn, *Fascism and the Right in Europe, 1919–1945* (Essex: Longman, 2000), pp. 8–16.

25. A clear example was the *Weltpolitik* pursued by Germany's II Reich, which was accompanied by the establishment of autonomous populist imperialist organizations such as the navy and the Pan-German Leagues. See Hughes, *Nationalism and Society*, pp. 139–42; Wehler, *The German Empire*, pp. 162–6, 173–9.

26. Rosario de la Torre, 'Los Noventa y Ocho', *Siglo XX. Historia Universal*, 1 (1983), pp. 49–66.

27. Manuel Tuñón de Lara, *España: La quiebra del 98* (Madrid: Sarpe, 1986), p. 13. Spain was at this time the only European country with a large population not considered, in diplomatic circles, a Great Power. See Hobsbawm, *Age of Empire*, p. 23.

28. It was the Aragonese essayist, Joaquín Costa, who first called for an 'iron surgeon' who was prepared to carry out radical surgery to save the nation. Francisco J. Romero Salvadó, *The Spanish Civil War. Origins, Course and Outcomes* (Basingstoke: Palgrave Macmillan, 2005), p. 2.

29. In France during the 19th century the situation had been similar. However, Eugen Weber argues that the link between the urban middle classes and the Left began to break down in the 1890s, first because the political programme of Republicanism had largely been enacted, and second because of the growing fear of social disorder. This was to provide a social base for far right-wing politics. Eugen Weber, 'France', in Hans Rogger and Eugen Webber (eds), *The European Right: A Historical Profile* (Berkeley and Los Angeles, 1966), pp. 71–127. In the case of Spain many Republican demands were yet to be enacted, and even when social conflict intensified from 1910 much of the Spanish urban petit bourgeoisie tended to sympathize with Republicanism.

30. Borja de Riquer, *Regionalistes i Nacionalistes, 1898–1931* (Barcelona: Dopesa, 1979), pp. 42–9.

31. Alvarez Junco, *Mater Dolorosa*, especially chs 4 and 5.

32. Examples of murky deals between Liberal notables and Lerroux can be found in Biblioteca de la Real Academia de la Historia, *Natalio Rivas's Papers* (hereafter ANR), Leg. 11–8898 (January 1910). Lerroux was an unprincipled but very able politician. After succeeding in creating a mass party and winning elections, he enjoyed the goodwill of Liberal governments.

33. Though it should be noted this more intense phase of nation-building was initiated with at least a 20-year time lag compared to the major capitalist powers. See, for example, Eric Hobsbawm, *Nations and Nationalism since 1780: Programme, Myth, Reality* (Cambridge: Cambridge University Press, 1990), chs 3 and 4.

34. According to María Jesús González Hernández, Maura was the only dynastic politician with a global project to foster citizenship and political participation; a project she describes as '*socialización conservadora*' (conservative socialization). See *El universo conservador de Antonio Maura* (Madrid: Biblioteca

Nueva, 1997), pp. 45–6, 133–7, and, 'Las manchas del leopardo: la difícil reforma desde el sistema y las estrategias de la socialización conservadora', in Suárez Cortina (ed.), *La Restauración*, pp. 167–70.

35. ANR, Leg. 8904 (29 October 1917).
36. A favourable biography of Canalejas can be found in Salvador Forner Muñoz, *Canalejas y el Partido Liberal Democrático* (Madrid: Cátedra, 1993). Socialist hostility towards Canalejas can be seen in Fundación Pablo Iglesias, *Cartas de Iglesias a Acevedo*, pp. 80–1.
37. Sebastian Balfour, *The End of the Spanish Empire, 1898–1923* (Oxford: Oxford University Press, 1997), p. 123.
38. Melchor Fernández Almagro, *Historia del Reinado de Alfonso XIII*, 4th edn (Barcelona: Montaner and Simón, 1977), pp. 190–2.
39. Rebellious, anti-system and on occasion even violent, they were called *Mauristas Callejeros* ('Street *Mauristas*'). In fact, they were ideologically a world apart from the 'legal' revolution from above preached by Maura. See María Jesús González Hernández, *Ciudadania y acción. El conservadurimo Maurista, 1907–1923* (Madrid: Siglo XXI, 1990), pp. 44–5, 122, 141–2; and Julio Pecharromán, *Conservadores y subversivos. La Derecha autoritaria Alfonsina, 1913–1936* (Madrid: Eudema, 1994), pp. 14–19, 31.
40. Callaghan, *The Catholic Church in Spain*, pp. 80–1.
41. Montserrat Bravo and Joan Palomas, 'Les corporacions industrials catalanes com a grup de pressió, 1875–1895', in *Congrés Internacional Catalunya i La Restauració, 1875–1923* (Manresa: Centre d'Estudis del Bages, 1992), pp. 259–64; Soledad Bengoechea, *Organització patronal i conflictivitat social a Catalunya* (Barcelona: Publicacions de La Abadia de Montserrat, 1994), pp. 284–313. On Catholic unions see Lannon, *Privilege, Persecution and Prophecy*, pp. 146–69; and Colin Winston, *Workers and the Right in Spain, 1900–1936* (Princeton, NJ: Princeton University Press, 1985), pp. 38–64. It should, however, be noted that at this time most large employers were content simply to keep their factories union free.
42. Sebastian Balfour, 'The Solitary Peak and the Dense Valley: Intellectuals and the Masses in Fin de Siècle Spain', *Journal of Iberian and Latin American Studies*, 1/1 (1994), pp. 1–19.
43. Francisco J. Romero Salvadó, 'The Failure of the Liberal Project of the Spanish Nation-State, 1909–1923', in Clare Mar-Molinero and Angel Smith (eds), *Nationalism and the Nation in the Iberian Peninsula* (Oxford: Berg, 1996), p. 121; Balfour, *The End*, pp. 164–87.
44. Carolyn P. Boyd, *Praetorian Politics in Liberal Spain* (Chapel Hill: University of North Carolina Press, 1979), p. 21.
45. Carolyn P. Boyd, 'El Rey-Soldado', in Javier Moreno Luzón (ed.), *Alfonso XIII* (Madrid: Marcial Pons, 2003), pp. 216–18.
46. Pecharromán, *Conservadores y subversivos*, p. 21.
47. Chris Wrigley, 'Introducción', in Chris Wrigley (ed.), *Challenges of Labour: Central and Western Europe, 1917–1920* (London: Routledge, 1993), p. 18.
48. Francisco J. Romero Salvadó, *The Foundations of Civil War: Revolution, Social Conflict and Reaction in Liberal Spain, 1916–1923* (London: Routledge and Cañada Blanch, 2008), p. 93.
49. Vladimir. I. Lenin, *Imperialism: The Highest Stage of Capitalism* (New York: International Publishers, 1990 [1917]), pp. 81 and 96–7. See also Neil

Harding, *Lenin's Political Thought: Theory and Practice in the Democratic and Socialist Revolutions*, 2 vols (London: Macmillan, 1986), vol. 2, pp. 58–9.

50. Wrigley, 'Introducción', pp. 16–19; Geary, *European Labour Protest*, pp. 134–45.

51. Angel Smith, *Anarchism, Revolution and Reaction: Catalan Labour and the Crisis of the Spanish State* (Oxford: Berghahn, 2007), p. 246. This redistribution of income from capital to labour also occurred in other European Countries. Maier (*Recasting Bourgeois Europe*, pp. 43, 77–8) calls it a 'silent revolution'.

52. Gerald Meaker, *The Revolutionary Left in Spain, 1914–23* (Stanford, CA: Stanford University Press, 1974), pp. 478–83.

53. Romero Salvadó, *The Foundations*, pp. 93–4.

54. *El Sol* (19 March 1919).

55. Kevin McDermott and Jeremy Agnew, *The Comintern: History of International Communism from Lenin to Stalin* (London: Macmillan: 1996), pp. 27–34.

56. Maier, *Recasting Bourgeois Europe*, pp. 9–11, 353–4.

57. This ambiguity has been emphasized (perhaps overemphasized) in Javier Tusell and Juan Avilés, *La derecha española contemporánea. Sus orígenes: el Maurismo* (Madrid: Espasa Calpe, 1986), pp. 78–9, 261–7.

58. For Fascism as an eclectic movement see Adrian Lyttelton, *The Seizure of Power: Fascism in Italy, 1919–29*, 2nd edn (London: Butler and Tanner Ltd, 1987), pp. 42–50.

59. For the Fascist squads see Mimmo Franzinelli, *Squadristi. Protagonisti e Techniche della Violenza Fascista, 1919–1922* (Milan: Arnoldo, 2003). The input of revolutionary syndicalists in early Fascism in covered in David D. Roberts, *The Syndicalist Tradition and Italian Fascism* (Manchester: Manchester University Press, 1979), pp. 165–81. See also Lyttelton, *The Seizure of Power*, pp. 52–4. It should be noted that the origins of the Italian Syndicalists were very different from those of the Spanish Anarcho-Syndicalists who led the CNT. The former tended to come from middle-class backgrounds and their links with the labour movement were limited. Hence, it was easy for them to reconsider their views, taking on board Italian nationalist ideas, during the First World War.

60. The Liberal-moderate hegemony during the Risorgimento is analysed by Gramsci in his 'Notes on Italian History', in Hoare and Nowell-Smith (eds), *Selections from the Prison Notebooks*, pp. 57–61, 104–6. It was the Piedmontese governing classes that through cunning diplomatic and political moves achieved the unification of Italy and not its armed forces that were often defeated in the battlefield.

61. Suárez Cortina, 'Demócratas', p. 365.

62. Francesc Cambó claimed that the dictatorship was born in Barcelona. Quoted in Jesús Pabón, *Cambó, 1876–1947* (Barcelona: Alpha, 1999), p. 921.

63. Angel Smith, 'The Catalan Counter-revolutionary Coalition and the Primo de Rivera Coup, 1917–1923', *European History Quarterly*, 37/1 (2007), pp. 15–16.

64. Archivo del Fomento del Trabajo Nacional, *Federación Patronal de Cataluña: Memoria de los trabajos realizados en su primer periodo activo*, p. 28.

65. Soledad Bengoechea, '1919: La Barcelona colpista; L'aliança de patrons i militars contra el sistema liberal', *Afers*, 23/24 (1996), p. 311.

66. Eduardo González Calleja and Fernando del Rey Reguillo, *La defensa armada contra la revolución* (Madrid: Consejo Superior de Investigaciones Científicas, 1995).
67. Smith 'Counter-Revolutionary Coalition', pp. 13–14; Alejandro Quiroga in this volume, pp. 203–7.
68. De Grand, *The Italian Nationalist Association*, pp. 159–60.
69. Maier, *Recasting Bourgeois Europe*, pp. 322–50.
70. Antonio Gramsci, 'On Fascism, 1921', in David Beetham (ed.), *Marxists in the Face of Fascism* (Manchester: Manchester University Press, 1983), pp. 82–3.
71. For additional details see Smith, 'Counter-Revolutionary Coalition', pp. 21–6.
72. J. Scheiderman, *Sergei Zubatov and Revolutionary Marxism: The Struggle for the Working Class in Tsarist Russia* (Ithaca, NY: Cornell University Press, 1976). The alliance between Martínez Anido and the Libres is recognized by the latter's biographer Feliciano Baratech, *Los Sindicatos Libres de España* (Barcelona: Cortel, 1927), pp. 90–1.
73. Smith, *Anarchism, Revolution and Reaction*, p. 331.
74. Javier Tusell, *Radiografía de un golpe de estado: El ascenso al poder del General Primo de Rivera* (Madrid: Alianza, 1987), p. 21; Smith, *Anarchism, Revolution and Reaction*, pp. 345–53.
75. Tusell, *Radiografía de un golpe de estado*, 71–83; Mª Teresa González Calbet, *La dictadura de Primo de Rivera. El Directorio Militar* (Madrid: El Arquero, 1987), pp. 72–4.
76. Hobsbawm, *Age of Empire*, p. 149.
77. Conde de Romanones, *Notas de una vida* (Madrid: Marcial Pons, 1999), p. 465.
78. Rafael Borrás Betriu, *El Rey perjuro. Don Alfonso y la caída de la Monarquía*, 2nd edn (Barcelona: Plaza & Janés, 1997), pp. 98–9.

2
The Government, Parties and the King, 1913–23

Javier Moreno Luzón

Introduction

This interpretative essay is based on recent developments in the Spanish historiography concerning the crisis of the Cánovas Restoration which have challenged interpretations advanced previously.[1] Here, two complementary propositions are defended. In the first place, the importance of endogenous political factors in the interpretation of the crisis of the liberal regime in Spain. Historians have overemphasized explanations attributing the main causes of that crisis to transformations in the socio-economic sphere, such as the tensions suffered by the Spanish economy as a result of the First World War, the subsequent emergence of a powerful workers' movement, and the class-based reaction to this. At times, the stress on these elements has led to a degree of determinism. Without wishing to discount these factors, in order to integrate them in a global and balanced explanation one has to bear in mind the evolution of the political sphere in the strictest sense of the word and respect its autonomy. Put succinctly, strikes were important but they did not directly bring down a single government. Internal party divisions and military pressure supported by the king accomplished this task.

It is therefore necessary to look in detail at elements such as the party system, institutional relations, the behaviour of the various political actors, including the army and the king, their interests, ideas and strategies, and the weight and the limitations of the political culture, of organizational bodies and of leadership. In short, one must analyse the struggle for power, which forms the fundamental nucleus of political life, while attempting to discern changing trends. Frequently, the political sphere in this period has been characterized as a capricious and arbitrary succession of governments, which lacks any interest. And until quite recently it has even been possible to undertake historical synthe- ses which discounted the importance of the main protagonists of the drama, the parties in government – the Conservatives and the Liberals – and the king – that is to say, those who effectively held power. Such interpretations have, fortunately, been rectified over the last decade.[2]

Second, the idea, which frequently appears in books on the history of Spain, that the collapse of the liberal regime was inevitable, that it was predetermined since 1913 or since 1917, or even since 1898, is rejected.[3] The constitutional reign of Alfonso XIII, which lasted for more than 20 years (1902–23), cannot be seen as a permanent crisis. The liberal monarchy was capable of surviving extremely difficult situations and lasting a long time, adapting to changing circumstances, introducing reforms and overcoming challenges as serious as the attacks emanating from a revolutionary workers' movement, from an army imbued with an air of authoritarianism, from parties whose aim was the proclam- ation of a republic, from anti-liberal Catholics and from various region- alist movements. These challenges were also present in other European countries, where similar regimes were also to succumb, often before that of Spain. If this period is presented as one of complete collapse, how should we interpret the Second Republic in the 1930s, a regime that barely survived five years and that was beset by even more serious upheavals? In one of his books, Sebastian Balfour expresses his surprise, and rightly so, that the Restoration regime should have survived for so long.[4] This needs explanation.

Consequently, the assumption that the period between 1917 and 1923 represented a mere prelude to dictatorship needs revision. It is one thing to explain the causes of the coup d'état of 1923 but quite another to see the entire period in teleological terms, as – in the words of Carlos Seco Serrano when referring to the final two years (1922–3) – 'a steep slope towards dictatorship'.[5] The crisis of the Restoration has only been stud- ied in terms of the final result, in the same way as the post-war period in Italy, between 1918 and 1922, is generally interpreted as merely a phase in the rise of Fascism, or the Spanish Second Republic itself is often seen as the prelude to the civil war of 1936–9. However, all deserve an impartial treatment. The period of the crisis of the Restoration has its own relevance and interest, independently of what was to come later, and can be seen as an era of complex conflict between different polit- ical options with a potentially open ending.

It is therefore essential to understand the dynamics of the party sys- tem and of institutional relations between political leaders, parliament and the king. In particular, it is important to highlight two parallel phenomena. The first of these was the fundamental relevance that the fragmentation of the major political parties was to acquire during the crisis years of the Restoration, brought about by conflicts which originally revolved around questions of leadership and which throughout were concerned with access to power. These leaders harboured differing programmes and strategies, which it was possible for them to implement because of the strength of their clientelist base in most of Spain. Furthermore, there was an inversely proportional relationship between the fragmentation of parties in government and the intervention of the crown in political disputes. In other words, the greater the divisions within government the greater the margin of influence enjoyed by the king, whose interference was not counteracted by the growth of mass parties in a democratic setting. Hence Alfonso XIII was crucial for the future of Spanish politics. The second point is that the options of the main political players of the age revolved around a central dilemma: either the two-party system was to be maintained, which carried with it a periodic rotation of power between the Conservatives and Liberals, or, on the contrary, other formulas for government had to be tried out in order to face the great problems of the day and to defend the regime from its many enemies. In consonance, two political groupings faced each other: those favourable to the reconstruction of a system of alternation between two parties or coalitions (generally, the majority factions of the old Conservative and Liberal parties), and those who were hostile to any two-party solution (the minority factions of these parties, in league with external groups – which were capable of being integrated into the regime – such as the Catalan Lliga Regionalista). The king fluctuated between these two elements, only to opt in the end for the liquidation of liberal parliamentarianism.

The bases of the political system: The crown and government parties

The Restoration regime was based on a number of fundamental pillars. To start with, the 1876 Constitution established a political system which synthesized the doctrinal features of 19th-century Spanish Liberalism. It incorporated the rights and democratic freedoms, previously defended by the Partido Progresista (Progressive Party), but its prime axis was the moderate principle of shared or co-sovereignty (*cosoberanía*) between the Cortes and the king, and this would convert the crown into the arbiter of political life. The monarch embodied the historical continuity of the nation and interpreted the national will with the same legitimacy as parliament. He was therefore able to intervene in the executive, legislature and judiciary, besides being commander-in-chief of the army and of the navy. He convened and dissolved the Cortes and he nominated and freely dismissed ministers, although any mandate for this could not come into force without the signature of one of them.[6] This bestowed on him enormous power.

The party system rested on the formation, finally achieved in the 1880s, of two great political forces: the Conservative Party and the Liberal Fusionist Party (usually known, purely and simply, as the Liberal Party). They inherited the country's various liberal traditions, the followers of which had previously competed against each other, causing, in the process, intense constitutional and governmental instability. The peaceful alternation of both parties in power – the *turno* – was the main political innovation of the Restoration and the key to its relative stability. Both to the Right and to the Left were to be found the marginalized political groups, the Republicans and Traditionalists, sectors of which became integrated into the regime in the late 19th century: the Partido Republicano Posibilista (Possibilist Republican Party) joined the Liberal Party, and some Traditionalists, who wanted a Catholic state, joined forces with the Conservative Party via the Unión Católica (Catholic Union).

In practice, the political process worked the other way round from other liberal regimes. As had occurred in Spain at least since the 1840s, governments always won the elections and then gained a parliamentary majority in the Cortes. To do this they utilized the centralized structure of the state, copied from the French model. When there was an election, the minister of the interior (*gobernación*) instructed the provincial governors, and they, in turn, directed the mayors in order to ensure that everything turned out in line with the wishes of the executive. This was possible thanks to high levels of passivity and abstentionism of the electorate, who left the field free for fraud on a massive scale.[7] This model, which had been adopted in moderate, progressive and even republican periods in the decades before the Restoration, did not change quickly, even after universal male suffrage was introduced in 1890. What was new about the Restoration was that the electoral results that the government manufactured were based on a pact, negotiated by Conservatives and Liberals before the election, through the so-called *encasillado*. The agreement was then applied by the authorities. In practice this fraud, organized from above, relied on the help of powerful local figures, known as *caciques*, who went along with it as long as they could control local affairs and receive administrative favours. The abuses committed by these people meant that the entire system became known as *caciquil* and that the expression *caciquismo* was used to discredit it.[8]

It was therefore the crown, not the people by means of parliamentary elections, who decided when the party in government would be replaced. However, the king could not do as he wished. Rather, he had to abide by a series of rules developed through custom: he had to consult the political leaders, weigh up their respective support and only take it upon himself to change things when a critical political situation had come about or when there was a split in one of the parties, which therefore no longer enjoyed a majority in the Cortes. In order to guarantee the effective operation of the regime, the two parties had to maintain internal cohesion around a clear leader, trying to ensure that any disagreements would only last for a short time. This was not easy, given that the parties in government in Spain, like their equivalents in other European countries, consisted of groupings of personal clienteles which spread from parliament to the four corners of the country and were not overly fond of discipline. They were formed by local notables and *caciques*: elite figures well connected with their respective local surroundings, who lived off the resources of the various state administrations. These elites belonged in general to the middle or upper classes of each place, comprising an *alta mesocracia* made up of landowners, professional people and businessmen with links to the most dynamic sectors of the local economy.[9]

These parties operated within a clientelist-based political culture, based on relations between bosses and their clients, in a world in which the antechamber (where those wanting to see some powerful notable waited to ask for a favour) enjoyed as much weight as the chamber itself (parliament). The parties had at their disposal a basic structure, with clubs and local committees in the best of cases, and, very importantly, numerous newspapers, whose widespread influence was facilitated by the operation of freedom of speech throughout most of the Restoration period. The many links established by these parties at local level refute claims that the political system was 'artificial'. It may be described as representing a 'politics of notables' similar to that of other liberal European countries, and alien to the politics of mass mobilization.[10] This system of politics continued until the end of the Restoration and even beyond. It should be remembered that as late as 1930, when Primo de Rivera's dictatorship fell, the government prepared an *encasillado* as if nothing had happened.[11] And one could even see examples of clientelist political relations during the Second Republic.[12]

The Restoration regime suffered its first major crisis at the end of the 19th century, after defeat in the colonial war with the United States in 1898. This defeat, known as 'the Disaster', caused widespread national soul-searching among the Spanish elites, and the publication of many possible prescriptions for curing Spain of the paralysis into which it had sunk. This helped accentuate criticism of the Restoration, which many intellectuals and politicians denounced as oligarchic and corrupt, and responsible for the country's backwardness and decadence.[13] In 1902, Alfonso XIII, a monarch much more politically active than either of his parents, came of age. In line with regenerationist rhetoric (so-called *regeneracionismo*) he adopted a Spanish nationalist discourse, and he wanted to turn Spain into a modern power respected in Europe, even if this meant intervening more in party politics.[14] At the same time, the first mass political parties appeared, which, taking advantage of the opportunities that universal suffrage offered, challenged the government parties in some cities. They enjoyed success especially in Barcelona, where the Catalanists of the Lliga Regionalista demanded recognition of Catalonia's status as a nation, and the republican followers of Alejandro Lerroux (the Lerrouxistas, who formed the Partido Republicano Radical [Radical Republican Party] in 1908) mobilized the left-wing electorate with their demagogic and anticlerical speeches.[15]

The period spanning 1897 to 1902 also brought the death of the historic Conservative and Liberal leaders and the search for new leaders and programmes by both parties. Despite the blow dealt by the 'Disaster' and the internal conflicts resulting from the struggle for leadership, both parties were able to renew themselves and elaborate reforming programmes. This process of renewal culminated between 1907 and 1912, when able leaders came to the fore who put their ideas into practice from within government. In the Conservative Party, Antonio Maura pushed through a programme which attempted to eliminate corrupt practices and 'uproot *caciquismo*' ('*descuajar el caciquismo*') through more transparent electoral procedures and by giving greater autonomy to local administration.[16] In the Liberal Party, first Segismundo Moret and then José Canalejas adopted a programme that was secular and interventionist in tone, on the lines of the New Liberalism in Britain and of French republican radicalism.[17] These programmes, which involved the mobilization of sectors of public opinion along the lines of such contentious issues as centralism versus regionalism, or clericalism versus anticlericalism, ended up with both parties clashing and becoming incompatible with each other. The paradox of the Restoration regime, which had been conceived as a delicate game of checks and balances, was that it

could only evolve towards democracy through recourse to public opinion, but when this occurred, albeit to a limited extent, its basic machinery began to break down.

1913 as a dividing line: Party fragmentation and political involvement of the king

This renewed two-party politics suffered a harsh setback as a result of
the assassination, towards the end of 1912, of the Liberal leader José
Canalejas at the hands of an anarchist terrorist. When the king had to
decide who should succeed him, not only did the Conservatives and
Liberals clash, but also both parties again split and some of their supporters cast doubt on essential rules of the Restoration settlement, such
as the *turno*. The political situation became polarized, especially with
regard to the possible return to power of Antonio Maura, who had fallen
from office in 1909 due to the repression of the so-called Tragic Week,
a bloody anticlerical riot in Barcelona. Maura's downfall, brought about
by Alfonso XIII, had been influenced by two factors: international protests at the execution of the pedagogue and freethinker Francisco Ferrer,
who was tried and found guilty by a military tribunal despite little
proof, and the demand, by the Liberal and Republican opposition, for
someone to blame for this scandal. In 1913, as in 1909, Maura was hated
by the Left, with the result that the politically active citizenry tended
to divide into two irreconcilable camps: those who backed the slogan
¡Maura no! (Maura No!) and those who backed *¡Maura sí!* (Maura Yes!).
The former saw Maura as the personification of clerical and authoritarian reaction, the latter saw him as a godsend, destined to save Spain
from its revolutionary enemies.

One part of the Conservative Party, under the leadership of Maura
himself, considered the attitude of the Liberal Monarchists from 1908
to 1909 to be unacceptable, as they had allied with the Republicans –
the very people opposed to the monarchy – against him. In response
Maura demanded, in 1913, an end to the collaboration between the
leftist Monarchists and the Republicans, and the Liberals naturally
were not prepared to accept such a humiliation. This led Maura to ref-
use to operate the *turno* with the Liberals – that is to say, he broke the
fundamental axis around which the system rotated. And this in turn
caused a Conservative split between those who maintained their allegiance to the *turno*, now under the leadership of Eduardo Dato (the
idóneos), and the so-called Mauristas who challenged it. The Mauristas
not only refused to play the political game of alternating in power, but

also bitterly criticized Alfonso XIII. Furthermore, although they started from the premise that legality should be strictly adhered to, they were to evolve towards the far Right.[18]

On the other hand, after the disappearance of their leader, the Liberals engaged in a new bout of in-fighting for the leadership and split into two groups: the Liberal majority led by Álvaro de Figueroa y Torres, the Count of Romanones, and the 'democrat' minority whose leader was Manuel García Prieto, the Marquis of Álhucemas. Some ideological differences separated them: Romanones was more sympathetic towards Catalanism and favoured closer relations with the Republicans, while Alhucemas was more of a Spanish nationalist centralist and rejected republicanism advances. Nevertheless, the key factor behind the rivalry was the struggle for leadership.[19] At the outset the Romanones faction, who sought an understanding with the more moderate Republicans of the Partido Reformista (Reformist Party), came out on top. The Reformists were prepared to back the liberal monarchy as long as it moved in a democratic direction. For this reason they referred to themselves as 'accidentalists', that is indifferent to the type of regime – be it republican or monarchical – as long as it incorporated democratic features – non-existent in the Restoration Constitution – such as freedom of thought and government responsibility towards parliament.[20] The party, which above all was made up of professional strata, had little weight in parliament but much influence in the sphere of public debate. In particular it enjoyed the support of a group of intellectuals who would become known as the Generation of 1914, at the head of which was José Ortega y Gasset, who was to become the best-known Spanish thinker of the 20th century and was at the time engaged in organizing 'intellectual leagues' whose aim was to make an impact on the political climate in order to stimulate the democratization of the monarchy.[21]

A central element of these years, given the divisions within the Liberal and Conservative Parties, was the enormous role played by the king, whose decision to maintain the Liberals in power during most of 1913 was openly debated in parliament.[22] As the government parties did not seek democratic legitimacy they tended to place the solution to their quarrels in the hands of the king, especially those that affected party leadership, and their political lives depended on the king's will. Even though occasionally they mobilized public opinion in search of support among the middle classes, the speeches made by their leaders at mass rallies were in reality a plea to the king for power. All this took place in an atmosphere of intrigue, plots, fears, and even hysterical and paranoid reaction whenever the monarch offered an opinion or it was rumoured that he was going to act in a particular way.[23] The supreme political game consisted of wooing the king to obtain a decree dissolving parliament. This automatically granted the means to manufacture, through fraudulent elections, a favourable parliamentary majority for the government.

The Monarchists were not alone in courting the king to win his favour. This practice was also adopted by the Republicans and later by Lliga Regionalista. The curious thing about the conjuncture of 1913 was that the main defenders of Alfonso XIII were the Reformists, who praised to the heavens the royal veto on Maura, thereby fomenting the monarch's political interventionism.[24] In this way they showed their powerlessness to change the political system by means of an open struggle in the electoral arena. Like the Monarchists they preferred to obtain a decree from the king dissolving parliament. In fact, the electoral route was by no means completely closed to the democratic opposition to the regime, as was demonstrated by the occasional triumphs of the republican and regionalist forces in a number of larger towns and cities. However, given that they only had influence in a few largely urban electoral districts, to try and win power through elections meant embarking on a slow, difficult task. This weakness of the democratic opposition, which oscillated between rapprochement with the king and a more revolutionary stance, would influence the crisis of the Restoration.

From 1913, therefore, the king was more than ever the central pivot of the system. In Spain, those elements which contributed so much to reducing the political role of the crown in other European monarchies – for example, in Great Britain – had yet to be consolidated. If the Spanish case is compared with that of Great Britain, it is clear that in Spain two crucial factors are missing. First, Spain lacked large, united, political parties built around a leader, whose solid structures represented much more than a mere aggregation of client personalities. The tendency of the Spanish parties towards factionalism offered Alfonso XIII a political influence that his contemporaries Edward VII and George V did not have. Second, in Great Britain the legal expansion of the electorate – which, in fact, took place later and less markedly than in Spain – was accompanied by high levels of participation and self-identification in the representative process. This conferred greater legitimacy on parliament and on the governments which emanated from it, when faced with any possible interference from the king. The Spanish Cortes were important – and at times had an influential role – in the political system, but they did not take any crucial decisions.[25] Therefore the Spanish monarch did not become a neutral player on the political stage, enjoying a status above the partisan quarrels, and the Spanish political parties, although occasionally turning to public opinion and launching campaigns, tended to look to the king, and not the electorate, when attempting to win power.

1913–17: Attempts to bring back the *Turno*

In the years following the break-up of the government parties in 1913, the majority factions of both camps – the Count of Romanones' Liberals and Eduardo Dato's Conservatives – attempted to rebuild the *turno* system (see Table 2.1). Although they achieved a certain degree of stability, the division of their respective parties affected their strategies. Matters were further complicated by the repercussions on Spain of the First World War. During the war Spain remained officially neutral, owing to the weak state of its armed forces and domestic disagreements as to which of the two sides in the conflict was deserving of support. However, as Francisco Romero Salvadó has written, 'Spain did not enter the war, but the war entered Spain'.[26] This was in part a result of the war's economic impact, which led to an era of great prosperity, but also to an unequal share-out of that prosperity and growing inflation which helped to heighten social conflict. It also had powerful ideological repercussions, sharpening internal nationalist tensions and creating a sharp division in public opinion between supporters of the Allies (francophiles) and supporters of the Central Powers (germanophiles), provoking what Gerald Meaker has called 'a civil war of words'.[27] All of this transformed the political scene.

As regards parliamentary politics, the division of the parties made the formation and maintenance of a parliamentary majority difficult for whoever was in power, which then led governments frequently to close the Cortes to avoid problems (although the constitution required that parliament meet every year, a minimum period of time was not fixed so governments could keep it closed for months on end). Between the beginning of 1914 and the end of 1915 Dato's orthodox Conservative government was dependent on the benevolence of Romanones' Liberals in parliament and therefore hardly any legislation was passed. The most important reform was the decree setting up the Catalan Mancomunitat, an administrative institution which brought together the four Catalan provincial councils and therefore granted the Catalanists one of their main objectives: the territorial unity of Catalonia. The Mancomunitat, governed from the start by the Lliga Regionalista, devoted itself to the educational, cultural and political task of Catalan nation-building.[28] Otherwise, the Dato government,

Table 2.1 Elections and make-up of the Congreso De Los Diputados (1914–23)

Date	08/03/1914	09/04/1916	24/02/1918	01/06/1919	19/12/1920	29/04/1923
(Govt)	Conservatives	Liberals	Nat salvation	Maurist Conserv	Conservative	Liberal
Conserv	216	111	147	190	221	115
Liberals	119	224	170	130	112	182
Other Monarchists	001	000	003	009	006	005
Traditionalists/ Carlists	006	010	009	007	005	004
Regionalists & Nationalists	013	015	033	019	019	021
Reformists	012	013	009	007	009	018
Republicans	019	020	015	016	012	013
Socialists	001	001	006	006	003	007
Independents	011	006	009	004	009	013
Not known	006	008	004	005	007	005
Total	404	408	405	393	403	383

Sources: M. Cabrera (ed.), Con luz y taquígrafos. El Parlamento en la Restauración (1913–1923) (Madrid: Taurus, 1998), p. 355; and author's own work.

preoccupied above all with the maintenance of neutrality, limited itself to surviving.

From 1915 to 1916 a re-formed Liberal majority government, under the leadership of Romanones, was able to operate more effectively, and, although its discipline left a lot to be desired, it undertook some important reforms. The economic consequences of the First World War meant that the Liberals sidelined the clericalism/anticlericalism question that had preoccupied them so much previously, and concentrated more on public finances and social problems. After the economic contraction caused by the initial uncertainty, the Spanish economy showed itself capable of reacting and took advantage of the country's neutrality to supply raw materials and manufactured goods to the countries at war. In this environment the rising star of Liberal politics became Santiago Alba, who combined a strongly Spanish nationalist and anti-Catalanist discourse with an interventionist programme on the lines of British New Liberalism. His tax plans stood out especially, centring on a tax on the extraordinary profits obtained by industry (mostly located in Catalonia and the Basque Country) during the wartime boom, and a complete reorganization of the Treasury to make the state the true engine of the country's modernization. As Alba realized, only economic and tax reform of this magnitude would give the weak Spanish state the resources to provide the country with the necessary infrastructure in sectors such as public works, education and social services.[29]

During this time minority groups appeared on the scene in the Spanish parliament, determined to break with the system. The Lliga Regionalista in particular became an increasingly important presence. It was determined to undermine the bipartisan *turno* in order to increase its influence and achieve recognition of a distinctive Catalan reality. The party's objectives evolved from simple administrative decentralization to political autonomy and it now adopted a clearly Catalan nationalist language. With their leader Francesc Cambó to the fore, the Lliga capitalized on the mobilization by business against Alba's plans and made maximum use of all the possibilities that the regulations of the old liberal parliament gave it to obstruct his legislative reforms in the Cortes. Miguel Matorell has studied extensively these mechanisms, which allowed a determined movement like the Lliga to effectively block parliamentary legislation.[30] Although the regulations' objective was to safeguard the prerogatives of the parliamentarians, in reality the practice of obstruction, exacerbated by the fragmentation of the political parties, the indiscipline of the parliamentarians and the periodic closure of the lower and upper houses, led to parliament being inoperative. One only has to remember that between 1914 and 1920 not one budget was approved.

At the same time, the struggle between the francophiles and the germanophiles monopolized public debate and built up pressure to break the official stance of neutrality and to tilt foreign policy in favour of one side or the other. While the francophiles – in general, those on the Left – called for governments to favour the Western powers or even for entry into the war on the side of the Allies, the germanophiles – who were almost always on the Right of the political spectrum – preferred maintenance of strict neutrality, since an open alignment with Germany was not viable because of Spain's geographical location and strategic interests. As the war went on, tensions increased, spilled out onto the streets and affected the government parties. Both sides called rallies with massive audiences, like those given by Maura on the one hand, and those held by various left-wing orators on the other, in the Madrid bullring in the spring of 1917. With regard to the Monarchist parties, these divisions affected above all the Liberal Party while it remained in government. The pro-German press – among which there were Liberal elements who belonged to critical currents within the party – devoted itself to mercilessly attacking Romanones, the Monarchist leader with the strongest pro-Allied outlook. These divisions put paid to his government and to the fragile Liberal unity in the spring of 1917. The party once again, and definitively, split into two factions, although García Prieto's 'democrats' now became the majority and were in a stronger position to remain in power thanks to the king's favour, while Romanones was now in a minority, his pro-Allied sympathies ensuring his marginalization. Both factions had the support of their respective local clientelist base.[31]

The king's stance was again crucial at this point, particularly as his initial sympathy for the Allies, which was in line with Spanish foreign policy since the end of the 19th century, was replaced by a defence of the out-and-out neutrality that the pro-German factions had been preaching. This shift reflected his own ideological evolution towards the Right and his fear that upon entry into the war (which appeared possible if Romanones stayed in power and responded vigorously to German submarine attacks on Spanish shipping) a revolution would be unleashed that would unseat the monarchy. Alfonso XIII was particularly shocked by events in Russia in the February and March of 1917; he discussed them frequently and they were to greatly influence his political attitude thereafter. They convinced him not only that the Allies did not yet have the war won, but also that a revolution could be imminent in Spain.[32]

1917–19: Governments of national unity and governments beset by factions

The precarious attempt to reconstruct the *turno* between Conservatives and Liberals was dynamited in the summer of 1917, when a number of rebellions, some of them with revolutionary aims, challenged the *caciquista* two-party set-up, the constitutional order based on the Constitution of 1876 and the monarchy itself. From a long-term perspective, perhaps the most important political event was the sudden appearance of the military defence committees, the *Juntas Militares de Defensa*, which, with the intermittent support of the king, became a crucial factor in destabilizing the political system. In the absence of a modern police force, those in power depended on the army for the maintenance of public order, which meant that confrontation with significant sectors of the armed forces became very difficult for any government.[33] This was particularly the case because from 1917, on several occasions, weak and minority governments were targeted by the *Juntas*, and the king sided with the military against the civil authorities.

Other subversive forces, such as the Lliga and other Catalan groups, and the trade unions, temporarily joined forces with the *Juntas*. They did not manage to reach any lasting agreements, because each had their own distinctive aims, and the government was able to respond successfully to the rebellion and quashed an attempted general strike in August 1917. But an assembly of rebel parliamentarians, which met first in Barcelona and then in Madrid, brought up the need for a constitutional reform that would make the system more answerable to parliament and democratize the regime, with a full commitment to national sovereignty and serious limitations on the king's powers, the secularization of the state and the granting of regional autonomies. Among the assembly members, contrary to what many historians have led us to understand, there were also members of the government parties, especially the Liberals, who also supported change.[34]

Constitutional reform did not materialize, mostly because of the determined opposition of the king and the Conservatives, but also due to the political weakness of those groups most committed to reform, such as the Partido Reformista. However, the crisis of 1917 had profound effects on the political system. The main result was the disappearance of the two-party *turno*. Over the following years two distinct sides were to emerge on the Spanish political scene. On the one hand, there were those opposed to the *turno* set-up. They included most of the members of the parliamentary assembly, such as the Catalanists, who had done all in their power to break the *turno*, and also the minority groups within the two big Monarchist parties, which would emerge as losers should the two-party system be re-established, but which could perform an important role in government should it be replaced by new mechanisms for the exercise of power based on other formulas such as multi-party governments. These groups were basically led by the triumvirate of Cambó-Maura-Romanones. From 1917 they vehemently criticized the old parties and the bipartite *turno*, which they saw as both inoperable and past its sell-by date. On the other hand, there were those who, despite everything, could not see any alternative to an updated variant of the classic alternation of power between two large blocks on the Right and Left. This position was defended by the majority groups in both pro-monarchy parties: Dato's Conservatives and García Prieto's 'democrats'. Until 1919 the former group were in the ascendancy; after this date the latter would impose their will.[35]

The immediate political effect of the revolutionary summer of 1917 was the triumph of those calling for multi-party solutions. In principle this had the great advantage over preceding formulas in that it widened support for the constitutional monarchy by integrating political forces which until then had been confined to the margins of the regime. These included moderate left- and right-wing Catalanist forces, which entered the first multi-party government founded at the end of 1917, presided over by García Prieto. Its mission was to call fair elections, without the fraudulent government *encasillado*. This had been one of the demands most frequently made in democrat circles.

The *fair* elections of 1918 are of great importance because they make it possible to calibrate political influence at a local level in Spain. In particular, although governmental pressure on the localities did not disappear completely, these elections are a good indicator of a significant phenomenon in Spanish political life, the growing importance of so-called *distritos propios*. These were districts under the domination of one party or faction, in which either one of the party's members was systematically re-elected, or in which the political weight of the said party or faction continuously determined the election result.

There were two kinds of *distritos propios*, which existed for different reasons. On the one hand, some constituencies had broken free from the *cacique* system. This was especially the case in urban areas, which, during the crisis of the Restoration, increasingly opted for the Partido Socialista Obrero Español (Spanish Socialist Workers' Party –PSOE) to the detriment of the Republicans – who were in freefall – and also, in some cities, for Catalan and now also Basque nationalists and the followers of Maura. On the other hand, in rural areas solid *cacique* strongholds with clientelist roots had established themselves independently of the government of the day. In other words, figures known to a particular area were able to take control of its affairs by basing their influence on the defence of local interests and on the sharing of public resources among their clients. To quote Maura, they comprised 'the professional groups and had set up their traps and had their friends in every province and in every town'.[36] A vicious circle was therefore being established: the districts themselves became a refuge for influential politicians against government instability and volatility, and their spread, at the same time, had an impact on the parties, making their fragmentation more acute and insoluble.

The growth of these districts thereby revealed a greater politicization of Spanish society, which traditionally had been marked by indifference to political life. This was the case not only in the cities, where competition was becoming more open and genuine, but also in country areas, where interest in politics began to grow among the middle and upper classes, although often this was expressed by means of a locality-centred clientelist political culture. In this case the individual or collective favour that the local notable or powerful *cacique* could bestow attracted greater attention than far-reaching ideological programmes. Nevertheless, this situation represented a break with the former passivity the government had encountered in rural areas and made the management of the regime more complex.

Bearing in mind the rural *distritos propios* as a whole, the Monarchists held sway. Nevertheless, there were rural districts in the hands of the opposition, from the Catalan nationalists in Catalonia, through to Reformists in Asturias. The electoral map of 1918 also confirmed the growing strength of autonomous client-based *cacique* politics, though in some of the electoral districts mass-based left- and right-wing parties had begun to make an impact. Within these parameters, a certain renewal of the parliamentary elite could also be observed, with the rise of young professionals who did not, like their predecessors, have to first climb the ladder of local politics (the so-called *cursus honorum*). A strengthening of family ties between the parliamentarians was also discernible and was related to the search for cohesion within the party factions.[37]

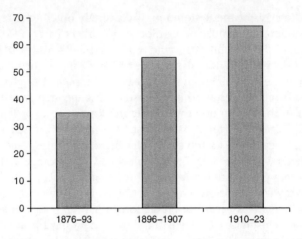

Figure 2.1   Percentage of seats in the Lower House of Parliament which were *Distritos Propios*, 1876–1923

Sources: J. Varela Ortega (ed.), *El poder de la influencia. Geografía del caciquismo en España (1875–1923)* (Madrid: Centro de Estudios Políticos y Constitucionales/Marcial Pons Historia, 2001), Appendix, pp. 651–776; and the author's own work.

Figure 2.1 illustrates the evolution of the *distritos propios* during the Restoration. The regime has been divided into three stages or phases, in each of which there were seven elections to the Cortes. An electoral circumscription is classified as a *distrito propio* when it elects, in at least five of the seven elections in a phase, the same deputy or a deputy from the same party. As can be gleaned from Figure 2.1, the percentage of these *distritos propios* grew considerably: from 35 per cent in the first phase (1876–93), to 55 per cent in the second phase (1896–1907) and 66 per cent in the third stage, which more or less coincides with the crisis of the Restoration (1910–23).

This growth of *distritos propios* made it much more difficult for governments to manage elections. They could no longer eliminate dissidents within their own party in the elections, nor could they fabricate the great majorities that they were able to in the first years of the Restoration. And this was made even more difficult by the fragmentation of the Conservative and Liberal parties. That is to say, governments, when writing the election book, could no longer fill in blank pages, but rather had to come face to face with pages that had already been filled in. In the 1918 election, where government interference was reduced markedly because of the effects of the crisis of 1917, the result was a fragmented and paralysed Cortes. This election also served as an antidote to possible experiments in the electoral arena: the risks brought by any absence of control became apparent, and in future no government would renounce the traditional mechanisms of the *encasillado* and governmental interference in elections, no matter how difficult it would be to apply such methods in this new phase.

Based on the logic that governments of national unity were a necessity, after these elections a government of 'national salvation' was formed. It was encouraged by the king, who had by now achieved a high degree of political influence. It consisted of all the Monarchist leaders and was presided over by Antonio Maura, who, having previously been ostracized, now returned as a quasi-providential saviour. His so-called national government represented a great victory for the enemies of the *turno*: the followers of Maura and Romanones, and Cambó's Lliga Regionalista, which had been integrated into the Restoration regime. This government, which aroused great expectations, undertook an important legislative programme. Its state employees' law put an end to the temporary employment of these workers, which had been the basis of a spoils system that had helped to oil the clientelist political machine. The reform of the regulations of the lower house, by introducing a maximum time period or guillotine to settle debates, speeded up parliamentary work.[38] Cambó initiated a public works programme. And Alba's education reforms created advanced educational institutions and led to the drafting of an ambitious plan for the building of primary schools, which the country needed. Yet the implication from the outset was that such a national government was exceptional and therefore provisional. It only lasted for a few months because its components were jockeying for position in anticipation of what, it was expected, would be a new political scenario after the end of the First World War.

Despite some opposition, further anti-*turno* administrations followed on from the national government. These now took the form of governments by a single-party faction, which, despite not enjoying the support of the majority groups in the Cortes, had the advantage of possessing great internal cohesiveness. First, the Allied victory and the upsurge in Catalanist agitation again put Romanones – a francophile in favour of Catalan autonomy – in power. The Catalan and Basque nationalists, like their European counterparts, demanded political sovereignty, encouraged by the triumph of the principle of self-determination at the end of the war. Indeed, under Romanones an opportunity for the approval of a statute of Catalan autonomy was lost because of the clash between hard-line Catalan and Spanish nationalists.[39] However, Romanones' cabinet fell for another reason.

Its readiness to negotiate with the Anarcho-Syndicalist Confederación Nacional del Trabajo (National Labour Confederation – CNT) following the outbreak of the big La Canadiense strike in Barcelona early in 1919, exacerbated tensions with a hostile army, which was both anti-Catalanist and defended the maintenance of law and order at all costs. The Liberal government's rapprochement with the working-class movement included, for example, the approval by decree of an eight-hour working day – Spain was one of the first countries in the world to adopt this measure – and a regulation establishing retirement pensions. But the armed forces humiliated the civil authorities in Barcelona and received the backing of the king, who was by this time an out-and-out militarist and counter-revolutionary.[40]

The Liberal faction of the Count of Romanones was succeeded in government by Maura's Conservative faction, which, despite adopting a much tougher counter-revolutionary stance, continued to enjoy the support of the anti-*turno* elements, including Romanones' Liberals. Even though only just over a year had elapsed since the last election, this Maura-led cabinet obtained a decree from the king to dissolve parliament, and, although it employed every trick in the book, attained the dubious honour of being the first Spanish government since the 1840s to lose an election. This resulted in its dramatic fall as soon as it was subjected to a vote in parliament. It had become obvious that the tools employed by the ministry of the interior to 'make' elections were unable to counteract the backing for the political factions in their respective *distritos propios*.

1919–23: The formation of two coalitions and political reforms

The period between 1919 and 1923 can be regarded as representing a final stage in which the failure of the governments of national unity and of factions led to the formation of a new bipolar political landscape. This was no longer based on two parties, since the old monarchic organizations had broken up, but on two broad coalitions: a Conservative one, under the leadership of Maura or Dato – and from Dato's assassination in 1921 his orthodox Conservative heir, José Sánchez Guerra – and a Liberal one under García Prieto, which was able to incorporate both the followers of Romanones on the Right and reform-minded Republicans on the Left. While the *Juntas Militares de Defensa* remained strong they acted as a veto on the Liberals, who did not wish to hand over any further power to the military and were considered by the *Juntas* as excessively tolerant in the face of revolutionary challenges to the regime. This helps explain why the various governments which succeeded each other between 1919 and 1922 were mainly Conservative.

At least two options presented themselves to the Conservatives. On the one hand, as previously, the orthodox Conservatives aimed to provide the monarchy with a broad-based disciplined force, which could reconstruct the *turno* and stabilize the regime. On the other hand, the group behind Maura, helped by the authoritarian Conservative Juan de la Cierva – who had his own small faction of followers – wanted to construct a *counter-revolutionary* front. From 1921, the king tried, without much success, to unite both wings into a single political force. But these years also saw a proliferation of attempts to form a broad coalition of the Spanish Right by elements as diverse as Carlists and orthodox Conservatives. Such plans won the support of the Catholic Church, the nobility and the king. Their ideological pillars were Catholic nationalism, social reaction and the defence of the monarchy backed by the military. Their strategy was linked to the mobilization of the Church-inspired vote by the Catholic associations or leagues (*ligas*) that had appeared in different parts of Spain, as well as agrarian-based Catholic trade unions.[41] This pointed to the Church's great capacity to mobilize, and while this was not yet fully realized (as would occur during the Second Republic in the 1930s), its potential became clear. At the same time, Spanish nationalist Monarchist parties made their appearance in the Basque Country and Catalonia.

The strength of the Maurista movement should be stressed. It was a peculiar phenomenon in that it was the only mass political movement born of a government Monarchist party in Spain. Within it were two distinct wings: the moderates, who adopted a philosophy akin to that of the Christian Democrats in other parts of Europe, and the extremists who held Fascist sympathies and turned to street activism. The Mauristas had much success among the urban middle classes – especially in Madrid – and tried to make inroads into the workers' world: up to 1919–20 they operated workers' teaching centres and friendly societies. The right-wing Mauristas, who were in a majority, employed a nationalist, Monarchist, Catholic, anti-*caciquista* and, above all, a counter-revolutionary language. This discourse was attractive to the so-called *gente de orden* (law and order crowd).[42] Thus they developed important connections with the business world, the Catalan Carlist-inspired Sindicatos Libres (Free Trade Unions), the citizens' militias which sprang up in some cities and, generally, with those circles that would subsequently provide the cadres for the Primo de Rivera dictatorship.[43] Their ideology was anti-liberal, like those which were spreading in other European countries in the same period. They detested liberal regimes for being too weak when faced by the challenges of the post-war world, advocated force in order to overthrow them, and a new political system based on corporative representation.

The Gordian knot of Spanish politics in this period was in the relationship between civil and military power, with the weakness of civil power directly proportional to the pressure wielded by the army with the support of the king. Conservative cabinets, like the one presided over by Joaquín Sánchez de Toca at the end of 1919, fell when coming face to face with the *Juntas Militares de Defensa*. The conflict had a two-fold scenario, Barcelona and Morocco. In Barcelona, the question was whether to employ a strategy of negotiation with the CNT, to which the military authorities, *Juntas*, business and Lliga Regionalista were all opposed; or adopt an out-and-out repressive strategy, as they wanted. Conservative governments swayed between the two options without making up their minds. While the Mauristas adopted a tough stance, the orthodox Conservatives appeared more inclined to negotiate as part of a broader strategy aimed at stabilizing labour relations through the new Ministry of Labour. However, Dato himself shifted from a conciliatory to a repressive policy during 1920 and his anarchist assassins justified their crime in 1921 by accusing him of having sponsored the so-called *ley de fugas*, the killing of those arrested by the forces of law and order with the excuse that they had tried to escape custody.[44]

Then the Morocco problem burst into life with a vengeance as a result of the so-called 'Annual Disaster', in which about 10,000 Spanish soldiers lost their lives in the summer of 1921.[45] This catastrophic event brought Maura back into power. His 'national mini-cabinet', formed in an alliance with Cambó, undertook important economic reforms, as Fidel Gómez Ochoa has shown, such as, for example, the new tariff aimed at protecting industry, which was now in crisis after the boom period of the First World War had turned to burst.[46] From then on the question of who was responsible for the events of the 'Annual' moved centre stage. It was debated openly in parliament, with the PSOE directly accusing the king of having promoted the military operations that had led to the fiasco.[47] Political struggles in the Conservative camp resulted in the orthodox option winning the day. This implied shying away from a broad right-wing coalition, while adopting a more moderate ideological stance, respectful of parliamentary protocol, committed to liberalism and civil power and opposed to any temptation to stage a coup. This position was embodied in Sánchez Guerra's 1922

Conservative government. He managed to bring some normality to the political situation by reinstating constitutional guarantees, which had been suspended for three years, and putting an end once and for all to the repressive state of emergency in Barcelona and to the subversive *Juntas Militares de Defensa*. It was also Sánchez Guerra's government which submitted the so-called Picasso inquiry, an official report on the 'Annual', for debate in parliament.

The Sánchez Guerra government represented the culmination of a period of relative normalization in Spanish political life, marked by less direct intervention by the military and with parliament making a greater impact. This is indicated by the changing causes behind government crises, analysed in Figure 2.2, for the period 1912 to 1923. The term crisis is used when the prime minister fell (although the crisis at the end of 1912, when the Liberal Romanones was reconfirmed in power, has also been included because of its political relevance). The figure points to the political protagonists who had a crucial part in the origin and resolution of each crisis. There were four distinct players: the army (A), the king (K), the notables of the government parties (G) and parliament (P). It indicates that the most relevant factor in crises suffered by the government was the intervention of major notables (a determining role in 12 of the 18 crises), followed by the king (in 10), parliament (in 7) and the army (in 6). While the intervention of parliament was linked to that of the notables, whose power rested on the parliamentary factions,

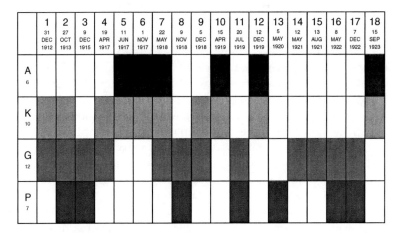

Figure 2.2 Government crises, 1912–23

Source: Author's own work.

the power of the army was closely allied to that of the king, who acted as an arbiter in conflicts between the military and civil powers. An ebb and flow in the causes of crises can be observed. While the army and king were the determining factors in the government crises between 1917 and 1919, their influence subsequently weakened, and between 1920 and 1922 the intervention of major figures, linked to parliament, became more important. As noted, this reveals a degree of stabilization of the political situation, related to the beginnings of a new *turno* between Conservative and Liberal coalitions.

Opposing the Conservatives, the Liberal Party, which had been marginalized from power for some years – except for periodic participation in governments of national unity – evolved in a democratic and interventionist direction in the constitutional, educational, economic and social spheres, and with respect to the relationship between civil power and the army. However, the Liberals experienced difficulties in reaching agreements amongst themselves. Three different attitudes stand out. On the Right, Romanones' followers were very reluctant to form a Liberal coalition and in favour of supporting the multi-party efforts and counter-revolutionary politics of Maura and Cambó. In the centre, the majority grouping, García Prieto's 'democrats', wanted to form a coalition in which they would play the central role and were ready to alternate in power with the Conservatives. Their moderate position, which was acceptable to the king and well supported in provincial clientelist circles, would win out. On the Left, Alba's backers wanted a leftward-leaning coalition that would include Reformists and even the PSOE, with a wide programme of socio-economic reform which was open to constitutional reform. The Socialists, who were open enemies of the monarchy, refused to be drawn in. However, the Reformists, who had turned their back on revolutionary adventures like that of 1917, now in reality functioned as a faction within the monarchic Liberal camp, though they still flew the flag of constitutional reform.[48]

The Liberals mobilized support by means of propaganda campaigns and finally united when they saw the possibility of returning to power, a task made easier by the work undertaken by Sánchez Guerra to strengthen civil power. Finally, at the end of 1922, a Liberal coalition formed a government and for the first time the Reformists joined it. With this, it could be argued, both the Catalanists of the Lliga Regionalista and the Reformists – the 'decentralizers and reformists' whom Ortega y Gasset had identified in 1918 as the greatest hopes for renewal in Spanish politics[49] – had been absorbed by the regime. It was evidently not as stagnant as some historians have often claimed. Meanwhile, the king had taken an increasingly clear position in favour of authoritarian options, adopting a counter-revolutionary, nationalistic, Catholic and militarist ideology. Alfonso XIII, the hero of the Liberal and Reformist Left and pilloried by the Mauristas in 1913, had become the hope of the Right and a scapegoat for the Left in 1923. The monarch's opinions were revealed in various private interviews and public interventions in which he discredited the political parties and parliament and advocated an authoritarian solution to the country's political problems. As a detailed study by José Luis Gómez-Navarro has shown, Alfonso XIII saw himself as the saviour of the fatherland, as a man who entertained great ideas and enjoyed the support of his people, but who found himself a prisoner of constitutional mechanisms, of ministers, parties and parliament.[50]

An old dilemma of Spanish historiography is the question of whether it was the fragmentation of the parties which propelled Alfonso XIII to intervene in public life, or whether it was the king himself who unleashed party division. There are arguments in favour of each of these theses, but, as has been shown here, it was party fragmentation which opened the way to interference by the throne. However, this does not mean that the king allowed himself to be dragged along by circumstances, as Javier Tusell has claimed on several occasions.[51] What was really the core of the problem was that the monarch seized the opportunities that presented themselves increasingly to intervene and, imbued with a reactionary traditionalist nationalism, he did so in such a way as to stymie any consolidation of civil power, because he backed the military when it challenged government, and to hinder the democratization of the regime, given his opposition to constitutional reform and distrust of parliament. The Liberal unity government of 1922–3 always lived under the threat of intervention by the military and the king, who continually played with the idea of launching a coup d'état himself and then abdicating if it backfired on him. Morocco was at the centre of tensions because of the determination of the government to establish a civilian protectorate, because of the military strategy it wished to follow in the colony, and also because its petition that parliament deal with the responsibilities issue would harm the military and would end up affecting the monarch himself.

The Liberal government aspired to introduce a wide programme of reform that, as well as the measures noted above, included constitutional reform to guarantee that the Cortes would sit at least four months per year, making the Senate more democratic in its composition and election, and reducing the government's discretionary powers to suspend constitutional guarantees. Furthermore, it intended to introduce religious freedom, but this was quickly blocked by the Church. Finally, it planned a series of economic and social measures, among which agrarian reform stood out, and it also wanted to replace the electoral system with proportional suffrage. These proposals represented the aspirations of the different elements that made up the government coalition. The 1923 elections were as fraudulent as those that had gone before, but they opened the door to a reform of the political system, if only in the long term. However, the programme remained virtually unimplemented, partly because internal divisions within the Liberal camp once again raised their heads and partly because within a few months of the new parliament being opened, the coup d'état of General Miguel Primo de Rivera took place. It had the support of the king, the only person who could make it succeed. In this way, Alfonso XIII, though obliged to defend the constitution, did away with almost 50 years of constitutional rule to embark on an authoritarian adventure which would end very badly for him.[52]

Final considerations

The significance of Primo de Rivera's coup in contemporary Spanish history has given rise to a famous controversy, which has pitted two groups of historians against each other. On the one side, those whom we might call the 'optimists', who, like Raymond Carr and Shlomo Ben-Ami, have argued that the coup suffocated a newborn child, that is to say a political system which, in 1923, was showing signs of democratizing.[53] On the other side are the 'pessimists', with Carlos Seco Serrano and Javier Tusell at their head, who have insisted that the political system of the Restoration represented a dead end, and that Primo de Rivera finished off a dying man.[54] In this chapter an intermediate position has been taken, but rather closer to that of the 'optimists'. To speak of the democratization of the constitutional regime in 1923 is to exaggerate somewhat. No mass political mobilization capable of breaking the *cacique* networks had taken place, and neither had constitutional reform – which had been demanded by a section of the political forces since the beginning of the century and especially since 1917 – been achieved. That is to say, any democratic opening was inhibited by the lack of electoral mobilization of public opinion headed by government or opposition parties. Nor was there any attempt to rewrite the laws of the political game, which perhaps would have helped achieve a full-blown parliamentary regime. All of this meant that the regime's direction often depended on a monarch who, from 1917, had been leaning towards anti-parliamentary solutions.

But one can also point to four main areas in which the regime did change and reform. First, it proved adaptable and its protagonists searched for new solutions to the problems it encountered. Thus the governments of national unity first, and then the move towards two alternative coalitions, to a certain extent succeeded in giving it stability. In 1923 the political landscape was less agitated than it had been in 1917 or in 1919. Second, despite the enormous instability of the time, some important reforms were undertaken, especially in the economic and social spheres, from new tariffs to the eight-hour working day. By 1923, the economic crisis had blown over and social conflict had lessened. Third, old anti-system parties such as the Lliga Regionalista and the Reformists had been integrated, while the extreme anti-liberal Right, the Republicans and even the PSOE found themselves in a very precarious situation electorally. And fourth, there were positive developments in the area of parliamentary procedures. The Cortes was reformed, putting an end to its chronic inefficiency, and parliamentary debates, especially as a result of the Annual disaster, acquired major political importance.

However, this incipient strengthening of parliamentary government did not imply immediate democratization, although it did facilitate it. Furthermore, as the case of Italy shows, neither did democratization necessarily produce a stable parliamentary regime or protection from authoritarian threats.[55] Some practitioners of virtual history have insisted that, but for Primo de Rivera's coup, the constitutional monarchy would probably have evolved to become a parliamentary monarchy which would have brought with it a stable democracy, or perhaps it would have given birth to a moderate republic with more chance of consolidation than the one which was proclaimed in 1931.[56] Without submerging ourselves in counterfactual exercises, what can be stated is that in early September 1923 nothing was decided and many options were still open.

Notes

This chapter was translated by Phil O'Hare and revised by Angel Smith. All translations from Spanish to English are by us.

1. There are no recent historiographic summaries dealing with this period. However, there are two important works from 1991 and 1994: Fidel Gómez Ochoa, 'La crisis final de la Restauración (1917–1923) en la

historiografía española', in Germán Rueda (ed.), *Doce estudios de historiografía contemporánea* (Santander: Universidad de Cantabria/Asamblea Regional de Cantabria, 1991), pp. 183–209; and Ignacio Olábarri, 'Actores políticos y actores sociales en la crisis de la Restauración (1914–1931). I. Los actores políticos', *Investigaciones históricas*, 14 (1994), pp. 197–219.

2. Teresa Carnero Arbat (ed.), *El reinado de Alfonso XIII*, monographic number of *Ayer. Revista de Historia Contemporánea*, 28 (1997).

3. See, for example, Juan Pro, 'La política en tiempos del *Desastre*', in Juan Pan-Montojo (coord.), *Más se perdió en Cuba. España, 1898 y la crisis de fin de siglo* (Madrid: Alianza Editorial, 1998), pp. 151–260. Pro refers to 'an end already forecast' from 1898 (p. 248).

4. Sebastian Balfour, *El fin del imperio español (1898–1923)* (Barcelona: Crítica, 1997), p. 231 (there is an English edition, Oxford, 1997).

5. Carlos Seco Serrano, 'El plano inclinado hacia la dictadura (1922–1923)', in José María Jover Zamora (ed.), *Historia de España Menéndez Pidal, 38/2: La España de Alfonso XIII. El Estado y la política (1902–1931). Del plano inclinado hacia la dictadura al final de la monarquía, 1922–1931* (Madrid: Espasa Calpe, 1995), pp. 9–130.

6. Mercedes Cabrera, 'El rey constitucional', in Javier Moreno Luzón (ed.), *Alfonso XIII. Un político en el trono* (Madrid: Marcial Pons Historia, 2003), pp. 83–110.

7. Carlos Dardé, 'Fraud and the Passivity of the Electorate in Spain, 1875–1923', in Eduardo Posada-Carbó (ed.), *Elections before Democracy: The History of Elections in Europe and Latin America* (London: ILAS-University of London, 1996), pp. 201–21.

8. Javier Moreno-Luzón, 'Political Clientelism, Elites, and *caciquismo* in Restoration Spain (1875–1923)', *European History Quarterly*, 37/3 (2007), pp. 417–41.

9. José Varela Ortega (ed.), *El poder de la influencia. Geografía del caciquismo en España (1875–1923)* (Madrid: Centro de Estudios Políticos y Constitucionales/ Marcial Pons Historia, 2001).

10. See, for example, Paolo Pombeni (ed.), *La trasformazione politica nell'Europa liberale 1870–1890* (Bologna: Il Mulino, 1986).

11. Javier Tusell, 'El encasillado de 1930', *Revista del Centro de Estudios Constitucionales*, 21 (1995) pp. 23–54.

12. Nigel Townson, 'La vieja política bajo la II República: caciquismo, clientelismo y control electoral', in Mercedes Gutiérrez Sánchez and Diego Palacios Cerezales (eds), *Conflicto político, democracia y dictadura. Portugal y España en la década de 1930* (Madrid: Centro de Estudios Políticos y Constitucionales, 2007), pp. 155–77.

13. Mercedes Cabrera and Javier Moreno Luzón (eds), *Regeneración y reforma. España a comienzos del siglo XX* (Madrid: Fundación BBVA, 2002).

14. Morgan C. Hall, *Alfonso XIII y el ocaso de la monarquía liberal, 1902–1923* (Madrid: Alianza Editorial, 2005); Javier Moreno Luzón, 'El rey patriota. Alfonso XIII y el nacionalismo español', in Ángeles Lario (ed.), *Monarquía y República en la España contemporánea* (Madrid: Biblioteca Nueva/UNED, 2007), pp. 269–94.

15. Borja de Riquer i Permanyer, *Escolta Espanya. La cuestión catalana en la España liberal* (Madrid: Marcial Pons Historia, 2001); José Álvarez Junco,

The Emergence of Mass Politics in Spain: Populist Demagoguery and Republican Culture, 1890–1910 (Brighton: Sussex Academic Press, 2002).

16. María Jesús González Hernández, *El universo conservador de Antonio Maura. Biografía y proyecto de Estado* (Madrid: Biblioteca Nueva/Fundación Antonio Maura, 1997).

17. Carlos Ferrera, *La frontera democrática del liberalismo: Segismundo Moret (1838–1913)* (Madrid: Biblioteca Nueva/Universidad Autónoma de Madrid, 2002); Salvador Forner Muñoz, *Canalejas y el Partido Liberal Democrático (1900–1910)* (Madrid: Cátedra/Instituto de Cultura Juan Gil-Albert, 1993); Javier Moreno Luzón, 'José Canalejas. La democracia, el estado y la nación', in Javier Moreno Luzón (ed.), *Progresistas. Biografías de reformistas españoles* (Madrid: Taurus/Fundación Pablo Iglesias, 2006), pp. 161–93.

18. María Jesús González Hernández, *Ciudadanía y acción. El conservadurismo maurista, 1907–1923* (Madrid: Siglo XXI, 1990), pp. 30ff.

19. Javier Moreno Luzón, *Romanones. Caciquismo y política liberal* (Madrid: Alianza Editorial, 1998), pp. 290–301.

20. Manuel Suárez Cortina, *El reformismo en España. Republicanos y reformistas bajo la Monarquía de Alfonso XIII* (Madrid: Siglo XXI/Universidad de Cantabria, 1986), pp. 85–131.

21. Javier Zamora Bonilla, *Ortega y Gasset* (Barcelona: Plaza & Janés, 2002), pp. 134–45.

22. Luis Arranz has used parliamentary debates to study the crisis of 1913 in depth in 'El debate parlamentario sobre las crisis de Gobierno 1909–1913. Una crisis de eficacia', *Documentos de trabajo del Seminario de Historia Contemporánea del Instituto Ortega y Gasset*, 2/ 2 (1996), pp. 5–82.

23. This situation can be studied at length in one of the most reliable sources for assessing the internal life of the Conservative and Liberal parties, the diary of the Liberal politician Natalio Rivas, which is kept in the Archivo Natalio Rivas in the Real Academia de la Historia in Madrid.

24. María Jesús González Hernández, 'El rey de los conservadores', in Javier Moreno Luzón (ed.), *Alfonso XIII. Un político en el trono* (Madrid: Marcial Pons Historia, 2003), p. 149.

25. See, for example, as regards the British monarchy, Vernon Bogdanor, *The Monarchy and the Constitution* (Oxford: Clarendon Press, 1995).

26. Francisco Romero Salvadó, *Spain 1914–1918: Between War and Revolution* (London: Routledge, 1999), p. ix.

27. Gerald H. Meaker, 'A Civil War of Words: The Ideological Impact of First World War on Spain, 1914–1918', in Hans A. Schmitt (ed.), *Neutral Europe between War and Revolution, 1917–1923* (Richmond: University of Virginia Press, 1988), pp. 1–65.

28. Enric Ucelay da Cal, 'La Diputació i la Mancomunitat: 1914–1923', in Borja de Riquer (ed.), *Història de la Diputació de Barcelona* (Barcelona: Diputació, 1987), 2, pp. 93–139. Albert Balcells, Enric Pujol and Jordi Sabater, *La Mancomunitat de Catalunya i l'autonomia* (Barcelona: Institut d'Estudis Catalans, 1996). Further information on the Lliga is to be found in Smith in this volume, pp. 145–74.

29. Mercedes Cabrera Calvo-Sotelo, Francisco Comín Comín and José Luis García Delgado, *Santiago Alba. Un programa de reforma económica en la España del primer tercio del siglo XX* (Madrid: Instituto de Estudios Fiscales, 1989).

30. Miguel Ángel Martorell Linares, 'El fracaso del proyecto de ley de beneficios extraordinarios de Santiago Alba en 1916: una lectura política', *Revista de Historia Económica*, XVI (1998), pp. 521–55.

31. Romero Salvadó, *Spain 1914–1918*, pp. 83–4. Moreno Luzón, *Romanones*, pp. 329–43.

32. See, for example, the impression Alfonso XIII gave the British Ambassador, in Public Record Office, Foreign Office 371/3033, 19 May, 14 June and 3 July 1917.

33. Manuel Ballbé, *Orden público y militarismo en la España constitucional (1812–1983)* (Madrid: Alianza Editorial, 1983).

34. On the crisis of the summer of 1917 one can consult various sources, from the old account by Juan Antonio Lacomba, *La crisis española de 1917* (Madrid: Ciencia Nueva, 1970) to the more recent analysis by Romero Salvadó, *Spain 1914–1918*, pp. 85–134. Still useful is Fernando Soldevilla, *Tres revoluciones (Apuntes y notas). Las Juntas de Defensa. La Asamblea Parlamentaria. La huelga general* (Madrid: Julio Cosano, 1917). See also the chapter on 'the revolutionary crisis of 1917' by Romero Salvadó in this volume, pp. 175–201.

35. Javier Moreno Luzón, 'Partidos y Parlamento en la crisis de la Restauración', in Mercedes Cabrera (ed.), *Con luz y taquígrafos. El Parlamento en la Restauración (1913–1923)* (Madrid: Taurus, 1998), pp. 65–102.

36. Cited by Carlos Seco Serrano, *La España de Alfonso XIII. El Estado y la política (1902–1931). De los comienzos del reinado a los problemas de la posguerra*, in José María Jover Zamora (ed.), *Historia de España Menéndez Pidal* (Madrid: Espasa Calpe, 1995), 38/1, p. 569.

37. See José Luis Gómez-Navarro, Javier Moreno Luzón and Fernando del Rey Reguillo, 'La elite parlamentaria entre 1914 y 1923', in Cabrera (ed.), *Con luz y taquígrafos*, pp. 103–42.

38. Mercedes Cabrera, 'La reforma del reglamento de la cámara de diputados en 1918', *Revista de Estudios Políticos*, 93 (1996), pp. 359–79.

39. Javier Moreno Luzón, 'De agravios, pactos y símbolos. El nacionalismo español ante la autonomía de Cataluña (1918–1919)', *Ayer. Revista de Historia Contemporánea*, 63 (2006), pp. 119–51.

40. Moreno Luzón, *Romanones*, pp. 365–71. One can also consult an account which is much more favourable to the military: Carlos Seco Serrano, *Militarismo y civilismo en la España contemporánea* (Madrid: Instituto de Estudios Económicos, 1984), pp. 279–87.

41. On the Catholic leagues see, for example, José-Leonardo Ruiz Sánchez, *Política e Iglesia durante la Restauración. La Liga Católica de Sevilla (1901–1923)* (Sevilla: Diputación Provincial, 1995); and José-Leonardo Ruiz Sánchez,'El sindicalismo católico', in Juan José Castillo (ed.), *Propietarios muy pobres. Sobre la subordinación política del pequeño campesino en España* (Madrid: Ministerio de Agricultura, 1979).

42. González Hernández, *Ciudadanía y acción*; Javier Tusell and Juan Avilés, *La derecha española contemporánea. Sus orígenes: el maurismo* (Madrid: Espasa Calpe, 1986). One can also consult Fernando de Cristóbal González, *Maura, el maurismo y sus seguidores: la propaganda y la acción social del maurismo callejero (Madrid, 1917–1921)* (unpublished manuscript, 1992, stored in the Fundación Antonio Maura in Madrid). The role of the Maurista and Catholic

Right in the crisis of the Restoration is further explored in the chapter by Alejandro Quiroga in this volume, pp. 202–29.

43. Eduardo González Calleja and Fernando del Rey Reguillo, *La defensa armada contra la revolución. Una historia de las 'guardias cívicas' en la España del siglo XX* (Madrid: Consejo Superior de Investigaciones Científicas, 1995).

44. On anarcho-syndicalism and social conflict in Barcelona see Angel Smith, *Anarchism, Revolution and Reaction: Catalan Labour and the Crisis of the Spanish State, 1898–1923* (Oxford: Berghahn Books, 2007).

45. For the events of the 'Annual Disaster' see the comments by Pablo La Porte in this volume, pp. 230–54.

46. Fidel Gómez Ochoa, 'Por una nueva interpretación de la crisis final de la Restauración: el gobierno Maura de agosto de 1921 y la reforma económica de Cambó', *Investigaciones históricas: Época moderna y contemporánea*, 11 (1991), pp. 251–71, and 'La alianza Maura-Cambó de 1921: una experiencia de reformismo conservador durante el reinado de Alfonso XIII', *Revista de Historia Contemporánea*, 5 (1991), pp. 93–108.

47. Pablo La Porte, *La atracción del imán. El desastre de Annual y sus repercusiones en la política europea (1921–1923)* (Madrid: Biblioteca Nueva, 2001).

48. The role of the Liberal factions in the crisis of the Restoration is dealt with in more detail in Javier Moreno Luzón, 'Los políticos liberales y la crisis del liberalismo (1917–1923)', in Manuel Suárez Cortina (ed.), *Las máscaras de la libertad. El liberalismo español (1808–1950)* (Madrid: Marcial Pons Historia/ Fundación Práxedes Mateo Sagasta, 2003), pp. 359–98.

49. José Ortega y Gasset, 'La grave política de estos días', article published in *El Sol*, 25 November 1918, reproduced in José Ortega y Gasset, *Obras Completas. Tomo III, 1917/1925* (Madrid: Taurus/Fundación José Ortega y Gasset, 2005), pp. 155–9.

50. José Luis Gómez-Navarro, *El régimen de Primo de Rivera. Reyes, dictaduras y dictadores* (Madrid: Cátedra, 1991), pp. 101–49.

51. See, for example, Javier Tusell and Genoveva G. Queipo de Llano, *Alfonso XIII. El rey polémico* (Madrid: Taurus, 2001), p. 358.

52. Javier Moreno Luzón, 'El rey de los liberales', in Javier Moreno Luzón (ed.), *Alfonso XIII. Un político en el trono* (Madrid: Marcial Pons Historia, 2003), pp. 151–86.

53. Raymond Carr, *Spain, 1808–1975* (Oxford: Clarendon Press, 1982); Shlomo Ben-Ami, *Fascism from Above: The Dictatorship of Primo de Rivera in Spain, 1923–1930* (Oxford: Clarendon Press, 1983).

54. Carlos Seco Serrano, *Alfonso XIII y la crisis de la Restauración*, 3rd edn (Madrid; Rialp, 1992); Javier Tusell, *Radiografía de un golpe de estado. El ascenso al poder del general Primo de Rivera* (Madrid: Alianza Editorial, 1987).

55. Fidel Gómez Ochoa, 'Democratización y crisis del liberalismo en Italia: análisis y aplicación al caso español', in Manuel Suárez Cortina (ed.), *La crisis del Estado liberal en la Europa del Sur (II Encuentro de Historia de la Restauración)* (Santander: Sociedad Menéndez Pelayo, 2000), pp. 79–108.

56. Fernando del Rey Reguillo, '¿Qué habría sucedido si Alfonso XIII hubiera rechazado el golpe de Primo de Rivera en 1923?', in Nigel Townson (ed.), *Historia virtual de España (1870–2004). ¿Qué hubiera pasado si...?* (Madrid: Taurus, 2004), pp. 93–137.

3
Spain's Revolutionary Crisis of 1917: A Reckless Gamble

Francisco J. Romero Salvadó

Between war and revolution

When war broke out in the summer of 1914, most of Europe's governing classes thought the conflict would be over by Christmas. Many even regarded a quick military campaign as a necessary step in order to rally popular support and silence, if not crush, the leftist opposition at home while gaining continental hegemony. However, as the conflict dragged on, the war became essentially a revolutionary force. Bitterness at the brutal slaughter of the cream of European youth in a military cataclysm that most people did not understand, combined with increasing social and economic dislocation, exacerbated the popular discontent and opposition to their respective rulers that had existed before the outbreak of hostilities.

The gathering storm exploded in 1917. Workers' restraint of the previous years gave way to rising industrial militancy and the troops' discipline began to crumble. The French army was shaken in the spring when some 54 divisions were affected by rebellion and unrest. The German Social-Democratic Party, supportive of the war effort, underwent a split in April with the creation of the Independent Social-Democratic Party that included the embryo of the future German Communist Party, the *Spartakus* League. The Austro-Hungarian Empire was shaken by internal disintegration and war-weariness. Italy experienced food riots and barricade fighting in Turin in August. Russia, whose appalling military defeats were accompanied by galloping inflation and imperial court scandals, was at the epicentre of the revolutionary fervour. Europe was startled in March with news of the overthrow of Tsar Nicholas II. In November, the Bolsheviks, under the leadership of Vladimir Ilich Ulianov (Lenin), having gained enough popular support for their opposition to the imperialist war and calls for power to the Soviets (Councils of Soldiers, Workers and Peasants) and land redistribution, toppled with hardly any resistance the Provisional Government that had failed to fill the power vacuum left by the fall of tsarism.[1] Russia's March and November Revolutions became inspiring examples for militants across the continent. If Russia's downtrodden masses had overthrown the most repressive regime of all, the experience could surely be repeated in other countries.

Even though neutrality shielded her from the human carnage, Spain was also rocked by massive economic disruption, social upheaval and political effervescence that finally exploded in 1917. Nevertheless, the Spanish revolution of 1917 lacked the sweeping impact of Russia's spontaneous popular insurrection of March, let alone the clinical efficiency of the Bolshevik seizure of power of November. Spain underwent, in 1917, a lengthy tragicomedy in three acts that could not be further from Lenin's description of revolutionary insurrection as an art.[2] They presented a combination of theatrical hysteria with bitter bloodshed during which both the ruling regime and the opposition forces gambled recklessly.[3] Unlike Russia, Spain's revolutionary dreams were brutally crushed. This histrionic drama, however, did not leave things static but actually closed with an epilogue which confirmed the precarious foundations on which the governing classes rested. There was, furthermore, a feeling of unfinished business; times of political instability, civil strife and social violence lay ahead.

Times, they are changing

Despite all its constitutional trappings, the liberal order ushered into power in Spain in December 1874 was far from a genuine democracy. During this period, two dynastic parties – Conservatives and Liberals – monopolized power and rotated in office in such a systematic practice that it was referred to as the *turno pacífico* (peaceful alternation). Their political hegemony was not dependent on grass-roots support but widespread apathy, clientelism and the adulteration of the suffrage by the local bigwigs (*caciques*).[4] The regime's de facto disenfranchisement of a majority of the population and the denial of demands for social justice meant the existence of constant civil strife and the subsequent suspension of the constitution that left public order in the 'capable' hands of the army.[5]

The regime's legitimacy came increasingly under question following the traumatic colonial disaster of 1898 and then the start of a new imperialist adventure in Morocco, whose huge unpopularity became evident in 1909 when the call-up of reservists to put down a rebellion there provoked a week of riots and church-burning in Barcelona. Labour protest, peripheral nationalism and praetorian intervention in politics gained momentum during the first decade of the 20th century. They became a threat to the regime after the outbreak of the First World War.

Following the outbreak of hostilities, Spain experienced financial disruption, growing difficulties in obtaining raw materials and rising unemployment due to the return of Spanish workers from belligerent countries. As the war progressed, the country enjoyed simultaneously a massive economic boom and widespread social distress. A significant drop in imports, together with the upsurge in foreign demand, turned the chronic deficit in the balance of trade into a period of fabulous profits.[6] As prices continued to spiral, a golden period for speculators, industrial barons and financial tycoons began. By contrast, these were years of hardship for the average citizen as the growing exports of staple products and rising prices brought about galloping inflation, shortages of basic goods and widened the extremely unfair distribution of income.[7]

Catalan industrial interests, largely represented in political terms by the Lliga Regionalista,[8] were amongst the main beneficiaries of the economic bonanza. They were, however, exasperated when their petitions for special economic legislation were refused.[9] Resentment turned to anger when, following the return to power of the Liberals, the party most associated with Spanish centralism,[10] the new minister of the interior, Santiago Alba, organized a coalition which even included Republicans (Pacto de la Castellana) to beat the Lliga in the elections of April 1916.[11]

The attempt to defeat the Catalan Regionalists in their own stronghold proved a fiasco: the Lliga increased its vote and returned 13 deputies, one more than in the elections two years previously.[12] It represented a turning point for political Catalanism.[13] Spurred by the favourable results and aware of the growing strength of Catalan industry, the Lliga went on to shock the governing classes when, for the first time, it championed home rule in parliament.[14] The Lliga was, however, not a separatist party. Demanding autonomy was just part of a carefully devised gamble, the objective of which was not only to consolidate political hegemony in Catalonia but also ultimately to play a crucial role in the government of the state. For this to be achieved, the monopoly of power held by the two dynastic parties had to end.[15]

The Lliga's plan was facilitated by the ambitions of Santiago Alba, coupled with the factional character of dynastic politics. The Lliga's leader, Francesc Cambó, stressed in his memoirs how Alba's defeat was imperative. Alba was perceived, especially after his recent stance as minister of the interior, as 'an obstacle to Catalan participation in the government of Spain and hence should be stopped and prevented from seizing the leadership of his party'.[16] This became more urgent when Alba moved from interior to finance, a post that offered him the possibility of acquiring a formidable reputation. Alba appeared to confirm his rising status when, in early June 1916, he introduced in parliament a vast ten-year programme of national regeneration that amounted to a total expenditure of 2,134 million pesetas, which was to be paid for by a windfall tax on war profits earned by industry and trade but ignored those made by agriculture.[17]

During the next months, Catalan industrial interests and Lliga MPs succeeded in mounting a massive mobilization against Alba's legislation. Newspapers and industrialists lambasted Alba as an irresponsible economic dictator whose grandiose illusions would lead to Spain's financial ruin. In the chamber, the minister was on the defensive before the constant grilling by the well-prepared Lliga deputies.[18]

Many dynastic politicians, who had either grown restless at the nationwide industrial reaction or were simply happy to see the ambitious Alba fall, collaborated with the Catalanists.[19] Also Alba's plans failed to raise any support in labour quarters. On the contrary, they were regarded with suspicion, if not cynicism, as merely the usual theatrics of the regime. In contrast, Cambó's critical position was seen in a comparatively favourable light and described as necessary to destroy the obsolete regime. On 2 July, Cambó was even invited by the Partido Socialista Obrero Español (Spanish Socialist Workers' Party – PSOE) to give a speech at the Casa del Pueblo in Madrid. There he won over his audience when he declared that the only real forces in the nation were Catalan nationalism and socialism.[20] By December 1916, Alba had not only seen his grandiose plans destroyed but also had failed to pass the annual budget. The Liberal Party was bitterly demoralized.[21]

Parallel to the campaign orchestrated by the Lliga, the regime had to face the angry mobilization of the proletariat. As the governing class proved unwilling or unable to mitigate the rising social distress, class conflict worsened due to the blatant disparity between the workers' gloom and the extravagant lifestyle of the bourgeoisie. Hard-fought piecemeal gains were often rapidly eroded by an unrestrained galloping inflation.[22] From 1915, cities began to experience rising industrial action, together with assaults on shops, food riots and clashes in markets. To add insult to injury, workers' poor housing conditions were now stretched to breaking point when thousands migrated to cities, attracted by the industrial boom. The social upheaval was such that the two bitterly rival labour organizations – the Socialist Unión General de Trabajadores (UGT) and the Anarcho-Syndicalist Confederación Nacional del Trabajo (CNT) – sealed a historic pact in Zaragoza in July 1916.

Spain's labour movement lacked a revolutionary organization of the Bolshevik sort. Following on from Marx's premise that revolutions are the locomotives of history, Lenin added that revolutionary leaders should show the masses the most direct route to complete, absolute and decisive victory.[23] With that objective in mind, the Bolshevik Party emerged from a split in Russia's Social Democratic Party during a congress in exile in London in 1903. The Mensheviks (or the minority in that moment) sought the establishment of a mass movement that would collaborate with the bourgeoisie in the creation of a democratic republic. By contrast, the majority (Bolsheviks) led by Lenin believed it possible to establish the dictatorship of the proletariat and the peasantry without going through a previous bourgeois stage. Furthermore, under the influence of 19th-century Russian populism, Lenin aimed to create a new type of party: centralized, disciplined and composed of an elite of professionals of the revolution.[24]

Under the repressive tsarist autocracy, where labour militants risked their lives by taking part in trade union or political activism, there was no possible compromise formula with the regime. The leaders of the political opposition were frequently intellectuals, authors and gifted speakers able to master several foreign languages due to their ostracism and exile. The ideology and nature of Spanish socialism was radically different. Known as *pablismo* due to the influence of its historic leader, Pablo Iglesias, it was more in tune with other European Marxist parties of the Second International. Led by reformist politicians and members of the trade union bureaucracy, happily anchored in economic determinism and thus the inevitable final triumph of socialism, its official discourse was bellicose and radical. However, instead of spending their energies on preparing the distant revolution, they pursued a strategy of negotiation and gradual achievement of short-term reforms that implied a tacit acceptance of the reigning legality. This allowed them to consolidate certain parcels of influence in the labour movement, municipal life and – hardly in the Spanish case – state politics.[25]

Thus the ever-cautious Spanish Socialist leaders were far from happy about co-operating with the CNT 'troublemakers'. Nevertheless, they could not ignore the increasing demands for labour collaboration from the rank-and-file or the overwhelming vote in favour of a resolution along those lines introduced by the Asturian delegation during the UGT's XII Congress (17–24 May 1916).[26] Socialist misgivings were, to a certain extent, overcome first by the belief that there was now a new generation of pragmatic Catalan Anarcho-Syndicalists and, second, by the awareness that their greater numerical and nationwide strength – the CNT had 30,000 members, mainly concentrated in Catalonia, while the UGT had over 100,000 militants more widely spread across the peninsula – left them in charge of the united labour movement.[27]

Of course, discrepancies about strategies and objectives remained. The Socialists were thinking in terms of a long campaign of education and mobilization through rallies and demonstrations across Spain intended to force the governing classes and parliament to take urgent measures to solve the economic crisis. If there was no forthcoming positive response within the following months, more aggressive and direct tactics would be considered.[28] They were not hard-core revolutionaries plotting an insurrection to overthrow the regime. Ministers only needed to read *El Socialista* to be acquainted with the plans of the Socialists.

A gradualist strategy was not what many Anarcho-Syndicalists wanted to pursue. On the contrary, many greeted the labour pact as a sign that the revolution was imminent. Instead of the Socialists' idea of a slow but steadily organized movement, in collaboration with other political forces, many *cenetistas* had something drastically different in mind. According to the witty and charismatic Anarcho-Syndicalist leader, Angel Pestaña, following the labour pact, his organization worked feverishly and spent every last peseta in acquiring weapons and making bombs.[29] Thus the Socialists in their dealings with the CNT's secretary Francisco Jordán, during the autumn of 1916, had often to restrain his more impetuous plans.[30] Nevertheless, despite all their prudence, the Socialists had endorsed an initiative with huge revolutionary potential. The labour movement was more united than ever before and crucially, for the first time in the Restoration era, the constant but disparate local protest was being channelled into a movement against not just local injustices but the state that presided over them.[31]

Gradually, even the Socialists realized that the labour movement was on a collision course with the regime. Baffled at the incompetence of the administration to mitigate the social havoc, and probably dreading what that meant for Spanish socialism, the founder and father-figure of the PSOE, Pablo Iglesias, argued in *El Socialista* that it appeared as if the king had gone to a mental hospital and chosen the nine most dangerous patients to form a government.[32] Thus a more aggressive approach began with a one-day nationwide stoppage on 18 December 1916.[33] In March 1917, news of the Russian Revolution helped harden the stance: the fall of the hitherto mighty tsarist regime in Russia opened the possibility of a similar event taking place in Spain.[34] Hence both the UGT and CNT approved that month a manifesto that blamed the ruling system for being the cause of widespread popular distress and even forewarned that the proletariat would overthrow the regime, at the right time, by means of a general strike.[35] The Socialists were far from thinking in terms of a social revolution but had been stressing for months that their objective was to bring about the modernization of the state by removing an oligarchic regime.[36]

Crippling inflation and shortages not only hit the working classes but also savaged the hitherto fairly secure living standards of those working in the public sector including the armed forces. As well as being hurt by the economic dislocation, the military became increasingly anxious at being dragged into the continental war. Their incapability to compete with their now embattled neighbours was no secret. The British military attaché Jocelyn Grant compared the effectiveness of the Spanish army with that of Romania and concluded that it did not represent a threat to anybody, except possibly Portugal.[37] Thus, alarm bells began to ring when the government passed a new military bill in 1915 that intended to modernize the armed forces by introducing tests of physical and intellectual ability in order to cut down the inflated officer corps and, with the savings, acquire new equipment and increase the number of troops.[38]

From late 1916, angry officers up to the rank of colonel began to join the so-called *Juntas Militares de Defensa*, a kind of military trade union whose primary objective was to defend the collective interests of the corps: better pay and the imposition of the *escala cerrada* (promotion according to seniority).[39] Their mouthpiece, *La Correspondencia Militar*, lambasted both the oligarchic nature of a regime that was presiding over the ruin of workers and military alike and the favouritism shown towards those privileged officers either based in the king's military household or serving in Africa where, from their point of view, the reigning nepotism had facilitated the award of medals and promotion.[40]

Fatal neutrality

The mobilization of workers, Catalan Regionalists and army officers constituted a dangerous storm gathering against the regime. It was, however, not the deteriorating domestic situation but the question of Spain's neutrality in the war, combined with two decisive royal encroachments on governmental affairs, which initiated the chain of revolutionary events that marked 1917.

As the armed hostilities in Europe dragged on, the initial almost unanimously welcomed neutrality began to polarize Spain. Whereas the great majority of the population failed to understand the issues at stake, for the urban cultural and political elites the war became a question of obsessive concern. With some significant exceptions, the landed classes, the army, the Church and the Court were Germanophiles since they regarded a victory of the Central Powers as a triumph for traditional values such as monarchism, authority and a hierarchical social order. By contrast, the Catalan Regionalists, the Republicans, the Socialists and intellectuals were Francophiles since they considered a triumph for the Allies a victory for democracy and secularism. The polemic between both camps was so passionate that it acquired the quality of a dialectic civil war, with bitter arguments and even the termination of old friendships.[41]

Following the return to power of the Liberals, in December 1915, the polarization around the neutrality question reached dramatic levels. Unlike most dynastic politicians who had done their utmost to ignore (and be ignored by) the war, the new prime minister, Count Romanones, shocked the country, as early as August 1914, with the publication in his newspaper, *El Diario Universal*, of a controversial article –'Neutralidades que matan' (Fatal Neutralities) – which advocated a closer alignment with the Allies. Aware of its explosive reception, the ever-shrewd Count sought to distance himself from the article.[42] Once in office, all his official speeches adhered to strict neutrality, but the damage was already done and his dismissal remained the main target of Germanophile Spain.[43]

Germany's ruthless behaviour exacerbated matters drastically. Indeed, while flattering its Germanophile friends with promises of territorial gains and a central role to play in the post-war new order in exchange for mere strict neutrality,[44] she flagrantly converted Spain into a theatre of operations. The exorbitant rise in the price of paper opened the possibility to invest in and so influence the editorials of a large number of journals. These newspapers therefore lambasted any criticism of Germany as warmongering while condoning her campaign of destabilization and sabotage; a campaign which included the establishment of an extremely efficient spy network, submarine attacks against merchant shipping, the infiltration of anarchist groups so as to disrupt by any means industrial production serving the Allies, and the supply of money and weapons to rebel natives in Spanish Morocco to foster rebellion in the French zone.[45]

Germany's insulting contempt for Spanish neutrality followed by her announcement of a dramatic increase in her submarine campaign in February 1917, persuaded Romanones that the time had come to follow the US example and break diplomatic relations. That month a German sailor was arrested in Cartagena with two suitcases full of explosives that, Romanones wrote, would have been enough 'to blow up all the fleets in the world and all Spain's factories'.[46] The Spanish prime minister confided to the French ambassador, Leon Geoffray, that the final straw was the torpedoing of the steamer *San Fulgencio* on 9 April. By then, Germany had already sunk 31 Spanish vessels. According to the Count, 'the moment had arrived to abandon strict neutrality otherwise Spain might sink to the level of an insignificant power such as the Netherlands'.[47]

However, Romanones' plans were never put into practice. On 19 April, he was replaced by another Liberal cabinet led by a rival party baron, Manuel García Prieto, the Marquis of Alhucemas. Spain's Germanophiles were ecstatic. One of its most blatant newspapers even pictured the Count with his heart pierced by a sword named neutrality in a cartoon sarcastically titled 'Fatal Neutralities'.[48]

Act I: Royal meddling and praetorian defiance

In his resignation note, Romanones alleged that his fall had been due to the opposition of members of his party and of public opinion to his foreign policy. The explanation did not ring true. Given the factional nature of the regime, the question of neutrality had certainly led some Liberal notables to support the candidacy of the more malleable Marquis of Alhucemas. However, public opinion did not have any major input into decision-making (otherwise the unpopular war in Morocco would have concluded long ago) or in forcing the collapse of governments. In fact, in Restoration Spain, cabinets often fell due to the attitude of the ultimate power in the country, King Alfonso XIII, and this time was no different.[49]

The bitter polarization on the neutrality debate combined with the explosive domestic situation constituted a powder keg on which the regime was sitting. Unfortunately for its well-being, two hasty royal interventions were to light the fuse. Ironically, the king appeared to have leaned towards the Allies at the outset of the war. Romanones claimed that Alfonso was in total agreement with the spirit of 'Fatal Neutralities'. Yet as the conflict dragged on, the identification of the enemies of the regime with the Allies, combined with Germany's territorial promises and the efficiency of her military machine, began to take its toll. Ultimately, it was the Russian Revolution and the Allies' abandonment of the tsar that placed Alfonso firmly in the pro-German camp.[50] The king concluded that it was necessary to get rid of a prime minister who risked pushing Spain into a war for which the country was neither militarily nor economically prepared.

Dismissal of his government was soon followed by another royal encroachment upon governmental prerogatives. The Spanish monarch, terrified by the events in Russia, kept drawing parallels between the officers' desertion of Nicholas II and the reformist rhetoric that emanated from the Spanish *Juntas*.[51] He felt the need to act promptly when, during a massive pro-Allied gathering in Madrid, on 27 May 1917, he was singled out as the leading Germanophile force in Spain and warned that if he continued to oppose the rupture of diplomatic relations with Germany, he would follow the fate of his Russian cousin Nicholas II.[52] In a frenzied state, Alfonso ordered his minister of war, General Manuel Aguilera, to ensure the disbandment of the *Juntas*.[53]

The leaders of the central *Junta* in Barcelona were arrested, but immediately a new provisional *Junta* emerged and officers in all the peninsular garrisons, in an act of solidarity, presented themselves to their commanders for imprisonment. Praetorian indiscipline and defiance reached a new dimension with the drafting of a manifesto on 1 June. It proved a turning point. The officers not only justified their rebellious attitude but gave the government a 12-hour deadline to release those in prison, to give guarantees that there would be no future reprisals and to recognize the existence of the *Juntas* by the approval of their statutes.[54]

The Alhucemas cabinet was faced with a potential full-scale rebellion. The officers had plotted, in case of resistance, a full-scale coup: the regional *Juntas* received instructions from Barcelona to take over the military governorships and army headquarters of their areas at 3 p.m. the following day.[55] The government conceded defeat and released the leading *Junteros*, but all attempts to preserve an atmosphere of constitutional normality crumbled when *La Correspondencia Militar* boasted in its editorials that 'the glorious feat' achieved by the officers constituted a death warrant for the 'repulsive rule of *caciques* and oligarchs'.[56] After less than two months in office, Alhucemas resigned and was succeeded by a Conservative ministry headed by Eduardo Dato. The old political fox Romanones was correct when he noted that the successful frontal assault against civil supremacy had effectively left the army as the virtual owners of the country.[57]

Act II: Revolution from above (historic or hysteric day)

In June 1917, there was a widespread belief that the regime was in its death throes; a belief which appeared to be borne out by the existing dire situation: the collapse in quick succession of two Liberal cabinets, the successful praetorian defiance and the spread of the corporatist revolt as *Juntas* began to spring up across the civil service and amongst non-commissioned officers. A newspaper close to the Liberals, *El Heraldo de Madrid*, claimed, on 6 June, that the revolution had already begun. These alarmist editorials emanating from newspapers close to the regime contrasted sharply with the euphoria that prevailed amongst its enemies; euphoria that was reinvigorated daily by editorials in *La Correspondencia Militar*, calling for new men and new politics as well as constant assertions that the governing oligarchy only served the interests of *caciques* and was leading Spain to moral decline and economic ruin.[58] The officers' successful defiance had shown the fragility of the regime, as even the normally cautious Pablo Iglesias cheerfully noted.[59] Socialists and Republicans saw this as a signal to step up their activities. However, amidst the reigning uncertainty, it was both the Catalan Regionalists and the Maurista movement and its leader Antonio Maura who took centre stage in the second act of Spain's revolutionary drama.

After a public statement, on 14 June 1917, claiming that the officers' disobedience had made it impossible to continue with the fictional character of the regime, the Lliga called for support for those parties with a real mass following to wrest power.[60] When the government refused to open parliament and sheltered behind the suspension of constitutional guarantees and strict censorship, the Catalan Regionalists responded by first summoning all the Catalan parliamentarians to Barcelona's City Hall on 5 July and then by extending the invitation to the rest of the Spanish MPs to attend an Assembly in Barcelona on 19 July to discuss the existing crisis.[61] The Lliga did not seek to storm the Bastille but to carry out a peaceful political revolution in order to pre-empt a deeper social revolt that, it felt, would be a consequence of maintaining an unreformed regime. Cambó even claimed that to become a revolutionary was the most conservative thing to do.[62] The Assembly was rapidly supported by Republicans and Socialists.

The unfolding events granted a pivotal role to Antonio Maura. A former Conservative leader and prime minister, Maura had been abandoned by the bulk of the party for his criticism of dynastic politics, in October 1913, but, exceptionally within the regime, won a genuine following of young Monarchists who even named themselves after him (Mauristas). As the key politician to whom both *Juntas* and Catalan Regionalists turned for backing, his stance was therefore fundamental. As his son Gabriel noted, most Mauristas were prepared at this stage to follow his father against the crown if necessary.[63] They had been enraged when, following the collapse of the Alhucemas cabinet on 9 June, the king had not turned to Maura but decided to stick to the *turno* routine. Dismayed at realizing that their ostracism was to continue and at seeing that the mainstream Conservatives led by the despised Eduardo Dato had been recalled to power, the Mauristas orchestrated vociferous demonstrations outside the royal palace.[64]

Indeed, the officers, unaware of how to channel their might, turned to Maura for guidance. The rabidly anti-Catalanist, Catalan Maurista Gustavo Peyrá, acted as go-between with the *Juntas* and encouraged his leader to seize office with the support of the officers who, according to him, 'were neither rebels nor anti-monarchists, just loathed the governing oligarchy as much as the Mauristas'.[65] Other leading Mauristas, such as the former governor of Barcelona, Angel Ossorio, and the Catalan Joaquín María Nadal were eager to take part in the Assembly which they regarded as akin to the necessary revolution from above preached by Maura. At this stage, Maura's sons Gabriel and Miguel were also urging him to act promptly otherwise, they claimed, the 'clumsy' Dato would sink Spain into a state of irreparable chaos. Simultaneously, Cambó was asking Gabriel Maura to join forces to renovate the country. He was, of course, aware that without having the Mauristas aboard the Assembly would be depicted as a project masterminded by separatists and left-wing revolutionaries and hence unlikely to win any sympathy in military barracks.[66]

It was in Maura's hands, during the summer of 1917, to become the necessary link between parliamentarians and officers against the governing oligarchy. Yet, notwithstanding all his previous passionate attacks on the *turno* and ignoring the constant prompting by his followers, he refused to endorse what he perceived as either a military rebellion or a seditious initiative. He noted how his philosophy was averse to obtaining power by illegal means, described with contempt the *Juntas* as an '*engendro monstruoso de añeja depravación*' (monstrous freak of ancient depravity) and even refused to receive a messenger from Barcelona, leaving him waiting in heavy rain.[67] Equally, despite his cordial relations with Cambó, Maura was adamant against lending his support to the Assembly, which he compared with a *'zoco profesional'* (professional flea market), and which besides, as he explained to Ossorio, was a 'subversive road and an adventure for which he did not have the vocation'.[68]

In a sense, Maura epitomized the greatest contradiction of Restoration politics: even though he saw the need for political reform, he was unwilling to sanction it. Maura's passive stance contributed to the destruction of Maurismo as a renovating force and exposed the internal tensions of a movement that contained reformists willing to participate in a democratic experience (the Assembly) as well as a nationalist and anti-liberal tendency happy to find common ground with the army.[69] The impasse also helped crown and government to regain the initiative.

Aware of the worsening crisis, the king sought to safeguard the throne, bypassing the government if necessary. Given the army's essential role as the main bulwark of the throne, he rapidly ditched his previous stance and began to speak in public about the officers' patriotism and, through key go-betweens such as Spain's most senior general, Valeriano Weyler, assured them of his willingness to meet their demands.[70] He also established contacts with Catalan Regionalists and even some Republicans to deflect the challenge presented by the Assembly. It is important to bear in mind that for the first time the king expressed a willingness to liquidate the *turno* by offering portfolios to Catalanists in return for abandoning their current partners.[71]

Meanwhile, the Dato government was using any means and methods in order to win its struggle with the parliamentarians. Maura's self-elimination from the scene appeared to have solved the worst nightmare: the potential alliance (even if temporary) between middle-class parties (Republicans and Catalan Regionalists), the labour movement and the rebellious officers. As Gustavo Peyrá noted, it was highly unlikely that the army would back an initiative (the Assembly) controlled by Catalanists, Republicans and Socialists.[72] Steps were thus taken quickly to ensure the support of the *Juntas*. As a government circular put it: 'some 16 or 17 million pesetas should be thrown to soothe the roaring beast'. And, indeed, the *Juntas*' statutes were promptly approved, the defence budget increased, reprisals against blacklisted generals carried out, and the civil governor of Barcelona, Leopoldo Matos, acted as a go-between.[73] Simultaneously, the government embarked upon a campaign of misinformation in order to discredit the parliamentarians. It was claimed that the Assembly was the product of a deal hatched between revolutionaries and separatists, and agents provocateurs handed out incendiary pamphlets, purporting to emanate from the parliamentarians, in order to frighten the Catalan middle classes.[74]

The Assembly gathering, on 19 July 1917, contained historic moments. Both the political nature of the participants and their reformist aspirations can be seen as a dress rehearsal for the Second Republic of April 1931. Nevertheless, the ludicrous vicissitudes surrounding the affair were worthy of vaudeville. The editorial of the Maurista mouthpiece, *La Acción*, described the events as a hysteric time.[75] With the city occupied by troops and cut off from the rest of Spain by a cordon sanitaire, the day began with a hide-and-seek game in which the parliamentarians first lost their police shadows in a series of taxi chases, and then proceeded to lunch at the Casino del Parque, where the restaurant had been hired under the pretext of a wedding party. From there they only had to walk over to the Palacio del Gobernador del Parque de la Ciudadela. The leading member of the Lliga, Lluís Durán i Ventosa, acted as the outside link with the press and received up-to-the-minute information from Cambó on the development of events.[76] There were 55 deputies and 13 senators – 46 of them from Catalonia. They denounced the hollowness of the regime and demanded the summoning of a constituent Cortes, after general elections presided over by a government representing the will of the nation. Three subcommittees were created to study constitutional reform and municipal autonomy; to deal with the issues of national defence, education and the administration of justice; and to examine economic problems. The gathering was suddenly interrupted by the abrupt entry of the police headed by the civil governor Matos. After a theatrical show of resistance, the parliamentarians finally agreed to yield to force and the act closed in a ridiculous fashion: Governor Matos symbolically arrested the parliamentarians by placing his hand on the shoulder of each one of them. They were released from custody outside the building.[77]

That same evening the minister of the interior, José Sánchez Guerra, boasted to the assorted press that the timely intervention of the governor had broken up the meeting before it had time to transact any business.[78] A no less buoyant prime minister, in conversation with the British ambassador, chuckled about the fashion in which the Assembly had been dispersed and affirmed that the 'bubble of the Barcelona revolution had been pricked'. A confident Dato even mentioned that he planned to ask the king for the decree of dissolution of parliament so as to be returned to power with a larger majority.[79] Events were soon to shatter these rosy expectations and force the government to take extraordinary steps.

Act III: Revolution from below (Gambling for high stakes)

Despite the tight censorship, journals from practically all political leanings agreed on the political significance of the gathering in Barcelona and condemned the government's methods of misinformation.[80] The parliamentarians, sensing that the momentum was on their side, announced a new meeting to be held in Oviedo on 16 August.[81] Such was the atmosphere in favour of the Assembly that Maura was beginning to recognize his inability to stop some of his followers from attending the new gathering. Crucial figures in the Maurista movement, such as Angel Ossorio and even Maura's son Miguel, were openly in favour of participating in the Assembly. According to them, the time had arrived to choose between supporting the governing oligarchy they had criticized for years or joining the camp seeking national renovation.[82] Still, the biggest shock to the government came when it was rumoured that a messenger sent by the *Juntas* had submitted a document to the king, then on holiday in Santander, advising him to lead the revolution that the entire nation was hoping for. This should begin with the introduction of new governing methods and new politicians.[83]

Finding itself against the ropes, the Dato administration took a reckless gamble. It involved tearing apart the opposition by luring the proletariat into carrying out its threat of a general strike. Confronted thus with the spectre of revolution, the scared middle classes would stop supporting any reformist schemes, the army would quell the disturbances and the government could then claim to be the saviour of Spain and the guarantor of law and order.[84]

Coinciding with the celebration of the Assembly, the outbreak of a railway strike in Valencia, seemingly encouraged by local Republicans, provided the government with the opportunity to stage a deadly showdown with the labour movement.[85] Having endured a massive defeat, exactly one year earlier, the leading railway company (Compañía del Norte) was seeking revenge.[86] Thus, once the situation was brought under control in Valencia after the imposition of martial law, the company took bitter reprisals that included its refusal to rehire 36 workers sacked during the conflict. The railway workers' trade union responded by threatening an all-out nationwide transport strike to begin on 10 August.[87] The UGT looked for a compromise but all its attempts at finding a negotiated solution met with the company's intransigence; an attitude that was encouraged by the government. In short, the UGT leadership was given a stark choice: accept utter defeat or go along with the strike announced for 10 August.[88]

Blind euphoria surrounded Spain's labour movement. Following the officers' rebellion in June and the parliamentarian defiance in July, there was such optimism that, for once, the Socialists even refused to listen to Pablo Iglesias, who, from his sickbed, argued for limiting the strike to a show of solidarity with the railway workers.[89] There was widespread belief that the Bourbon dynasty was about to follow the fate of the Romanovs and yet they had seriously misread the conditions that had produced the downfall of tsarism.

While Spain had been spared the dramatic human and material impact of the war by her neutrality, the hegemony of the mighty tsarist regime crumbled fast after the outbreak of hostilities as its vast but overall poor empire was not prepared for a conflict of such scale. As the mobilization of 15 million peasants and workers destroyed the traditional fabric of Russian society, the country's industrial infrastructure proved unable to meet the military needs of modern warfare.[90] The precarious transport system virtually collapsed and the army, handicapped by poor leadership as well as shortages of clothing, rifles and munitions, despite intermittent victories on the Austrian front, suffered appalling defeats and brutal losses. Simultaneously, mounting inflation and food and fuel rationing shattered the home front, turning the initial patriotism into widespread agitation against the regime.

By early 1917, the army, demoralized and plagued by the mounting numbers of desertions, was close to collapse.[91] In March, the garrison in Petrograd – 150,000 downtrodden recruits crammed in barracks for 20,000 men – sided with the popular revolt and ensured the downfall of the dynasty.[92] Now soldiers, like peasants and workers, were part of the revolutionary storm released by the collapse of the old hierarchical society. Land and peace were their primary objectives.

Lenin's original role after his return from exile was to expose with singular clarity the great paradox of the March Revolution. The fall of the throne had unleashed the masses' revolutionary expectations. The street insurrections had placed real power in the hands of the Soviets, whose leaders, however, refused to exert it and instead had permitted the formation of a Provisional Government, dominated by Monarchist deputies, who postponed vital issues such as the distribution of the land, continued the tsarist imperialist war and sought to turn back the advances of the revolution.[93] Nevertheless, aware that the opportune moment to launch their bid for power had not yet arrived, the Bolsheviks decided to hold back the angry masses in

Petrograd following the start of another highly unpopular military offensive in July 1917.[94]

The Provisional Government bet on a decisive military victory. It attempted to transform the brutal conflict into a democratic war in defence of the revolution. A victory, it was thought, would restore discipline to the armed forces and consolidate the new regime. The outcome was the opposite. The subsequent debacle sealed the fate of the Provisional Government.[95] The Bolsheviks, the party associated with an end to the war, emerged strengthened. Three months later, with much deeper nationwide support, they overthrew the Provisional Government with relative ease.

By contrast, Spain's hastily prepared revolutionary strike was a very costly failure. As one *cenetista* commented, rather than a revolution, it looked like they were planning a party. Largo Caballero, in an astonishingly anti-revolutionary statement, affirmed in parliament in May 1918 that they had kept governments informed of all their plans since May 1916.[96] The Dato administration was indeed prepared and had taken the pertinent measures.[97]

The Socialists chose to throw their traditional caution to the wind. The PSOE and UGT Executive Committees agreed to link the transport dispute with the revolutionary strike announced earlier in March. A strike committee was formed by Julián Besteiro and Andrés Saborit (for the PSOE) and Francisco Largo Caballero and Daniel Anguiano (for the UGT). Plans were made to co-ordinate the movement with their Anarcho-Syndicalist and Republican partners.[98] In fact, during recent trips to Barcelona, Iglesias, and the Madrid UGT leader, Largo Caballero, had been left in no doubt about the CNT's demands for action.[99]

The Socialists felt caught in the vanguard of an insurrectionary process, in which government intransigence as well as the impulsiveness of their Anarcho-Syndicalist and some Republican partners forced them to assume the role of protagonists. Normally averse to gambling the well-being of the organization on revolutionary adventures, they accepted the gauntlet thrown down by the administration and embarked upon a revolutionary road for which they were ill-prepared. It was as if they were trying to demonstrate that they could be genuine revolutionaries.[100]

The manifesto drawn up to justify the revolutionary initiative was extremely moderate. It merely endorsed the Assembly's objectives of summoning a Constituent parliament following clean elections presided over by a provisional government.[101] The Socialists wanted to usher in a progressive democratic republic and not to subvert the social order. However, despite all the calls for restraint, it was only natural that violent clashes developed when pickets attempted to bring the cities to a standstill. After all, the Socialists were seeking to overthrow the regime by means of a general strike.[102]

Once the revolutionary strike broke out, on 13 August, everything went according to the government's plans. Any chance of collusion between the Assembly, the officers and the proletariat was soon dashed. Catalan Regionalists and most of their parliamentarian partners initially sat on the fence waiting to see how events unfolded. Had the revolution succeeded, they would have expected to be catapulted to power. But they hastened to distance themselves from the revolution as soon as it became glaringly obvious that the strike was failing.[103] Ultimately, the fate of the regime was in the hands of the troops and they acted as they always had in the past, quelling any threat to the social order with massive brutality. Unlike the scenes of fraternization between soldiers and strikers in Petrograd in February, the August days in Spain developed into a shooting gallery, in which workers threw stones and were answered by volleys of bullets. Spain's peasant-soldier troops, not traumatized by the war-weariness of their Russian counterparts, obeyed the orders of their officers, who, in turn, forgot all their anti-oligarchic language of the previous two months and followed the instructions of their generals. Rumours spread by the government that foreign gold was behind the disturbances and that the triumph of the revolution would lead to participation in the war removed their final hesitations. Most officers believed that it was better to shoot workers in Spain than to dig trenches in France. In a week, the revolution had been drowned in blood everywhere but in Asturias where miners still resisted for a couple of weeks. The fact that the countryside had remained mostly quiet facilitated the mopping-up operations.[104]

Epilogue: A twist of fate

Spain's 1917 revolutionary drama ended with a telling twist. By unleashing the might of the army against the workers, Dato won a brief reprieve for the regime but sealed the fate of his government and undermined the constitutional order. In the aftermath of the August events, the dreaded collusion between the labour movement, the Assembly and the army officers crystallized, if only in their mutual contempt for the government.

With hundreds of their militants imprisoned, the labour movement suffered the brunt of the repression. Still, the trial against the strike committee provided an opportunity to attack the regime. Iglesias' lieutenant, the eloquent professor of logic at Madrid University, Julián Besteiro, acting as spokesman, denounced the Dato administration for having turned the railways dispute into a general strike.[105]

Simultaneously, Cambó was lambasting the government along the same lines. On 22 October, he made one of his most incisive speeches to date at the Centro Autonomista de Dependientes in Barcelona. There, he not only accused the Dato cabinet of representing bankrupt old politics but also of immorality by having sowed intrigue in order to provoke a general strike which the army had to crush.[106] In fact, an astute politician like Cambó, not exactly sorry to see the field cleared of some of his previous left-wing partners, embarked upon a frenetic campaign to restore the spirit of July and breach the dynastic citadel. According to him, the revolutionary strike had been an error; a 'grotesque adventure' as he described it in a new vain attempt to persuade Maura to abandon the passivity which had helped prop up an ailing regime.[107] Taking advantage of the restoration of the constitutional guarantees, in early October, a second gathering of parliamentarians took place in Madrid in the middle of the month where they confirmed their commitment to carry out the conclusions adopted in July.[108]

More alarming for the government, the officers reverted to the hostile position they held before the strike. In general, they were not eager to police the streets and take charge of maintaining public order. However, once given the task, they did not want political interference or criticism. They were therefore mortified when the ministers, overwhelmed by the scale of the repression, sought to distance themselves from the unfolding bloody events.[109] By September, the military began to voice their suspicions that they had been manipulated into putting down a rebellion that the government had provoked by its mishandling of the transport dispute. They demanded the lifting of martial law, the re-establishment of constitutional guarantees and the acceptance of governmental responsibility for the repression.[110] Already furious that the recent events orchestrated by the government had resulted in their loss of popularity, the officers were livid when they then intercepted a cable from Sánchez Guerra telling the civil governors to be ready for the moment when the government could turn against the *Juntas*.[111]

Despite growing military unrest, Dato appeared to have believed that he could cling on to power. After all, he thought that by putting down the revolutionary strike he had saved the throne and thus could count on royal confidence.[112] To Dato's chagrin, the monarch was now more than ever before conscious that the throne depended on the position of the army. So he had no second thoughts about what to do when the 'bayonets finally spoke'. On 26 October, a message approved by all army corps was submitted to the king demanding the removal of the existing administration. In return, the officers guaranteed the dissolution (by force, if necessary) of any new parliament that might represent a challenge to the dynasty.[113]

Spain's liberal regime was tottering. With both dynastic parties torn apart by factionalism and expelled from office by the army, the *turno pacífico*, the foundations of the smooth functioning of the system for over 40 years, had to be abandoned. The political vacuum lasted a record eight days and was finally filled by a monarchist coalition presided over by the weak Marquis of Alhucemas. It included members of different dynastic factions and, for the first time, Catalan Regionalism held two portfolios, while the *Juntas* were represented by the new war minister, Juan de la Cierva, the leader of a small dynastic faction on the right of the Conservative Party, to ensure that their corporatist demands were met.[114] Far from being a long-lasting settlement, the solution achieved in November 1917 – described by the ever-wise Romanones as *'engendro caótico'* (a chaotic freak) even when his faction had one minister – only marked the beginning of a period of political instability and social violence.[115]

By November 1917, hopes for democratic change were all but dashed. Attempts to usher in democracy from below had suffered a fatal blow in August. Afterwards, traumatized by the bloody outcome and despite the growing social strife and the echoes of the Bolshevik Revolution, the Socialists returned to their traditional prudent stance, leaving the CNT to profit from the radicalization of the era and thus become Spain's hegemonic labour force in the post-war years. However, despite their massive mobilizing power, the Anarcho-Syndicalists concentrated on the economic struggle and not on challenging state power. Political renovation from above, embodied by the Assembly, also perished in autumn 1917, by the hand of its own creator, the Lliga. The about-turn of the Catalan Regionalists, from leading opponent to bedfellow of the governing oligarchy, was not shocking but followed the behaviour of many social-conservative parties in a moment of growing upheaval at home and abroad. Constitutional reform was one thing, while an assault on the monarchy was another.[116] Furthermore, the Lliga achieved some key objectives: seizure of two portfolios which included control of the economy and destruction of the political monopoly enjoyed by the dynastic parties.[117]

The irony of Spain's revolutionary drama of 1917 was that while the regime scored an important victory by craftily exploiting the

contradictions between those forces seeking its removal, its foundations ultimately were drastically undermined. The relative social demobilization and political apathy upon which its governing oligarchy so
heavily relied had been brought to an abrupt end by the dramatic transformations produced by the war. The fall of tsarism and the subsequent
Bolshevik takeover heralded the age of mass politics and the intensification of popular demands and social struggle. The ruling order had overcome revolution but the danger lay within. Constitutional practices
remained in place but the existence of an increasingly politically active
officer corps, with the backing of an interventionist crown, struck an
ominous note for the future. Indeed, the regime owed its survival, in
the summer of 1917, to praetorian forcefulness. But if the officers had
thwarted the revolution, who was going to stop the army?

Notes

I would like to thank Angel Smith for his comments on earlier drafts.

1. William Henry Chamberlin, *The Russian Revolution, 1917–1921*, 2 vols
   (Princeton, NJ: Princeton University Press, 1987 [1935]), vol. 1, pp. 311–13.
2. Vladimir I. Lenin, 'Marxism and Insurrection', in *Lenin's Selected Works*
   (London: Lawrence and Wishart, 1971 [1917]), p. 357.
3. This chapter differs from the conclusions reached by the otherwise lucid
   and pioneer analysis of the Spanish labour movement by Gerald Meaker, *The
   Revolutionary Left in Spain 1914–23* (Stanford, CA: Stanford University Press,
   1974). This author seems to have overestimated the role of the Russian peasantry. In fact, the revolution was led in Spain as well as in Russia (and indeed
   France in 1789) by urban-based movements. The Bolsheviks seized Petrograd
   first and then gradually expanded their authority over the countryside at
   the cost of a bloody civil war. This work is indebted (as any dealing with this
   period) to Juan Antonio Lacomba's classic study *La crisis española de 1917*
   (Málaga: Ciencia Nueva, 1970). It agrees with his overall view of the year
   1917 as the great missed opportunity to have changed the course of Spain's
   history. However, Lacomba overlooks the optimism of the labour movement
   hoping to establish a new political order in a deadly gamble in which it was
   clearly outmanoeuvred by the government. Instead, his analysis displays an
   excessive emphasis on labour's deterministic acceptance of fate (pp. 248–50,
   281–2).
4. A re-evaluation of the liberal regime has been suggested by Mercedes Cabrera
   and Fernando del Rey, 'De la Oligarquía y el caciquismo a la política de
   intereses. Por una relectura de la Restauración', in Manuel Suárez Cortina
   (ed.), *Las máscaras de la libertad. El Liberalismo Español, 1808–1950* (Madrid:
   Marcial Pons, 2003), pp. 289–325. Unlike the traditional Manichean view
   of the Restoration as a repressive political order that reflected the interests of privileged elites, they note that the regime was representative to an
   extent and showed the capability to absorb persons and groups outside the

system. Accurate and thought-provoking though these suggestions are, they need to be put in the overall framework underlined in works such as that of María Jesús González Hernández, 'Las manchas del leopardo: la difícil reforma desde el sistema y las estrategías de la socialización conservadora', in Manuel Suárez Cortina (ed.), *La Restauración, entre el liberalismo y la democracia* (Madrid: Alianza, 1997), pp. 164–5: 'the regime was ultimately and thoroughly based on nepotism, patronage and clientelism; a leopard unable to change its spots'. See also the chapter in this volume by Javier Moreno Luzón, pp. 32–61.

5. Fundación Antonio Maura, *Antonio Maura's Papers* (hereafter AAM), Leg. 273, Carp. 4: constitutional guarantees were suspended in part or all of the country 25 times between December 1875 and March 1919.

6. Ignacio Bernís, *Consecuencias económicas de la guerra* (Madrid: Estanislao Maestre, 1923), p. 116.

7. Instituto de Reformas Sociales, *Movimientos de precios al por menor en España durante la guerra y la posguerra* (Madrid: Sobrinos de la Sociedad de M. Minuesa, 1923), pp. 7, 10–11, 36.

8. The Lliga Regionalista is dealt with in the chapter by Angel Smith, this volume, pp. 145–74.

9. Jesús Pabón, *Cambó, 1876–1947* (Barcelona: Alpha, 1999 [1952]), pp. 348–51.

10. In general, the Catalan Regionalists had much better relations with the Conservatives. The two historic leaders, Francesc Cambó and Enric Prat de la Riba, had a very good personal rapport with the Conservative statesman Antonio Maura. See in the Instituto Francesc Cambó (hereafter IFC) the correspondence between Maura and Cambó and box 3/2, no. 14 (2–3): 'Maura had opinion behind him the Liberals had never had' (June 1914); Cambó's memoirs (*Memorias*, Madrid: Alianza, 1987, pp. 133, 151, 172); and Arxiu Nacional de Catalunya (hereafter ANC), *Enric Prat de la Riba's Papers* (hereafter AEPR), undated. It had been a Conservative government that in 1913 had granted, by royal decree, the Catalan *Mancomunitat* (an institution with some administrative autonomous powers).

11. Catalonia was one of the exceptional areas in Spain where ballot-rigging no longer worked. Deals between Alba and the Republican leader Alejandro Lerroux can be seen in Biblioteca de la Real Academia de la Historia (hereafter BRAH), *Santiago Alba's Papers* (hereafter ASA), Leg. 9/8081, 8/105–4 (22 and 24 December 1915). Alba's initiative is seen in a positive light in José María Marín Arce, *Santiago Alba y la crisis de la Restauración, 1913–30* (Madrid: UNED, 1990), pp. 35–6. For the Lliga's reaction see AEPR (April 1916) and *La Veu de Catalunya* (3–7 April 1916). See also Pabón, *Cambó*, pp. 359–63; Miquel Ferrer, *De la Fundació de la Lliga Regionalista a la Primera Guerra Mundial, 1901–18* (Barcelona: Dalmau, 1977), pp. 35–41; and Borja de Riquer, *Regionalistes i Nacionalistes, 1898–1931* (Barcelona: Dopesa, 1979), pp. 90–2.

12. *La Veu de Catalunya* called the results 'The triumph of Catalonia' (10 April 1916). Albert Balcells, Joan B. Cullá and Conxita Mir, *Les eleccions generals a Catalunya, 1901–23* (Barcelona: Estudis Electorals, 1982), p. 234.

13. Catalanism is used to refer to political parties that stand for Catalan nationalist (or regionalist) goals.

14. Francesc Cambó, 'El problema catalá' (7–8, 15 June, 1, 8 July 1916), *Discursos parlamentaris, 1907–35* (Barcelona: Alpha, 1991), pp. 311–73.
15. Something confirmed by Cambó in his memoirs (*Memorias*, p. 227) and in Pabón, *Cambó*, p. 386. This strategy is analysed in Borja de Riquer, 'Francesc Cambó: un regeneracionista desbordado por la política de masas', *Ayer*, 28 (1997), pp. 103–4; Francisco J. Romero Salvadó, *Spain, 1914–18: Between War and Revolution* (London: Routledge/Cañada Blanch, 1999), pp. 45–6; and Charles E. Ehrlich, '*Per Catalunya i l'Espanya Gran*': Catalan Regionalism on the Offensive, 1911–19', *European History Quarterly*, 28/ 2 (April 1998), pp. 190–1.
16. AEPR, Cambó to Prat de la Riba (9 July 1916): 'Our battle with Alba is decisive... it will decide our prestige and force vis-à-vis the government of Spain (unless otherwise mentioned, all translations are mine).' See also Cambó, *Memorias*, pp. 223–4, 235–6.
17. The best study of Alba's economic plans is Mercedes Cabrera, Francisco Comín and José Luis García Delgado, *Santiago Alba. Un programa de reforma económica en la España del primer tercio del siglo XX* (Madrid: Instituto de Estudios Fiscales, 1989), pp. 251–426. See also Maximiano García Venero, *Santiago Alba* (Madrid: Aguilar, 1963), pp. 110–19.
18. Spain's main industrial and business organizations joined the offensive against Alba's legislation. For Cambó's leading role see IFC, box 3/2, nos. 16–17 (October–November 1916); Cambó, *Discursos*, 'Debat sobre el pressupost extraordinary o de reconstrucció nacional' (31 October and 3 November 1916), pp. 417–46; AEPR, Cambó to Prat de la Riba (5 November 1916); and ASA, Leg. 9/8080, 7/91–3 (November 1916). See also Cabrera et al., *Santiago Alba*, pp. 375–406; Pabón, *Cambó*, pp. 372–9; and Marín Arce, *Santiago Alba*, pp. 42–7.
19. According to Cambó (*Memorias*, p. 240), the Liberal Prime Minister, Count Romanones, fearful for his leadership, had to make efforts not to applaud the storm of criticism against his own minister.
20. *El Socialista* (6–7 and 27 June and 1 October 1916); *España*, nos. 72–5, 79, 89, 91 and 94 (8, 15, 22 and 29 June, 27 July, 5 and 19 October, 9 November 1916).
21. This feeling of disarray in the Liberal ranks is well captured by the party notable and Alba's close friend, Natalio Rivas: BRAH, *Natalio Rivas's Papers*, Leg. 11–8903 (13–14 December 1916). See also Marín Arce, *Santiago Alba*, pp. 55–6.
22. Instituto de Reformas Sociales, *Movimientos*, p. 36: The gap between prices and salaries widened from 1914, being at its worst in 1918–19.
23. Vladimir I. Lenin, *Two Tactics of Social-Democracy in the Democratic Revolution*, in Lenin (ed.), *Selected Words* (London: Lawrence & Wishart, 1971 [1905]), pp. 125–6.
24. These ideas had already appeared in Lenin's crucial book (originally published in February 1902), *What is to Be Done?* (London: Penguin, 1988), pp. 162–212. Tellingly, Lenin had borrowed the title from the classic work of one of the best-known leaders of Russia's revolutionary populist movement, Nikolai Chernichevski (1863).
25. The analysis of Spanish socialism as a basically centrist movement follows that of Meaker (*The Revolutionary Left*, pp. 195–6). For the synthesis of

doctrinal extremism and reformist practice in the Second International see the chapter by Gerhart Niemeyer, 'The Second International, 1889–1914', in Milorad M. Drachkovitch (ed.), *The Revolutionary Internationals, 1864–1943* (Oxford: Oxford University Press, 1966). See also P. Heywood, *Marxism and the Failure of Organized Socialism in Spain, 1879–1936* (Cambridge: Cambridge University Press, 1990), pp. 1–3; M. Pérez Ledesma, *Pensamiento Socialista español a comienzos de siglo* (Madrid: Centro, 1974), pp. 26–54; S. Juliá, *Los Socialistas en la política española, 1879–1982* (Madrid: Taurus, 1997), pp. 16–49. For bureaucratic tendencies in European Marxism see, Dick Geary, *European Labour Protest, 1848–1939* (London: Methuen, 1984), pp. 112–13.

26. Socialist rank-and-file pressure for labour unity can be seen in Fundación Pablo Iglesias (hereafter FPI), *Archivo Amaro del Rosal* (hereafter AAR), *UGT's Executive Committee Minutes, 1916–1918* (hereafter AARD-IX, 4 and 23 May 1916) and *History of the UGT* (hereafter AARD-330-2, May 1916): Amongst others, the Madrid bricklayers' union and the marble workers' union had demanded that the UGT leaders seek collaboration with the CNT. According to a member of the UGT's Executive Committee, Andrés Saborit, the XII Congress overwhelmingly passed a resolution from the Asturian delegates, Isidoro Acevedo and Manuel Llaneza, calling for collaboration with the Anarcho-Syndicalists. Ironically, Acevedo and Llaneza did not believe in an alliance with the CNT but had been obliged to table such a resolution by the votes of the Asturian miners whom they represented. See, FPI, *Andrés Saborit Colomer's Papers* (hereafter AASC), 1915–17 (33), pp. 1963–4; and Andrés Saborit, *Julián Besteiro* (Buenos Aires: Losada, 1967), pp. 87–8. In turn, the CNT's federation of Gijón (Asturias) suggested, in April 1916, an alliance between both unions, and one month later an Anarcho-Syndicalist assembly in Valencia agreed to officially approach the Socialists: AARD-IX (11 May 1916). See also Ángeles Barrios Alonso, *Anarquismo y Anarcosindicalismo en Asturias, 1890–1936* (Madrid: Siglo XXI, 1988), p. 140.

27. AARD-IX, view of the UGT's secretary Vicente Barrio (21 July 1916). See also Heywood, *Marxism*, pp. 40–2.

28. The conclusions approved by the UGT's XII Congress had been the result of a compromise reached by the UGT leaders on the eve of the congress. AARD-IX (15–16 May 1916).

29. Ángel Pestaña, *Lo que aprendí en la vida*, 2 vols (Murcia: Zero, 1971 [1933]), vol. 1, p. 59. See also Meaker, *The Revolutionary Left*, p. 51; and José Luis Gómez Llorente, *Aproximación a la historia del movimiento socialista español* (Madrid: Edicusa, 1976), pp. 292–4.

30. AARD-IX (19, 26 October, 2, 16 and 19 November 1916). The most important confrontation took place (19 November) when the demands of Jordán and two anarchists, Gabriel Calleja and José Villanova (representing Zaragoza's labour federation and Barcelona's textile workers respectively), for a general strike were turned down.

31. Carlos Gil Andrés, *Echarse a la calle. Amotinados, huelguistas y revolucionarios, La Rioja, 1890–1936* (Zaragoza: Prensas Universitarias, 2000), p. 120.

32. *El Socialista* (8 January 1917).

33. *El Liberal* (19 December 1916).

34. AARD-330-2 (March 1917).

35. *El Socialista* (28 March 1917).
36. *El Socialista* (16 and 20 December 1916; 15 January, 17 and 27 March 1917); AARD-330–2 (March 1917); and AARD-IX (22 March 1917).
37. The National Archives, *Foreign Office Papers* (FO), 371–3030/11488 (9 January 1917).
38. Carolyn P. Boyd, *Praetorian Politics in Liberal Spain* (Chapel Hill: University of North Carolina Press, 1979), p. 51. The bill of military reform, introduced first by the Minister of War General Ramón Echague, is in Archivo del Palacio Real (hereafter APR), Sec. 15,614, Exp. 6 (9 November 1915).
39. José Buxadé, *España en crisis. La bullanga misteriosa de 1917* (Barcelona: Bauzá, 1918), pp. 33–4. For more details on the *Juntas Militares de Defensa* see the chapter by Sebastian Balfour, this volume, pp. 255–74.
40. The editorials against the military reforms and existing privileges are numerous. For instance, see those of 1, 4–5, 9 and 16 January 1917 alone.
41. For Spain's divisions see FO 371–2471/73,963 and 2760/20,756, Secret reports (29 July 1915 and 17 April 1916). For examples of secondary literature see Jesús Longares Alonso, 'Germanófilos y aliadófilos españoles en la Primera Guerra Mundial', *Tiempo de Historia*, 21 (1976), pp. 38–45 and 'España 1914: La difícil neutralidad', *Tiempos de Historia*, 27 (1977), pp. 54–61; Manuel Espadas Burgos, 'España y la guerra', *Historia*, 16/51 (1983), pp. 89–104; Gerald Meaker, 'A Civil War of Words', in Hans A. Schmitt (ed.), *Neutral Europe between War and Revolution, 1917–1923* (Charlottesville: University of Virginia Press, 1988), pp. 1–41; and the works by Romero Salvadó, *Spain 1914–1918*, pp. 10–17 and 'Fatal Neutrality: Pragmatism or Capitulation? Spain's Foreign Policy during the Great War', *European History Quarterly*, 33/3 (2003), pp. 296–7.
42. Javier Moreno Luzón, *Romanones: Caciquismo y política liberal* (Madrid: Alianza, 1998), pp. 309–10.
43. In all his interventions in parliament (10 May, 6 June, 13 October and 4 November 1916) Romanones declared his intention of adhering to the policy of strict neutrality formulated by the previous government. The struggle between Romanones and the Germanophiles is examined in Romero Salvadó, 'Fatal Neutrality', pp. 297–304.
44. Germany's territorial offers included Gibraltar, Tangiers, Portugal and in some cases even large chunks of the French North African empire. See FO 371–2472/159,874 (28 October 1915) and 371–2761/31,988 (17 March 1916). See also Romanones, *Notas de una vida, 1912–1931* (Madrid: Marcial Pons, 1999 [1947]), pp. 385–6; and Ron M. Carden, *German Policy Towards Neutral Spain, 1914–18* (New York: Garland, 1987), pp. 92–9.
45. A complete summary of German subversive activities is in BRAH, *Romanones's Papers* (hereafter AR), Leg. 63, Exp. 46 (April 1917). See also secret reports by the Political Intelligence Department in FO 371–2760/20,756 (2 February 1916) and FO 371–3372/118,836 (6 July 1918), and dispatches by British Ambassador Arthur Hardinge, FO 371–3373/44846 and 54288 (9 and 14 March 1918). For a further analysis of the subject see Romero Salvadó, *Spain 1914–1918*, pp. 67–74; and Carden, *German Policy*, pp. 100–2.
46. AR, II I A, Romanones to Spanish Embassy in Berlin (28 February 1917).
47. The confidence to the French ambassador is in FO 371–3035/75548, Vaughan to Balfour (12 April 1917). For the decision to break off diplomatic relations with Germany see AR, II I A, Romanones to León y Castillo (14 April

1917) and to Fermín Calbetón (18 April 1917). See also Carden, *German Policy*, pp. 172–6. For submarine attacks on the Spanish merchant fleet see Anon., *Algunos datos sobre la guerra submarina* (Madrid: Hijos de Tello, 1918), pp. 45–7.
48. *La Acción* (21 April 1917).
49. Political crises were known as *'orientales'*, as they were produced and resolved at the Palacio de Oriente, Alfonso's residence. See Carolyn P. Boyd, 'El Rey-Soldado', in Javier Moreno Luzón (ed.), *Alfonso XIII* (Madrid: Marcial Pons, 2003), p. 218. The resignation note is in *La Época* (19 April 1917). There is a good analysis of the king's role in the dismissal of the government in *España*, no. 118, *'Una crisis Germanófila'* ('A Germanophile Crisis', 26 April 1917).
50. Romanones, *Notas de una vida*, pp. 379, 384–5.
51. FO 185–1344/268, Hardinge to Balfour (19 May 1917).
52. *El País* (28 May 1917).
53. Romanones, *Notas de una vida*, pp. 413–14.
54. For the manifesto and circumstances surrounding the officers' defiance see Benito Márquez and Jose María Capó, *Las juntas militares de defensa* (La Habana: Porvenir, 1923), pp. 31–9, appendix 2, pp. 178–9; and Buxadé, *España en crisis*, pp. 43–7, 50–9; Fernando Soldevilla, *El año político de 1917* (Madrid: Julio Cosano, 1918), pp. 193–213.
55. An account of the planned coup is in a letter by Captain of Artillery Salvador Furiol to Maura in AAM, Leg. 402, Carp. 22 (5 June 1917).
56. *La Correspondencia Militar* (6 and 8 June 1917); the officers' confidence was such that their leader, Colonel Márquez, after being released from prison, declared that they owed their freedom to no one but themselves (Márquez and Capó, *Las juntas*, p. 39).
57. Romanones, *Notas de una vida*, p. 416.
58. *La Correspondencia Militar* (12, 14–15 June 1917).
59. *El Socialista* (12 June 1917).
60. *La Veu de Catalunya* (15 June 1917).
61. Pabón, *Cambó*, p. 399; and Lacomba, *La crisis española*, pp. 176–9.
62. Lacomba, *La crisis española*, pp. 167, 201.
63. Gabriel Maura and Melchor Fernández Almagro, *Por qué cayó Alfonso XIII: Evolución y disolución de los partidos históricos durante su reinado* (Madrid: Ambos Mundos, 1948), p. 302. Examples of Mauristas asking for advice: AAM, Leg. 390, Carp. 7, Centre Maurista at Chamberí in Madrid (4 July 1917) and Leg. 185, Maurista Youth of Barcelona (15 July 1917).
64. AAM, Leg. 399, Carp. 18 (11–12 June 1917).
65. As early as 6 June 1917, two officers wrote to Maura suggesting that he was the man the nation needed (AAM, Leg. 402, Carp. 2). For mail from Peyrá see AAM, Leg. 389, Carp. 10 (20, 25 and 28 June 1917) and Leg. 402, Carp. 22 (20 June 1917). Confirmation of officers' willingness to press the king to give power to Maura is in AAM, Leg. 402, Carp. 22, Gabriel to Antonio Maura (22 June 1917).
66. AAM: Leg. 185 Nadal to Maura (6 and 11 July 1917); Leg. 80, Ossorio to Maura (9 July 1917); Leg. 362, Carp. 2, Miguel to Antonio Maura (24 June 1917), Gabriel to Antonio Maura (26 June, 3, 8, 13 and 14 July 1917); and Leg. 19, Cambó to Gabriel Maura (10 July 1917).

67. Maura and Fernández Almagro, *Por qué cayó Alfonso XIII*, Antonio to Gabriel Maura (23 and 30 June 1917), pp. 488–9.
68. Maura and Fernández Almagro, *Por qué cayó Alfonso XIII*, Antonio to Gabriel Maura (6 July 1917) pp. 489–90; AAM, Leg. 397, Carp. 7, Maura to Ossorio (12 July 1917).
69. María Jesús González Hernández, *Ciudadanía y Acción. El Conservadurismo Maurista, 1901–1923* (Madrid: Siglo XXI, 1990), pp. 39–40. Fundación Antonio Maura, *Gabriel Maura's Papers*, Leg. 113, Carp. 4: Gabriel Maura informs Cambó's lieutenant, Raimon D'Abadal, that, despite their holding many common views, he had to decline the invitation to Barcelona (17 July 1917).
70. Melchor Fernández Almagro, *Historia del reinado de Alfonso XIII*, 4th edn (Barcelona: Montaner & Simón, 1977), pp. 234–6; Soldevilla, *El año político de 1917*, pp. 222, 238–9.
71. Meeting with the Republican Gumersindo de Azcárate is in APR, Sec. 15, Exp. 7 (July 1917). For contacts with Catalan Regionalists see Joaquín María Nadal, *Memóries*, 2nd edn (Barcelona: Aedos, 1965), pp. 269–70; and Márquez and Capó, *Las juntas*, pp. 48–50. After being informed by the Catalan Maurista Nadal of the royal offers, Angel Ossorio wrote to Maura (AAM, Leg. 362, Carp. 2, 13 July 1917) that it was just another example of the royal skill of deceiving everyone. Ossorio's view of the king appears to be borne out by the monarch's own confidence to the then Conservative foreign minister, the Marquis of Lema, that allowing Catalanists into the government could lead to the latter's division. See BRAH, *Eduardo Dato's Papers* (hereafter AED), Lema to Dato (27 July 1917).
72. AAM, Leg. 402, Carp. 22, Peyrá to Maura (10 July 1917).
73. AED, Leg. *Juntas y Movimiento revolucionario de 1917* (June–July 1917). For the activities of the civil governor see Archivo Histórico Nacional (hereafter AHN), *Leopoldo Matos's Papers*, Leg. 3115, nos. 26–31.
74. AHN, Leg. 42 A, Exp. 1, no. 1, Instructions relative to surveillance, censorship and preventive measures (8–19 July 1917). See also Mauro Bajatierra, *Desde las barricadas: Una semana de revolución en España. Las jornadas de Madrid en Agosto de 1917* (Madrid: n.p., 1918), pp. 20, 34–5; and Buxadé, *España en crisis*, pp. 148–51.
75. *La Acción* (19–20 July 1917).
76. ANC, *Lluís Durán i Ventosa's Papers* (hereafter ADV), two notes from Cambó to Ventosa (19 July 1917).
77. Luis Simarro, *Los sucesos de agosto en el parlamento* (Madrid: LIF, 1918), appendix 2C, pp. 365–77. AR, Leg.14, Exp. 19, 5, Collection of documents and pamphlets (July 1917).
78. Sánchez Guerra's boasts were, of course, reproduced in the press organ of the Conservative Party, *La Época* (20 July 1917). AHN, Leg. 42 A, Exp. 1, no. 1, Instructions to civil governors to spread the news that the parliamentarians had been dissolved before passing any resolutions (19 July 1917).
79. FO 371–3033/143,746, Hardinge to Balfour (20 July 1917).
80. A crucial turning point was the accusation on 21 July of dishonesty by the government by Cánovas Cervantes, the maverick MP for Almadén and also editor of *La Tribuna*, who had attended the Assembly.
81. Cambó, *Memorias*, p. 257.

82. AAM, Leg. 362, Carp. 2, Miguel to Antonio Maura (30 July 1917); and AAM, Leg. 80, Ossorio to Maura (1 August 1917). A subdued Maura replied to Ossorio (AAM, Leg. 80), on 7 August, that he was not prepared to collaborate in a movement that could lead to the ousting of the monarchy and which included many political groups that had been fighting him for years. However, he noted he would not stand in the way of those Mauristas who wanted to participate in the Assembly.
83. Márquez and Capó, *Las juntas*, appendix 13, pp. 204–8.
84. Francisco J. Romero Salvadó, *The Foundations of Civil War: Revolution, Social Conflict and Reaction in Spain* (London: Routledge/Cañada Blanch, 2008), pp. 86–7.
85. Some contemporary authors (such as Buxadé, *España en crisis*, p. 138) called it 'the mysterious railway workers' strike' and hinted that agents provocateurs had provoked it. However, two Socialists, Manuel Cordero (*Los Socialistas y la revolución*, Madrid: Impresa Torrent, 1932, pp. 30–3) and Andrés Saborit (*La huelga de agosto de 1917*, México D. F.: Pablo Iglesias, 1967, p. 67) blamed the imprudence of local Republicans, such as the vehement Félix Azzati.
86. In July 1916, the railway workers had succeeded in their dispute against the Compañía del Norte. Their demands included not only the usual pay rises but also the official recognition of their trade union's legal right to represent its members. The decisive moment came when, in an exceptional display of audacity (and against the orders of the UGT's Executive Committee, of which he was a member), Andrés Saborit, surprised in Asturias by the outbreak of the strike, persuaded the miners there to come out in solidarity with the railway workers. On that occasion, the Romanones government intervened and all the conflicting parties accepted the mediation of the Institute of Social Reforms that ruled in favour of the workers. See AARD-IX (27 July 1916); and AASC-XXXIII, pp. 1968–9.
87. Saborit, *La huelga*, pp. 67–8.
88. The members of the strike committee, Largo Caballero (pp. 9, 13–14) and Anguiano (pp. 27, 43–4), both in Simarro, *Los sucesos*, accused the government in parliament in May 1918, of provoking the strike.
89. This revolutionary optimism was stressed by Besteiro's speech in parliament (Simarro, *Los sucesos*, pp. 169, 175–6). For the ignoring of Iglesias's advice see Juan José Morato, *Pablo Iglesias* (Barcelona: Ariel, 2000 [1931]), pp. 202–3; Cordero, *Los Socialistas*, pp. 32–4; and Saborit, *La huelga*, pp. 68–9.
90. James D. White, *The Russian Revolution, 1917–1921* (London: Arnold, 1994), p. 49.
91. Russia suffered more casualties (8 million) than any other belligerent country. Chamberlin, *The Russian Revolution*, vol. 1, p. 65.
92. The crucial moment took place during the third night of popular disturbances (11 March). Troops of the Volynsky Regiment, who during that day had taken a leading role in shooting the demonstrators, mutinied and sent envoys to the other regiments. The following morning, the majority of the Petrograd garrison had deserted the authorities. See Orlando Figes, *A People's Tragedy: The Russian Revolution, 1891–1924* (London: Jonathan Cape, 1996), pp. 312–17; and Chamberlin, *The Russian Revolution*, vol. 1, pp. 77–80.
93. V. I. Lenin, *The Tasks of the Proletariat in Our Revolution* (London: Lawrence & Wishart Ltd, undated [1917]), pp. 3–8, 15–16. This paradox was underlined

in Leon Trotsky, *The History of the Russian Revolution* (New York: Monad Press, 1961 [1932]), vol. 1, pp. 157–8, 164, 168.

94. The so-called 'July Days' (16–18 July) remain a highly complex subject. Some, like Richard Pipes (*The Russian Revolution, 1899–1919*, London: Fontana, 1990, pp. 429–30), regard them as a failed Bolshevik coup. In fact, the popular uprising in the capital appeared to have been spontaneous as in March. The Bolsheviks (like the Mensheviks and Socialist-Revolutionaries then dominant in the Soviets) were surprised by its intensity and scope and could easily have taken power, if they had intended, in Petrograd. This is the conclusion reached by the leading Menshevik Nikolai N. Himmer (Sukhanov), *The Russian Revolution, 1917* (London: Oxford University Press, 1955), pp. 425, 429–31, 480. With the benefit of hindsight, Sukhanov notes the madness of his fellow Mensheviks and Socialist-Revolutionaries bent on sharing power with the bourgeoisie against the demands of the masses who, up to that moment, were their own supporters. See also Robert Service, *Lenin: A Biography* (Basingstoke: Macmillan, 2000), pp. 282–4.

95. Figes, *A People's Tragedy*, pp. 408–9.

96. Baltasar Porcel, *La revuelta permanente* (Barcelona: Espejo de España, 1978), p. 83. For Largo Caballero's statement see Simarro, *Los sucesos*, pp. 9–10. The CNT Secretary Jordán had complained at the Socialists' constant meetings with ministers (AARD-IX, 19 November 1916).

97. Even while negotiations continued, the minister of the interior was already giving instructions to the civil governors to draw up lists of leading revolutionary elements, so as to make their arrests easier as soon as the strike began, and to form armed groups with the reliable people of their regions: AHN, Leg. 42 A, Exp. 1, no. 1 (8–12 August 1917).

98. Francisco Largo Caballero, *Mis recuerdos* (México D. F.: Ediciones Unidas, 1976), pp. 51–2; and Saborit, *La huelga*, pp. 68–9.

99. According to Pestaña (*Lo que aprendí*, vol. 1, pp. 60–3), Iglesias met some leading *cenetistas* during his attendance at the Barcelona Assembly. He offended them when he told them: 'for you, manual workers, it is easy to defend violent methods, but for us, intellectuals, it is different'. Largo Caballero also met a group of Anarcho-Syndicalists when he hurried to Barcelona to prevent any hasty action. Pestaña claimed that the UGT leader must have undergone one of the worst experiences of his life when, at the rendezvous, a hideout on the outskirts of the city, he was abused verbally by some militants brandishing weapons, who accused the Socialists of connivance with bourgeois parties. Largo Caballero (*Mis recuerdos*, pp. 49–50) paints a calmer picture although confirms there was some reckless gun-toting.

100. Joan Serrallonga, 'Motines y revolución. España 1917', *Ayer*, 4 (1991), p. 187.

101. Saborit, *Besteiro*, pp. 100–2.

102. Gómez Llorente, *Aproximación a la historia*, pp. 222, 258–60.

103. Pabón, *Cambó*, pp. 440–1.

104. A narrative of the events is in Soldevilla, *El año político de 1917*, pp. 370–403. On claims that the disturbances were the work of foreign gold see FO 185–1346/433 and 371–3034/175,803, Hardinge to Balfour (24 and 31 August 1917).

105. Anon., *La condena del comité de huelga* (Madrid: n.p., 1918).
106. *La Veu de Catalunya* (25 October 1917).
107. AAM, Leg. 19, Carp. 22, Cambó to Maura (19 September 1917). See also Pabón, *Cambó*, p. 443.
108. AR, Leg. 14, Exp. 19 (15–17 October 1917).
109. AAM, Leg. 362, Carp. 2, Miguel to Antonio Maura (16–17 August and 7 September 1917) and Gabriel to Antonio Maura (16 and 20 August 1917); AED, Leg. *Juntas y Movimiento Revolucionario de 1917* (August–October 1917).
110. Soldevilla, *El año político de 1917*, pp. 438–42.
111. AAM, Leg. 389, Carp 10 (undated but likely to be from late September or early October 1917); and Márquez and Capó, *Las juntas*, p. 68.
112. Dato's optimism was reported by the British ambassador in FO 185–347/522 (28 October 1917). It was well-founded on symbolic royal actions such as the flattering description of his prime minister in a conversation with the Marquis of Lema (AED, 3 October 1917) or the sending of a supportive message, on 20 October, coinciding with Dato's saint day (Fernández Almagro, *Historia*, p. 250).
113. The message is in Márquez and Capó, *Las juntas*, appendix 16, pp. 216–23. The term 'bayonets' was used by Peyrá in a letter to Maura, AAM, Leg. 402, Carp. 22 (26 October 1917).
114. For details of these eight days see Lacomba, *La crisis española*, pp. 304–18.
115. Romanones, *Notas de una vida*, p. 420.
116. Ángeles Barrio Alonso, *La modernización de España, 1917–1939* (Madrid: Síntesis, 2004), p. 16. See also the chapter on the Lliga by Angel Smith, this volume, pp. 145–74.
117. Cambó's thoughts can be seen in ADV, letters to Durán i Ventosa (28 October–3 November 1917). Cambó's cunning opportunism was described as 'gypsy-bargaining' by Saborit (*La huelga*, p. 83) and superbly analysed at the time by the Republican journalist Luis Bello in *España*, nos. 137 and 140 (22 November and 13 December 1917). Further analysis can be seen in Pabón, *Cambó*, pp. 469–70; Boyd, *Praetorian*, p. 91; José Antonio González Casanova, *Federalismo y autonomía* (Barcelona: Crítica, 1979), pp. 205–6; Riquer, 'Francesc Cambó', pp. 106–7; and Romero Salvadó, *Foundations*, pp. 102–4.

4
An Impossible Unity: Revolution, Reform and Counter-Revolution and the Spanish Left, 1917–23

Chris Ealham

Labour politics, 1917–23

The history of the Left during these years was, in no small part, dictated by the tale of two revolutions in 1917 – the Bolshevik Revolution, the epitome of 20th-century revolutions, and a much lesser known aborted Spanish revolution.[1] The year 1917 initiated a process of political definition and realignment on the Left, a process that was both organizationally fissiparous and divisive and witnessed the emergence of new Communist movements. Thus we will see how the Left was in a state of crisis and transition during the crucial period leading up to the 1923 military coup.[2]

Prior to 1917, the Left was split essentially between reformist Socialist and revolutionary anti-state currents. On the Socialist side, the Partido Socialista Obrero Español (Spanish Socialist Workers' Party – PSOE) and Unión General de Trabajadores (General Workers' Union – UGT) were both quite typical of European social democracy of the period.[3] The Socialist movement was more influenced by Kautsky and Guesde than by the untrammelled reformism of Bernstein, its occasional and fleeting revolutionary rhetoric, its talk of the march towards socialism, masking an essentially reformist practice that was, among certain factions of the party, more republican than Marxist. In contrast, the anti-state trend, represented by the revolutionary unionism of the Confederación Nacional del Trabajo (National Confederation of Workers – CNT) after its foundation in 1910, was always far more complex, difficult to characterize and open to misinterpretation.[4]

The division of the Left was perhaps inevitable in a country like Spain, with its profound regional differences, its unevenly developed economy, and its divergences between the urban and rural economies. The division also reflected the internal and occupational differentiation of the working class.

What is also remarkable, however, is that after years of division, the Left managed to reach a new understanding in 1916 in a bid to fight rising prices and inflation, and promote united union mobilizations in favour of improving working-class living standards, a degree of unity in action that was unprecedented and utterly unimaginable in earlier times. But in the context of Spain's repressive monarchy, economic struggles were quickly politicized. Thus, in 1917 a united Left challenged Spain's corrupt monarchy frontally with a general strike that was conceived as part of a wider bid to establish a democratic, parliamentary republic. The failure of this revolutionary movement, coupled with the impact of the Russian Revolution,[5] brought this brief essay in unity to an end. Moreover, 1917 radically reshaped the balance of forces on the Left: its main organizations became increasingly estranged from one another, and also underwent a series of debilitating schisms. It is this panorama that, in part, explains why the Left failed to present a united response to the 1923 coup.

And yet, much seemed to suggest that Spain might follow Russia along the road to revolution during 1917–23. First of all, there is much evidence that throughout this period there was great support among the grass roots of the main left-wing groups for broad, working-class unity.[6] Ultimately, this popular desire for unity was stymied by the organizational rivalries of the main leftist groups and the growing divisions over the question of how to make the revolution, or indeed whether revolution was necessary at all.

Meanwhile, this period was one of unprecedented social and political conflict and mobilization. For the first time the working class emerged as a major player on the national political stage; previously it had largely exerted influence in Barcelona and the Basque Country, the main industrial centres, but now it was possible to talk of a modern class struggle, as popular dissent and more spontaneous protest forms, such as the bread riot, gave way to more organized and structured conflicts based around unions and political parties, although, of course, the two protest repertoires continued to coexist. Despite Spain's wartime neutrality, towards the end of the war and in subsequent years, the state was rocked by the same conflicts that reverberated in the belligerent nations of Europe.[7] We can make comparisons with the revolutionary factory occupations that occurred in Northern Italy; we can point to Russian-style land occupations in the south, during the so-called 'Bolshevik triennium';

we can also see the emergence of right-wing militia and parallel police forces; and finally this protest cycle was largely abrogated by the 1923 coup and the dictatorship that emerged in its wake.[8]

The first frontal challenge to the state was seen in 1917.[9] The elitist and repressive constitutional monarchy so pandered to oligarchic interests that large sectors of society were increasingly alienated by their social and political exclusion. The 1917 crisis had its immediate origin in the growing strength of the working and bourgeois classes during the wartime economic boom, occasioned by Spain's privileged neutrality, which allowed its exports to reach both warring camps. Urban manufacturing interests, especially in Catalonia, wished for a government that might be more responsive to the needs of business, and their protest appeared to dovetail with that of dissident, junior army officers in search of more pay, and whose demands were dressed up in democratic language. At the same time, the organized labour movement appeared ready to provide the muscle that would topple the monarchy with a general revolutionary strike. As urban social groups increased their demands for political representation in the summer of 1917, the narrow social basis of the regime was thrown into sharp relief. Increasingly isolated and bereft of broad support, sections of the moderate Left believed the monarchy might be superseded by a democratic republic. However, as crises unfolded in Spain and in Russia, army dissidents and Catalan industrialists recognized that their interests would be poorly served by a clash with the state and the unpredictable consequences this presupposed. Inevitably, following the August 1917 general strike, businessmen and army officers preferred to rally to the old order, leaving their erstwhile allies on the Left to face a fierce repression that left 71 dead, 156 wounded and over 2,000 imprisoned.

So what was the impact of Spain's 1917 for the Left? For the Socialists it was incredibly traumatic.[10] The Socialist revolutionary committee failed to take adequate security measures and was detained early on in central Madrid, their centre of operations ironically located in a flat in Calle Desengaño (Disappointment Street). The official version of the arrests released to the press could not have impressed their erstwhile revolutionary allies in the CNT: according to one account, the Socialist leaders were hiding – one was found in a wardrobe, another under a bed, and two others inside large flowerpots.[11] All were sentenced to death, although these were commuted to life in prison. Meanwhile, in the streets, the Socialists clearly expected that important sections of the army would side with the people or at least adopt a neutral position. Shortly before the general strike, there had been a wave of bread protests and the army and police periodically had held back from the fray. Yet there was a world of difference between sporadic food conflicts and a political strike that challenged the continuity of state power. The repressive denouement of the 1917 revolutionary movement drove home to Socialists the costs of revolutionary conflict with the state.[12]

The Socialists were deeply scarred by what they viewed as their reckless involvement in a risky revolutionary venture. As if to underscore the malaise within their ranks, Pablo Iglesias, the founder of the PSOE, its 'pope', known affectionately within the movement as the 'Grandfather', fell ill the same year, a circumstance that did little to steady the path of the PSOE.[13]

In keeping with their timid, reformist nature, the leaders reverted to a stoical legalism, fearing any frontal confrontation with the state that might endanger the future of their cherished movement. Inevitably, the tactical chasm between the Socialist movement and the CNT opened up once more, as the Socialist leadership hoped to let the repressive storm run its course, whereupon they could slowly set about building up their strength in anticipation of a future democratic opening that would allow them more of a say in the political process. But on this count, they were set for further disappointment.

The extra-parliamentary street actions of armed workers witnessed during the Bolshevik Revolution of October 1917 and in Spain's 1917, constituted a frontal challenge to the gradual, reformist political strategies of the Socialists. Unsurprisingly, the party elders did not welcome the Russian Revolution. Iglesias, on his sickbed, was profoundly distressed, referring to it as 'tragic' and 'inopportune'. We should bear in mind that the Socialists were vehemently anti-German and pro-Allies, and feared the Bolsheviks would sue for a separate peace with Germany. Remarkably, *El Socialista*, the party's main newspaper, imposed a news blackout on Russian events: it did not even report the Bolshevik seizure of power until 18 March 1918.[14] There are several possible reasons. Party leaders were certainly concerned about the militancy of the rank and file, and wished to stymie copycat radicalization or even a new revolutionary attempt in Spain. But perhaps more than anything, silence reflected growing strategic divisions inside the party about how to react to the Bolshevik revolutionary model. In a sense, the party was immobilized by the internal tensions generated by the supporters and opponents of the Russian Revolution. The PSOE became profoundly introspective, to a significant degree withdrawing from political life in the years that followed, as it thrashed out its future relationship with the Bolsheviks and the new, Moscow-based Third International.

Between 1919 and 1921 this introspection was manifest in three extraordinary congresses. At the first, in December 1919, the party discussed Trotsky's invitation for it to enter the Comintern. The Iglesias leadership, unsurprisingly, prevailed and congress resolved to remain in the Second, reformist, International, which, in the eyes of pro-Bolsheviks in the party, had acquiesced in the slaughter of millions of workers during the war. Keen to avoid a split in the party's ranks, the leadership expressed vague and contradictory platitudes about the provisional nature of this decision, how it would monitor the new Third International, and even work to achieve the unification of the old and new Internationals. Given that the Third International was just a few months old and was created on the premise that its precursor was historically bankrupt, and considering that the Second International had been disbanded in 1916, and would only be reconstituted the following year, in 1920, this piece of nonsense rightly convinced nobody, least of all the Socialist youth movement, which had been radicalized by the 1917 revolutions. The youthful *énragés* were utterly smitten with the Bolshevik way, and wanted action, not words. They duly broke away to form the Partido Comunista de España (Spanish Communist Party – PCE) in April 1920, a small party that was known pejoratively as 'the party of the 100 children'.[15]

Yet no sooner had the split occurred than the Socialist leadership faced a second rebellion of pro-Bolsheviks within their ranks. These were the so-called *terceristas*, the supporters of the 'Third Way' embodied by the new (Third) International. By spring 1920, a majority of party activists sympathized with the *terceristas*, and succeeded in pushing for a new extraordinary congress to reopen the issue of the party's relationship with Moscow. Thus, at the June 1920 extraordinary congress it was decided by a slim majority – 8,269 voted in favour, 5,016 against and 1,615 abstained – to join the Comintern conditionally. Yet the conditional element was key. It was a new fudge. To satisfy the various factions in the party, an emissary from each of the main factions was sent to Moscow to negotiate the party's entrance to the Comintern and to find out more about the famous Twenty-One Conditions that governed all member parties. Daniel Anguiano, a railwayman, leader of the 1917 general strike and political lightweight, represented the pro-Soviet trend. He was accompanied by Fernando de los Ríos, a somewhat foppish professor of philosophy from Granada University, who espoused a brand of Fabian-humanist socialism. Arriving in Russia at the height of 'War Communism', de los Ríos infuriated his Bolshevik hosts by arguing that the PSOE should have full autonomy from Moscow and defending its right to pick from the Twenty-One Conditions as it saw fit. Upon their return to Spain, a third, and final, extraordinary congress was called for April 1921 to discuss their perceptions of the nascent Bolshevik state. Inevitably the two delegates disagreed fundamentally on what they had seen, and this divergence was mirrored at the congress by increased tensions within the party. However, by now the pro-Bolshevik tide had abated somewhat and the leadership won the day, albeit by a small minority (8,808 delegates voted to leave the Comintern, against 6,025, who wished to remain). The PSOE turned its back on Moscow, preferring to join the centrist Vienna, or 'Two-and-a-half', International, and prompting a second split within the party and the creation of a second Communist Party, the Partido Comunista Obrero Español (Spanish Communist Workers' Party – PCOE), on 13 April 1921, almost exactly a year after the creation of the first Spanish Communist Party.[16] Whereas the first split was the work of the radical Socialist youth movement, the second was championed by militant trade unionists from within the UGT.

This period was, beyond doubt, very debilitating for the Socialist movement, as it was for organized labour as a whole. In the short term, the PSOE was immobilized by its internal divisions; and this came in the wake of the trauma of the post-1917 repression. It meant that the PSOE was a relative bystander in the years after the Russian Revolution and during the crisis that led up to the 1923 coup. Moreover, and notwithstanding brief attempts at forging a broader alliance, the experience of the twin revolutions of 1917 and their aftermath militated against the revival of the ephemeral unity pact with the CNT, to which the UGT had subscribed in 1916. The path of unity was seen as a dangerous one that held unforeseen and hazardous consequences, and, if the party bureaucracy periodically made platonic declarations about the need for unity, this was more a desire to appease its own supporters than a genuine declaration of intent.

Yet despite the splits, the all-important movement, the party organization and its structures survived largely intact, and, while it is true that the Spanish Socialists never secured the same degree of penetration as their European counterparts (only during the Second Republic did they make a significant intervention in politics), this had more to do with the political context in Spain and the limited opportunities for a reformist party.

On one level, the leadership strategy of doing or deciding little or nothing helped neutralize internal tensions. On balance, despite the departure of pro-Communists from the Socialist Party, in many crucial respects the PSOE emerged relatively unscathed from the fallout of the Bolshevik Revolution. For instance, not all the pro-Bolsheviks left the Socialist Party during 1920 and 1921. A significant number remained out of loyalty and, while this meant the persistence of certain divisions, the unstable radicalism of the rank-and-file was easily quelled by periodic doses of verbal radicalism. Thus, the majority of party cadre was retained and the PSOE continued to be Spain's leading left-wing political party. Equally, the traditional reformist line of the Socialist leadership emerged strengthened by the departure of the most vocal opponents of the reformist leadership. This allowed for a more uninhibited reformism, and eventually we see the Socialist movement collaborating with Primo de Rivera's dictatorship, something that increased still further the distance between the UGT and the CNT.

If we now turn to the other pole of the labour movement, the so-called anti-authoritarian or anti-state wing, we see the irony that it was here that the impact and consequences of the Bolshevik Revolution were most profoundly felt. Certain caveats need first to be made about the CNT.[17] It is frequently described as an anarchist union or, sometimes, interchangeably as anarchist and anarcho-syndicalist, the differences between the two elided. More accurately, the CNT was revolutionary syndicalist, at least until 1919.[18] But, above all, the CNT was an anti-capitalist, direct action labour union. (Direct action signified class struggle without external arbitration or intervention by third parties.) Founded in Barcelona in 1910, and forged by the city's peculiar industrial relations context, the union consisted of an amalgam of anarchists, anarcho-syndicalists, Socialists, republicans and trade unionists. The essential membership requirement was a readiness to *unite* with other workers, regardless of ideology, to fight capitalism. So we can note two essential features of the early CNT: first, it was overwhelmingly comprised of anti-capitalist workers, not anarchists or anarcho-syndicalists; second, unity was a key element of its early identity and organizational culture.

This flexible, organizational model accommodated a diversity of tendencies within the CNT's base and cadre and proved extremely successful, with union membership expanding vertiginously during the war. At the CNT's 1919 congress it claimed to have three-quarters of a million members, this just nine years after its formation, during most of which time it had been illegal.[19]

So how did the CNT respond to the Russian Revolution? In contrast to the trepidation of the Socialists, for *cenetistas* Russia seemed to show the way forward. As *Solidaridad Obrera*, the main CNT paper proclaimed: 'The Russians are showing us the path to follow...[We] can learn from their actions in order to triumph ourselves, taking by force what is denied to us.'[20] What is more striking still is that the early supporters of the Bolsheviks in Spain were even greater in number among the anarchists, an irony given what would be the violent rupture between the Communists and anarchists in Russia after 1917. But meanwhile, *Tierra y Libertad*, Barcelona's leading anarchist publication, not only justified the Bolshevik Revolution,[21] it celebrated what it claimed was its anarchist content,[22] and even went as far as acknowledging the 'utility' of dictatorship when dealing with the enemies of the Revolution.[23] There was no exaggeration, therefore, in the opinion of Manuel Buenacasa, a prominent anarchist of this era, that 'for many of us – the majority even – the Russian Bolshevik was a kind of demi-God, the carrier of freedom and human happiness'.[24]

This was clearly a huge step for 'anti-authoritarians' to take. Most academic studies explain this in terms of the anarchists being seduced by the successful revolutionary example provided by the Bolsheviks. Doubtless the libertarians were impressed by the beacon of the world's first workers' revolution and the birth of new organs of proletarian democracy, such as the Soviets, open assemblies that approximated the mass workers' unions.[25] Moreover, *The State and Revolution*, Lenin's most libertarian work, had recently been translated into Spanish and, as a once prominent Spanish Communist noted, 'had the virtue of reconciling a large number of anarchists with Bolshevism'.[26]

This pro-Bolshevik trend reached its apotheosis at the CNT's December 1919 Madrid congress. One of the early resolutions presented to the congress read thus:

> The Russian revolution, in principle, embodies the ideal of revolutionary syndicalism. That it abolished class and caste privileges and gave power to the proletariat, so that it could by itself gain the happiness and welfare to which it is entitled, imposing a transitional proletarian dictatorship in order to guarantee the success of the revolution...[27]

This declaration lays bare the deep impact of Russian events within the CNT. It also underscores a fascinating moment in the development of the revolutionary movement in Spain. It marks a moment of clarity, a recognition that the revolution required new institutions, that historical circumstances required some new form of organizing, repressive authority. But, in addition, it also reflected a deep-rooted tension between liberty and authority within anarchist ideology and practice. How should the anarchist revolution be made? What was the most efficacious way of suppressing the old order while simultaneously safeguarding the greatest level of freedom? These issues of liberty and authority would remain thorny dilemmas in anarchist and CNT circles, bedevilling the movement into the 1930s. Indeed, while growing libertarian revulsion towards the Russian experience meant that 'authoritarian' politics were increasingly rejected, there were always some within the movement guided by what anarchist 'purists' denounced as 'authoritarianism'.[28] We have the examples in the mid-1920s of the so-called 'anarcho-Bolsheviks', who advocated the seizure of power by an audacious vanguard.[29] Meanwhile, in the 1930s Marín Civera attempted to transcend the gulf between anarcho-syndicalism and Marxism, a schism he regarded as a barrier to any future revolutionary victory.[30] While such 'bridging' projects were muted by anarchist anti-communism, the practical quest for a revolutionary structure endured, as witnessed by the establishment of the 'Sollana Soviet' in the course of an anarchist uprising in late January 1932.[31] Moreover, after the July 1936 revolution, these unresolved issues of revolutionary power bedevilled the anarchist movement. Thus, in the heat of the civil war, the Friends of Durruti Group openly advocated a 'revolutionary junta', in other words, a workers' state.[32]

Many commentators, including anarchist ones, correctly point to the absence of theoretical clarity within the CNT at different moments in its history.[33] Indeed, the forte of the CNT was its capacity for struggle: it was an organ of combat and action rather than a revolutionary think-tank. For all the popularity of anarchism in Spain, Iberians do not occupy pride of place within the intellectual elite of the European anarchist movement.

Returning to the 1919 congress, while significant factions within the CNT openly flirted with proletarian dictatorship, a majority of delegates accepted a proposal that the ultimate objective be defined as 'libertarian communism'. This was naturally a great success for the anarchists, since previously the CNT had never subscribed to a specific ideology. At the same time, however, congress voted to take the CNT into the newly created Third International, albeit on a provisional basis.

The acceptance of apparently incompatible goals – Comintern membership, 'transitional proletarian dictatorship' and 'libertarian communism' – reflected the free play between the various political tendencies operating within the CNT, all of which were pulling in distinct directions within the same organization. To get a greater appreciation of this we need to look inside the CNT a little more. At the 1919 congress we can discern four main tendencies inside the CNT: the anarchists, the anarcho-syndicalists, the syndicalists and a new faction, the self-proclaimed 'revolutionary syndicalists', although, as we will see, this last tendency was, in very important respects, different from the revolutionary syndicalism that had developed in France after the Charte d'Amiens and after the creation of the CNT in 1910.[34]

Dubbed 'communist-syndicalist' by one commentator,[35] this last faction was the most enduringly and emphatically pro-Soviet and consisted of the most determined pro-Bolsheviks within the CNT. Its most prominent figures were Andreu Nin and Joaquim Maurín, two schoolteachers who rose to prominence within the CNT's Liberal Professions' Union in 1920. For Nin and Maurín, the revolutionary events of 1917 in Spain and Russia constituted a radical learning curve marked by a series of accelerated political experiences and lessons: appalled by what he saw as its 'sickening reformism', Nin left the PSOE, while Maurín quit the Republican movement. Upon entering the CNT, both initially sided with the syndicalist faction led by Salvador Seguí, arguably the most astute and popular labour leader of this era, and a great partisan of workers' unity.[36] As such, they were very hostile to the anarchist control of the CNT, even though they accepted that anarchists, like any other tendency, had a role to play within the unions.

The first public evidence of this trend came with Nin's address to the 1919 congress:

> I am an enthusiast of action, of the revolution. I believe in actions more than in distant ideologies and abstract questions. I am an admirer of the Russian Revolution because it is a reality. I am a supporter of the Third International because it is also a reality, because over and above ideologies it represents a principle of action, a principle of coexistence for all the genuinely revolutionary groups that seek the immediate establishment of communism.[37]

This quote bears all the hallmarks of the revolutionary syndicalists: their abiding obsession with insurrectionary action over and above ideological and theoretical debates; the conviction that the revolution was an immediate priority for the working class; and the importance of unity, the sine qua non of all revolutionary action. Unity, in particular, became the cornerstone of the practice of the revolutionary syndicalists.[38]

Nin and Maurín quickly rose to prominence in the Catalan CNT, and later nationally, during what was an especially bleak period in the history of the union. As will be discussed further below, between 1919 and 1923 the authorities resolved to destroy the union, taking the war to the CNT's Catalan heartlands, where parallel police and right-wing terrorist groups assassinated *cenetistas* with impunity. This was combined with classic union-busting tactics like the lockout of unionists. When, in the spring of 1921, the CNT leadership was decapitated by mass arrests, Nin and Maurín stepped into the breach: Nin, 29 years old at the time, became Secretary of the CNT National Committee, while Maurín, aged 25, sat on the powerful Catalan Regional Committee, although circumstances obliged him to replace Nin as Secretary later that year. At this time, all prominent CNT militants were obliged to carry pistols and often be accompanied by union bodyguards. Nin and Maurín risked their lives to keep the CNT alive in what was a fierce struggle for organizational and physical survival. Nin's predecessor had been assassinated, and Nin himself narrowly escaped an attack by right-wing gunmen that left one of his close allies dead. Meanwhile, Maurín's activism led to him being shot and wounded by the police, and jailed on more than one occasion.

The adverse climate facing *cenetistas* deteriorated further under the watch of the revolutionary syndicalists. Just a few days after Nin took over as CNT Secretary, a CNT 'action group' assassinated Prime Minister Dato, who had been in office during the revolutionary crisis of 1917, when his role in the subsequent repression earned him huge opprobrium in left-wing circles. But Dato's death was sealed by his tolerance of the more recent repression, which saw the systematic hunting and slaying of CNT activists. It is hard to know Nin's exact role in the assassination.[39] Ideologically, Nin was opposed to individual terror, but this assassination was not a traditional anarchist *attentat*. Rather, it was launched by a group of young workers from the CNT Barcelona metalworkers' union who travelled to Madrid to 'settle scores' with the prime minister. As such, it might be argued to fit with the Sorelian formula of 'collective revolutionary violence' so lauded by the revolutionary syndicalists. Yet the police had no doubts about Nin's complicity, forcing him into exile in the Soviet Union to evade a widening repressive net, at which point he was replaced by Maurín as National Secretary in October 1921 until his arrest in February 1922.

According to Gerald Meaker, the history of the revolutionary syndicalists 'remains poorly documented and, indeed, obscure'.[40] Certainly, their role in the CNT has been distorted, simplified and misunderstood.

Cold War narratives of 'Communist subversion' have further muddied the waters, particularly when it comes to their politics. For instance, Meaker, a US historian writing in the 1970s, depicted the revolutionary syndicalists simply as a 'Leninist' group. He suggests they converted to Bolshevism very swiftly, claiming that as early as 1921 they were ortho- dox Bolsheviks, 'greatly preoccupied with the need for centralized lead- ership and organizational discipline'.[41]

But this judgement does not tally with Maurín's writings, both then and later, just as it clashes with the testimonies of the pro-Bolsheviks within the CNT and with the judgement of the leading authority on this group.[42] The overwhelming evidence therefore suggests the revolu- tionary syndicalists were in a state of political limbo, a space in-between syndicalism and Marxism. So, in 1921, the year in which Meaker claims the CNT's pro-Bolsheviks were already 'Leninist', Maurín was as much influenced by Georges Sorel, and 'the systematization of the doctrine of collective violence', as by Lenin.[43] While Maurín and his comrades felt an 'idealization of proletarian dictatorship', they remained hostile towards party discipline and political parties in a way that placed them more within the syndicalist tradition.[44] Maurín also criticized what he called 'neo-Marxists' and their stress on Soviets, which, he believed, could not play the same role locally as they had in Russia. Maurín was explicit: CNT strength meant that communism in Spain would be attained through 'revolutionary syndicalism', with the 'trade union apparatus, the organization of the producers, as the base on which com- munist society will rest'.[45] Even at the end of 1922, Maurín declared that he and his followers were 'neither Communist nor anarchist'.[46] Finally, only in 1924 did Maurín join the PCE, only to leave shortly afterwards to become a leading anti-Stalinist Marxist.[47] Moreover, while arguably Spain's most gifted Marxist theoretician, there are some indi- cations that Maurín never entirely shook off his revolutionary syndical- ist past: he retained deep sentimental ties with the CNT and, as late as 1931, when he led a dissident Communist Party, he called on the CNT to seize power.[48]

The other great myth surrounding the revolutionary syndicalists is that they rose to power within the CNT having orchestrated some kind of coup within the union organization. In the opinion of Robert Kern, another US scholar also writing in the 1970s, the Nin–Maurín group was a Trojan horse for Communists bent on subverting the CNT from within.[49] For Kern, they did this by 'capitalizing on the Confederation's disarray'[50] during a time of state repression. Meaker concurs, noting that 'the CNT had indeed fallen under the control of a small minority of communist-syndicalists',[51] with values alien to those of the CNT.[52] This view is supported by suggestions that the revolutionary syndicalists used 'irregular procedures', packing CNT meetings and assemblies with loyalists to manufacture majorities and relying on methods later identified with Stalinism.

Such perspectives were clearly inflected by Cold War narratives. Meaker and Kern also base their accounts heavily on anarchist sources, which to a significant extent shared this anti-Soviet narrative, especially after their experience of the Spanish Civil War, which saw vertiginous Communist growth within the Republican zone, much to the detriment of the Socialist and anarchist movements. Thus, anarchist writers have emphasized the 'cunning', 'sophistry' and 'manoeuvres'[53] of 'Moscow agents' who briefly 'took over' the CNT.[54]

This perspective is based on several flawed premises. First of all, it is anchored in a profound misrepresentation of the CNT, a direct democracy union without any bureaucracy or apparatus that might be seized by an ambitious, power-hungry Svengali. Moreover, had the revolutionary syndicalists 'seized power' using devious, Machiavellian means, we need an explanation for their subsequent negligent loss of power. More realistically, the pro-Bolsheviks rose to prominence due to a variety of factors, ranging from the arrest and assassination of older CNT leaders across to, it has to be acknowledged, the brief love affair that existed among important sections of the *cenetista* rank-and-file with the Bolshevik Revolution. Once the passion subsided, so too did the brief hegemony of the revolutionary syndicalists, a reversal of fortunes that was further aided by Nin's enforced Soviet exile and Maurín's incarceration in Barcelona. Nevertheless, by mid-1921, when news of the Kronstadt uprising and the brutal repression of Russian anarchists by the Bolsheviks had reached Spain, the Nin–Maurín group were fighting a rearguard action within the CNT.

All the same, the revolutionary syndicalists were firmly rooted within CNT traditions. For them, the CNT was 'the great organization of the Spanish proletariat in which all social tendencies can co-exist',[55] it was the union of all anti-capitalists, regardless of their politics. For example, when, in April 1921, the CNT sent a delegation to Moscow, the revolutionary syndicalists, then at the head of the organization, ensured all factions, including the anarchists, were represented in the four-man delegation, even though it was glaringly obvious that their presence would result in criticism and censure of the Soviet regime and, potentially, compromise the standing of the pro-Bolsheviks within the CNT.[56] Indeed, while in Moscow, two CNT delegates, Hilario Arlandis and 'Gastón Leval' (Pierre Robert Pillar), signed a document criticizing Bolshevik repression of the Russian anarchist movement.[57] Undeterred, the leading pro-Bolshevik newspaper, *Lucha Social*, which was also briefly the main CNT paper, was anything but a sectarian organ: it publicized anarchist pamphlets, as well as those produced by other CNT factions; it was strikingly open to all revolutionary tendencies, carrying articles by anarchists critical of the pro-Bolsheviks,[58] and reflected Maurín's faith in 'the great universal family of workers'.[59]

Yet this family became increasingly strife-ridden, in no small part due to the growing sectarianism and anti-communism of the radical anarchists, who, from 1922, were on the ascendancy within the CNT. Although the moderates remained at the helm of the CNT until the summer of 1923, at the June 1922 Zaragoza Conference radical anarchists pushed through an initiative that saw the Confederation withdraw from the Comintern, even though, formally speaking, a congress was required to reach decisions of such import.[60] There is, moreover, evidence that the departure of the CNT from the Third International had less to do with the sentiments of the union grass roots and was more linked to the pressure of anarchist activists. For instance, just two months after the Zaragoza Conference, the orthodox anarchist publicist Teresa Mañé i Miravet, who was always impervious to the pull of the Russian Revolution, published a brutally frank appraisal of the CNT rank-and-file, in which she concluded that 'the trade union mass is not anarchist'. Worse still, in the opinion of Mañé i Miravet:

> The majority [of the CNT] is closer to the dictatorship of Lenin than to the concepts of Kropotkin or Reclus... [T]o simple minds, the Russian revolution is above all else a revolution... they answer you that the laws and statutes which we, the anarchists, want to destroy, have already been destroyed in Russia.[61]

The growing rupture between the anarchists and the Bolshevik state had far-reaching implications for the labour movement in Spain. As the anarchists inveighed against the Russian model, we see an outpouring of anti-communism. So, despite the numerous sacrifices of the revolutionary syndicalists to sustain the CNT in impossible circumstances, preserving the union's institutions and its internal democracy, anti-Communist opprobrium was directed unswervingly against them: in mid-1922 anarchists called for an 'intensive labour' to exclude 'the Communists disguised as syndicalists' from the CNT,[62] and the following year, the year of the coup, we see the first expulsions of pro-Bolsheviks from the Confederation.[63]

Thus, with the ascendancy of the radical anarchists, for the first time we see a conscious attempt to marginalize and isolate one of the tendencies within the CNT. Here, therefore, we have a break with CNT traditions of freedom of tendency and tolerance, a state of affairs that prompted the pro-Bolsheviks to accuse the anti-authoritarian anarchists of establishing their own 'dictatorship' within the unions.

Certainly, this anti-communism was not shared by all *cenetistas*. For instance, the syndicalist current, led by Seguí, from which the revolutionary syndicalists had emerged, was more inclusive and open to joint initiatives with the pro-Bolsheviks. In one sense, the sharp anti-Communist turn of the anarchists reflected their own sense of ideological weakness and vulnerability. As we saw earlier, it was they who had been the first and most enthusiastic supporters of the Russian revolutionary experiment and some were briefly seduced by 'authoritarian' solutions to questions posed by the revolution. Unable to face up to their dangerous liaison with the Bolshevik state, when they woke from what they saw as a bad dream, they lashed out at the former object of their fascination. Hence, Buenacasa, previously one of the most fervent advocates of the Bolshevik cause, now became one of their fiercest critics.[64]

In the context of labour politics in the period leading up to the 1923 coup, this was inopportune. The rise of the radical anarchists was a further hammer blow to the prospects of working-class unity and further divided the Left. By 1922 the radical anarchists were convinced they represented the only true revolutionary force. This self-image had much to do with the two revolutions of 1917. First of all, they were appalled by the timidity of their erstwhile Socialist allies after the aborted Spanish revolution that year. Meanwhile, the CNT was the receptacle for the wave of radicalization that swept across the working class after 1917 – by 1919 its membership was possibly four times greater than the cadre of its Socialist rival. Buoyed up by this newfound strength, the anarchists pushed through a motion at the December 1919 CNT Congress giving the UGT an ultimatum to merge with the Confederation or be treated as a 'yellow' union. In effect, Socialist trade unionists were expected to suppress their identity and personality and be absorbed by the CNT.

Second, if the anarchists had been seduced by the return of Marxism to its revolutionary origins in 1917–18, by 1922 they had concluded that Bolshevism could only result in a new dictatorship to oppress the workers and therefore had to be combated. But the growing marginalization of the revolutionary syndicalists was a disaster for the CNT and for the

An Impossible Unity 107

labour movement as a whole, for of all the groups on the fragmented Left, it was the Nin–Maurín group that showed greatest awareness of the Fascist menace, both internationally and in Spain.[65] The revolutionary syndicalists were also the most insistent defenders of working-class unity in the face of the onward march of reaction.

In sharp contrast, the official Communists did much to divide the labour movement and the Left before the 1923 coup.[66] The creation of Spain's Communist movement was immersed in confusion and controversy. The 'party of the proletariat' remained a minnow until the peculiar international and historical context of the Spanish Civil War allowed it to grow. Many problems flowed from the party's birth. The Bolshevik emissaries who served as midwives to the new party were deeply ignorant of Spanish conditions and the peculiarities of the local labour movement. The first Soviet agents on the scene – Mikhail Borodin and a certain 'Ramírez', whom many historians have claimed to be Mexican but who was, in fact, a US citizen – had little real interest in Spain; they were simply passing through on their way to Europe after a fruitless sojourn in Mexico.[67]

In more general terms, the ascetic, 'workerist' traditions of Spanish labour and revolutionary activists were at variance with Comintern agents who frequently failed to conceal their bourgeois origins. Juan Andrade, an early Spanish Communist who soon became a dissident Marxist, denounced 'Ramírez' to Moscow for his 'aristocratic habits' and 'extraordinary lifestyle', including excessive expenditure on tobacco and the seduction of cinema actresses.[68]

Successive Soviet representatives committed the tactical error of focusing their attention on the Socialist movement, even though mass opposition to reformism in Spain had always been inside the CNT and the anarchist movement. Consequently, Moscow's envoys did nothing to develop the enormous support for the Bolsheviks within the CNT. Simply put, the script issued by the Kremlin to its agents was based on Russia's revolutionary past: it precluded the possibility of a pro-Bolshevik trend emerging within a mass revolutionary syndicalist union. So, while revolutionary ideas might pass across the Pyrenees into Spain, imported revolutionary models did not travel as felicitously. This inability to adapt to local conditions was not unique to Spain: in the USA a similar process was seen with the Industrial Workers of the World (IWW), whose pro-Bolshevik current was effectively ignored by Comintern strategists.

In effect, the Comintern simply placed its money on the wrong horse in Spain.[69] It ordered the unification of the two Spanish Communist parties created during 1920–1 as the Partido Comunista de España but the radical youth and militant trade unionists who constituted the bulk of the two parties found it difficult to surmount their accumulated personal and organizational jealousies. Whereas Oscar Pérez Solís[70] and Mariano García Cortés, two of the early leaders of the PCE, later converted to authoritarian conservatism, Spain's most original and celebrated Marxist thinkers emerged from the pro-Bolshevik current within the CNT. It was Nin and Maurín who most astutely and intelligently employed the new political vocabulary and concepts that came into currency with the Russian Revolution. Yet their Marxism was dissident, anti-Stalinist, much richer than anything inside the official Communist movement, whose cadre was more concerned with repeating slogans and implementing Comintern formulas.

The politics of the orthodox Communists were similarly limited, characterized by a vehement sectarianism. Early on, in particular, some party activists resorted to heavy-handed intimidation of their erstwhile Socialist allies, resulting in gunfights and fatalities at several UGT and PSOE meetings and congresses.[71] When, finally, the PCE focused its attention on the CNT, it was obsessed with splitting the union, a line that brought discredit to the party, and increased the aloofness of the revolutionary syndicalists from the official Communist movement. This profound gulf between the CNT's pro-Bolsheviks and those who emerged from within the Socialist movement would continue to dog the evolution of Spanish communism into the 1930s.

The meltdown of labour relations

Wartime industrial expansion, the concomitant numerical expansion of the urban working class, new forms of union organization, rampant inflation and stagnant wages, along with the political crisis of the Restoration, all provided the context for an unprecedented wave of industrial conflict in the years before the 1923 coup. In effect, we see the meltdown of industrial relations, a decisive factor in cementing the military–industrial alliance in the prelude to Primo de Rivera's coup.

After 1918 it was possible, for the first time, to talk of a national or state-wide working class, providing a more solid basis for a labour movement that was now able to extend its influence across a wider geographical space. (The CNT was effectively a Barcelona-based union up until the end of the war, when, for the first time, urban and rural mobilizations were co-ordinated by the National Committee of an invigorated CNT organization.) Now, class struggle reached provincial centres such as Santander, Logroño and Palma de Mallorca, as well as more traditionally conservative areas, such as Valladolid, Castilla-La Mancha, the Campo de Gibraltar and the neighbouring British colony.[72] The political capital, Madrid, hitherto more an administrative than an industrial centre, was also rocked by the biggest wave of conflict and protest in the city's history until that time.[73] A similar pattern was seen in more traditional northern centres of industrial mobilization, such as in the Asturian coal mines[74] and among the heavy industry of the Basque Country.[75] And, as we see in Francisco Cobo's chapter in this volume, southern rural protest was generalized during these years.[76] The giddy development of this protest cycle was amply reflected in statistics produced by the Instituto de Reformas Sociales, according to which the days lost from strikes grew from 1,784,538 in 1917 to 7,261,764 in 1920, while the number of strikes increased from 71,440 to 244,684.[77]

Yet this protest cycle is most noteworthy for its qualitative dimensions, its part in undermining the foundations of the Restoration regime, the nature and substance of the demands articulated by strikers, and their scope. Protest was not purely industrial but combined consumption issues relating to inflation as well as traditional demands for a 'fair price' for bread.[78] Thus, for instance, the landscape of protest in Madrid was extensive, spanning tram burnings, industrial stoppages, general strikes, food riots, and both peaceful and direct action protest, including assassination.[79] Strikes also became more politicized. This was most marked in 1919, the high point of enthusiasm for the Russian Revolution, when organized labour was enthused by a wave of optimism, and when important sections of the CNT felt the revolution was nigh.[80] General strikes became more frequent; for instance, between 1917 and 1921 the anarchist stronghold of Zaragoza witnessed general strikes every year, reaching a crescendo in 1921, when there were three.[81]

This explosion of union militancy was intimately linked to the expansion of the CNT, which, as mentioned above, had around three-quarters of a million members by 1919. One of the keys to CNT success was that it actively fused two protest repertoires – a more traditional, direct action, insurrectionary methodology, and a more stable set of practices based on strike actions, meetings and demonstrations – to develop a variegated and combative arsenal in the post-war era.[82] (In contrast, the Socialists for the most part struggled to channel and neutralize this more traditional protest culture, albeit with varying degrees of success.[83])

Key to the CNT's new gamut of tactics was the Sindicato Único (Single Union), an Iberian version of the IWW's 'One Big Union': the *Únicos* were local unions, uniting workers in any given town or industrial sector, skilled and unskilled alike, in the same union, thus transcending the craft divisions and sectionalism of the old workers' societies. This innovation was announced at the July 1918 Catalan CNT regional congress (in Barcelona), before being adopted nationally.[84] The Sindicato Único had a profoundly radicalizing effect on CNT unions, as the more circumspect or moderate sections were often outnumbered by the overwhelmingly militant mass membership. Moreover, since members of each Sindicato Único knew they could rely on other unions for support in the event of a strike, the 'free rider' problem was largely resolved.[85]

Before the war, employers were largely accustomed to having it all their own way in their factories; now, in the post-war years, not only did they face a combative and well-organized labour movement but, more worryingly still from their perspective, revitalized unions, buoyed up by the numerical expansion of the working class during the war, were now capable of winning industrial strikes. This was also facilitated by the creation of armed groups that ensured that growing numbers of workers backed industrial action. At the same time, the geographical expansion of social conflict undermined the confidence of the old elites in the ability of the Restoration system to protect their interests from the growing challenge from below. In addition, the CNT now co-ordinated what had previously been largely isolated rural collective action with its urban protest movements. As one Catalan industrialist wrote, these were 'times of fear'.[86]

Elite trepidation focused on Catalonia, where the CNT had over 400,000 members in 1919, accounting for nearly half the overall membership, a third of which (over 250,00 members) was massed in the Barcelona area.[87] The power of Barcelona's *Sindicatos Únicos* was most dramatically glimpsed in early 1919 at the Ebro Irrigation and Power Company, an Anglo-Canadian concern known locally as La Canadiense.[88] Conflict began in early 1919 with the sacking of a handful of CNT white-collar workers. Unionized workers – blue- and white-collar alike – walked off the job and appealed for solidarity from the local CNT. In this way, a fairly insignificant dispute was transformed into a titanic struggle between a vast coalition spanning the city and state authorities and national and international capital, on the one hand, and the Barcelona CNT, on the other. Much of the state's repressive arsenal was mobilized; martial law was implemented and, following the militarization of essential services, soldiers replaced strikers;

some 4,000 workers were jailed. Regardless, cuts in the energy supply paralysed industry across Barcelona province for 44 days. Amidst food shortages, power cuts and torchlit nocturnal army patrols, the Catalan capital seemed like a city at war. Finally, Prime Minister Romanones attempted to calm the labour situation in Barcelona, sending an emissary, José Morote, to broker a deal between unions and employers. After pressure from Morote, La Canadiense management bowed to the CNT's demands, which included a wage rise, the payment of the strikers' lost wages and a complete amnesty for pickets. In an attempt to forestall further class conflict, the Madrid government became the first in the world to legislate the eight-hour day in industry. Despite opposition from radicals within the CNT, Seguí sold the package to activists at a monster rally on 17 March. This triumph heralded the coming of age of the CNT – it had arrived as a major player in the industrial arena.

Yet the La Canadiense conflict had polarized the social context, unleashing key processes that sounded the death knell of the Restoration. The authoritarian Barcelona Employers' Federation, which represented the most militant elements within the industrial elite, had entered into an alliance with extremists within the local military.[89] In a blatant act of rebellion against the government, the then head of the Barcelona garrison, General Joaquín Milans del Bosch, backed by the infantry officers' association, the *junteros*, and egged on by the Employers' Federation, refused to release CNT prisoners in army custody, in a bid to scupper La Canadiense settlement and provoke a showdown with the unions. The middle ground caved away. The new situation confirmed the stance of the radicals in the CNT, which launched a general strike on 24 March to secure the freedom of its prisoners. The Romanones government was obliged to repress the movement, declaring martial law in Barcelona and suspending civil liberties throughout Spain. Under a tumult of sharp criticism from the Employers' Federation and the rattling of sabres in the Barcelona garrison, the discredited civil governor and police chief were dismissed; they then fled to Madrid, where Romanones later resigned.[90]

The year 1919 brutally exposed the inability of the Restoration authorities to pacify an increasingly conflictive industrial relations context through negotiation or reform. The Spanish government signed up to the Versailles Treaty, a move that raised hopes among many Republicans and Socialists that the International Labour Organization might bolster an institutionalized system of trade unionism and herald the gradual democratization of the political system.[91] Yet any such utopian aspirations floundered on the traditional hostility of capitalists to state intervention in industry,[92] and on the bedrock of the hardening authoritarian stance of the most reactionary groups of Spanish society. Evidence of this came in September, when the syndicalist wing of the Barcelona CNT and complaisant elements within the bourgeoisie agreed to submit disputes to the Mixed Commission (*Comisión mixta*), a state-sponsored arbitration committee, their hopes scotched by a flare-up of social and industrial conflict after the Barcelona Employers' Federation declared an 84-day lockout of some 300,000 workers, lasting from 3 November 1919 to 26 January 1920.[93]

The experience of Barcelona's labour relations increasingly inspired a reactionary utopia of pacifying industrial relations *manu militari*. The Employers' Federation sought to destroy the CNT in a bid to reassert its unfettered right to determine working conditions. As growing circles of capitalists became alienated from the Restoration state, the underlying feeling among the Employers' Federation was that the Madrid authorities lacked the political will to take on the unions and that the distant central power was out of touch with their concerns. Salvation for a section of the bourgeoisie lay with the military, and this group opted to act autonomously of central government, a freedom of manoeuvre that peaked with the September 1923 coup.

In the interim period, the social war in Barcelona gathered pace. In autumn 1919, the Sindicatos Libres (Free Trade Unions) was established with the support of the Employers' Federation and the Barcelona garrison. An extreme right-wing, Catholic union, the *Libres* was committed to breaking the power of the CNT, mainly through strike-breaking activities that were backed up by its paramilitary wing.[94] With *cenetistas* increasingly demonized as 'felons' in the conservative press, new authoritarian civic groups such as the Somatén militia and Acción Ciudadana augmented police patrols on the streets in order to 'banish criminal types from Barcelona'.[95] In practice, while the CNT was not a prescribed organization, anyone found with a membership card faced the prospect of being sacked, arrested or beaten, as the strident pursuit of a 'law-and-order' agenda produced numerous infringements of civil rights, including the freedom of workers to join the union of their choice. Now, preventive arrest, internment without trial and internal deportation were the order of the day.[96]

The assault on the CNT gathered pace after 8 November 1920, with the appointment of General Severiano Martínez Anido, the military governor of the Barcelona garrison, as civil governor, following intensive lobbying by the Employers' Federation and military top brass. Having served previously in Morocco and the Philippines, Martínez Anido ruled

Barcelona as if it were a colonial fiefdom, appointing General Miguel Arlegui as city police chief, and unleashing a two-year reign of terror based on the *ley de fugas*, a programme of selective assassination of CNT militants. At the height of the violence, in 1921, 113 people were killed and 95 wounded, the majority Barcelona *cenetistas*.[97] It is noteworthy that the admirers of this bloody tactic included General Miguel Primo de Rivera, then head of the Valencia garrison.[98]

The CNT now experienced more or less constant repression until the 1923 coup. There was a brief respite under the government of José Sánchez Guerra, who removed Martínez Anido and Arlegui, but even then the CNT's freedom of manoeuvre was curtailed. The intense repression took its toll: not only were key figures in the organization assassinated (Seguí suffered this fate in March 1923), but the everyday climate of fear and the disarticulation of CNT structures produced a haemorrhage of members.[99] By September 1923, CNT membership has been estimated at 'between 300 and 400,000'.[100] Some 45 years later, one astute anarchist analyst of the CNT reflected that by this time the CNT was 'almost bled dry', the La Canadiense strike 'had been our Waterloo'.[101]

While the ferocious anti-union offensive could not finish with the CNT, it nevertheless exerted a profound impact on the internal balance of forces within the Confederation, aiding the ascendancy of the radical anarchists, validating their paramilitary activities and the tactical shift away from mass union mobilizations towards small group activity, such as the assassination of politicians and employers. When the authorities prevented the CNT from collecting union dues from members, thus compromising the Confederation's principles of active solidarity, which included helping the jailed comrades and their families through the Comité pro-presos (Prisoners' Support Groups), armed groups responded with a string of spectacular bank raids to strengthen union funds on the brink of collapse.[102] This climate of violence – 'permanent disorder' in the view of one scholar[103] – generated immense insecurity among the elite and became an important factor in the build-up to the 1923 coup, and it is significant that General Primo de Rivera was captain general of Catalonia during this time, where the armed anarchist groups were most active.[104]

Conclusion

Communism was widely debated on the Left in the years immediately after the war. The topic was given full vent in the anarchist press, later in the Socialist press, and, of course, in Communist newspapers. The elites could readily conclude that Communist fever was gripping the country. This was all the more troubling as this phenomenon dovetailed with the widespread growth of mass mobilization. For the first time, labour conflicts were occurring across the state.

Yet the growing strength of labour masked fissiparous tendencies on the Left. By 1923, leftist divisions, coupled with widespread popular revulsion towards the Restoration state, which had repressed and excluded broad sectors of the masses, clearly aided the success of the coup. Indeed, such was the intensity of the anti-leftist assault after 1917 that many understandably felt they were already experiencing dictatorship before 1923. Any popular defence of such a discredited system was unimaginable. The memory of the easy coup of 1923 was very much in the mind of the Right in 1936, when sections of the army and their Fascist civilian supporters expected a swift, effortless victory. There was no rerun in 1936. Besides the desire to halt the onward march of Fascism, the Left had learnt from its earlier disunity, even if it was a slow learning process. All the same, it was a learning curve shaped crucially by the revolutionary syndicalists of the 1920s, who ten years on emerged as the most ardent purveyors of revolutionary left-wing unity. While their politics of unity fell on deaf ears in the 1920s, in the 1930s they found an echo just in time to enable a divided Left to forge anti-Fascist alliances and challenge the aspirations of the authoritarian Right.

Notes

An earlier version of this chapter was delivered at the Modern European History Research Seminar, Cambridge University, in February 2008. I am indebted to Andy Durgan, Francisco J. Romero Salvadó and Angel Smith for their incisive written comments on earlier drafts. All the translations into English in this Chapter are by myself.

1. For Spain's 1917, see the chapter by Francisco J. Romero Salvadó in this volume.
2. For general surveys of the Left during these years, see Benjamin Martin, *The Agony of Modernization: Labor and Industrialization in Spain* (Ithaca, NY: Cornell University Press, 1990); Manuel Tuñón de Lara, *El movimiento obrero en la historia de España* (Madrid: Taurus, 1972).
3. Carlos Forcadell, *Parlamentarismo y bolchevización: el movimiento obrero español, 1914–1918* (Barcelona: Crítica, 1978); Paul Heywood, *Marxism and the Failure of Organised Socialism in Spain, 1879–1936* (Cambridge: Cambridge University Press, 1990). For the UGT, see Amaro del Rosal, *Historia de la UGT de España, 1901–1939* (Barcelona: Grijalbo, 1977).

4. Antonio Bar, *La CNT en los años rojos: del sindicalismo revolucionario al anarcosindicalismo, 1910–1926* (Madrid: Akal, 1981).
5. As one pro-Bolshevik noted, the Russian Revolution 'was like a new dawn rising in the East that gave hope to us all' (Adolfo Bueso, *Recuerdos de un cenetista. De la Semana Trágica (1909) a la Segunda República (1931)* (Esplugues de Llobregat: Ariel, 1976), 1, p. 100). See Juan Avilés Farré, *La fe que vino de Rusia: la revolución bolchevique y los españoles, 1917–1931* (Madrid: UNED-Biblioteca Nueva, 1999).
6. The aim of those who founded the CNT was to unite with the UGT in order to unify the entire working class in a single organization. See Adolfo Bueso, *Como fundamos la CNT* (Barcelona: Avance, 1976), and Bar, *La CNT*, pp. 32–6.
7. See especially Francisco J. Romero Salvadó, *Spain 1914–1918: Between War and Revolution* (London: Routledge, 1999).
8. Albert Balcells, 'Violencia y terrorismo en la lucha de clases en Barcelona de 1913 a 1923', *Estudios de Historia Social*, 42–3 (1984), pp. 37–79; Julio Aróstegui, 'El insurreccionalismo en la crisis de la Restauración', in José Luis García Delgado (ed.), *La crisis de la Restauración. España, entre la primera guerra mundial y la II República* (Madrid: Siglo XXI, 1986), pp. 75–100; Eduardo González Calleja, *El máuser y el sufragio. Orden público, subversión y violencia política en la crisis de la Restauración, 1917–1931* (Madrid: Consejo Superior de Investigaciones Científicas, 1999).
9. Juan Antonio Lacomba, *La crisis española de 1917* (Madrid: Ciencia Nueva, 1970).
10. Heywood, *Marxism*, pp. 53–4.
11. Though unfounded, this version of events was widely circulated at the time and certainly affected anarchist perceptions of the Socialists. See Francisco J. Romero Salvadó, *The Foundations of Civil War: Revolution, Social Conflict and Reaction in Liberal Spain, 1916–1923* (London: Routledge, 2008), p. 91.
12. David Ruiz, 'La crisis de 1917', in Manuel Tuñón de Lara (ed.), *Revolución burguesa, oligarquía y constitucionalismo (1834–1923)*, Historia de España, 8, 2nd edn (Barcelona: Labor, 1987), p. 502.
13. Manuel Pérez Ledesma, '¿Pablo Iglesias, santo?', in 'Pablo Iglesias. El socialismo en España', *Anthropos*, 45 (1985), pp. 171–5.
14. Heywood, *Marxism*, p. 55; Forcadell, *Parlamentarismo y bolchevización*, pp. 241–50.
15. See Luis Arranz Notario, 'Los "cien niños" y la formación del PCE', in Various Authors, *Contribuciones a la historia del PCE* (Madrid: Fundación de Investigaciones Marxistas, 2004), pp. 95–174. For first-hand accounts of the new party, see Luis Portela, 'El nacimiento y los primeros pasos del movimiento comunista en España', *Estudios de Historia Social*, 14 (1980), pp. 191–217; Juan Andrade, *Recuerdos personales* (Barcelona: Ediciones del Serbal, 1983), pp. 137–74; and Albert Pèrez Baró, *Els 'Feliços' anys vint. Memòries d'un militant obrer, 1918–1926* (Palma de Mallorca: Moll), 1974, pp. 45–51.
16. This fragmentation within the early Communist movement was replicated, to varying degrees, in the USA, Germany and Italy, to give just three examples.
17. For an organizational history of the union's early years, see Bar, *La CNT*.
18. Bueso, *Como fundamos*, pp. 32–6.

116   *Chris Ealham*

19. Confederación Nacional del Trabajo, *Memoria del Congreso celebrado en el Teatro de la Comedia de Madrid los días 10 al 18 de diciembre de 1919* (Barcelona: CNT, 1932), pp. 221–53.
20. *Solidaridad Obrera* (11 November 1917).
21. *Tierra y Libertad* (14 November 1917).
22. *Tierra y Libertad* (28 November 1917).
23. *Tierra y Libertad* (26 December 1917).
24. Manuel Buenacasa, *El movimiento obrero español, 1886–1926. Historia y crítica* (Madrid: Ediciones Júcar, 1977 [1928]), p. 50.
25. Joaquim Maurín, *Revolución y contrarrevolución en España* (Paris: Ruedo Ibérico, 1966 [1935]), p. 246.
26. Andreu Nin, *La revolución rusa* (Barcelona: Fontamara, 1979), p. 111. See also Forcadell, *Parlamentarismo y bolchevización*, p. 259.
27. Confederación Nacional del Trabajo, *Memoria del Congreso celebrado*, p. 341.
28. See, for instance, *Solidaridad Obrera* (17 May 1924), where the aim of the CNT was defined as 'combatting all political conceptions, without distinction, that tend to perpetuate the state'.
29. See César Lorenzo, *Los anarquistas españoles y el poder, 1868–1969* (Paris: Ruedo Ibérico, 1972), pp. 47–8. Interestingly, in a book concerned with the relationship between anarchism and the issue of power, no reference is made to the 1919 Congress debate about the possible role of a 'transitional dictatorship'.
30. For Civera's project, see *Orto (1932–1934): Revista de documentación social* (Valencia: Fundación Instituto de Historia Social, 2001). See also Xavier Paniagua, *La sociedad libertaria. Agrarismo e industrialización en el anarquismo español, 1930–1939* (Barcelona: Crítica, 1982), pp. 182–90 and Francesc Artal, Emili Gasch, Carme Massana and Francesc Roca, *El pensament economic català durant la República i la Guerra* (Barcelona: Edicions 62, 1976), pp. 151–4.
31. I am grateful to Richard Purkiss for drawing my attention to the events at Sollana.
32. *Los Amigos de Durruti, Hacia la nueva revolución* (Barcelona: Etcétera. 1997 [1937]).
33. For critiques of *cenetismo*, see the works by José Peirats, *La práctica federalista como verdadera afirmación de principios* (Paris: CNT, 1964) and *Examen Crítico-Constructivo del Movimiento Libertario Español* (Mexico: Mexicanos Reunidos, 1967).
34. Bar, *La CNT*, pp. 560–1, describes them simply as the 'pro-Bolsheviks'. For their evolution, see Andy Durgan, *BOC, 1930–1936: El Bloque Obrero y Campesino* (Barcelona: Laertes, 1996), pp. 20–34.
35. Gerald Meaker, *The Revolutionary Left in Spain, 1914–1923* (Stanford, CA: Stanford University Press, 1974), pp. 385–403.
36. Manuel Cruells, *Salvador Seguí, el noi del sucre* (Barcelona: Ariel, 1974); Josep Maria Huertas Claveria, *'El noi del sucre.' Materiales para una biografía* (Barcelona: Laia, 1976); Antonio Elorza (ed.), *Artículos madrileños de Salvador Seguí* (Madrid: Cuadernos para el Diálogo, 1976).
37. Confederación Nacional del Trabajo, *Memoria del Congreso celebrado*, pp. 373–4.
38. For a first-hand account, see Bueso, *Recuerdos*, 1, pp. 205–11.

39. On balance, it seems likely that Nin and Maurín knew a 'major act' was planned, but were ignorant of the detail; see Bueso, *Recuerdos*, 1, p. 140.
40. Meaker, *The Revolutionary Left*, p. 390.
41. Ibid., p. 385.
42. As Durgan, *BOC, 1930–1936*, p. 20, noted: 'The most important pro-Communist group in Catalonia emerged from within the CNT and had no formal link with the Communist Party.'
43. Joaquim Maurín, *El Sindicalismo a la luz de la revolución rusa* (Lleida: Lucha Social, 1922), p. 51.
44. Ibid., p. 106. See, also, how Bueso (*Recuerdos*, 1, pp. 205–11) continued to define himself as a 'revolutionary syndicalist' who, while pro-Bolshevik and involved in organizational work for the PCE, baulked at joining the party.
45. *Lucha Social* (18 March 1922).
46. *La Batalla* (21 December 1922).
47. Meaker (*The Revolutionary Left*, p. 425) claims Maurín joined the PCE in 1923, yet at the same time recognizes that 'the precise nature of his activity until that time remains unclear', inferring he might have been a secret member.
48. *La Batalla* (30 July and 3 September 1931), in which an editorial, 'The Duty of the Confederation', almost certainly written by Maurín, concluded 'The Confederation must take power'.
49. Robert Kern, *Red Years/Black Years: A Political History of Spanish Anarchism, 1911–1937* (Philadelphia, PA: Institute for the Study of Human Issues, 1978), p. 56.
50. Ibid., p. 386.
51. Meaker, *The Revolutionary Left*, pp. 391–2.
52. Ibid., p. 389.
53. José García Pradas, *¡Teníamos que perder!* (Madrid: G. del Toro, 1974), pp. 55, 57 and 59. Here, the CNT infatuation with the Russian Revolution is attributed to Lenin's 'fraud' (p. 57).
54. Buenacasa, *El movimiento obrero español*, pp. 73–4. See also Francisco Olaya Morales, *Historia del Movimiento Obrero español, 1900–1936* (Madrid: Solidaridad Obrera, 2006), p. 458.
55. *Lucha Social* (24 June 1922).
56. The anarchist delegate to Moscow, 'Gastón Leval' (Pierre Robert Pillar), acknowledged that the procedures involved in organizing the CNT mission to the Soviet Union were utterly regular. Another anarchist source recognized that the CNT delegates were selected as they 'had distinguished themselves [by their actions] *and were willing to go to Moscow* [original italics]'. See José Peirats, *Figuras de la revolución española* (Barcelona: Picazo, 1978), pp. 153–9; the quote is from p. 155.
57. Other signatories included prominent Russian anarchists Alexander Berkman and Alexander Schapiro (José Peirats, *Emma Goldman: Anarquista de ambos mundos* (Madrid: Campo Abierto, 1978), p. 126).
58. *Lucha Social* (11 February 1922).
59. *Lucha Social* (29 October 1921).
60. *Vida Nueva* (13, 14 and 15 June 1922).

118   Chris Ealham

61. 'Soledad Gustavo' (Teresa Mañé i Miravet), 'La masa sindicalista, no es anarquista', *Redención* (17 August 1922), cited in Richard Purkiss, 'Anarchism and Anarcho-Syndicalism in the City and Province of Valencia, 1918–36', unpublished doctoral thesis, Lancaster University, 2009.
62. *Vida Nueva* (14 June 1922).
63. This situation was repeated in the 1930s, with a wave of expulsions of anti-anarchist syndicalist, anarcho-syndicalist and pro-Communist union federations. See Eulàlia Vega i Massana, *Anarquistas y sindicalistas, 1931–1936* (Valencia: Institut Alfons el Magnànim, 1987) and *El trentisme a Catalunya. Divergències ideòlogiques en la CNT, 1930–1933* (Barcelona: Curial, 1980).
64. Buenacasa, *El movimiento obrero español*, pp. 73–4. A recent book by an anarchist historian portrayed Maurín as little more than a tool of the authorities to split the CNT (Olaya Morales, *Historia.*, p. 510).
65. See the warning of the Fascist danger in Spain after Mussolini's March on Rome (*La Batalla*, 21 December 1922).
66. Bueso, *Recuerdos*, 1, p. 212.
67. Meaker, *The Revolutionary Left*, pp. 250–1.
68. Andrade, *Recuerdos personales*, p. 160.
69. Interestingly, Borodin, one of the Comintern agents in Spain, was later instrumental in developing the Comintern's disastrous line of seeking a rapprochement with Chiang Kai-shek; see Juan Avilés Farré, 'El impacto de la revolución rusa en las organizaciones obreras españolas (1817–1923)', *Espacio, tiempo y forma. Serie V, Historia contemporánea*, 13, (2000), pp. 22–3.
70. See his somewhat tendentious memoir, *Memorias de mi amigo Oscar Perea* (Madrid: Renacimiento, 1931).
71. Fernando Hernández Sánchez, 'La formación del PCE. Juventud y violencia política (1920–1931)', *Historia*, 16/380 (2007), pp. 56–73; Julián Gorkín, *El revolucionario profesional. Testimonio de un hombre de acción* (Barcelona: Aymá, 1975), p. 54.
72. Carlos Gil Andrés, *Echarse a la calle. Amotinados, huelguistas y revolucionarios. La Rioja, 1890–1936* (Zaragoza: Prensas Universitarias de Zaragoza, 2000), pp. 136–57; José Luis Gutiérrez Molina, *Valeriano Orobón Fernández: Anarcosindicalismo y revolución en Europa* (Valladolid: Libre Pensamiento, 2002), pp. 20–1; Óscar Bascuñán Añover, *Protesta y supervivencia. Movilización y desorden en una sociedad rural: Castilla-La Mancha, 1875–1923* (Valencia: Biblioteca Historia Social, 2008), pp. 188–96; Martin, *Agony of Modernization*, p. 209; Gareth Stockey, *Gibraltar: 'A Dagger in the Spine of Spain?'* (Brighton: Sussex Academic Press), 2009, pp. 40–2.
73. Francisco Sánchez Pérez, *La protesta de un pueblo. Acción colectiva y organización obrera. Madrid, 1901–1923* (Madrid: Cinca, 2005).
74. Ángeles Barrio Alonso, *Anarquismo y anarcosindicalismo en Asturias, 1890–1936* (Madrid: Siglo XXI, 1988), pp. 183–259 and Adrian Shubert, *The Road to Revolution in Spain: The Coal Miners of Asturias, 1860–1934* (Urbana, IL: University of Illinois, 1987), pp. 115–28.
75. Luis Castells, *Los trabajadores en el País Vasco (1876–1923)* (Madrid: Siglo XXI, 1993), pp. 33–88.
76. The classic study remains Juan Díaz del Moral, *Historia de las agitaciones campesinas andaluzas* (Madrid: Alianza, 1973 [1929]).

77. Cited in Martin, *Agony of Modernization*, p. 206. It is generally accepted these figures underestimate the real degree of conflict, although they capture its ascendent curve.
78. Gutiérrez Molina, *Valeriano Orobón Fernández*, pp. 20–1.
79. Sánchez Pérez, *La protesta de un pueblo.*
80. Ángeles González Fernández, *Utopia y Realidad. Anarquismo, Anarcosindicalismo y Organizaciones Obreras. Sevilla, 1900–1923* (Sevilla: Diputación de Sevilla, 1996), pp. 267–397.
81. Jesús Ignacio Bueno Madurga, *Zaragoza, 1917–1936. De la movilización popular y obrera a la reacción conservadora* (Zaragoza: Institución 'Fernando el Católico', 2000), pp. 283–5.
82. Chris Ealham, *Class, Culture and Conflict in Barcelona, 1898–1937* (London: Routledge, 2004), pp. 23–53.
83. Bascuñán Añover, *Protesta y supervivencia*, pp. 209–11.
84. Manuel Lladonosa, *El Congrès de Sants* (Barcelona: Nova Terra, 1975).
85. All the same, coercion was still necessary. One militant spoke of the existence of 'strong committees to collect dues' (Buenacasa, *El movimiento obrero español*, p. 52).
86. Pere Gual Villalbí, *Memorias de un industrial de nuestro tiempo* (Barcelona: Juventud, 1922), pp. 157–246.
87. Susana Tavera and Eulàlia Vega i Massana, 'L'afiliació sindical i a la CRT de Catalunya: entre l'eufòria revolucionnària i l'ensulsiada confederal, 1919–1936', in *Col.loqui Internacional 'Revolució i Socialisme'* (Barcelona: Departament d'Història Moderna i Contemporània de la Universitat Autònoma de Barcelona, 1989), 2, p. 358.
88. See Paulino Díez, *Un anarcosindicalista de acción* (Caracas: Editexto, 1976), pp. 34–47; Joaquim Ferrer ('Simó Piera'), *Simó Piera: Perfil d'un sindicalista. Records i experiències* (Barcelona: Pòrtic, 1975), pp. 78–96; and Carolyn P. Boyd, *La política pretoriana en el reinado de Alfonso XIII* (Madrid: Alianza, 1990), pp. 152–9.
89. Soledad Bengoechea, *El locaut de Barcelona (1919–1920)* (Barcelona: Curial, 1998), p. 17.
90. Ángeles Barrio Alonso, 'La oportunidad perdida: 1919, mito y realidad del poder sindical', *Ayer*, 63/3 (2006), pp. 174–7.
91. Barrio Alonso, 'La oportunidad perdida', pp. 153–84.
92. Fernando del Rey Reguillo, 'La polémica sobre el control obrero. Los orígenes en España', *Sociología del Trabajo*, 8 (1989–90), pp. 135–65.
93. Ibid., p. 180; Bengoechea, *El locaut de Barcelona*, pp. 61–79 and 106–22.
94. Ángel Smith, *Anarchism, Revolution and Reaction: Catalan Labour and the Crisis of the Spanish State, 1898–1923* (Oxford: Berghahn, 2007), pp. 324–6.
95. Cited in Bengoechea, *El locaut de Barcelona*, p. 168.
96. Ealham, *Class, Culture and Conflict*, pp. 18–21.
97. Smith, *Anarchism*, p. 335.
98. Romero Salvadó, *Foundations of the Civil War*, p. 231.
99. Bar, *La CNT*, pp. 558–9. In Gibraltar a curious alliance of the Spanish and British authorities, supported by the Trades and General Workers' Union, worked to isolate the CNT (Stockey, *Gibralter*, pp. 40–2).
100. Bar, *La CNT*, p. 563.

101. Peirats, *Examen Crítico*, p. 20.
102. Bar, *La CNT*, p. 559; Juan García Oliver, *El eco de los pasos* (Paris: Ruedo Ibérico, 1978), p. 633.
103. Bengoechea, *El locaut de Barcelona*, p. 215.
104. Ealham, *Class, Culture and Conflict*, and Smith, *Anarchism*. As Sidney Tarrow notes: 'The attraction of violence is that it is easy for people without political resources to initiate. But the difficulty of violence is that, once it has begun, it legitimates repression, polarises the public and ultimately depends on a small core of militants for whom violence has become the main form of politics. When that happens, organisers are trapped in a military confrontation with authorities that it is virtually impossible for them to win' (*Power in Movement: Social Movements, Collective Action and Politics*, Cambridge: Cambridge University Press, 1994, p. 105).

5

'The Red Dawn' of the Andalusian Countryside: Peasant Protest during the 'Bolshevik Triennium', 1918–20

Francisco Cobo Romero

What was the Andalusian 'Trienio Bolchevique'?

The years 1918–20 were fundamental in the modern history of the Andalusian peasant movement. The post-war economic dislocation and the rocketing prices of basic commodities brought about by Spain's neutrality during the First World War resulted in a dramatic deterioration in the living conditions of a vast legion of landless peasants (*jornaleros* or *braceros*)[1] from the south of the Iberian peninsula. In Andalusia, agrarian capitalism made giant strides with the gradual incorporation of small and medium-sized holdings into a market economy sustained by a large and impoverished labour force.[2] This made possible the rapid extension in contractual relationships between *jornaleros* and small landowners and sharecroppers resulting in higher numbers of disputes between these groups due to the post-war inflationary cycle. Furthermore, in a still poorly mechanized agricultural sector, the profits of the big landowners depended on the maintenance of extremely low salaries. Better pay demands from *jornaleros*, progressively more organized in trade unions, were therefore systematically refused.

Growing labour tensions, well illustrated by the explosion of strike activity during the years 1918–20, lent credence to the belief in the collapse of the 'old bourgeois world', fuelled by the Bolshevik Revolution and the sudden defeat of the Central Powers. Amidst a highly charged atmosphere infused with political proclamations announcing the 'definitive demise' of the 'liberal capitalist order', the Andalusian *jornaleros'* Socialist and Anarchist trade unions initiated a vast campaign of social agitation[3] that was to play a significant role in undermining the foundations of the Restoration regime. The echoes of the Bolshevik Revolution of 1917 and the deep emotional impact produced by the expropriation of the land of the nobility and its subsequent handover to the Russian peasantry, awakened intense hopes and expectations amongst the *braceros*. Juan Díaz del Moral, a leading *agrarista*[4] and a direct witness of this period of labour mobilization dubbed it '*el trienio bolchevique*' ('the Bolshevik Triennium').[5]

The agrarian bourgeoisie and the rural oligarchy reacted with panic to the outbreak of the revolt and launched a virulent propaganda campaign in which the strike activity and the *jornaleros'* demands were equated with the symptoms of the feared social revolution.[6] From 1918 a powerful wave of social mobilization and popular protest engulfed practically all of Spain's southern provinces, hitting Jaén, Málaga and Sevilla with particular intensity. Although the agitation mainly sought to improve salaries and existing agrarian conditions, some *jornaleros'* trade union leaders, both Anarchists and Socialists, were carried away by the 'collective euphoria' and proclaimed the start of a genuine 'revolutionary red dawn'.[7] They believed that they were witnessing an 'awakening' that would not only end the hegemony of the hated landowners but would also establish a new moral, political and social order.[8] This 'new era' would lead to land redistribution, the formal recognition of the *jornaleros'* unions' collective bargaining rights and the establishment of labour contracts highly favourable to the interests of the peasantry.

Prologue: Agrarian modernization and peasant mobilization

The Andalusian peasantry underwent significant transformations during the last years of the 19th century and the first of the 20th century. The de facto privatization of important tracts of land, hitherto of common use, prevented the rural population from obtaining those staple products that had previously been freely available to them.[9] This led to a greater dependence of small landowners and sharecroppers on the commercial power of the market, while condemning the *jornaleros* to survive only on the wages offered by their agrarian employers.[10] At the same time, the expansion in some labour-intensive crops, increasingly orientated towards market demand, allowed small landowners to increase their turnover.[11]

Hence, like many other regions of Southern and Western Europe, between the 1870s and 1930s Andalusian agriculture experienced a powerful reorientation towards the needs of the international markets.

This led to positive innovations: a greater specialization in those crops that offered better returns. The number of landowners who profited from the expansion of labour-intensive crops such as olives, grapes and fruits grew significantly, particularly in eastern Andalusia. These crops were highly adaptable to small agrarian enterprises and family-based peasant economies, and therefore spurred the growth in the number of small landowners and sharecroppers as well as *jornaleros*.[12] The urgency to harvest certain crops and the demand for an abundant labour force led small landowners and sharecroppers to hire *jornaleros* with increasing frequency and, consequently, to a rise in labour interactions.[13]

Spain's neutrality in the First World War provided the critical conditions, in nearly all of Andalusia, for an increase in strikes and conflicts aimed at obtaining improved wages and working conditions for the *jornaleros*.[14] This new focus on concrete demands led the reformist or gradualist principles held by the Socialists of the Unión General de Trabajadores (General Workers' Union – UGT) and the Partido Socialista Obrero Español (Spanish Socialist Workers' Party – PSOE) to become more appealing to many of the *jornaleros'* associations that had emerged at the start of the 20th century. This explains the unusually fast growth of Socialist organizations in the provinces of Córdoba, Jaén, Almería, Granada and Málaga during the years 1918–20.[15] At the same time, there were signs of glaring divisions within the peasantry as small sharecroppers began to adopt positions close to those defended by the big landowners, especially when it came to maximizing profits.

Parallel to the aforementioned process of agrarian and labour modernization, a profound reorganization of electoral and political participation took place in Andalusia. From the early 20th century, both Republicans and Socialists strove for a genuine democratization of local power.[16] They sought to cleanse municipal politics and to transform town halls into places responsive to the interests of poor peasants and *jornaleros*. In their attempt to mobilize rural society politically, the Socialists won the support of large numbers of these *jornaleros*. Their growing politicization awakened a corresponding interest in national politics amongst small landowners and sharecroppers in a context in which, in an increasingly commercialized agrarian economy, market prices often depended on state decisions in areas such as tariff barriers, regulation of wages, working hours and taxation.[17]

It was, above all, during the 'Bolshevik Triennium' when the final internal fracture of the Andalusian peasantry took place. Growing social tensions were reflected in the different attitudes adopted by the distinct sectors of the agrarian population. It was a decisive moment in the politicization of the rural world as *jornaleros* joined trade unions in order to strengthen their bargaining power in the labour market and to obtain better wages to cope with the rising living costs and the mounting prices of staple products. Left-wing parties, particularly the PSOE, took advantage of the situation to tap into the hitherto largely spontaneous *jornaleros'* political mobilization. In turn, the growing political activism of the *jornaleros* stimulated small farmers and sharecroppers to follow suit, although they oscillated between backing political organizations of conservative, traditionalist or Catholic leanings, all dominated by the rich landowners.[18] All these issues will now be considered in greater detail.

The actors, the international context, the *Jornaleros'* new trade unionism and the allegorical building of the revolution

The impact of the First World War on the Spanish economy: The crisis of staple products

The wave of rural strikes and social conflict during the years 1918–20 in Andalusia resulted from the extraordinary conditions brought about by Spain's neutrality during the First World War. Galloping inflation resulted in the deterioration of living standards due to the inability of wages to keep up with the rocketing prices of staple products. This highly inflationary situation facilitated the sudden transformation of existing social tensions into significantly greater and more intense labour struggles. Simultaneously, landowners gained massive profits from the high prices achieved by a large number of essential products, mainly due to the unprecedented external demand from the belligerent countries.[19]

Statistics on the social conflicts of the years 1918–20 show that most strike activity was over wages, followed by demands for substantial improvements in working conditions, for the official recognition of collective bargaining by the trade unions, and finally in solidarity with other workers' associations. The strike wave of 1918–20 made possible a significant increase in the average wages paid for agrarian labour, as can be seen in Table 5.1.

The reorganization of the *Jornaleros'* trade union movement and the symbolic resurgence of strike activity

The politics of mass mobilization gained momentum after the end of the First World War. This is well illustrated by the increasing number of demands put forward by various popular movements. At the same time,

Table 5.1 Agrarian salaries in Spain, 1910–26

Year	Average wages (pesetas/day)*	Index (1910 = 100)	% of variability
1910	1.96	100	–
1914	1.96	100	± 0.00
1915	2.19	112	+ 11.73
1916	2.34	119	+ 6.84
1918	3.09	157	+ 32.05
1919	4.53	231	+ 46.40
1920	4.97	253	+ 9.71
1921	4.90	250	− 1.40
1922	5.35	273	+ 9.18
1925	5.23	267	− 2.24
1926	5.12	261	− 2.10

Note: * Average wages expressed in pesetas of the era.
Source: Miguel Ángel Gutiérrez Bringas, 'Un intento de reconstruir una variante del nivel de vida del campesinado: los salarios agrícolas en España, 1756–1935', in *Preactas del VIII Congreso de Historia Agraria*, (Salamanca: Universidad de Salamanca, 1997), p. 77. My elaboration.

the political violence, radicalism and dehumanization of the enemy, generated by the tragic experience of mass slaughter that surrounded the First World War, led to support for a more revolutionary strategy by the Left.[20] Indeed, encouraged by the discrediting of the old pre-war liberal oligarchies, a protest wave – and deep social upheaval – engulfed a good deal of Europe.[21] Within these new parameters, the stability of the liberal order on which the traditional hegemony of the bourgeoisie had rested, was under serious threat.[22] During the second decade of the 20th century, and particularly following the end of the First World War, a sudden and vast cycle of protest erupted in most industrialized countries. In agrarian economies with a large presence of *jornaleros*, the creation of increasingly depersonalized large labour markets took place.[23] Such economies were marked by profound inequalities in the incomes of the different social groups, by the political domination exerted by the rich landowners' oligarchy and by the high degree of concentration of the land. While old contractual relations were breaking down, a new rich agrarian bourgeoisie emerged and market-based models of labour contracts came into place.[24] All these factors accelerated the establishment, amongst *jornaleros* and *braceros*, of permanent and well-structured unions.

In areas of Mediterranean agriculture characterized by a historic concentration of the land and the high numbers of landless workers, new models of Socialist and/or Anarchist trade unionism emerged. In

Italy, both the powerful Socialist agrarian leagues and the revolutionary Anarcho-Syndicalists embraced formulas of combat against the
employers that went far beyond the old-fashioned local strikes.[25] At the
same time, new regulations in the labour market, hugely beneficial to
the workers, appeared in some regions dominated by landed estates and
very productive export-orientated agriculture such as the Mezzogiorno
(Apulia and Campania), and the northern area of the Po Valley (Emilia-
Romagna, Lombardy and the Piedmont). Amongst them, we should
mention the *imponíbile di manodòpera* (the compulsory hiring of a specific number of rural workers) and the *collocamento di classe* (the fair distribution of employment opportunities amongst the *jornaleros* of each
area). Some of these measures were adopted as their strike demands by
the rural Socialist unions, and to a lesser extent by the Anarchists, in
rural Andalusia from the beginning of the 20th century.

   Within this new framework, the rural class struggle in Andalusia during the years 1918–1920 witnessed the sudden emergence of demands
for the radical transformation of the capitalist order in the countryside.
It largely responded to the echoes of the Bolshevik Revolution (with
its land collectivization and redistribution amongst the peasantry), as
well as to the radicalization of a revolutionary syndicalism characteris-
tic of an agrarian capitalism with a strong *jornalero* element. It was the
Anarchists in Andalusia who, above all, contributed to the combining
of many of these revolutionary proposals, merging them with strikes
and demands for reforms. In doing so, they believed that popular mobilization to obtain small gains constituted a genuine *'gimnasia sindicalista'*[26] to prepare the workers for the expected 'revolutionary general
strike' that ultimately would give rise to a new social order based on the
principles of collectivism, equality and fair distribution of the wealth
generated by the land.[27]

   The consolidation of all these concepts amongst rural Andalusian
Anarchists was facilitated by their reception of the ideological principles and programme of 'revolutionary syndicalism', which had made its
mark on the international trade union world since the start of the 20th
century. The revolutionary syndicalist model contained a rich symbolic
construction of the class struggle and the seizure of power in capitalist
societies. At the same time, it recreated an idealized vision of the titanic
struggle to destroy capitalism and the bourgeoisie founded on the deifi-
cation of the working class, the sublimation of direct action,[28] and the
hope for the revolutionary transformation of capitalism through the
establishment of a new socio-moral order based on workers' control of
a collectivized economy.[29]

The political landscape: Opportunities and framework for collective action

Growing political opportunities

The so-called Spanish 'crisis of neutrality' of the years 1914–18 acceler-ated the political difficulties of the traditional liberal elites. It resulted largely from the economic dislocation produced by the First World War, the reorientation of trade and the shortages of basic products. This led to rising strike activity, the heightening of social tensions and the occu-pation of the public space by the popular classes and their political and union representatives. Amidst a framework of political turmoil and distress, the anti-monarchist forces built up a seductive discourse that singled out 'the corrupt governments' of the 'decrepit' ruling order for all the evils suffered by the population. Consequently, left-wing forces (Republicans, Socialists and Anarchists) increased their mobilizing cap-acity and hence their opportunity to bring about political change.

New political opportunities resulted from the 'crisis' of 1917 and the governments' growing instability in the last period of the liberal state. The mounting discredit of the liberal governing class went hand in hand with the frontal rejection of the corrupt practices of Restoration Spain. In 1918, when the PSOE partially returned to its reformist tactics,[30] it launched a 'crusade' to bring morality to local politics and directed its efforts to fighting the political and electoral corruption ingrained in town halls and rural life.

For their part, encouraged by the radicalized class struggle, the Anarchists of the Confederación Nacional del Trabajo (National Labour Confederation – CNT) promoted a vast strike movement in industri-alized Barcelona,[31] and in the southern areas with capitalist agricul-ture. Since the Congress of Sants (Barcelona, 28 June–1 July 1918), the Anarchists had embraced the tactics of revolutionary syndicalism and the general strike.[32] They also undertook an intense reorganiza-tion based on the adoption of the so-called *Sindicatos Únicos* (unions that embraced all those branches that belonged to the same industrial sector).

The parliamentary deadlock also facilitated the growth of political dissidence. The immediate result was the sharpening of political con-frontation, the most perceptible consequence of which was the ritual identification of the anti-dynastic political culture as the embodiment of the generic interests of 'the people', while the representatives of the ruling order were identified with the mean interests of the old oligarchy and its notables.

New mobilization patterns and changing frameworks

a) The Anarchist interpretation of revolution in the countryside

From the 1880s, the Spanish Anarchists reconsidered their ideological programme and embraced the defence of collectivism and the joint ownership of the means of production in agriculture. Such a position was already in the process of being adopted at the famous 1881 congress in Barcelona that established the Federación de Trabajadores de la Región Española (Federation of Workers of the Spanish Region – FTRE). The following year at the FTRE's Sevilla congress, Spanish Anarchism broke with Proudhonian ideas – advocating the democratic takeover of the means of production by workers' communes – and adopted the more radical collectivist stance defended by Michael Bakunin. Simultaneously, the ancestral 'formula of [land] redistribution' was idealistically recreated. The ultimate dream was the construction of an idyllic future society based on a federation of independent peasants' collectives to be responsible for managing all the available resources.[33]

From the early 20th century, revolutionary syndicalist currents began to influence Andalusian Anarchism to a greater degree. Thus, intense propaganda campaigns during 1902 and 1903 contributed to the forging of a new union model better adapted to the expanding capitalist agrarian markets.[34] Through the use of a new discourse, the Anarchists managed to spread a symbolic and ritualized view of themselves as a crucial part of a vast front immersed in a brutal and merciless struggle against the bourgeoisie and capitalism. Indeed, the idealized image of the Andalusian peasantry contained surprisingly large numbers of quasi-religious, mythic and messianic elements.[35] Consequently, the Anarchists' forecast that the working class would be saved from the capitalist yoke became a powerful tool of social and union mobilization and agitation.[36] The assimilation by the Spanish Anarchists of rural insurrectionary tactics facilitated the intense upheaval experienced by the Andalusian peasantry during the years 1903–5 and after 1918.

It can thus be affirmed that from the beginning of the 20th century the Andalusian Anarchists embarked upon a process of adaptation, attempting, with greater or lesser success, to confront the changing nature of capitalist relations in the agrarian world and that of the agrarian labour markets. They abandoned the tactics of individual terrorism and propaganda by the deed and instead sought the constitution of stable, disciplined and well-rooted campaigns, with revolutionary syndicalism as their hegemonic strategy.[37]

They experienced impressive growth following the Córdoba congress of 17–20 April 1913, which set up the Federación Nacional de Obreros

Agricultores de España (Spanish Federation of Landworkers – FNOA). The FNOA, in which the Andalusian Anarchists took the lead, embraced revolutionary syndicalist ideals and counted amongst its ultimate objectives the establishment of an anarchist society, to be achieved by a 'revolutionary general strike'. The collective ownership of the land and the suppression of private property became basic tenants from the outset. 'The land for those who work it' was the maxim par excellence of rural Anarchist trade unionism. This final aspiration went hand in hand with the task of educating the peasantry. Furthermore, the struggle for small reforms was seen as a worthwhile practice that would strengthen the peasantry in its ethical and organizational preparation for the final clash against the bourgeoisie and agrarian capitalism.[38]

After the congress in Vilanova i la Geltrú (Barcelona) in 1916, the FNOA agreed that it should 'channel the propaganda campaign towards the achievement of wage rises and a reduction in the working day'. Even though the principal demand continued to be the handover of land to the peasants, they also pursued several additional goals: the illegalization of the labour of women and children below 14 years of age in the countryside, the lowering of the price of staple products, the establishment of a minimum wage (that, from 1918, was to be fixed by each workers' society according to the nature of the agrarian tasks in a given area), the extension of the Workplace Accidents Law from industry to the peasantry, the abolition of piecework and, finally, a reduction in the working day.[39] Embracing a programme of immediate reforms for agrarian workers, combined with their long-term objectives, proved to be a successful formula.

b) The Socialists' discourse on the 'agrarian question'

At the same time, the Socialists became leading protagonists in the political and union mobilization of the Andalusian *jornaleros*. From the early 20th century, the Spanish Socialists expressed a growing interest in recruiting activists amongst the peasantry. Nevertheless, their growth lagged behind the *jornaleros'* own spontaneous mobilization.[40] Left-wing parties and unions, and particularly the PSOE and the UGT, took advantage of the *jornaleros'* tendency to join trade unions to foster the political awareness of the agrarian workers. This facilitated their strategy of transforming the capitalist and liberal state through the democratization of town halls, local councils and even the national parliament.[41]

The Spanish Socialists adopted the analysis of the agrarian question dominant within Western European social democracy since the end of the 19th century.[42] Like their European counterparts,[43] they explained the development and transformation of the agrarian sector from an evolutionary perspective. They believed that the rise of market capitalism in the countryside would reveal the superior efficiency and competitiveness of large mechanized estates. They therefore defended the economic superiority of large agrarian enterprises and were convinced that the expansion of agrarian capitalism would contribute to the concentration of land.[44] Large properties were considered beneficial since once socialism had seized power the large landed estates would be expropriated and subsequently handed over to poor peasants and *jornaleros*, who were the main target of the Socialists' message regarding the structural transformation of capitalist agriculture. They explained the backwardness of Spain's agriculture by referring to the dualism of *latifundio–minifundio*,[45] and blamed the big landed estates, which had been strengthened by the land disentailment of the 19th century, for the poor returns of the primary sector, stressing the absenteeism of the agrarian bourgeoisie, and the big landowners' lack of interest in the modernization of their properties. In sum, the *latifundismo* of the southern agrarian regions was seen as the ultimate cause for the backwardness of Spain's agriculture.[46]

Well-known *agraristas* committed to innovative projects of agrarian reform, such as Pascual Carrión,[47] or Socialist leaders such as Fernando de los Ríos[48] or Antoni Fabra i Ribas,[49] totally endorsed this interpretative paradigm. They all singled out the unfair land distribution, the labour-intensive nature of the big landed estates and the alleged apathy shown by the speculative bourgeoisie with regard to the adoption of modernizing techniques. Hence the Spanish Socialists aimed at the mobilization of the *jornaleros* to achieve the elimination of agrarian capitalism and its worst features: *latifundismo* and bourgeois absenteeism. In the meantime, they would pursue a number of demands that would improve the living conditions of the agrarian workers, such as the eight-hour working day, the minimum wage, the abolition of piecework and the enjoyment by agrarian workers of insurance benefits in case of unemployment or accidents and also for old age. Nevertheless, given the persistence of family-owned farms, the UGT-PSOE also proposed, as laid out in its agrarian programme of 1918, a large number of measures in order to appeal to that constituency.[50] During the early 20th century, rural Socialists (particularly in Andalusia) therefore pursued a reformist strategy that ultimately was expected to lead to the socialization of the land and the means of production (with the exception of small landowners), and the end of the capitalist landowning regime.[51] The Socialists thus promoted a type of state-controlled agrarian reformism, combined with the formulation of new demands, strikes and the political mobilization of the *jornaleros*, to bring democracy to local politics.[52]

The actual development of events

During the triennium of 1918–20 labour conflicts attained an unprecedented level of co-ordination and intensity in nearly all of Andalusia (see Table 5.2) but this was particularly so in the provinces of Córdoba, Jaén and Málaga. The short-term cause for this new 'cycle of protest' was the impact of the inflation provoked by the First World War (rising prices of basic commodities, stagnation of salaries, the widening gap between wages and cost of living, etc.).[53] Other social, cultural and political factors, however, need to be added. Anarchists, Socialists, Republicans and Regionalists were protagonists of intense propaganda campaigns in rural Andalusia from 1902–3. These campaigns gained momentum first during 1916–18 and then in 1919–20.[54] They spread a modernizing discourse, denouncing the agrarian oligarchy and its unchanged *caciquista* practices. They also painted an image of a selfish bourgeoisie, whose monopoly of wealth and power resulted in the misery and deprivation of the working population.

Despite the workers' demands being couched in reformist terms during the 'Bolshevik Triennium', the rural employers invariably responded with extreme harshness. The conflicts took place immediately before the start of the two crucial harvests: cereals and the collection of olives.[55] The *jornaleros'* unions demanded wage rises, the regulation of breaks in the working day, the abolition of piecework, the reduction in the

Table 5.2 Strikes registered in four Andalusian provinces, 1917–22

Provinces	1917	1918	1919	1920	1921	1922
Córdoba	–	117	141	64	–	–
Granada	5	33	46	28	7	9
Jaén	9	37	69	73	8	5
Málaga	7	23	81	51	6	11
Total	21	210	337	216	21	25

Source: Ángeles González, 'La construcción de un mito. El trienio bolchevique en Andalucía', in Manuel González de Molina and Diego Caro Cancela (eds), *La utopía racional. Estudios sobre el movimiento obrero andaluz* (Granada: Editorial Universidad de Granada, 2001), pp. 175–219. My elaboration.

use of agricultural machinery and the restriction of the employment of 'foreigners' (workers coming from outside the locality of the employing landed estate). The employers reacted with the brutal persecution of the workers, the closing of their centres, the banning of demonstrations and the imprisonment of their leaders and propagandists.[56]

Córdoba and Jaén were especially important because of the intensity, symbolic character and number of conflicts. In the province of Córdoba, from June 1918, the employers' resistance to demands for improved labour contracts during the harvest triggered numerous strikes in the town of Castro del Río. These conflicts then spread to the other main towns of the province, worsening in July. Social upheaval increased with the constant demand for wage increases, employers' fulfilment of their traditional duty of feeding and lodging labourers, and rising petitions for measures to solve the issue of unemployment after the harvest. There were soon outbreaks of rural violence such as the burning of crops, pillaging and theft of cereals and livestock. From late October, a new cycle of peasant conflict spread across the province of Córdoba, marked particularly by the co-ordination of workers' demands, both among the different unions (Anarchists, Socialists or Republicans) and also between different regions.

Rising strike activity coincided with the organization of a congress in Castro del Río (Córdoba) between 25 and 27 October 1918. It was dominated by Anarcho-Syndicalists delegates, although there were also Republican representatives from 30 villages. Nearly all the delegates came from Córdoba, with a few from Sevilla and Jaén. During this crucial event agreement was reached on some general demands: better pay for harvesting the olives (wages of 5 pesetas), a reduction in the working day, longer breaks and the end of piecework.[57] Following these resolutions, new stoppages took place in large areas of the province of Córdoba, with 43 villages on strike in November and 17 disputes in December.[58]

The intensification and spread of the labour conflict from the autumn of 1918 provoked, as at the turn of the century, an intense debate in the regional and Madrid press on the increasingly grave 'Andalusian rural social problem'. As well as some leading politicians, distinguished members of the intellectual world such as José Ortega y Gasset, Pascual Carrión, Fabián Vidal, Julio Álvarez del Vayo and Blas Infante intervened. Meanwhile, the Conservative press wasted no time in creating a state of panic, stirred up by constant references to the Bolshevik Revolution. In early February 1919, the Instituto de Reformas Sociales[59] sent a commission to Córdoba to obtain first-hand reports on the attitudes of both sides.[60] This commission gathered many witness statements from workers' as well as employers' associations. Its conclusion – that arbitration should be used for pending conflicts – was reached just when the first strike wave had already left its deepest imprint.

Spurred by the employers' intransigence towards the *jornaleros'* demands, a general strike was declared during the second half of May 1919, just before that year's harvest. This time the stoppage spread throughout the Guadalquivir valley, hitting the provinces of Córdoba, Jaén and Sevilla. In the province of Córdoba alone, over 30 towns responded to the strike call. The gravity of the situation provoked the declaration, on 29 May, of martial law in the province. The interior minister sent 20,000 troops headed by the general of the Civil Guard, Manuel de la Barrera. The army occupied the villages, closed the workers' centres and deported large numbers of leading militants.[61] The military's severe repression resulted in a tragic tally of many workers' leaders imprisoned, others beaten and some strikers killed.[62]

Despite the powerful governmental response, the employers' refusal to fulfil the agreements previously reached provoked the resumption of strike action throughout the summer in several provinces, particularly in Córdoba, where the stoppage again acquired a violent dimension. A striker shot dead the mayor of Moriles. Almost simultaneously, acts of sabotage were committed everywhere, including crop burning in places such as Espiel (where the estate 'El Plata' was destroyed), Villafranca (where the farmhouse 'La Posadilla' was wrecked), Almodóvar, Cabra, Posadas, Bujalance, Castro del Río and many more.[63] Demands from rural employers for decisive measures were heeded: implacable military intervention on behalf of landowners, arrests and deportation of workers' leaders, immediate closure of meeting places, censorship of their newspapers and troops used to help with the harvesting.

Events in Jaén, one of the provinces most deeply shaken by the strike wave of this period, are equally revealing. There was a significant increase in political and social conflict throughout 1918. The year began with a workers' gathering in the town of Linares which concluded with the demand for cheaper staple products and the summoning of a demonstration that was attended by 3,000 people.[64] Rural strikes took place in, amongst other towns, Villampordo and Mancha Real. There were demonstrations against *caciques'* and employers' abuses of power in Cambil, and similar events occurred in Jaén and Linares in July and August.

Events in 1919 were even more prolific in terms of social conflict. There were frequent meetings between workers and employers to discuss

labour contracts. They established the peasants' right to collective bargaining and the procedures by which employers could hire manpower.
These results, which were only obtained with threats of strike action,
caused fear amongst Jaén's landowning class. Thus the brutal repression
against the most active militants that ensued in 1919–20 was marked
by all types of coercive practices and the constant use of the police.
Alarming messages from the landowners to the civil governor revealed
their deeply ingrained fear at the spread and radicalization of the social
conflict. The Bolshevik Revolution and the immense impact of the revolutionary changes taking place in the Russian countryside sparked a
mood of euphoria and exaltation among the *jornaleros* that coloured the
tense relations between them and employers during the years 1919 and
1920. The employers' reaction was not long in coming and disproportionate. From the spring of 1919, the civil governor decreed a number
of harsh measures. Workers' centres were closed, the Socialist press was
banned, workers' meeting places were under constant surveillance, and
the Civil Guard was used to search for weapons. The repression served
to exacerbate existing tensions. A new wave of strikes and disturbances
began in May in Higuera de Arjona and soon spread to the towns of
Arjona, Baeza, Lopera and Porcuna. In the latter two towns, numerous groups of *jornaleros* – 2,000 in Lopera – demanded pay increases
and better labour contracts. The approaching summer cereal harvest
increased the intensity of the conflict. There were strikes and labour
disturbances in Lopera, Escañuela, Arjona and Mancha Real. In the latter two towns the employers responded by closing the workers' centres. Further clashes led to the burning of cornfields in Arjona, Lopera,
Andújar, Las Casillas de Martos and Jabalquinto. A harvesting machine
was deliberately wrecked in Higuera de Calatrava.[65] The start of the
quiet season (after the summer) for agriculture provoked an increase in
unemployment but did nothing to ease the employers' fears. A general
strike took place in October in the provincial capital of Jaén.

In November, the Workers' Provincial Federation of Jaén (affiliated to
the UGT) expressed its solidarity with the growing discomfort felt by
workers in that province and protested on behalf of its nearly 20,000
members against the outrages committed against the workers' centres
of Baeza, Porcuna and Mancha Real, as well as against the arrests and
deportations of labour leaders. It was, however, the onset of the olive
harvest when rural disturbances reached their height. The rising living
costs and the employers' resolve to keep wages low provoked a proliferation of social unrest over nearly all the province. There were incidents and strikes in Lopera, Arjona, Arjonilla, Alcaudete, Mancha Real,

Jaén, Martos, Baeza, Torredelcampo and Torredonjimeno. Amidst this upheaval, the Workers' Provincial Federation backed a campaign for the suspension of piecework, the payment of a minimum wage of 5 pesetas for men and 2.50 for women and children.

Violent clashes between strikers and the Civil Guard soon took place. The rising tension provoked an enraged response from employers. In some cases, the repression was brutal. Workers were beaten in Cambil, Villacarrillo and Villanueva del Arzobispo; there were also beatings and arrests in Baeza and Arjona. In the middle of a general strike, there were violent clashes between the striking *jornaleros* and the Civil Guard, with 18 workers injured and a little girl killed in a shooting. The Civil Guard also used firepower in Porcuna where over 100 strikers were arrested. In Torredonjimeno, women participated in pickets against piecework. The Civil Guard stormed the workers' centre in Baeza creating havoc, while in Arcona an irate crowd set upon a couple of Civil Guards leading to a shoot-out.[66]

The wave of strikes began to decline in 1920. This year was also marked by a dramatic increase in the number of Socialists elected to Andalusian town halls – a total of 204 were returned in the municipal elections held in February of that year. They obtained 28 per cent of the votes in Jaén, gaining 68 councillors, and even managed to get the typographer José Morales Robles elected as mayor of the provincial capital.

Developments: The erosion of *Caciquismo* and the agrarian employers' corporate and authoritarian temptation

The most obvious consequence of the wave of strikes that took place during the years 1918–20 was probably the rapid rise in the number of *jornaleros* joining agrarian Socialist or Anarchist trade unions. With regard to the Anarchist trade unions, following an intense propaganda campaign in rural areas, the number of workers affiliated to CNT unions rose from 3,623 in September 1918 to the amazing figure of 113,214 in December 1919.[67] At the same time, workers' and peasants' provincial federations affiliated to the UGT were formed in all the Andalusian provinces except for Huelva and Cádiz.[68] By the end of 1919, there were 68,596 *jornaleros* and peasants in Socialist organizations (a figure which fell to some 30,617 in 1920).[69] PSOE membership also underwent a significant increase, from 2,689 in 1917 to a total of 25,577 in 1919 (see Table 5.3).[70]

The growth in Socialist membership culminated with the holding of the Peasant Congress of Andalusia and Extremadura in October 1920 in the capital of Jaén. Steps were then taken – although ultimately

Table 5.3   Members of the Socialist and Anarchist unions in Andalusia, 1918–22

	UGT			CNT	
Province	1918[1]	1920[2]	1922[2]	1918[1]	1919[1]
Almería	162	1,619	99	–	192
Cádiz	527	–	600	410	24,597
Córdoba	6,357	13,934	3,932	857	17,551
Granada	70	1,532	1,738	–	922
Huelva	30	–	–	340	3,093
Jaén	998	5,308	894	136	1,081
Málaga	413	6,910	3,689	640	24,597
Sevilla	105	1,314	693	1,240	36,154
Total	8,572	30,617	11,645	3,623	113,214

Notes: [1] Members belonging to all types of trades and branches of production. [2] Members belonging to the agrarian sector (*jornaleros* and poor peasants).
Sources: Antonio Bar, *La CNT en los años rojos. Del sindicalismo revolucionario al anarcosindicalismo, 1910–1926* (Madrid: Akal, 1981); Paloma Biglino, *El socialismo español y la cuestión agraria, 1890–1936* (Madrid: Ministerio de Trabajo, 1986); Antonio María Calero, 'Movimiento obrero y sindicalismo', in Antonio Miguel Bernal (ed.), *Historia de Andalucía*, 8 (Barcelona: Planeta, 1983); and Ángeles González, 'La construcción de un mito. El trienio bolchevique en Andalucía', in Manuel González de Molina and Diego Caro Cancela (eds), *La utopía racional. Estudios sobre el movimiento obrero andaluz* (Granada: Editorial Universidad de Granada, 2001). My elaboration.

frustrated – to set up a Socialist *jornaleros'* national agrarian federation.[71] There was euphoria amongst the Socialist rank and file, especially since there had been a spectacular growth in the UGT's agrarian provincial federations in 1919 and 1920, mostly based in eastern Andalusia. Even though the creation of a national agrarian federation had to be postponed until 1930, due, amongst other reasons, to the plummeting membership suffered by the peasant movement from 1922, the Peasant Congress of October 1920 marked a watershed in the history of rural Socialist trade unionism.

Sixty delegates, representing 150 agrarian workers' societies and 67,000 members (25,000 of them from the two provinces from Extremadura) gathered in Jaén.[72] There are no reliable figures for the number of militants from each of the provinces represented at the congress: Córdoba, Granada, Jaén, Málaga, Cáceres and Badajoz. However, the high number of members in attendance shows the strength of the rural Socialist unions at that time.

The growing unionization of *jornaleros* and poor peasants in much of Andalusia went hand in hand with the growing politicization of the rural population. Anarchists, reformist Socialists and Republicans enjoyed, during this hot period of social conflict (1918–20), a rare opportunity to spread their political principles. By linking the Restoration political order with the employers and the agrarian bourgeoisie, they could offer a bitterly negative view of the ruling regime. In sum, employers and right-wing dynastic politicians were blamed for sustaining the *caciquista* network that corrupted public municipal life and for their selfish backing of a crooked, undemocratic and unpopular political system devised precisely to defend the privileges of a minority of oligarchs and tycoons. The symbolic contrast between the working class and the culture of the employers amongst the southern *jornaleros* accompanied the intense rural conflict. In this way, the rural workers' growing interest in local politics and the struggle against 'the hated agrarian employers' was conveniently channelled towards political mobilization. The rhetoric used by the PSOE and the UGT was orientated towards the defence of specific political principles that demanded the cleansing of municipal life and the destruction of *caciquista* practices.

The support of the Socialist organizations for the strike wave in the Andalusian countryside during the so-called 'Bolshevik Triennium' not only helped them to recruit amongst the *jornaleros* but also to channel the tide of sympathy towards political goals. Indeed, it allowed them to increase their political representation in town halls and continue their commitment to uproot *caciquista* practices in local affairs.[73] The spectacular rise in electoral support for Socialist candidates in vast areas of Andalusia is indicated in Table 5.4.

Table 5.4 Socialist councillors elected in the eight Andalusian provinces, 1905–20

Province	1905	1909	1911	1915	1916	1917	1918	1920
Almería	–	–	1	–	–	–	–	6
Cádiz	–	2	–	2	–	–	–	14
Córdoba	–	1	2	5	3	5	3	37
Granada	–	–	5	–	–	1	1	25
Huelva	–	–	–	25	1	5	1	17
Jaén	1	2	4	10	9	12	6	68
Málaga	–	1	5	9	2	2	–	24
Sevilla	–	–	–	–	–	1	–	13
Andalusia	1	6	17	51	15	26	11	204
Spain	49	–	–	176	62	136	82	946

Source: Calero, 'Movimiento obrero y sindicalismo', p. 136.

Parallel to the distrust and rancour felt by many *jornaleros* and poor peasants towards the employers – and their traditional right-wing dynastic representatives –, the rural bourgeoisie and the big land-owners were determined to hold back the rising political power being acquired by the anti-dynastic political forces (Socialists, Republicans, Regionalists, etc.). Between 1918 and 1923 the old oligarchies and their political representatives increasingly resorted to all kinds of pseudo-legal chicanery and methods of coercion against their electoral rivals.[74]

During these years, practically all the Andalusian provinces experienced a litany of fraudulent and coercive actions carried out by the Monarchist forces. The general elections of 1919, for instance, saw massive irregularities. Also in this year the Socialists' vote grew at a formidable rate, resulting in the return of their first ever Andalusian deputy, Fernando de los Ríos, for Granada. Nevertheless, fraudulent practices occurred nearly everywhere, for example, from sunrise on election day the town of Linares in Jaén was occupied by the police, intimidation was rife and the purchase of votes took place. Several Socialist delegates were imprisoned and in Espeluy the electoral returns were filed before the votes had been cast. Similar violent activities to prevent electoral support for Socialist or Republican candidates were frequent in many areas of the province of Sevilla. Leading Socialists were arrested and held incommunicado on the eve of the vote in Puebla de Cazalla; the Civil Guard charged a leftist gathering in Cazalla de la Sierra; the workers' centres were closed in Écija and Cañada del Rosal; ballot boxes were smashed by gangs armed with clubs in Guadalcanal; and Republican sympathizers were searched and insulted at the door of an electoral college in Fuentes de Andalusia.[75]

The use of article 29 of the electoral law also became more frequent in the turbulent elections of 1919–23,[76] emphasizing the determination of the 'old *caciquista* networks' to deny the anti-dynastic candidates their lawful access to political representation. As an example, article 29 was applied in all the constituencies of Almería and Córdoba in 1923. As a result, in these elections – where attempts to prevent the people's electoral participation were at their most blatant – 45.8 per cent of the Andalusian electorate effectively lost their right to vote.[77]

Furthermore, the mobilization of the *jornaleros* and the growing electoral support acquired by the Socialists and Republicans caused turmoil and scepticism amongst employers and the rural bourgeoisie, with a large number of their leaders becoming increasingly detached from their traditional loyalty towards the normal channels of political and parliamentarian representation. Employers' corporative organizations sprang up everywhere. Twenty of them with 7,000 members were established between March and August 1919 in Jaén alone, and an Employers' Agrarian Federation was established in Córdoba following the general strike in May of that year.[78] In these circumstances a growing feeling of mistrust towards the ruling liberal oligarchic order spread amongst important sectors of the wealthy landed classes.[79] The unstoppable process of *jornalero* mobilization and the electoral progress of the anti-dynastic forces resulted in the devaluation and erosion of the governing class in the eyes of significant circles of the powerful rural bourgeoisie.

Finally, yet no less important, Andalusian rural employers increasingly adopted an independent strategy, outside the legal channels of self-defence, aimed at defending their interests. There was a tendency amongst the agrarian oligarchy to bypass the political and coercive instruments of parliamentarian liberalism, deemed by them as redundant and ineffective. Thus, as in the rest of Europe during the interwar years,[80] agrarian employers established armed citizens' militias (*guardias cívicas*). In this way, they expected to face down the growing social conflict, the rising political mobilization, and the revolutionary ideals embraced by *jornaleros* and working classes. In 1919, the most recalcitrant of the rural employers established a rifle association, the Sociedad de Tiro Nacional de Jaén.[81] And agrarian employers and the most combative young members of the rich rural bourgeoisie set up armed groups and Somatenes[82] in the provinces of Granada (1919), Málaga (1919) and Sevilla (1921).[83] The formation of armed groups in the service of rich landowners had especially serious consequences in the province of Córdoba, in places such as Puente Genil and Luque, where clashes between strikers and employers reached an unprecedented level of ferocity.

Leading figures from the rural bourgeoisie and large landed estates, such as Antonio Medina y Garvey in Sevilla, Count Tovar in Granada, the Marquis of Casa Domecq in Jerez de la Frontera and Count Guadalhorce in Málaga, headed the Andalusian sections of the Somatén from its early days. Recourse to these bourgeois militias indicates that the corporative and authoritarian flirtations of the rural employers, and their break with the Restoration regime, were signs of the general attitudes amongst the Andalusian agrarian oligarchy. This can be seen in the warm welcome with which the large associations representing the corporate interests of the rural employers received the seizure of power by General Miguel Primo de Rivera in much of rural Andalusia.[84]

Notes

Translated by Francisco J. Romero Salvadó.

1. Translator's note: *Jornaleros* are those working for a fixed salary or *jornal*, and *braceros* are those working with their arms or *brazos*.
2. Manuel González de Molina and Miguel Gómez Oliver (eds), *Historia contemporánea de Andalucía. Nuevos contenidos para su estudio* (Granada: Junta de Andalucía, 2000), pp. 233–7.
3. Juan Díaz del Moral, *Historia de las agitaciones campesinas andaluzas* (Madrid: Alianza Editorial, 1979), pp. 270–4.
4. Translator's note: *agrarista* refers to experts on agriculture from the worlds of politics, academia or the civil service. They believed the state should work for the improvement of agrarian conditions and productivity.
5. Díaz del Moral, *Historia de las agitaciones*, p. 265.
6. Instituto de Reformas Sociales, *Información sobre el problema agrario en la provincia de Córdoba* (Madrid: Sucesores de M. Minuesa, 1919), pp. 19, 95 and 98; José Luis Martín Ramos, *Historia de la UGT. Entre la revolución y el reformismo, 1914–1931* (Madrid: Siglo XXI, 2008), pp. 71–2.
7. Antonio María Calero, 'Movimiento obrero y sindicalismo', in Antonio Miguel Bernal (ed.), *Historia de Andalucía* (Barcelona: Planeta, 1983), 8, p. 149; Díaz del Moral, *Historia de las agitaciones*, pp. 270–4.
8. Francisco J. Romero Salvadó, *The Foundations of Civil War: Revolution, Social Conflict and Reaction in Liberal Spain, 1916–1923* (London: Routledge, 2008), p. 157.
9. Grupo de Estudios de Historia Rural, 'Más allá de la "propiedad perfecta". El proceso de privatización de los montes públicos españoles (1859–1926)', *Noticiario de Historia Agraria*, 8 (1994), pp. 99–152; Francisco Cobo Romero, Salvador Cruz Artacho and Manuel González de Molina, 'Privatización del monte y protesta campesina en Andalucía Oriental (1836–1920)', *Agricultura y Sociedad*, 65 (1992), pp. 253–302.
10. González de Molina and Gómez Oliver, *Historia contemporánea*, pp. 249–52.
11. Francisco Zambrana Pineda, *Crisis y modernización del olivar* (Madrid: Ministerio de Agricultura, 1987).
12. Francisco Cobo Romero, *Conflicto rural y violencia política. El largo camino hacia la dictadura. Jaén, 1917–1950* (Jaén: Universidad de Jaén, 1998), pp. 104–9; Francisco Cobo Romero and Manuel González de Molina, 'Obrerismo y fragmentación del campesinado en los orígenes de la Guerra Civil en Andalucía', in Manuel González de Molina and Diego Caro Cancela (eds), *La utopía racional. Estudios sobre el movimiento obrero andaluz* (Granada: Editorial Universidad de Granada, 2001), pp. 238–45.
13. Antonio López Estudillo, 'Los mercados de trabajo desde una perspectiva histórica: El trabajo asalariado agrario en la Andalucía Bética (la provincia de Córdoba)', *Revista Española de Estudios Agrosociales y Pesqueros*, 211/3 (2006), pp. 63–119.
14. José Rodríguez Labandeira, *El trabajo rural en España, 1876–1936* (Barcelona: Anthropos-Ministerio de Agricultura, 1991), pp. 206–9; González de Molina and Gómez Oliver, *Historia contemporánea*, pp. 258–9.

15. Calero, 'Movimiento obrero'; Manuel Tuñón de Lara, *Luchas obreras y campesinas en la Andalucía del Siglo XX. Jaén, 1917–1920, Sevilla, 1930–1932* (Madrid: Siglo XXI, 1978); Paloma Biglino, *El socialismo español y la cuestión agraria, 1890–1936* (Madrid: Ministerio de Trabajo, 1986).

16. For the Republicans see Antonio López Estudillo, *Republicanismo y anarquismo en Andalucía. Conflictividad social agraria y crisis finisecular, 1868–1900* (Córdoba: La Posada, 2001).

17. Francisco Cobo Romero, 'Labradores y granjeros ante las urnas. El comportamiento político del pequeño campesinado en la Europa Occidental de entreguerras', *Historia Agraria*, 38 (2006), pp. 47–73.

18. Ángeles González, 'La construcción de un mito. El trienio bolchevique en Andalucía', in Manuel González de Molina and Diego Caro Cancela (eds), *La utopía racional. Estudios sobre el movimiento obrero andaluz* (Granada: Editorial Universidad de Granada, 2001), pp. 204–5; Juan José Castillo, *Propietarios muy pobres. Sobre la subordinación política del pequeño campesino* (Madrid: Ministerio de Agricultura, 1979).

19. Albert Carreras and Xavier Tafunell, *Historia económica de la España contemporánea* (Barcelona: Crítica, 2003), pp. 223–34.

20. Geoff Eley, *Un mundo que ganar. Historia de la izquierda en Europa, 1850–2000* (Barcelona: Crítica, 2003) pp. 157–64.

21. Charles S. Maier, *Recasting Bourgeois Europe: Stabilization in France, Germany, and Italy in the Decade after World War I* (Princeton, NJ: Princeton University Press, 1988), pp. 3–9; Martín Ramos, *Historia de la UGT*, pp. 63–71.

22. Eduardo González Calleja, *El máuser y el sufragio. Orden público, subversión y violencia política en la crisis de la Restauración, 1917–1931* (Madrid: Consejo Superior de Investigaciones Científicas, 1999), pp. 19–24.

23. Marcel Van der Linden and Wayne Thorpe, 'Auge y decadencia del sindicalismo revolucionario', *Historia Social*, 12 (1992), pp. 3–29.

24. See works by Frank M. Snowden: 'The City of the Sun: Red Cerignola, 1900–1915', in Ralph Gibson and Martin Blinkhorn (eds), *Landownership and Power in Modern Europe* (New York: Harper Collins, 1991), pp. 199–215; *The Fascist Revolution in Tuscany 1919–1922* (Cambridge: Cambridge University Press, 1989); and *Violence and Great Estates in the South of Italy, Apulia, 1900–1922* (Cambridge: Cambridge University Press, 1986). See also Anthony L. Cardoza, 'Commercial Agriculture and the Crisis of Landed Power: Bologna, 1880–1930', in Gibson and Blinkhorn (eds), *Landownership*, pp. 181–98.

25. Renato Zangheri (ed.), *Lotte agrarie in Italia. La Federazione nazionale dei lavoratori della terra, 1901–1926* (Milan: Feltrinelli, 1960).

26. Translator's note: *gimnasia sindicalista* was the constant flexing of muscles by the *sindicatos* (trade unions) by engaging in constant strike action. Anarchists, especially in the 1930s, talked more precisely of 'revolutionary gymnastics'.

27. José Álvarez Junco, *La ideología política del anarquismo español, 1868–1910* (Madrid: Siglo XXI, 1991), pp. 547–73.

28. Translator's note: *Acción Directa* (Direct Action), embraced by revolutionary syndicalists, meant the struggle of the proletariat vis-à-vis the bourgeoisie without the mediation or the intervention of third parties, that is, the state.

29. Van der Linden and Thorpe, 'Auge y decadencia'.
30. Francisco J. Romero Salvadó, *España, 1914–1918. Entre la Guerra y la Revolución* (Barcelona: Crítica, 2002), p. 179.
31. Angel Smith, *Anarchism, Revolution and Reaction: Catalan Labour and the Crisis of the Spanish State, 1898–1923* (Oxford: Berghahn, 2007), pp. 245–9.
32. Antonio Bar, *La CNT en los años rojos. Del sindicalismo revolucionario al anarcosindicalismo, 1910–1926* (Madrid: Akal, 1981), pp. 543–50.
33. Álvarez Junco, *La ideología política*, pp. 355–68.
34. Díaz del Moral, *Historia de las agitaciones*, pp. 182–90; José Luis Gutiérrez Molina, 'De la utopía social al sindicalismo', in Antonio Miguel Bernal (ed.), *Historia de Andalucía. Andalucía Liberal* (Barcelona: Planeta, 2006), p. 244.
35. Álvarez Junco, *La ideología política*, pp. 115–28.
36. Díaz del Moral, *Historia de las agitaciones*, pp. 168–72.
37. Jacques Maurice, *El anarquismo andaluz, una vez más* (Granada: Editorial Universidad de Granada, 2007), pp. 127–35.
38. Jacques Maurice, *El anarquismo andaluz. Campesinos y sindicalistas, 1868–1936* (Barcelona: Crítica, 1990), pp. 260–6.
39. Bar, *La CNT*, pp. 316–38.
40. Biglino, *El socialismo español*, pp. 47–51.
41. José Manuel Macarro, 'El socialismo en Andalucía', in Santos Juliá (ed.), *El socialismo en las nacionalidades y regiones* (Madrid: Fundación Pablo Iglesias, 1988), pp. 109–11.
42. Vladimir I. Lenin, *Desarrollo del capitalismo en Rusia* (Madrid: Ayuso, 1975); Eduardo Sevilla Guzmán, 'Los marcos teóricos del pensamiento social agrario', in Cristobal Gómez Benito and Juan Jesús González Rodríguez (eds), *Agricultura y sociedad en la España contemporánea* (Madrid: Ministerio de Agricultura, 1997), pp. 25–69.
43. Gerolamo Gatti, *Le socialisme et l'agriculture* (Paris: V. Giard et E. Brière, 1901); Karl Kautsky, *La politique agraire du Parti Socialiste* (Paris: V. Giard et E. Brière, 1903).
44. Salvador Cruz Artacho, 'El socialismo español y la cuestión agraria (1879–1923). Luces y sombras en el debate teórico y en la práctica sindical y política', *Ayer*, 54/2 (2004), p. 146.
45. Translator's note: *latifundios* or big landed estates and *minifundios* or tiny plots of land.
46. Artacho et al., 'El socialismo español', p. 148.
47. Ibid., pp. 111–15.
48. Fernando de los Ríos, 'Le problème agraire en Espagne', *Revue International du Travail*, 11/6 (1925), pp. 877–901; Miguel Gómez Oliver and Manuel González de Molina, 'Fernando de los Ríos y la "cuestión agraria" en Andalucía', in Manuel Morales Muñoz (ed.), *Fernando de los Ríos y el socialismo andaluz* (Málaga: Diputación Provincial, 2001), pp. 75–108 and 'Fernando de los Ríos y la cuestión agraria', in Gregorio Cámara Villar (ed.), *Fernando de los Ríos y su tiempo* (Granada: Editorial Universidad de Granada, 2001), pp. 371–99.
49. Artacho et al., 'El socialismo español', p. 148.
50. Biglino, *El socialismo español*, pp. 167–77.
51. Ibid., pp. 171–3.
52. Artacho et al., 'El socialismo español', pp. 149–51.
53. Martín Ramos, *Historia de la UGT*, pp. 72–4.

54. Eloy Vaquero, *Del drama de Andalucía. Recuerdos de luchas rurales y ciudadanas* (Córdoba: Ayuntamiento de Córdoba, 1987), pp. 139–58.
55. Calero, 'Movimiento obrero', pp. 148–51.
56. Antonio Barragán Moriana, *Conflictividad social y desarticulación política en la provincia de Córdoba, 1918–1920* (Córdoba: Ayuntamiento de Córdoba, 1990), pp. 120–7; Tuñón de Lara, *Luchas obreras*, pp. 78–84; Calero, 'Movimiento obrero', p. 149.
57. Barragán Moriana, *Conflictividad social*, pp. 90–3; Constancio Bernaldo de Quirós, *El espartaquismo agrario y otros ensayos sobre la estructura económica y social de Andalucía* (Madrid: Ediciones de la Revista de Trabajo, 1978), pp. 183–5; Vaquero, *Del drama de Andalucía*, pp. 139–41.
58. Instituto de Reformas Sociales, *Información sobre*, pp. 11–14; Bernaldo de Quirós, *El espartaquismo agrario*, pp. 184–5; Barragán Moriana, *Conflictividad social*, p. 98.
59. Translator's note: The Instituto de Reformas Sociales was created in 1902 to advise on and promote social legislation. It was composed of 18 government nominees, 6 employers and 6 labour representatives.
60. Instituto de Reformas Sociales, *Información sobre*.
61. González Calleja, *El máuser y el sufragio*, pp. 43–4.
62. Barragán Moriana, *Conflictividad social*, pp. 118–22.
63. Ibid., p. 121.
64. Tuñón de Lara, *Luchas obreras*, p. 74.
65. Ibid., pp. 71–9.
66. Ibid., pp. 82–3.
67. Bar, *La CNT*, pp. 763–6.
68. González, 'La construcción de un mito', pp. 195–7.
69. Biglino, *El socialismo español*, pp. 194–5.
70. Diego Caro Cancela, *Los socialistas en la historia de Andalucía. La construcción del partido obrero en Andalucía, 1900–1936* (Cádiz: Fundación Pablo Iglesias, 2006), p. 120.
71. Luis Garrido González, *Riqueza y tragedia social. Historia de la clase obrera en la provincia de Jaén, 1820–1939* (Jaén: Diputación Provincial, 1990), 2, p. 158.
72. Tuñón de Lara, *Luchas obreras*, pp. 96–7.
73. Almudena Delgado Larios, '¿Problema agrario andaluz o cuestión nacional? El mito del Trienio Bolchevique en Andalucía (1918–1920)', *Cuadernos de Historia Contemporánea*, 13 (1991), pp. 113–15.
74. Salvador Cruz Artacho, *Caciques y Campesinos. Poder político, modernización agraria y conflictividad rural en Granada, 1890–1923* (Madrid: Ediciones Libertarias, 1994), pp. 454–9.
75. Caro Cancela, *Los socialistas*, pp. 138–165; Tuñón de Lara, *Luchas obreras*, pp. 75–6.
76. This article included in the Electoral Law of 1907 conferred the automatic election of candidates in those constituencies where their number was equal to or less than the available places.
77. Barragán Moriana, *Conflictividad social*, p. 327; González de Molina, *Historia, Identidad y Construcción de la Ciudadanía. Por una relectura de la Historia Contemporánea de Andalucía* (Sevilla: Fundación Centro de Estudios Andaluces, 2007), p. 36–8.

Francisco Cobo Romero

144   *Francisco Cobo Romero*

6
The Lliga Regionalista, the Catalan Right and the Making of the Primo de Rivera Dictatorship, 1916–23

Angel Smith

Between 1916 and 1923 Spain see-sawed between three political alternatives: a democratization of its political structures, a revolution led by the working-class Left, and a military-inspired reaction. Barcelona was at the centre of all these movements and Catalonia's major political party, the Lliga Regionalista, played a major role throughout. It was at the forefront of the campaign both to democratize Spain and achieve political autonomy for Catalonia between 1916 and 1918. It played a key part in organizing Catalonia's middle-class citizens against the anarchist-syndicalist threat in 1919, and it supported the military coup by General Miguel Primo de Rivera in September 1923. This chapter aims to explain the Lliga's changing stance over this period and the impact this had on the Spanish polity.

This not only has relevance to the Spanish case. A key factor in the rise of power of authoritarian right-wing and Fascist leaders in interwar Europe was the complicity of liberal-conservative individuals and parties. Faced with the threat of proletarian revolution they could easily move in an authoritarian direction and link up with more Radical Right options. Amongst these groups there was a widespread over-optimistic assumption that the authoritarian forces unleashed in the aftermath of the First World War could be channelled and controlled; that they were a useful tool in combating left-wing subversion but that the genie could subsequently be put back into the bottle.[1]

The Lliga Regionalista: Ideology and political praxis

The Lliga Regionalista was founded in Barcelona in 1901 in the context of intensifying agitation against the Restoration regime following

145

'the Disaster' of 1898 – a devastating military defeat at the hands of the United States which precipitated the loss of Spain's colonies in the Caribbean and Pacific. Its leadership comprised a group of Catalanist ideologues, who were supported by leading figures within the business community, upset by what they saw as the state's neglect of Catalan interests, but the party had also gained the sympathy of broader sections of the Barcelona urban middle class in the aftermath of the 1899 protest movement by small businesses and shopkeepers against additional government taxes known as the *tancament de caixes*.[2]

At its inception the party had conservative and liberal wings. However, by 1904 the Conservatives had established their dominance. Their ideology had strong Catholic-corporatist roots. Very influential in the intellectual formation of leading figures like Enric Prat de la Riba and Francesc Cambó were French anti-liberal ideas, as represented by the likes of Maurice Barrès and Charles Maurras (who were viewed as fellow regionalists). Yet the ideological tradition from which they hailed did not, like that of the ultra-Catholic Carlists, reject industrialization. On the contrary, it looked to make corporatism compatible with the modern world. Indeed, the emergence of Catalan nationalism from the 1880s was strongly linked to the belief that dynamic Catalonia was being held back by the backward Spanish state. This made possible the confluence between the Catalanists and key business and landed interests between 1899 and 1901.[3] The compromise was reflected in the decision to call the party regionalist rather than nationalist or Catalanist, in order not to frighten away timorous business and other elites.[4]

The Lliga leadership tended to come from wealthy middle- or upper-class backgrounds and, once the party had established itself, moved in elite Catalan cultural and social circles, comprising the interlocking worlds of the *forces vives* (live forces), made up of key political figures and representatives of business and cultural associations, and the haute bourgeois and aristocratic *bones famílies* (good families). The *forces vives* would frequently be called in to see the civil governor to discuss political problems and served together on a whole series of commissions and committees, while the cultural circuit of the *bones famílies* was made up of society balls, elite theatres, the Liceu Opera House and, from 1918, horse races at the Barcelona Hippodrome.[5]

The Lliga at first called for regional decentralization and then went on to demand political home rule, which, it maintained, should also be extended to other parts of Spain. Castilian domination of the peoples of Spain, it believed, had stifled their creative energy. It was the historic role of the Catalan 'people' (*poble*) to lead the struggle to throw off Castilian oppression. Yet this did not imply separation from Spain. Rather, the party's key ideologue, Enric Prat de la Riba, built on ideas developed in 19th-century Catalan business circles, and, influenced by the economic nationalism of Friedrich List and the interventionist model of German capitalism, argued that in consonance with Catalonia's status as the country's industrial centre it was its mission to save Spain by modernizing the country and turning it, once more, into a major European power.[6]

The idea that Catalonia's mission was to transform and industrialize Spain was taken up during the First World War by Francesc Cambó, the party's key political strategist and effective leader after the death of Prat de la Riba in August 1917. On the basis of Prat de la Riba's analysis, Cambó and his supporters eulogized business as the front line in the struggle to transform the country.[7] And economic reforms, such as higher tariff barriers, export subsidies and a free port for Barcelona, which the party argued benefited not just industrial Catalonia but Spain as a whole, were always at the forefront of its demands. There were strong social Darwinist and imperialist components to this perspective. Cambó maintained that the commercial war that would follow the First World War would determine which countries would wither and die and which would prosper and extend their empires.[8] The whole emphasis was on the need to build a more effective capitalist state, which could hold its own against the Great Powers.

Two rather contradictory ideological strands therefore developed within the Lliga. On the one hand, it drank from the cup of 19th-century anti-state nationalism, with its stress on the struggles of the peoples of Europe against autocratic regimes and multinational empires. On the other, it drew on the aggressive statist nationalism which grew up from the 1880s.[9] When stressing the former the reference points were the Greek, Polish and Hungarian nationalist movements; when focusing on the latter they became the figures of Theodore Roosevelt, Joseph Chamberlain and Kaiser Wilhelm II.[10] In the former case the emphasis was on the liberating potential of the *poble*; in the latter particular weight was given to the business elite. The former would require a strategy centred on Catalan nation-building; the latter more focus on reconstructing the Spanish state.[11]

Despite the key role assigned to business, not all social elites joined the Lliga. Most of the landed aristocracy and even important elements in the business community remained attached to the dynastic Conservative and Liberal parties. Furthermore, particularly in rural areas and in Catholic circles, Carlism remained a significant force. However, the

Lliga was, from the turn of the century, also able to tap into a region-alist sentiment widespread within Monarchist and Traditionalist sec-tors of elite Catalan society. Such sentiment was rooted in opposition to 'Jacobin centralization', and in the generalized belief that central Spanish governments were a dead weight, holding Catalonia back. It was reflected in the widespread backing amongst Catalan Monarchists for the Mancomunitat – a Catalan administrative body set up under pressure from the Lliga in 1914 which took over many of the functions of the four Catalan Diputacions (county councils) – and in support for the Lliga's economic programme. The Lliga also gained the sympathy of these groups through its advocacy of a more efficient interventionist central state, which would not only promote industrialization but also build a modern police force in order to combat subversion and terrorism more effectively. The consensus on a number of issues between the Lliga and Catalan dynastic regionalists was facilitated by the existence of the elite cultural and social milieu, noted above, in which leading figures from both the Lliga and the Monarchists would frequently meet.

Yet while the Lliga had strong conservative roots it was also a modern mass party which was born on the back of a protest movement against the Restoration regime and which mobilized against the 'official' Conservative and Liberal Monarchist parties. Like other 'regeneration-ist' groups, it located the responsibility for Spain's supposed decadence at a political level, bitterly criticizing the Monarchists for their manipu-lation of the electoral process, and the inefficient, corrupt nature of their rule. Hence it demanded an overhaul of the political system which would displace the 'oligarchy'.[12]

Nevertheless, the Lliga's leaders were elitists, who wished to undertake this transformation via a peaceful, ordered 'revolution from above'. As far as possible, therefore, they implemented a gradualist strategy, based on negotiations with central government. The party's major achieve-ment in this regard was the concession of the Catalan Mancomunitat by central government. Indeed, it was the apparent success of this stance which turned it into Catalonia's major political force. Its leaders were well aware of the need, on occasion, to mobilize its middle-class base to put pressure on the government, but they were careful to ensure that such movements were controlled and choreographed by the party. Cambó and other key figures were always afraid that the Catalanist rank and file would escape their control, hindering negotiation and political resolution. Even worse, in their opinion, were chaotic movements by the 'frenzied mob' and the 'all or nothing ... [syndicalist] masses', which could only lead to disaster.[13]

Similar ambiguity could be seen in the party's political ideology. In the 1900s it increasingly embraced liberal democracy in the heat of electoral contests and mobilizations for 'Catalan liberty'. This took it into alliance with much of the Catalan and Spanish Republican movement between 1905 and 1909 in the Solidaritat Catalana campaign against military intervention in civil life and in favour of regional decentralization. Its growing liberalism was reflected in the voluntarist component in its Catalanist ideology. Though the party's ideologues viewed the Catalan nation as an organic cultural whole, and maintained that the people needed educating and directing by the political elite, they also affirmed that only through the people's struggles could Catalanist demands be achieved.[14] As part of this process the Lliga presented itself as a more 'modern' and 'progressive' social and political force than the 'oligarchic parties', in favour of 'advanced' social legislation and collective bargaining. Industrial progress, Cambó emphasized, could not be built on the misery of the proletariat.[15]

1916–18: The defeat of the democratic offensive

During the First World War the party felt strong enough to pursue a more aggressive strategy in favour of constitutional reform. Several reasons for this can be discerned. Dislocation caused by the war encouraged it and its business supporters to push their economic demands more forcefully. Furthermore, in Catalonia support for the Allies, who were identified with the rights of the 'small nations' of Central and Eastern Europe, was predominant, and as the war turned in their favour there was a widespread belief that 'freedom' and 'liberty' for the peoples of Europe would be its outcome. This stimulated demands for political autonomy. Finally, the Restoration regime was beginning to fall apart. Angered by high inflation, in 1916 the Socialist Unión General de Trabajadores (General Workers' Union – UGT) and anarchist-syndicalist Confederación Nacional del Trabajo (National Labour Confederation –CNT) allied, and in March 1917 threatened a general strike should the regime fail to enact wide-ranging reforms. May–June 1917 then witnessed a revolt by infantry officers, who had formed Juntas Militares de Defensa (Military Defence Committees) and located their central committee in Barcelona.

Francesc Cambó believed that he could take advantage of this situation to force constitutional reform on the king and Restoration parties. Rather than a general strike, with parliament shut he called an assembly of deputies and senators in Barcelona to elaborate proposals for reform. During this campaign the party seemed to have fully embraced liberal democracy. Had the strategy succeeded it would have signified the passage from a liberal-constitutionalist but in many respects non-democratic regime to a full-blown democracy which would grant political autonomy to Catalonia (along with any other territory that it so desired).[16]

This was a bold move on Cambó's part, which contradicted the party's previous policy of working with Restoration elites where possible. Crucially, he was able to get Prat de la Riba onside, but his strategy frightened other Lliga leaders, who baulked at the party's tacit alliance with left-wingers and would have preferred that he negotiate with the Conservative prime minister, Eduardo Dato.[17] Cambó, however, stressed that he wanted to bring more conservative sectors of Spanish and Catalan society with him, and that his programme was aimed at instigating a 'revolution from above' which would ward off any 'revolution from below'.[18] Hence he reassured King Alfonso XIII that his aim was a constitutional monarchy. Furthermore, he tried to get the key reforming figure within the dynastic parties, the dissident Conservative Antonio Maura, on board. Like the Lliga, Maura had adopted a regenerationist rhetoric and stressed the need to 'dignify' Spanish politics.

Cambó was able to reach out to important sectors of the Left, most notably the Republicans and the Socialist party and union, the Partido Socialista Obrero Español (Spanish Socialist Workers' Party – PSOE) and UGT. Even the CNT, which started to grow significantly in Catalonia during 1917, gave the movement its tacit approval. At the other end of the political spectrum, though most Catalan Monarchists backed away, the Lliga retained the support of a significant group of 'Liberal Autonomists'. This, unfortunately, was not enough to ensure the assembly movement's success in the summer of 1917. Cambó had hoped that the army officers would give it their backing. This proved not to be the case. Despite the fact that they had also adopted a regenerationist language, most officers were conservative centralists who would not support a movement in which Catalanists and leftists were prominent.[19] He was also turned down by Antonio Maura, who was frightened by the movement's audacity and feared that it might call the monarchy into question. And in such circumstances, though it had great support in Catalonia, it was not strong enough to force the king and government to capitulate.

The failure of the peaceful revolution of July 1917 was a great blow to hopes for democratic renewal. In August the working-class Left then essayed a general strike in order to force through the Assembly's demands. It was, however, put down by the military. This was the first indication of the massive impact growing social tensions would have on the political landscape. In Catalanist circles the strike was at first greeted with enthusiasm, the hope being that if the army remained aloof the government would have to accept the assembly movement's demands.[20] Army intervention produced consternation. In conservative milieux there was a sense that the agitation begun by the assembly movement had unleashed social unrest. The right-wing Catalan Maurista, Gustavo Peyrá, advised his leader that 'those socially conservative Catalanists ... are nervous regarding the course of the boat which they have boarded', and Cambó later admitted that the strike had 'cooled the enthusiasm of the conservative elements, even within the Lliga'.[21] The major business organizations gave their total support to the Conservative government. Subsequently, there was talk of the president of the major Catalan business association, the Foment del Treball Nacional (Development of National Labour – FTN), the Liberal Monarchist Josep Caralt, forming a coalition of order in opposition to the Lliga in forthcoming municipal elections.[22] Nothing came of this, but it did serve to emphasize that the Lliga could by no means automatically count on the backing of conservative middle-class Barcelona, especially business interests. Aware of the danger that the strike posed to his party, Cambó distanced himself once the army had intervened, affirming that the Assembly of parliamentarians had had no role in the strike's gestation, in turn producing anger on the Left.

Faced with unexpectedly strong resistance from the regime and fearful at the possibility of losing upper-middle-class and elite support the Lliga leadership now essayed a less risky strategy of reform. In November 1917 it abandoned the assembly movement and joined a coalition government, headed by the Liberal leader Manuel García Prieto, the Marquis of Alhucemas. The Lliga's price was that at the next election the government would not, as was customary, engineer a majority. This allowed Cambó to argue that they had broken the *turno* and were pursuing the demands of the Assembly through parliamentary means. As long as they campaigned effectively through to the general elections the new parliament would, in reality, operate as a constituent assembly which would introduce major political reforms.[23] In addition, he argued that had they not taken this step the result would have been an 'anarchic situation'.[24] This comment was important. After the August general strike the threat of 'revolution from below' would weigh heavily in the political decisions adopted by the Lliga.

Cambó's strategy at first appeared successful. The fact that there was a major Catalan presence in a Spanish government was greeted with satisfaction by much Barcelona public opinion.[25] Cambó tried to build support for regionalist candidates outside Catalonia. The problem was that in the run-up to the election, while the minister of the interior stayed aloof from electoral manipulation, García Prieto, Eduardo Dato and Juan de La Cierva did not. And in many rural areas local power brokers (*caciques*) had the ability to deliver the candidate of their choice.[26] This confirmed that with the failure of the 1917 assembly movement the chance of major democratic political reform had gone. Without a radical reform of Spanish political life it would be difficult, if not impossible, to break the link between the state and the *caciques*, and without a thoroughgoing transformation of power relations in the localities, especially in rural areas, the *caciques* would remain in control.

The upshot was that in the February 1918 elections, though the Lliga won in Catalonia, in other areas the Monarchists were largely dominant. However, because the *turno* had not operated effectively, no Monarchist grouping had a majority. The result was chaos with, when the government fell in March, no clear alternative. And in these circumstances the Lliga was pulled into the Restoration regime further. Given that there was no effective anti-Restoration power block in which the Lliga could feel comfortable, and with the king threatening to abdicate, it agreed to form part of a coalition 'government of talents' under Antonio Maura, in which Cambó was minister of development (*fomento*), in order to 'save Spain'.[27] Previously the Lliga had affirmed that it would only participate in a government that implemented a regionalist programme, but it was concerned that if it was left out the Monarchists would simply try and reconstruct the *turno*. Furthermore, it was, once again, afraid that should no solution be found, 'anarchy' beckoned, especially in the aftermath of the Bolshevik Revolution in Russia. It was the belief of Cambó's right-hand man, Joan Ventosa i Calvell, that 'the political problem of Spain can be seen in these terms, to be or not to be' and he confided that in elite political circles 'the sinister example of Russia played on the minds of everyone'.[28] These comments are indicative of the growing fear of revolution in conservative milieux.

Cambó, ever the optimist, was more upbeat, believing that in tandem with Maura he could do much good work, the implication being it would be laying the basis for the 'revolution from above'.[29] After the failures of the previous year he seems to have been convinced that this could only be brought about by working within the Restoration regime, and that Maura was the only person with sufficient prestige throughout

Spain to carry it through. Moreover, throughout his political career Cambó had been interested, above all, in the exercise of power and saw his new role as allowing him to commence the industrial transformation of Spain. Hence he threw himself with gusto into a whole series of reform projects, most notably the overhaul of Spain's antiquated railway network.[30] Bombastically, he affirmed on a visit with Alfonso XIII to Covadonga (supposedly the spot from whence the 'reconquest' of Spain from the Moors had begun) that while he would not renege on his Catalanist ideals he was determined to create a strong interventionist state in order to initiate 'the new reconquest of Spain'.[31]

However, Cambó's new strategy overestimated Maura's reforming zeal and underestimated the level of opposition he would face. Indeed, the coalition fell in October in good measure because most Monarchists had decided to work together tacitly to rebuild the old party system without Cambó being able to get most of his reforms onto the statute book. An attempt by him to allow the Mancomunitat more financial autonomy was indeed rejected by his cabinet colleagues. These setbacks led the optimism felt in Catalanist circles at Lliga participation in government to fade. Criticisms from the Catalanist Left that Cambó had sold out to the central oligarchy intensified.

The period between 1916 and 1918 had therefore seen the Lliga backtrack on radical constitutional reform. Unable to gain the support of Antonio Maura and the military, and increasingly fearful of losing bourgeois support after the August general strike, Cambó hoped to force through a 'revolution from above' from within the confines of the Restoration regime. This was always going to be an arduous if not impossible task. Moreover, the goalposts of this 'revolution from above' began to shift. Cambó seemed increasingly willing to subordinate demands for democratization and Catalan autonomy to a programme of Spanish economic modernization. In the process, the attempt to hold together the party's inter-class base, which stretched from elite right-wing regionalists to lower-middle-class Catalan nationalists, came under pressure. Over the next three years, heightened social conflict would make its maintenance impossible.

1918–22: The construction of a counter-revolutionary coalition

Late 1918 would see the Lliga apparently adopt a more radical-reforming stance for one last time. The break-up of the Maura coalition was accompanied by growing Catalanist agitation in the aftermath of the publication of President Woodrow Wilson's 14 points, recognizing minority national rights, and then the Allied victory. On this occasion the Left had taken the lead, prompting fears within the Lliga that it would be outflanked. King Alfonso XIII, concerned by the increasingly revolutionary situation in Europe, told Cambó that he would tacitly back a Lliga-led campaign which led the Catalan masses down the path of autonomy rather than revolution. Cambó's hope was that he would then use the agitation to force the new liberal government to give Catalonia home rule by decree.[32]

As in the summer of 1917, events did not go to plan. An anti-Catalan-ist offensive, which took in much of the military, frightened the king away from the path of reform. In addition, when the prime minister, Count Romanones, agreed to form an extra-parliamentary committee to draw up a home-rule bill, more radical Catalanists rejected the idea, prompting the Lliga not to participate.[33] However, all these debates seemed increasingly irrelevant as social conflict escalated. The Catalan CNT had grown extraordinarily rapidly since the autumn of 1918. In mid-February 1919 it called a strike in the territory's main power-gen-erating company, popularly known as La Canadiense. Over the follow-ing weeks the strike spread to the entire sector, with Barcelona, on one occasion, being plunged into darkness. The government negotiated a compromise favourable to the workers. But the Barcelona captain gen-eral, Joaquín Milans del Bosch, then emerged as the employers' cham-pion. His refusal to release a number of CNT prisoners scuppered the agreement and provoked the declaration of a general strike. He then declared martial law and forced the workers back, provoking the resig-nation of the Romanones government in the process. This represented a key development in post-war Barcelona. An alliance between business and the military had been forged in order to deal with the syndicalist challenge, if need be in defiance of the central state.[34]

As in August 1917 this left the Lliga in a difficult position. Cambó recognized that the strike had produced a 'profound conserva-tive reaction'.[35] Throughout conservative middle- and upper-class Barcelona fear of revolution took hold, exacerbated by the fact that the Catalan CNT had developed a terrorist wing which, over the previous months, had carried out a number of assassinations of employers and foremen. For the Lliga the situation was made worse because within business, and in broader conservative-Catholic circles, there was sus-picion that the Catalanist agitation had provoked the labour unrest, both because it had provided workers with an example to follow and because Romanones had reacted by instigating the strike in order to undermine the autonomy campaign.[36] As a result, in February, with the backing of Milans del Bosch, the most conservative sectors of the Catalan Monarchist establishment formed an alliance, called the Unión Monárquica Nacional (National Monarchist Union – UMN), whose battle cry would be the rejection of Catalan nationalism and the defence of order. Aristocrats, landowners and the business elite would be particularly well represented. Within business, in particular, a move away from the Lliga was visible.[37]

In response the Lliga shifted towards the right-wing camp. As Cambó was later to recognize, the Lliga leadership 'understood that the question of liberty had to be put off for a time when faced with the question of life itself'.[38] At the start of the La Canadiense dispute the Lliga had tried to take an equidistant position between workers and employers, but after the general strike had been declared it began to complain at government weakness in the face of the syndicalist threat. 'If Romanones cannot or will not govern another way,' the Lliga's mouthpiece, *La Veu de Catalunya*, sarcastically declared, 'he should once and for all hand power over to the *Noi del Sucre* [Salvador Seguí, the leader of the Catalan CNT], who will do a better job.'[39] This very much echoed criticism in business and military circles of the supposed weakness of the Romanones government.

Once the general strike had begun the Lliga tacitly supported Milans del Bosch, played a leading role in the extension of a bourgeois militia, called the Somatén, to central Barcelona, and backed employer demands for what was referred to as 'compulsory unionization' (*sindicación forzosa*).[40] Until this date much of Catalan big business had been anti-union, but employers now recognized that in some shape or form they would have to bargain with labour. However, they had no stomach for dealing with the CNT, suggesting instead that workers and employers should participate in compulsory state-sponsored union elections followed by the construction of trade- or industry-wide state-run arbitration boards.[41]

In the general strike's aftermath, *La Veu de Catalunya* declared that 'the city' had been subject to 'a hunger siege' and that it had struck back.[42] Hence, the anti-CNT coalition was portrayed as representing the legitimate citizens of Barcelona. The CNT's supporters were outside interlopers. As we shall see, this argument was soon to be given an ethnic-nationalist dimension. Cambó later admitted that the Lliga's emergence as a 'party of order' had produced tensions within the organization (making its more liberal and Catalan nationalist wings uncomfortable), and would in future make it impossible for it to link up with the political Left in any reform project.[43] The result was that rather than leading more conservative elements in a coalition for reform, the Lliga was now being pulled along by a counter-revolutionary coalition at the heart of which was the alliance between the Barcelona military and business. And this alliance, which constantly criticized Restoration governments for weakness in the face of the revolutionary threat, and had no compunction about bringing them down if need be, had clear authoritarian implications.[44]

A similar process of radicalization was once again visible between June 1919 and January 1920. After the fall of Romanones, much to the satisfaction of the Lliga, Maura took over at the head of a government of close colleagues. Maura was now convinced that before reform could be considered the subversive threat had to be dealt with and therefore kept martial law in place and repressed the CNT. However, when a new Conservative government under Joaquín Sánchez de Toca (a subordinate of Eduardo Dato) took office in the summer, it adopted the opposite stance of bringing the CNT out into the open and trying to integrate it into a state-sponsored arbitration board. This was accompanied by a rapid reorganization of the anarchist-syndicalist union from September. The Lliga at first went along with this and, briefly and reluctantly, even brought the elite business organization, the FTN, onboard. However, the hard-line Barcelona Employers' Federation was quickly reorganized in response and sabotaged the process. It overtly called for military intervention to bring the government down and, when this was not forthcoming, with the support of Milans del Bosch, launched two massive lockouts between 3 and 16 November 1919 and 1 December 1919 and 26 January 1920, in order both to break the back of the CNT and undermine the authorities.

At first *La Veu de Catalunya* opposed the lockout, stating that it backed the government decree of 11 October, creating an arbitration board on which the CNT had agreed to work.[45] This position was, however, countermanded by Cambó, who, while trying to distance himself from the employers – who he believed were too individualistic and materialistic –, stated that in the present circumstances he favoured the lockout because business had had to face up to syndicalist violence and terror without any protection from the state.[46] In one respect Cambó was correct. The Spanish liberal state had proved itself totally incapable of building anything approaching an effective police force, and this had clearly encouraged the syndicalist gunmen. In other respects his reading of the situation was not so accurate. The leader of Catalan syndicalism, Salvador Seguí, had in recent months brought the gunmen under control and it would be as a result of the lockout itself that young hotheads would, despite the leadership's opposition, launch a number of high-profile shootings from late December.[47]

As the lockout progressed, the Lliga closed ranks further with business interests, especially after the CNT began planting small explosive devices and then attacking employers and the security services. Governments, its mouthpiece suggested, were not only weak in the face of subversion, they might actually be in connivance with the CNT.[48] 'Barcelona' was once again under attack from the anarchists, who used violence and terror and wished to carry out a communist revolution, the results of which would be 'like the atavistic Asiatic regime essayed in Russia', and would provoke Catalonia's ruin.[49] This was echoed by Cambó in parliament. Spain was now, he claimed, in the midst of a struggle between 'those who propose to destroy present-day society', and those who 'defend the essential bases of our... civilization... a sense of Christian spirituality and democratic organization'.[50]

From the end of December this critique of the CNT was given an ethnic twist. It was claimed that there were parallels between the Republican movement which had been led by Alejandro Lerroux in the 1900s and the Catalan CNT leadership. Like the Lerrouxists the latter were at the very least de facto 'enemies of Catalonia', if not Castilian-speaking outsiders, who denied the existence of the motherland and whose use of violence had a certain 'ethnic flavour', incompatible with Catalan mentality. They had duped and frightened the Catalan workers into supporting them. Once this oppression was removed the latter would reveal themselves in their true colours; men whose 'love of useful work and ancestral blood' naturally made them Catalan patriots.[51] As for the solution to the dispute, on 23 December the president of the Mancomunitat, the mayor of Barcelona and the presidents of the four Catalan Diputacions produced a note in which they stated that it was up to the Employers' Federation to come up with a formula which would be acceptable to enough workers to restart work. The government then needed to introduce legislation putting the employer and worker unions on a legal footing.[52] The Mancomunitat president, it should be noted, was Josep Puig i Cadafalch, who, with Cambó now taking a more backseat role, would be a key figure in the party over the next four years. Several days later *La Veu de Catalunya* eulogized a note published by the employers, affirming that it constituted such a solution. The note stated that when they lifted the lockout the workers would have to sign individual contracts, but made the apparent concession that 'should there not be a legal deposition which improves it', they would subsequently participate in the formation of an arbitration board, as stipulated by the 11 October Royal Decree.[53] That is, the institutionalization of collective bargaining would take place on the ashes of the CNT. As it was, in the face of the employer lockout, the government resigned, the workers were finally forced back and the arbitration board failed to materialize.

During the lockout, then, the Lliga had, after some initial hesitation, once again integrated into the counter-revolutionary coalition. Two interrelated factors above all were involved. Its leaders were, no doubt, genuinely frightened by the CNT and participated in the view that order had to be restored, but they would also have been mindful of the fact that had they not taken such a stance, broader sectors of their conservative middle-class base would have been alienated.

Simultaneously, Cambó's discourse began to incorporate anti-parliamentary, Catholic-corporatist overtones. He criticized what he saw as the claims of the ideologues of the French Revolution, that only the state and the individual (as represented by political parties) were of significance. On the contrary, he maintained, it was increasingly clear that the European 'Jacobin' political parties (like the Spanish Conservatives and Liberals) represented no one. Hence, the war years had seen the rise of both new parties and professional organizations (above all employer and worker unions) which embodied concrete interests. Once 'legitimized', there was a need to incorporate these latter organizations, which were at present undermining governments, by making the Senate a chamber of the corporations. This perspective dovetailed with his support for *sindicación forzosa*, whose roots lay in Catholic-corporatist ideology (the need to overcome the atomization of society provoked by the liberal revolution), and which had marked a retreat from the party's backing for free collective bargaining, implying, at the very least, the withdrawal of bargaining rights from independent labour confederations, if not their outright illegalization.

At the same time, Cambó put emphasis on the need for a strong government, led (albeit temporarily) by a strong man, which would impose itself by decree and thereby be in a position to deal with the social problem. And in April 1920 he made clear that he believed Antonio Maura to be that man. The popularity such a government would gain would allow it to fight a successful election campaign, should parliament try and block it. He argued that in countries like Spain, where the lack of a 'civic culture' meant that elections were manipulated, parliaments were creatures of the ruling parties and did not represent public opinion. But he also seemed to believe that in the democracies in general, executive power needed strengthening. 'In France', he commented approvingly,

'[Georges] Clemenceau governs dictatorially against the parliament, which hates him', but it could do nothing because he had the backing of the people, with the result that he could 'abolish parliament without anyone noticing'.[54]

The reading of Cambó's position is complex. At one level it needs relating to the political circumstances of the day. To Cambó's dismay, Dato's Conservatives were trying to reconstruct the *turno*, and he was angling for a new Maura coalition government in which the Lliga would participate. In addition, his views must be seen in the context of debates within the European Right on the need for new instruments to contain industrial strife. Emphasis was on the need to reinforce executive power and put in place systems of state-sponsored collective bargaining. Some saw this as compatible with liberalism, while others looked towards more authoritarian political structures. Finally, widespread concern was expressed in European conservative circles at the instability of parliamentary government. Again, the far Right adopted an anti-liberal reading of such concerns.[55]

Cambó's perspective cannot be seen as overtly anti-liberal. The emphasis was on the reform of parliament rather than its destruction. His aim was to deal with concrete problems: the threat posed to parliamentary legitimacy by growing social strife (as made abundantly clearly in 1919), and also the growing difficulty faced by government in getting legislation though parliament after 1914 as a result of the growing crisis of the dynastic parties (a fact which, ironically, the Lliga took full advantage of in 1916 to derail Santiago Alba's fiscal reforms). Furthermore, Cambó also maintained that he wanted to see the Lower House regenerated through proportional representation, thereby undermining the hold the Conservatives and Liberals had over it (though such democratizing intentions no longer corresponded to the practice of the Lliga).

Nevertheless, most of Cambó's remedies, with their emphasis on the need for a strong executive and corporatist representation, combined with his language, redolent in some respects of 19th-century Traditionalism, clearly represented an opening to the Right, and in the political context of 1919–20 this added grist to the anti-parliamentary mill. At the heart of his vision was the construction of a powerful state machine which, along with fostering Spanish industrialization, would impose social control. This represented a stark contrast to the programme of the assembly movement in 1917 which centred on the need to strengthen parliament vis-à-vis the executive and monarch.[56] A similar corporatist evolution could be seen in the thought of Antonio Maura from 1919.[57]

In Catalonia other elements within the counter-revolutionary coalition were beginning, more overtly than Cambó, to question aspects of liberal constitutionalism. Within the Employers' Federation criticisms were voiced at the 'useless' parliament, and it was argued that questions relating to the world of work should be dealt with by a separate 'producers' parliament'. The FTN took a more regionalist-authoritarian tack, calling for a 'governing body' in Catalonia, run by a 'person of high reputation ... uncoupled from any political interests'. Ramon Rucabado, a Social Catholic who wrote regularly for *La Veu de Catalunya*, in some respects took a similar line, lamenting that Catalonia did not have its own authority, which could impose the only possible solution, the abolition of the right to strike or call lockouts and 'the designation of state representatives in each factory, to impose order and make sure that the laws and pacts are respected'. As noted, the Employers' Federation had also actively encouraged military intervention against 'weak' Restoration governments, and while some were looking back to the 19th-century tradition of liberal praetorianism, others invoked the memory of Donoso Cortés, who in the mid-19th century had affirmed that only a military dictatorship could stem the revolutionary tied unleashed by liberalism.[58] Outside Catalonia a similar trend could be discerned, with anti-parliamentary rhetoric visible in right-wing military, Catholic and Maurista circles, combined with calls for military intervention.[59]

Growing criticism of parliamentary government was encouraged by the Catholic-corporatist component still present within Spanish right-wing thought. The Lliga had not travelled as far down this path as some, but it was not unaffected. This was not, of course, a phenomenon limited to Spain. In Italy and France a Radical Right had emerged which overtly affirmed the need for a strong state in order to impose order, combined with the transformation of parliament into a corporatist institution subordinate to the authorities.[60]

In Catalonia similar themes would again raise their heads in the following year, when another Conservative government, under Eduardo Dato, once again entered negotiations with the CNT during the autumn of 1920. The vision of both the Spanish central governments in hock to the anarchist-syndicalists, and the latter as 'elements ... not belonging to our motherland', was confirmed.[61] The point was constantly made that Catalans, who really understood the situation on the ground, would do a far better job than non-native civil governors sent to Barcelona 'on the say so of Madrid'.[62] This did not stop the Lliga from backing the call by business and other elite institutions for the emollient civil governor Carlos Federico Bas to be replaced by the commander of the Barcelona garrison, General Severiano Martínez Anido, at the beginning of November. Indeed, Cambó was to play a key role in his appointment.[63]

La Veu de Catalunya stated hopefully that though born in Galicia, Martinez Anido 'left his native land when he was three years old, came to Catalonia when he was eight and since then he has resided here and pursued his career here'.[64] This could not hide the fact that he was, like most officers, a Spanish patriot who hated Catalan nationalism. Martínez Anido would, once in power, launch an all-out assault on the CNT. This included encouraging the development of a stratum of gunmen within a small right-wing populist-Catholic trade union, the Sindicatos Libres (Free Trade Unions), who were given arms and information by the military, police and Somatén in order to assassinate CNT activists. The Lliga responded by claiming that it opposed all forms of terrorism.[65] But over the next three years the anarchist-syndicalists, almost exclusively, were blamed for the shootings. For example, when at the beginning of December the CNT declared a general strike to protest at the assassination (almost certainly at the instigation of Martínez Anido) of the MP Francesc Layret, a far-left Catalanist with links to the syndicalists, the Lliga denounced the strike as a revolutionary assault on 'the city' by its enemies. It was grateful, it stated, to Martínez Anido for imposing order.[66]

This was a position ratified by Cambó in parliament. A 'parenthesis' was needed during which the CNT was destroyed, before proceeding to institutionalize labour relations.[67] It was to be a long parenthesis. Martínez Anido would remain in power until October 1922, during which time he consolidated a de facto authoritarian military regime in Catalonia, to an important degree outside central government control. Others went further than Cambó. From late 1918 Maura, though he still considered himself a liberal, began to contemplate the possible need for a military government to step in temporarily, given the crisis of the regime.[68] As noted, calls for military intervention became more widespread in 1919. Less attention was devoted to how to ensure that the military would return to their barracks after carrying out their supposed labour of cleansing the body politic. And rather than focusing on the anti-Catalanism of the CNT the Lliga would have been better advised to pay more attention to military attitudes towards Catalan nationalism. From the autonomy campaign at the end of 1918, frequent and extraordinarily aggressive anti-Catalanist rhetoric had been common currency in much of the military press.

As we have seen, Cambó maintained that a strong Maura government (in which he would, no doubt, play a key role) was the only hope for the 'revolution from above'. In December 1920 he publicly affirmed that he would only come aboard if Catalan autonomy was on the table.[69] However, when he accepted the role of finance minister in a new Maura emergency coalition government, formed in August 1921 in the aftermath of the military disaster of 'Annual' – while Martínez Anido was still civil governor – its objectives were more modest. As in 1918 Cambó emphasized the importance of concrete reforms which he believed would benefit the Catalan and Spanish economy. The Lliga's 'statist' nationalist project, aimed at Spanish regeneration, was clearly taking precedence over 'anti-state' Catalan nationalist demands.[70] The most important legacy of his period in office would be the ultra-protectionist 1922 'Cambó tariff'. At the same time, he was also mindful that his presence in government would help undermine the UMN, which, to a significant degree, depended on Maurista support. Finally, the ministry disinterred the Catalan employers' programme of *sindicación forzosa*. Interestingly, discussion between Maura and Cambó on an alternative project to stabilize labour relations proposed by Martínez Anido and based on the Sindicatos Libres, which de facto outlawed the right to strike, indicates Cambó had some sympathy for this position. He commented that although such a goal would be difficult to achieve through legislation, the illegalization of strikes in the public services represented 'an important advance'.[71]

However, the ministry fell in March 1922 before the government's proposals in his field could be enacted. Cambó suggested to Maura that they rule by decree. The latter's refusal now led Cambó to doubt whether 'reform from above' from within the regime would actually be possible.[72] The problem was that this left him and his party without any credible strategy. He allowed a Lliga representative, Josep Bertran i Musitu, to participate in a new Conservative government led by José Sánchez Guerra (the minister of the interior in the 1917 Dato administration which headed off the assembly movement). It now seemed to be Cambó's philosophy that to have a hand on the levers of power was always better than to be excluded. However, he would find it very difficult to justify such a stance to his Catalanist social base. The Lliga appeared to be operating as a satellite of right-wing Conservative (especially Maurista) governments. This became even clearer when Bertran i Musitu resigned after the government, under pressure from Liberals and the Left, restored constitutional guarantees (which had been suspended throughout Spain since March 1919) on 31 March 1922. This shone a light on the fact that the party was in reality backing semi-dictatorial rule in Catalonia.

Amongst the more Catalan nationalist and liberal sections of the Lliga there had been a growing frustration at this situation. This now boiled over. The Lliga youth wing broke away and, together with a number of moderate republican Catalanists, founded a new party called Acció Catalana (Catalan Action). Its key arguments were that the Lliga's intervention in central government had been a failure and that more attention should be paid to the cultural construction of the Catalan nation. This again brought to the fore the contradictions within the Lliga's nationalist ideology and the difficulty of holding together the social coalition which it represented. Cambó had tacked to the Right and to a significant degree headed off the threat of Catalan elites and the Catholic-conservative middle classes coalescing around the UMN. However, this was at the expense of its more liberal lower-middle- and middle-class supporters. In the April 1923 general elections and June 1923 provincial elections Acció Catalana ate into the Lliga electorate to a significant degree in Barcelona, provoking Cambó's retirement from active politics.[73]

1923: The counter-revolutionary coalition and the assault on the restoration regime

It is in the aftermath of the Maura government's fall in March 1922 that the final assault on the Restoration regime took place. More liberal governments, that were willing to contemplate negotiations with the CNT, once again came to power. Sánchez Guerra forced Martínez Anido to step down in October. Then, in December – following the rules of the *turno* – a Liberal coalition government was formed under the leadership of the García Prieto, in which Santiago Alba – considered by the Lliga as its most formidable enemy – became foreign minister. In conservative Catalan circles concerns further heightened in this month as the CNT began to reorganize. And in response, as in 1919 and 1920, the alliance between the industrialists and the military was reactivated. The Employers' Federation provoked a strike on the waterfront on 1 May 1923, which quickly escalated into an all-out transport strike, leaving Barcelona groaning under mountains of uncollected rubbish. This was also accompanied, from March that year, by escalating tit-for-tat killings between CNT and Sindicato Libre gunmen. And in the summer, groups of hard-line anarchist insurrectionaries undertook a number of spectacular hold-ups in order to raise funds for an uprising.[74]

This provoked a renewed assault by the counter-revolutionary coalition. Once again, after its spell in government had concluded, the Lliga turned on the authorities with venom. In a speech in the run-up to the April 1923 elections, Cambó presented an apocalyptic vision of the state of the government, judiciary, army and Spanish economy.[75] *La Veu de Catalunya* then laid into the government for supposedly allowing chaos to reign. This, it was now repeated continuously, was a deliberate policy undertaken – with Alba in the shadows pulling the strings – in complicity with the CNT (and even the terrorists) in order to undermine Catalanism.[76] A simple identification was made between terrorism and the CNT, despite the fact, all the indications are, that the shootings had been reignited by agent provocateurs linked to the Sindicatos Libres and paid for by a group of hard-line employers. And the decision by the Barcelona-based CNT leadership to call for a boycott of Catalan goods in the rest of Spain, in response to the employer offensive, was taken as proof that they were 'allies and accomplices of the enemies of Catalonia'. 'The boycott of Catalan products called for by *Solidaridad Obrera* [the mouthpiece of the CNT]', *La Veu de Catalunya* maintained, 'is the same as the boycott predicated by *ABC* [the anti-Catalanist right-wing Spanish daily].'[77]

A particular focus of their ire was the civil governor, Francisco Barber, who was trying to reach a negotiated settlement to the transport strike. Once again, a military figure emerged as the saviour in waiting of the conservative classes; in this case Miguel Primo de Rivera, who had been captain general of Barcelona from April 1922. And Primo de Rivera obliged, undermining the position of Barber and pushing for a solution favourable to the employers. With the general also enjoying the backing of wider military circles and the sympathy of the king, the government capitulated in June, bringing in a tougher civil governor, Manuel Portela Valladares, in order to oversee the repression of the strike. Yet Portela Valladares got little credit for his labours. Rather, on 13 July the mayor, Ferran Fabra i Puig, the Second Marquis of Alella, a Monarchist close to the Lliga, visited the captain general and other leading military figures to 'express the gratitude of the city'.[78]

The Lliga now turned its attention to other aspects of government policy of which it disapproved. It focused on the government's intention to negotiate trade agreements which would reduce tariff protection on industry, which it maintained represented an attack on Catalonia, its continued electoral manipulation and its supposed inability to implement the prudent strategy in the Moroccan war it had promised. Following what appeared to be the definitive failure of the Maura-Cambó 'revolution from above', in collaboration with the other components of the counter-revolutionary coalition, the Lliga was clearly determined to bring down the government and, it appeared increasingly, the entire Restoration regime. The government, *La Veu de Catalunya* declared in July 1923, was 'in decadence' and the regime was 'breaking up'.[79]

By this time Primo de Rivera had already begun to conspire. He had met a number of generals in June while in Madrid, when the decision was taken that he would organize a coup with their backing. These generals represented the opinion of *africanista* officers, angry at press criticism of the Moroccan war and keen to bury the whole responsibilities issue. This was important because such a position had the sympathy of the king and Primo de Rivera's alliance with the africanistas would give him wideranging military support. But it was Primo de Rivera who took the lead and crucial for him was the situation in Barcelona, especially the revolutionary threat presented by the CNT. At the same time, officers within the Barcelona garrison were also furious at the growth of radical Catalanism.[80]

Primo de Rivera was also buoyed up by the support he had received from 'the city'. Conservative Barcelona was united in praise for the job he had done in restoring order. The fact that he came from an influential, titled, military family was no doubt reassuring. He even took on board regionalist sentiment, stating that he respected the Catalan language and favoured decentralization. In this context a close relationship was established between the general, high society and the *forces vives*. The Republican journalist, Claudi Ametlla, recalled: 'There wasn't a party in the house of the Baroness of Maldà, a great dame in those years, to which Primo de Rivera did not add prestige through his presence. And no event held by the Marquis of Alella, the regionalist mayor of Barcelona, which he did not preside over, brighten up and amuse through his sometimes irreverent jokes, which were often acerbic criticisms of governments.'[81] It was in this atmosphere that, as Ametlla notes, a consensus was built up: on the need to do something about the supposed chaos enveloping the country, which was not, however, incompatible with 'autonomy properly understood' (i.e., mild regional decentralization).[82]

Puig i Cadafalch, who was a key figure at such gatherings, was later to recognize that Primo de Rivera often expressed the 'desire and intention' to overthrow the regime.[83] Clearly no one dissented. Primo de Rivera was actually closest to the leader of the UMN, Alfons Sala, and to the independent Conservative (with close Lliga contacts) Joan Antoni Güell i López, the Second Count of Güell, but he also took leading Lliga figures into his confidence. All the indications are that he held a meeting with Puig i Cadafalch and with Cambó's confidant Emili Junoy in August in Font Romeu in southern France at which they reached a tacit understanding: support for a coup in return for Catalan autonomy and high protectionist tariffs.[84] The 13 September coup attained total support in elite Catalan circles. Ever the shrewd politician, Cambó, who since the beginning of July had been travelling around the Near East on his yacht, on being informed called on the Lliga leadership not to give the coup their active backing.[85] It was too late. *La Veu de Catalunya*, from the outset, was favourably disposed. On the afternoon of the 13th, Puig i Cadafalch and Ventosa i Calvell were present at the inauguration of a furniture exhibition, at which the Marquis of Alella and Primo de Rivera gave speeches. Puig i Cadafalch then wrote a letter to Primo de Rivera on behalf of the Mancomunitat, giving him his support in return for the anticipated regionalist administrative reforms. A very cordial meeting followed.[86] The following evening Primo de Rivera was seen off to Madrid from Barcelona train station by a cheering crowd of around 4,000 'respectable citizens', including the Marquis of Alella (who embraced him), the bishop of Barcelona Dr Guillamet (who blessed him), Puig i Cadafalch, Ventosa i Calvell and leading figures from the business associations.[87]

To understand the Lliga's position one has to take into account its growing disenchantment that it could break the *turno* and reform the regime from within. In addition, like other sectors of the counter-revolutionary coalition, it feared the reorganization of the CNT. Cambó was later to recall that when he visited Italy in September 1922 it was 'in an anarchistic state' and 'I understood then that the coming of Fascism was inevitable'.[88] Many members of the Lliga hierarchy must have harboured similar thoughts with respect to the establishment of a Spanish dictatorship. Such views were encouraged by Primo de Rivera's assertion that his rule would be a 'parenthesis', during which he would both impose order and cleanse Spain of *caciques*, before handing power back to the civilians. In the meantime, one suspects, they hoped he would introduce the reforms Cambó saw as necessary to ensure social stability and an economic revival. It did not occur to the Lliga that, on the contrary, he might institutionalize his rule. Cambó made a similar mistake in the following year in a book analysing Italian Fascism. He was favourably disposed. Mussolini had both restored order and a patriotic sense of duty. But Cambó maintained that despite his anti-parliamentary rhetoric Mussolini would have to reach a compromise with parliament. He was, indeed, concerned that he would fall before he was able to introduce the necessary constitutional reforms to strengthen the executive.[89]

Other sectors of the coalition of order, while not necessarily advocating a total break with liberalism, were certainly looking to impose a more authoritarian settlement, in which the state would have new powers to maintain social control. From 1922 Mussolini was praised by both Social Catholics and by the Employers' Federation for re-establishing order, attacking the liberal political elite (seen as the equivalent of Spain's Restoration politicians) and left-wing labour unions, and promoting class collaborationism through the Fascist unions. In addition, once the Fascist militia, the Fascio de Combattimento, had been made a legal arm of the state in Italy there were suggestions within military, UMN and business circles that the Somatén might play a similar role in Spain. A smaller group of officers, in contrast, argued that the Sindicatos Libres could fulfil this task. Finally, business spokesmen also reiterated calls, first made in early 1920, for a 'non-political' autonomous institution to operate in Catalonia and maintain order.[90]

Conclusions

The August 1917 general strike put paid to Lliga pretensions to build a broad coalition, which included the Left, for democratic reform. With the rise of the CNT from the beginning of 1919, it then put demands for political autonomy on the back-burner, while supporting right-wing Conservative governments which kept the lid on social protest in Barcelona. The maintenance of social order now clearly took precedence over democratization and home rule. And when Cambó entered government it was on the economic reforms that pleased his most bourgeois backers that he concentrated. As a result, between March 1918 and March 1922 the Lliga, to a degree, integrated into the Restoration regime, its programme sharing much in common with the Maurista Conservatives.

Yet this collaboration was always unstable. The party's more liberal and nationalist wing was impatient for political autonomy, while its more right-wing supporters, most notably in the business community, were fiercely opposed to Restoration governments which tried to reach a compromise with the Catalan CNT and failed to pursue (what they perceived as) pro-business economic policies. It was a perspective that the Lliga came to share, with the result that periods of co-operation in government were followed by phases of virulent opposition, during which it formed part of what I have termed the Catalan counter-revolutionary coalition.

Cambó was well aware of these tensions in his party. Rhetorically, he frequently sided with the more radical Catalanists, noting early in 1917 that 'the business elements are by nature governmental and one cannot expect any great heroic acts from them. At times of struggle and persecution we find our strength in the Catalanist masses.'[91] Yet, as noted, the party leaders were elitists, who moved in the world of the *forces vives* and *bones famílies*, and who feared any social or political movement that they could not control. Furthermore, not to have acted in the way they did would have meant their marginalization from elite society and the loss of bourgeois backing. This was not an option for figures like Cambó, who saw the industrial bourgeoisie as spearheading society's modernization and Spain's transformation into an imperialist power. At one level the Lliga leaders' 'fear of the masses' put them at a crossroads between the old world of oligarchic liberalism and the new age of mass mobilization, and they retreated from mass politics as the social and political climate became more polarized.[92] Furthermore, the corporatist component in Cambó's thought, his glorification of economic struggle and empire, and stress on the industrial bourgeoisie as the agent of reform, also provided a possible bridge with more authoritarian and anti-liberal political options.

Under pressure from growing social conflict in the Catalan capital, and faced with the failure of the 'revolution from above', the Lliga leadership in 1923 broke totally with the Restoration regime and came to accept the need for a 'military parenthesis' by a 'regenerationist' military dictator. Its historic opposition to the Restoration regime and the regime's refusal to grant home rule no doubt made it psychologically much easier for the party to take such a step. But the evidence amassed in this chapter points to the Lliga's perceived need to remain in tune with Catalan bourgeois opinion as the key factor in its decision. After all, it had collaborated with Restoration governments which were not out of tune with conservative Catalan interests.

The party did not, as a result, jettison the liberal-democratic elements in its discourse. In the days after the coup, *La Veu de Catalunya* maintained that the new military directory's job was to 'destroy the political oligarchies, re-establish the principle of authority and the rule of law' before holding elections.[93] This can be analysed at a number of levels. For the Lliga it was both convenient and reassuring to believe that it could delegate the task of beginning the 'regeneration' of Spanish society to the hands of a general. Furthermore, the Lliga leadership also no doubt hoped Primo de Rivera would implement reforms such as the illegalization of the revolutionary Left, strengthen the executive and even implement decentralizing measures. Such a stance was commonplace amongst both conservative-liberal parties and conservative middle-class opinion in interwar Europe, and was of key importance in making dictatorship possible. In the case of Spain, the Lliga's attitude both broadened Primo de Rivera's tacit support base and muffled opposition to his assumption of power.

Notes

Research for this chapter was made possible by a Small Grant from the British Academy. I would like to thank Francisco J. Romero Salvadó for his comments on earlier drafts. All translations from Catalan and Spanish are by me.

1. See, for example, the comments in Hans Rogger and Eugen Weber (eds), *The European Right: A Historical Profile* (Berkeley, CA: University of California Press, 1966), pp. 1–28; Martin Blinkhorn (ed.), *Fascists and Conservatives: The Radical Right and the Establishment in Twentieth Century Europe* (London: Unwin Hyman, 1990), pp. 1–13.
2. For the Lliga's formation see, Borja de Riquer, *Lliga Regionalista: La burgesia catalana i el nacionalisme, 1898–1904* (Barcelona: Edicions 62, 1977). I have preferred to use the term Catalanist rather than Catalan nationalist because there is considerable ambiguity as to whether the Lliga's discourse and practice can be seen as nationalist or regionalist.
3. Jesús Pabón, *Cambó, 1876–1918* (Barcelona: Alpha, 1952), pp. 74–94; Jordi Sole Tura, *Catalanismo y revolución burguesa*, 2nd edn (Madrid: Cuadernos Para El Diálogo/Edicusa, 1974), pp. 126–34; Maties Ramisa, *Els orígins del catalanisme conservador i 'La Veu de Montserrat'* (Vic: Eumo, 1985).
4. Riquer, *Lliga Regionalista*, pp. 191–203; Francesc Cambó, *Confederencia pronunciada por D. Francisco Cambó en el Teatro Los Campos Elíseos de Bilbao el día 28 de enero de 1917* (Bilbao: Jesús Álvarez, n.d. [1917]), p. 15.
5. For the world of the *bones famílies* see, Gary Wray McDonogh, *Good Families of Barcelona: A Social History of Power in the Industrial Era* (Princeton, NJ: Princeton University Press, 1986); Borja de Riquer, 'Burgesos, polítics i caçics a la Catalunya de la Restauració', *L'Avenç*, 85 (1985), pp. 16–33. At the top of the social tree, until his death in 1918, was Count Güell, Eusebi Güell i Bacigalupi, who was close to the Lliga.
6. See Prat de la Riba's key work, 'La nacionalitat catalana' (1906), in Enric Prat de la Riba, *Obra completa, 1906–1914*, 3, ed. Albert Balcells i Josep Maria Ainard Lasarte (Barcelona: Proa and Institut d'Estudis Catalans, 1998), pp. 117–70.
7. See, for example, Francesc Cambó, *Actuació Regionalista. A propòsit d'un article de Don Gabriel Maura i Gamazo* (Barcelona: Publicacions de la *Lliga* Regionalista, 1915), p. 62; *La Veu de Catalunya* (hereafter LVC), (15 July 1915). *La Veu de Catalunya* was the daily mouthpiece of the Lliga.
8. LVC (13 July 1915). Charles E. Earlich correctly states that the Lliga cannot simply be seen as the party of industry. See: 'The Lliga Regionalista and the Catalan Industrial Bourgeoisie', *Journal of Contemporary History*, 33/3 (1998), pp. 399–418. Conservative Catalanists like Prat de la Riba and Cambó did not

hail from a business background, and sectors of the industrial elite remained linked to the Monarchist parties. However, it is important not to underestimate the influence that both business and landowning interests and demands had within the party. At first the Lliga gained the support of the major business corporations (with the Foment del Treball Nacional particularly important), and industrialists like Lluís Ferrer-Vidal, Albert Rusiñol and Lluís Sedó were weighty figures in the party. Similarly, the key landowners' association, the Institut Agrícola Català de Sant Isidre (the Sant Isidre Catalan Agrarian Institute) was a firm supporter, and its leading figure Carles de Camps, the Second Marquis of Camps, became a powerful voice. Furthermore, as noted above, the Lliga leadership moved in elite circles in which the need to back business interests was taken for granted. Most importantly, the party came to view businessmen as the nation's redemptors. Cambó's secretary, Rafael Marquina, noted that 'Cambó has always had a clear weakness...for the creators of wealth. Cambó has always admired them and believed that these energetic founders of businesses...were the foundation on which Catalonia's greatness was based'. Rafael Marquina, *Francesc Cambó* (Barcelona: Libreria Catalonia, n.d. [1925?]), p. 65. For links between the Lliga and business in the party's first years see Riquer, *Lliga Regionalista*, especially pp. 205–6. For the backing on landed interests, see Montserrat Caminal i Badia, 'La fundació de l'Institut Agrícola Català de Sant Isidre: els seus homes i les seves activitats (1851–1901)', *Recerques*, 22 (1989), especially p. 123. Co-ordination between the Lliga and the business associations in the formulation of economic policy is amply demonstrated in Joseph Harrison, 'Big Business and the Failure of Catalan Right-Wing Nationalism, 1901–1923', *The Historical Journal*, 19/4 (1976), pp. 901–18. These are points to which I shall return.

9. Peter Alter, *Nationalism*, 2nd edn (London: Edward Arnold, 1994), pp. 16–64; Eric J. Hobsbawm, *Nations and Nationalism since 1780: Programme, Myth and Reality*, 2nd edn (Cambridge: Cambridge University Press, 1992), pp. 80–130.

10. Prat de la Riba, 'La nacionalitat catalana', pp. 136, 164–8; Francesc Cambó, 'Catalunya devant de Castella. Conferència pronunciada al Círculo Mercantil de Salamanca el día 15 de març de 1908', in Francesc Cambó (ed.), *El catalanisme regeneracionista*, edició a cura de Jordi Casassas (Barcelona: Edicions La Malgrana/Diputació de Barcelona, 1990), p. 23.

11. This is why the celebrated jibe by the centralist Liberal Party MP Niceto Alcalá Zamora in the Spanish parliament in December 1918, that Cambó was attempting to play the role of Bolívar in Catalonia and Bismark in Madrid, made such an impact. Cambó admitted in his memoirs that 'it was a very effective personal blow which got to the heart of the truth'. Francesc Cambó, *Memòries, 1876–1936* (Barcelona: Alpha, 1981), p. 303.

12. For a broader discussion of regenerationism see the introductory chapter and the chapter by Javier Moreno Luzón in this volume, pp. 1–31 and pp. 32–61.

13. 'Manifest dels senadors i diputats regionalistes a propòsit dels successos de juliol de 1909', in Prat de la Riba (ed.), *Obra completa*, pp. 449–50; Francesc Cambó, *Conferència d'en Francesc Cambó diputat per Barcelona a l'Ateneu Democràtic Regionalista del Poble Nou* (Barcelona: Impenta de La Veu de

Catalunya, 1923), p. 5. Cambó's 'fear of the masses' is stressed in Borja de Riquer, 'Francesc Cambó: un regeneracionista desbordado por la política de masas', in Borja de Riquer, *Escolta Espanya. La cuestión catalana en la época liberal* (Madrid: Marcial Pons, 2001), pp. 205–41.

14. Francesc Cambó, *Catalunya i la Solidaritat. Conferència donada al Teatre Principal el dia 26 de maig de 1910* (Barcelona: Fills de D. Casanova, 1910), p. 91. Theorists of nationalism have emphasized the voluntarist element present in the ideology of liberal nationalist movements.
15. Pabón, *Cambó*, p. 592. For growing military interventionism and the Solidaritat Catalana see also Alejandro Quiroga and Sebastian Balfour in this volume, pp. 216–17 and pp. 260–3.
16. For more details on the Lliga's battles with central government over economic policy during 1916 and on the origins of the crisis of 1917 see Romero Salvadó, 'Spain's Revolutionary Crisis of 1917', in this volume, pp. 62–91.
17. Cambó, *Memòries*, pp. 261–2.
18. Pabón, *Cambó*, p. 546; Antoni Rovira i Virgili, *La crisi del regim. Crònica documentada dels darrrers esdeveniments de la política espanyola* (Barcelona: Editorial Catalana, 1918), p. 100.
19. For the anti-Catalanism of much of the officer corps see the comments by Balfour and Quiroga in this volume, pp. 261–2 and pp. 206–7.
20. Amadeu Hurtado, *Quaranta any d'advocat. Història del meu temps, 1894–1930* (Barcelona: Ariel, 1969), p. 313.
21. Archivo de Antonio Maura Muntaner (hereafter AMM), Fundación Maura, leg. 82, carp. 29, Peyrá to Maura (20 October 1917); Cambó, *Memòries*, p. 265.
22. For more details on the reaction of the business associations to the strike see, Angel Smith, 'The Catalan Counter-revolutionary Coalition and the Primo de Rivera Coup, 1917–23', *European History Quarterly*, 31/1 (2007), pp. 11–12. The president of the FTN had been a Lliga member for much of the period between 1901 and 1912, but between 1914 and 1923 the presidents would all be Monarchists.
23. LVC (9 November 1917).
24. Pabón, *Cambó*, p. 578.
25. Hurtado, *Quaranta any d'advocat*, p. 321.
26. Cambó, *Memòries*, pp. 272–3. For more details on this election and the power of the local *caciques*, see Javier Moreno Luzón, this volume, pp. 32–61.
27. In Maura's own words: see Cambó, *Memòries*, p. 275.
28. LVC (27 March 1918).
29. LVC (17 March 1918). Though Cambó subsequently also stated that it was a 'government of containment' to deal with 'an anarchic situation', and represented 'a truce' between the Lliga and the Restoration parties. See LVC, 10, 30 September 1918.
30. See Cambó's own account, *Vint mesos al ministeri del Foment. Ma gestió ministerial* (Barcelona: Editorial Catalana, 1918). There is a brief analysis in Harrison, 'Big Business', pp. 913–14.
31. Riquer, 'Francesc Cambó', p. 223.
32. Cambó, *Memòries*, pp. 292–9.
33. For an overview of the autonomy campaign see Josep M. Poblet, *El moviment autonomista a Catalunya dels anys 1918–1919* (Barcelona: Pòrtic,

1970). Important inside information is to be found in Cambó, *Memòries*, pp. 300–5.

34. Angel Smith, *Anarchism, Revolution and Reaction: Catalan Labour and the Crisis of the Spanish State, 1898–1923* (Oxford: Berghahn, 2007), pp. 290–7. See also the chapters by Romero Salvadó ('Si Vis Pacem Para Bellum') and Ealham in this volume, pp. 175–201 and pp. 92–120.

35. Cambó, *Memòries*, p. 317.

36. Hurtado, *Quaranta any d'advocat*, pp. 363–4. In a speech in the following year Cambó remarked on the ambiguous position of many businessmen: 'Who amongst you, Catalanists of the heart and propagandists of our ideals, speaking with industrialists, hasn't heard them say "why do you perturb Catalonia with these foolish ideas?"' LVC (13 November 1919). At the time, *La Veu de Catalunya* also claimed that 'the enemies of the Catalans' demands' had been spreading the rumour that 'the nationalists are to blame for the recent social conflicts and that we led the great syndicalist organization'. LVC (23 March 1919).

37. For more details on the UMN see Josep Puy, 'La Unión Monárquica Nacional frente al catalanismo de la *Lliga*, 1918–1923', *Estudios de Historia Social*, 28–9 (1984), pp. 467–73; Smith, 'Counter-revolutionary Coalition', pp. 19–20. See also the comments by Alejandro Quiroga in this volume, pp. 207–8

38. Cambó, *Memòries*, p. 329.

39. LVC (23 March 1919).

40. For Cambó's views on *sindicación forzosa* see the interview with him in LVC (7 March 1919).

41. Smith, 'Counter-revolutionary Coalition', pp. 15–16.

42. LVC (15 April 1919).

43. Cambó, *Memòries*, p. 316.

44. For further details see Romero Salvadó, 'Si Vis Pacem Para Bellum' in this volume, pp. 175–201.

45. LVC (28 October 1919).

46. LVC (13 November 1919). Cambó's talk was published as a separate pamphlet, *La crisi social a Catalunya* (Santiago de Xile: Germanor, 1920).

47. Smith, *Anarchism, Revolution and Reaction*, pp. 315–17.

48. LVC (24 December 1919).

49. LVC (18, 19, 24, 29, 31 December 1919; 1, 3, 7 January 1920).

50. *Diario de las Sesiones de las Cortes. Congreso de los Diputados* (hereafter DSC), (3 February 1920), p. 2235.

51. LVC (29, 30 December 1919).

52. LVC (24 December 1919).

53. LVC (28, 30 December 1919).

54. See 'La crisi social i la realitat catalana. El discurs d'en Cambó a Girona', LVC (18 November 1919), along with two somewhat different texts based on the same talk, Francesc Cambó, *Sexta conferencia pronunciada en el Teatro del Centro de Madrid el día 10 de Abril de 1920. Curso de conferencias organizadas por El Debate* (Madrid: n.p., n.d. [1920]); and 'L'actualitat social i política. Conferencia donada al Teatre del Centre de Madrid el día 10 d'abril de 1920', *La Novel.la Nova*, 135 (n.d.[1920]). It should, however, be noted that Cambó's analysis of the Conservative and Liberal parties was rather contradictory. When his focus was on Catalanist demands

they were transformed into agents of Castilian hegemony over the rest of Spain.

55. Charles S. Maier, *Recasting Bourgeois Europe: Stabilization in France, Germany and Italy in the Decade After World War I* (Princeton, NJ: Princeton University Press, 1975), especially pp. 353–4; Eric J. Hobsbawm, *The Age of Empire* (London: Abacus, 1994 [1987]), pp. 96–7. For additional details see the introduction to this volume, pp. 1–31.

56. LVC (15 July 1917). Moreover, Cambó had in the past affirmed that problems were solved more effectively when parliament was in session and they could be discussed. LVC (9 November 1915).

57. Fernando del Rey Reguillo, 'Las voces del antiparlamentarismo conservador', in Mercedes Cabrera (ed.), *Con luz y taquígrafos. El parlamento en la Restauración, 1913–1923* (Madrid: Taurus, 1998), p. 306.

58. For business see Smith 'Counter-revolutionary Coalition', pp. 17–21. Rucabado's article can be found in LVC (6 December 1919).

59. See the comments by Alejandro Quiroga and Sebastian Balfour in this volume, pp. 202–29 and pp. 255–74.

60. See the comments in the introduction to this volume, pp. 1–31.

61. LVC (20 October, 7 December 1920).

62. LVC (2, 6 November 1920).

63. See the comments by Romero Salvadó, 'Si Vis Pacem Para Bellum', in this volume, pp. 175–201.

64. LVC (9 November 1920).

65. LVC (1 December 1920).

66. LVC (10, 11 December 1920).

67. DSC (11 February 1921), pp. 396–7.

68. Javier Tusell, *Antonio Maura. Una biografía política* (Madrid: Alianza Editorial, 1994), p. 190.

69. LVC (14 December 1920), reproduced in the pamphlet, *El que pensa Francesc Cambó davant els problemes actuals* (Barcelona: Imprenta de la Veu de Catalunya, 1920).

70. Correspondence between Cambó and Maura between March and August 1921 indicated how keen the former was to become part of a Maura government. There was no mention of Catalan autonomy: Institut Cambó, *Correspondència Cambó–Maura/Maura–Cambó*, Cambó to Maura (11 March 1921), Cambó to Maura (15 August 1921), Maura to Cambó (16 August 1921).

71. AMM, leg. 444, carp. 7, Francesc Cambó 'Observaciones del proyecto del Sr Martínez Anido (5 October 1921)'.

72. Cambó, *Memòries*, pp. 353–4.

73. For the formation of Acció Catalana see, Montserrat Baras, *Acció Catalana, 1922–1936* (Barcelona: Curiel, 1984), pp. 11–50.

74. Smith, *Anarchism, Revolution and Reaction*, pp. 345–53.

75. Francesc Cambó, *Els problemes catalans i els problemes espanyols* (Barcelona: Imprenta de La Veu de Catalunya, 1923). It included the prescient observation: 'The prestige of parliament has fallen so low', that if it were 'dissolved by the boot of a military man or by the staff of a dictator no one would be sorry' (p. 2).

76. See, for example: LVC (22 May; 26, 12, 17, 27 June 1923).

77. LVC (30 June 1923).
78. LVC (14 July 1923).
79. LVC (5 July 1923).
80. On Primo de Rivera's outlook see Javier Tusell, *Radiografía de un golpe de estado. El ascenso al poder del general Primo de Rivera* (Madrid: Alianza Editorial, 1987), p. 79. For the repercussions of the 'Annual disaster' see Pablo La Porte in this volume, pp. 230–54.
81. Claudi Ametlla, *Memòries polítiques, 1918–1936* (Barcelona: Catalònia, 1979), 2, pp. 53–4. As noted, the Second Marquis de Alella was a Monarchist close to the Lliga.
82. Ibid., pp. 53–6.
83. Josep Puig i Cadafalch, 'La Mancomunitat de Catalunya i el dictator I', in LVC (27 February 1930).
84. Arturo Perucho, *Cataluña bajo la dictadura* (Madrid: Oriente, 1932), pp. 12–13. We also know that Joan Antoni Güell i López was informed of the proposed coup in early July and that Catalan business helped finance it. See Maximiano García Venero, *Historia del nacionalismo catalán* (Madrid: Editora Nacional, 1967), 2, pp. 306–8; Gabriel Maura Gamazo, *Bosquejo histórico de la dictadura*, 5th edn (Madrid: Tip de Archivos, 1930), p. 33. Claims that Primo de Rivera actually met up with Cambó before the coup, however, seem mistaken.
85. Though he was reported as saying: 'I consider the attitude of the military the only sweet we have tasted in these bitter years.' M. Teresa González Calbet, *La dictadura de Primo de Rivera: El Directorio Militar* (Madrid: El Arquero, 1987), p. 82.
86. Cambó, *Memòries*, pp. 377–8; LVC (13, 14, 19 September 1923); Josep Puig i Cadafalch, 'La Mancomunitat de Catalunya i el dictator II', LVC (28 February 1930); Tusell, *Radiografía*, p. 210.
87. *La Vanguardia* (15 September 1923); LVC (15 September 1923); Francisco J. Romero Salvadó, *The Foundations of Civil War: Revolution, Social Conflict and Reaction in Liberal Spain, 1916–1923* (London: Routledge, 2008), p. 291.
88. Cambó, *Memòries*, p. 330.
89. Francesc Cambó, *Entorn del feixisme italià. Meditacions i comentaris sobre problemes de política contemporània* (Barcelona: Editorial Catalana, 1924).
90. For additional details see, Smith, 'Counter-revolutionary Coalition', pp. 26–8, and Alejandro Quiroga in this volume, pp. 202–29.
91. Pabón, *Cambó*, p. 487.
92. See the interesting comments in this regard in Riquer, 'Francesc Cambó', especially pp. 239–41.
93. LVC (25 September 1923).

7

'Si Vis Pacem Para Bellum': The Catalan Employers' Dirty War, 1919–23

Francisco J. Romero Salvadó

In the early hours of 13 September 1923, Miguel Primo de Rivera, Captain General of Barcelona, staged a military coup that marked the death of the liberal regime which had ruled Spain since December 1874. In a manifesto addressed to the country and to the armed forces, he claimed the mantle of 'iron surgeon' prepared to undertake radical surgery to save the motherland. Significantly, the code to inform his allies in Madrid that the rebellion had begun was 'the patient has been operated upon'.[1]

Even if the medical analogy of the ruling order as an ailing body was correct, the coup of 1923 was not a generous act of euthanasia. When Primo de Rivera alleged its chronic ill-health to justify switching off the life support of the 'Liberal patient', he cynically concealed that the military political meddling abetted by the ruling economic sectors, particularly in Catalonia, was the cancer that had placed the regime in that state.

A lethal cocktail of opulence and gloom

Spain was caught, like the rest of Europe, in the post-war spiral of social unrest unleashed by the Bolshevik triumph in Russia. News of revolutionary activity from Berlin, Vienna, Budapest and other European capitals, combined with the establishment of the Comintern in March 1919, set alarm bells ringing amongst the Spanish ruling classes. Their collective hysteria appeared to be borne out by events both in the countryside and in the urban centres: between 1918 and 1920 Andalusia experienced a period of social effervescence, known as the 'Trienio

Bolchevique'. At the same time, the main cities were shaken by industrial disputes, food riots and demonstrations against the high cost of living and the dastardly gains made by profiteers. But it was Barcelona that stood out as the epicentre of the social explosion.

A former civil governor, Angel Ossorio, wrote that Barcelona was a place where revolution was always ready to take place.[2] Indeed, as Spain's economic powerhouse, Barcelona presented, as no other city, the critical combination of a large proletariat with an unequal tradition of social struggle, an intransigent employer class, nationalist feelings amongst significant sections of its middle classes, a restless officer corps and a widespread mistrust of the central administration. The epidemic of bombings and subsequent military repression in the 1890s, the general strike of 1902 and the Tragic Week of 1909 were ample evidence of Barcelona's powder keg status. The dramatic transformations brought about by the Great War lit the fuse.

The First World War produced in Spain, but particularly in Barcelona, a lethal cocktail of unprecedented opulence and widespread gloom; the perfect milieu for social violence. In fact, basking in Spain's neutrality, the Catalan capital underwent an exceptional industrial expansion generated by the high volume of exports to the warring countries.[3] The extraordinary profits enjoyed by Catalan industrial barons and businessmen were often frittered away in new property, luxuries or in the numerous cabarets, brothels and casinos that appeared in the city's richer quarters.[4] Simultaneously, the drastic cut of imports, shortages of staple products and galloping inflation brought misery to the working classes. The fabric of Catalan society, furthermore, was dramatically torn apart by the flood of immigrants that arrived, lured by the economic explosion. This poverty-stricken mass of labourers was in the majority a radicalized and unskilled workforce who found themselves crammed in filthy inner city tenements and exploited with derisory wages at the workplace.[5]

In 1918, Catalan industrialists were gripped by growing anxiety. They had observed how a new generation of Anarcho-Syndicalist leaders, taking advantage of increased working-class solidarity produced by strikes and consumer-based protests, had achieved the successful reorganization of the proletariat.[6] Such efforts culminated at the Congress of Sants (Barcelona) from 28 June to 1 July 1918, with the establishment of local industrial trade unions, *Sindicatos Únicos* (Single Trade Unions), to replace the old craft federations whose rivalries and overlapping had hitherto characterized the Catalan labour movement.[7]

To add insult to injury, employers were increasingly targeted in *atentados* (assassination attempts). In fact, they were the victims of two parallel but not always disconnected processes arising from the particular conditions of wartime Barcelona. First, the *atentados* were carried out by Anarchist Action Groups who had always existed on the fringes of the Libertarian milieu and now in the radicalized atmosphere surrounding the Catalan capital began to apply terror at the workplace in order to solve pending conflicts: the shooting of a few industrialists or foremen rapidly proved a convincing incentive to obtain concessions from the otherwise stubborn employers.[8] Second, some of these *atentados* were entangled with the murky world of spies and adventurers that flourished in Barcelona during this period as the German intelligence services sought to hinder industrial production for the Allies by means of sabotage and, if necessary, violence.[9]

Administrations in Madrid could neither ignore the Anarcho-Syndicalist Confederación Nacional del Trabajo (National Labour Confederation – CNT) expansion nor have missed the avalanche of demands from Catalan employers for punitive measures. The social explosion was, however, triggered by the authorities' misguided response to an altogether different question: the demands for Catalan home rule that gained momentum following the Allied victory and the US President Woodrow Wilson's call for the self-determination of small nations.

By the end of the year, with Barcelona experiencing daily demonstrations and clashes between autonomists and centralists, the Liberal government led by Count Romanones found itself caught between its desire to find a compromise with an autonomist movement that contained powerful economic interests and the need to appease the indignation of the local garrison.[10] The outcome was finally to suspend constitutional guarantees, on 16 January 1919, and direct then the repressive backlash towards the Anarcho-Syndicalists. Thus it was the labour movement, even though it had not been behind the disturbances of the previous weeks, whose press was shut down, its trade union centres closed and several of its high-ranking militants arrested.[11] Of course, the CNT, unlike the autonomists, could not boast ex-ministers of the crown or wealthy industrial backers in its ranks. However, Catalonia's home rule soon was relegated from the agenda by the magnitude of the social conflict that was about to erupt.

A macabre film: The Canadiense strike

In early February 1919, a wages dispute began at Barcelona's Ebro Irrigation and Power Company, popularly known as La Canadiense, the city's most important electricity supplier. After the sacking of eight employees, all CNT members, the strike turned into a protracted struggle between the Catalan labour movement and the industrial bourgeoisie. At stake was the balance of power at the workplace. The company pursued a hard line backed by the civil governor, Carlos González Rothwos, the Captain General Joaquín Milans del Bosch and the British Embassy. But the introduction of repressive measures such as the declaration of martial law, the arrest of hundreds of workers and even the militarization of basic services, proved useless against the working class mobilization, that, led by the Sindicato Único of Gas, Water and Electricity, brought the city to a standstill. With food riots rocking Madrid and other capitals, the southern countryside in revolt and the Socialists threatening to call a nationwide solidarity strike with the CNT, the government finally blinked first and opted for sending a new civil governor, Carlos Montañés, and even the cabinet secretary, José Morote, with special powers to negotiate a compromise. After 44 days, the strike ended with a stunning victory for the workers. The company agreed to accept the rehiring of its discharged employees (without penalties of any kind), to raise salaries, and the reimbursement of a fortnight's pay in February and a full month's wages for the days lost in March. In turn, the government conceded an amnesty for all those imprisoned and introduced an eight-hour working day in the construction sector (with a promise to extend this legislation to all industry).[12]

The Canadiense's outcome was the final straw for Catalan industrialists. It was not the violence of the strike (it had clearly been kept under control) nor any revolutionary demands (improvement of working conditions and wages) which frightened them but the discipline of the trade unions. Equating labour strength with Bolshevism, the employers were aghast at the CNT's ability to paralyse Barcelona and overcome by a collective feeling of despair.[13] The Foment del Treball Nacional (FTN), the powerful employers' association dominated by the Catalan grand bourgeoisie, called the recent events *una película macabra* (a macabre film).[14]

The employers prepare for war

Gripped by panic and insecurity, the industrialists felt indignant at what they considered the capitulation of the authorities in Madrid. According to the FTN, the government had not only left Catalan employers defenceless before the rising number of *atentados* but had even rewarded the very same criminals with the eight-hour working day, 'an economic *coup d'état* that damaged significantly the national economy'.[15] Consequently, increasing numbers of Catalonia's industrial barons concluded that the governing classes were unable to contain the revolutionary avalanche and defend the social order. In these times of acute danger, they had to close ranks regardless of diverse political leanings – including support or not for autonomist hopes – to defend their corporate interests and prepare for war: *Si Vis Pacem Para Bellum*.[16] To achieve this, a new employers' association, the Spanish Employers' Confederation (Confederación Patronal Española, CPE), was reorganized, in its own words, to fight against what it termed 'an insatiable beast feeding on destruction and collective misery', the Sindicato Único.[17]

Officially established at a congress held in Madrid in September 1914, the Patronal was led by hardliners and self-made employers, often from the construction sector (such as its president, Francisco Junoy, and its leading Catalan members, Felix Graupera and Joan Miró i Trepat). Like its enemies in the CNT, the CPE's most powerful branch was its Barcelona Federation (reorganized in March 1919 and then extended to the whole of Catalonia in July 1920: Federación Patronal de Cataluña). Unlike traditional employers' organizations, such as the Chamber of Industry and the FTN, the Patronal was equipped as an organ of combat to carry out the offensive against the unions. It was structured like the *Sindicatos Únicos*, with local industrial federations integrated into regional bodies. It claimed that it stood for law and order against those who wanted to destroy the traditional fabric of society, but borrowed from its class enemies the same weapons of boycott and pressure against those 'weak industrialists' failing to toe the line. Members were encouraged to take out insurance policies against violent death and 'unfair' strikes and to adopt radical measures, such as registries of workers, the compilation of blacklists and the establishment of special funds to support non-unionized labour and to finance lockouts.[18]

Some scholars suggest that there was a certain rivalry between the Patronal and long-established employers' associations such as the FTN over hegemony and leadership amongst Catalan employers. They also note the latter's lukewarm approach, if not opposition, towards the CPE's confrontational strategy. In fact, the FTN, manned by the crème de la crème of the Catalan bourgeoisie, was precluded by its statutes from taking part in the class struggle and instead was to focus on influencing the political elites. Nevertheless, evidence demonstrates that even if the FTN directors were usually to stay in the background, on most occasions they worked in tandem with the Patronal. While the FTN remained a formidable pressure group focusing on commercial objectives such as defending Catalan production and lobbying for protective tariffs, the Patronal constituted the employers' shock troops and handled the dirty business of facing the CNT head-on. Tellingly, the FTN's bulletin described the Patronal as an organization led by brave men, who, displaying love for Catalonia, were prepared to endanger their lives by facing the 'Bolshevik mob'.[19] Furthermore, sharing a similar dread of the red subversion embodied by the CNT, the FTN directors, including its two presidents during this period – Jaume Cussó until February 1922 and then Domingo Sert –, pursued the same corporatist objective: the compulsory unionization (*sindicación forzosa*) of employers and workers. Initially suggested in October 1917, this idea of *sindicación forzosa* gained momentum in 1919 amongst employers who kept demanding a *Ley de Sindicación Profesional* (a law of professional unionization). It consisted of the creation of joint workers' and employers' industrial unions which could be integrated into state-sponsored industrial tribunals and thus overcome class conflicts and deny the CNT labour representation.[20]

In order to launch their offensive, the employers could rely on backing from the local garrison. The recent separatist incidents, the escalation of *atentados* and constant industrial unrest had exhausted the military's patience with constitutional legality and appeared to confirm their mistrust towards the efficiency of the governing classes to defend the motherland.[21] Unlike the political squabbling and manoeuvring of the politicians, army officers were prepared to take effective steps to quash the power of the organized labour movement.

General Milans del Bosch took the extraordinary decision in early 1919 of transforming a rural militia, the Somatén, whose origins lay in medieval times when local villagers were armed to repel Muslim raids under the cry of *sometent* (be vigilant), into an urban paramilitary formation. The Somatén of Barcelona included humble shopkeepers and white-collar workers, but ultimately its leaders were members of the Catalan aristocracy and rich industrialists. It was, in all but name, an armed militia of 'respectable citizens' that under the banner of authority, religion and social order sought to wrest control of the streets from the perceived red threat. From spring 1919, the Somatén sprang up in other Spanish cities.[22] The Somatén constituted the Spanish variant of the patriotic leagues, bourgeois militias, counter-revolutionary movements and other organizations of 'respectable citizens' that emerged in the aftermath of the First World War in order to combat the perceived threat embodied by 'the red spectre' and social subversion. In the defence of their imperilled world, they were not only prepared to use violence to destroy the 'evils' of socialism but also were deeply hostile to liberalism itself, which they believed too feeble to impose social discipline and protect private property.[23]

In the dirty war against the CNT, employers also hired the services of armed gangs. The most notorious was led by the disgraced former police chief of Barcelona, Manuel Bravo Portillo. He had been arrested in June 1918 due to his involvement in the German spy network but was released in December of that year largely due to his military connections. Soon thereafter, with the support of the army's chief of the general staff, General Manuel Tourné, Bravo Portillo helped organize the Somatén as well as recruit a sort of employer's police amongst thugs from the Catalan underworld to carry out arrests, beatings and, occasionally, the murder of labour activists.[24]

Bravo Portillo also collaborated with the Somatén and military headquarters in an operation financed by secret army funds that consisted of keeping a card index of *Cenetistas* (the so-called *Fichero Lasarte*, named after its main keeper, the retired captain of the Civil Guard, Julio Lasarte). Based on information from police 'stool pigeons', its goal was to enable the detention of trade unionists, often upon trumped-up charges, and, if necessary, their assassination.[25] There was jubilation in proletarian quarters, on 5 September 1919, when news spread that Bravo Portillo had been shot dead outside one of his lovers' apartment.[26] His gang, however, still remained active under the leadership of a German adventurer and former spy, Fritz Stallmann, known as Baron Koening. On the whole, the Patronal did not finance the Baron's gang but under the protection of leading members of the Somatén and some hard-line industrialists, its members acted as bodyguards and agents provocateurs, and engaged in shootouts with *Cenetistas*. The gang was finally dissolved and Koening expelled from Spain in June 1920 as details unfolded that payments had been extracted from several employers through the invention of false death threats and blackmail.[27]

The seeds were also sown in the spring of 1919 to create a new trade union, the Sindicatos Libres (Free Unions). Tellingly, one of its leading architects was an army officer, Major Bartolomé de Roselló. The idea was to split the labour movement by recruiting amongst Catholic and Carlist workers who, although affiliated to the CNT, were repelled by its increasingly revolutionary character. Officially, the birth of the Libres took place at the Ateneo Obrero Legitimista, the stronghold of Catalan Carlism, on 10 October 1919.[28]

The spring of 1919 marked the point of no return; the start of the Catalan counter-revolution. Such would be its ferocity that the leading

Italian political thinker, Antonio Gramsci, noted that it constituted the precursor of Italian Fascism.[29]

The first phase: The leapfrog of civil governors

From March 1919 to November 1920, Barcelona experienced the consolidation of a parallel power operating in the shadows. Under the pretext of embodying the defence of social order against the perceived revolutionary threat, Catalan employers and army officers behaved as a veritable 'anti-state'. Governments thus faced the dilemma of being an accomplice – or feigning blindness – to the reactionary backlash, or enduring its subversive might. The result was a permanent *coup d'état* hanging over the central administrations that effectively placed civil sovereignty in the gutter: there were five civil governors in Barcelona during this period.

The employers' offensive began in earnest soon after the Canadiense. Incensed by the outcome of that dispute – perceived by industrialists and officers as a dangerous concession to Bolshevism –, the military provoked the CNT into a new general strike by refusing to obey the government instructions to release those militants they still held.[30]

On 24 March 1919, the Anarcho-Syndicalists again brought Barcelona to a standstill. However, the army and industrialists were now much better prepared. They collaborated over the opening of factories and agreed to demand legislation for the compulsory unionization of workers into professional bodies away from class-based organizations.[31] Right from the start, Milans del Bosch reimposed martial law. The following day, the Somatén came out in force and collaborated with the troops in forcing shops and markets to open their doors, preventing the paralysis of basic services. The Bravo Portillo gang helped the army to round up leading labour activists. By 7 April, the general strike was clearly petering out.[32]

The employers and the military agreed that Barcelona could only return to normality with the perpetuation of emergency measures and martial law.[33] Thus they were furious when the government made conciliatory overtures such as announcing a compulsory scheme of workers' pensions and the introduction of the eight-hour working day in all industrial sectors from 1 October. Such measures, according to industrialists, were detrimental to productivity and revealed yet again a bias in favour of the troublemakers.[34] This time, industrialists and army officers were determined to settle the conflict on their own terms and prevent political interference from sabotaging their efforts. Hence the civil governor's pacifying initiatives as well as the demands of the chief of police, Gerardo Doval, to dismantle Bravo Portillo's parallel force were rejected. Milans del Bosch twice offered his resignation, but not without stressing that the Catalan ruling classes and the entire officer corps would not accept it. The impasse was finally broken on 14 April, when the military governor, General Severiano Martínez Anido, and an officer of the Civil Guard, Colonel Aldir, on behalf of the local garrison, told Doval and Montañés to leave Barcelona. A few hours after their departure, the government resigned.[35]

The blatantly seditious stance pursued by employers and officers paid off: the Romanones Liberal administration was followed by a hard-line cabinet headed by the veteran leader Antonio Maura that was praised by the FTN's president as 'a ray of light on the horizon'.[36] Industrialists could not complain: martial law remained in place, while the new civil governor, the Marquis of Retortillo, was happy to take a backseat. However, the 'ray of light' soon faded. The government failed to obtain an overall majority in the elections of June 1919 and had to resign in mid-July.[37]

Employers initially welcomed the new civil governor Julio Amado, an army officer and editor of the military mouthpiece, *La Correspondencia Militar*. As that newspaper noted, they were rubbing their hands with glee since they expected Amado to give the unions 'a good thrashing' (*pegar de lo lindo*).[38] Their hopes, however, were shattered when it became apparent that he was working in tandem with the new Conservative minister of the interior, Manuel Burgos y Mazo, whose social reformist ideas threatened to unravel the repressive stance of the previous months.

Burgos y Mazo believed that the trade unions should be allowed to operate freely as the recognized representatives of the workers. Otherwise, their persecution and prolonged clandestine life was bound to strengthen the hand of the extremists.[39] Thus, instead of conducting a 'good thrashing', Amado began negotiations with high-ranking imprisoned *Cenetistas* and offered them a quick return to constitutional normality, including the liberation of the thousands of jailed militants, in return for an acceptance to initiate, without prerequisites, a dialogue with the employers.[40]

During September and October 1919, government and CNT fulfilled their side of the deal. Leading Anarcho-Syndicalists published a note condemning violence and pledged to solve pending disputes by negotiation. In turn, the authorities lifted martial law, granted a general amnesty, introduced officially the eight-hour working day in all the industrial sectors and finally, on 11 October 1919, established by royal decree a Comisión Mixta de Trabajo (Joint Employers–Labour Arbitration Commission), with an equal number of employers' and workers' representatives, which was, amongst other matters, to negotiate conflicts between labour and capital and to advise the government on social legislation.[41]

The employers, meanwhile, were only biding their time. Their response came during the CPE's second congress held in Barcelona on 20–6 October 1919. There, amidst apocalyptical warnings that Spain under the existing administration was about to follow in the steps of Russia, they agreed to launch a partial lockout (public services and the food sector were not affected) on 3 November, to starve the workers into abandoning the CNT and in the process to oust the government. Two thousand industrialists paid a courtesy visit to Milans del Bosch, at the end of the congress. Their intentions were revealed clearly by Felix Graupera when he declared at the congress that the captain general was the only guarantor of justice, order and tranquillity.[42]

Both Burgos y Mazo and Amado singled out the Catalan industrialists as the main obstacle to social peace in Barcelona.[43] The civil governor struggled to get the Joint Commission working but the employers were never seriously committed to the negotiations. In fact, they played a cat and mouse game intended to provoke the workers to break off the dialogue. On 12 November, a breakthrough appeared to have been made when both sides agreed on the need for new social legislation and the halting of existing strikes and lockouts. But hopes were soon dashed. Two days later, at the entrances to the reopened factories, managers carried out a selective purge of their workforce. Infuriated by this blatant mockery of the recent accord, the labour representatives withdrew from the Commission.[44] The government still endeavoured to solve the foundering situation by receiving workers' and employers' delegations in Madrid. However, once there Graupera only confirmed the intransigent position of the industrialists: unless there was a general clampdown on the CNT, including the arrest of the unions' leaders, the Catalan employers would resume (on 25 November) a lockout that (by 1 December) would affect all spheres of economic production.[45]

The lockout lasted until 26 January 1920 and counted on the connivance of the captain general, the sympathy of the crown and the backing of the FTN and the other main Catalan economic associations whose collusion was obviously imperative. It left nearly a quarter of a million people jobless and produced widespread misery amongst the working classes.[46] It did achieve one of its objectives: to help bring down the government in Madrid. In December 1919, the Patronal, for the first time, called for an 'iron surgeon', a national leader prepared to crush the threat of Bolshevism.[47] The die was cast. The cabinet finally collapsed on 9 December 1919.[48]

Nevertheless, the lockout did not lead to a massive departure of workers from the unions. Instead, it fuelled class hatred and undermined the grip on the CNT of the traditional labour leaders who favoured dialogue.[49] Spain in general, and Catalonia in particular, began to sink into a vicious cycle of terror. Of course, the anarchist groups were not behind all the violence. Koening's gang continued to act as agents provocateurs and to engage in shootouts with *Cenetistas*. The number of *atentados* against industrialists certainly increased. The most spectacular occurred on 5 January 1920, when the car in which Graupera and another Patronal director, Modesto Batlle, were travelling was sprayed with bullets in the city centre. The two industrialists, the driver and one police escort were wounded, and another policeman died. The funeral of the policeman produced a massive display of protest by the 'respectable citizens' of Barcelona. Some newspapers even demanded an all-out manhunt of Anarcho-Syndicalist 'beasts'.[50]

In February 1920, the employers lost their erstwhile ally Milans del Bosch, when private correspondence about his actions in the previous year was filtered to the upper chamber.[51] Both industrialists and the local garrison were incensed. With the backing of the Somatén, the former ordered the symbolic closing of all commerce for 24 hours and organized numerous acts of support for the captain general, including an appeal to the monarch. Amongst the army officers, there were discussions about what measures to adopt and some even commented that they would be seen as lacking 'balls' unless they acted forcefully. There were rumours of a military coup.[52]

Ultimately, the threatening rhetoric was not matched by deeds; or not yet! Milans del Bosch lacked the ambition to stage a coup and agreed to resign when a hesitant king, after pondering for days, signed his dismissal but rewarded him soon after with the prestigious post of head of the royal household. His replacement, General Valeriano Weyler, rapidly assured employers that he fully endorsed their interests and confirmed his collaboration with the Somatén in the repression of the labour movement. After all, he reminded them, he had already imposed law and order twice as captain general of Barcelona in equally traumatic times (the bombing wave of the 1890s and following the Tragic Week of 1909).[53] Nor could industrialists complain about the interim coalition formed in December 1919 under the Maurista Manuel Allendesalazar.

Indeed, the new cabinet swiftly appointed hard-line civil governors such as the Count Salvatierra in Barcelona who, on the pretext of the *atentado* on Graupera, initiated an all-out assault on the Catalan labour movement: on 6 January, he ordered the closing of all unions. With prisons crammed, ships in the harbour had to be used as jails. Even some Republicans acting as labour lawyers were detained.[54]

By substituting repression for dialogue, Salvatierra persuaded a still reluctant Patronal to lift the lockout on 26 January.[55] However, the resumption of office in May 1920 by the Conservatives headed by their leader Eduardo Dato brought new dismay to Catalan employers. The appointment of a moderate, Francisco Bergamín, at the Home Office, and of the engineer Federico Carlos Bas as civil governor of Barcelona, meant a new attempt at social conciliation.[56]

It was déjà vu for the industrialists. If anything, the escalation of violence was much worse than during the terms of Montañés or Amado. Random shootings of factory owners and shootouts between *Cenetistas* and Libres dominated newspaper headlines.[57] Finally, faced with the furore following the murder of Count Salvatierra, on 4 August, in Valencia, Dato replaced Bergamín with the hard-line Count Gabino Bugallal.[58] Bas's position was doomed. Industrialists demanded his scalp when, during a strike in the electrical sector in which the civil governor was attempting to mediate, the president of the employers of that industry was murdered. Besieged by petitions from Catalan industrial barons and politicians, Dato agreed, on 8 November 1920, to replace Bas with their candidate, General Severiano Martínez Anido.[59]

The second phase: Embracing a viceroy

A former colonial officer, Martínez Anido had been appointed military governor of Barcelona early in 1919 where, as Milans del Bosch's second in command, he stood out as a hardliner on questions of public order. Hence Catalan industrialists were euphoric when the post of civil governor was filled at last by someone prepared to 'give the unions a good thrashing': the FTN greeted him as the necessary person to restore tranquillity to Barcelona and the Patronal's bulletin forecast an age of social peace.[60] Martínez Anido would not disappoint them. During almost two years in office, he acted as a viceroy and, supported by General Miguel Arlegui as head of police, orchestrated an era of such terror it dwarfed the most brutal episodes of recent times. The vital difference was that now the overwhelming majority of the victims belonged to the labour movement.[61]

Before the end of his first month in office, most of the well-known union leaders had been rounded up and 36 of them imprisoned in the castle of La Mola in Mahón (Menorca). Ironically, Martínez Anido might have been telling the truth when he suggested to the assorted press that by imprisoning them he was saving their lives.[62] They could indeed consider themselves fortunate. The killing of the disabled Catalan Republican Deputy Francesc Layret, on 30 November 1920, showed that there were no limits to the onslaught. His crime was his close friendship with some labour leaders and his having raised in parliament the illegal activities of employers and officers.[63] He was not the last Republican to become the target of an assassin's bullets.[64] Hundreds of CNT militants were deported to their native provinces, making the long journey in chains and on foot. Barcelona and its industrial belt experienced scenes reminiscent of Chicago as gunmen sprayed with bullets places frequented by *Cenetistas*, and Anarchist groups engaged in street shoot-outs with Arlegui's squads or Libres' gangs.[65]

Anarchist groups still carried out some spectacular *atentados* such as the murder, on 8 March 1921, of Prime Minister Dato.[66] However, the overwhelming majority of the victims after November 1920 were *Cenetistas*. With General Arlegui in charge of public order, hired gunmen and Libres' hit squads colluded with police headquarters in the hunting of Anarcho-Syndicalists. Amongst the most infamous practices introduced was the so-called *Ley de Fugas* – the shooting of prisoners while they were allegedly trying to escape or overpower their guards.[67] Of course, the ongoing slaughter did not bring the usual apocalyptic outbursts in the conservative press or employers' circles. On the contrary, it was accepted as a necessary step to restore order. In parliament, the spokesmen for the Catalan parties linked to industrial interests insisted that Martínez Anido was irreplaceable and counted on the backing of all the 'respectable citizens' of Barcelona.[68]

The Catalan employers had nothing but praise for a civil governor whose brutal methods practically eliminated the physical presence of the CNT in Catalonia throughout 1921. Large number of workers even sought refuge in the Libres, which, at its peak in mid-1922, claimed some 175,000 members.[69] Industrialists' praise for their protector was continually sounded in official correspondence to Count Bugallal in Madrid.[70] They also attended various events in force to stress their support for the civil governor. For instance, in a glaring display of bourgeois strength, some 35,000 *Somatenistas* (including delegations from several cities) paraded, on 24 April 1921, before the cream of the business elites headed by Graupera and local authorities presided over by

Martínez Anido.[71] On 11 May, Jaume Cussó presented the civil governor with 32 albums containing 102,092 individual signatures and 253
corporate signatures (representing over 200,000 members and 83 city
halls) as a sign of their total support for him.[72] The following month the
FTN's directors even discussed a proposal to ask the king to bestow a
noble title on Martínez Anido and to make him an adoptive son of the
city as a reward for his services to the cause of order.[73]

The final phase: Desperately seeking an iron surgeon

The return to power in March 1922 of the Conservatives headed by
Dato's lieutenant, José Sánchez Guerra, initiated the final phase; the
moment during which the Catalan employers came to embrace the
idea of an authoritarian state.[74] They were dismayed by the signing of
new commercial treaties with Britain and France (in July and October
of 1922 respectively) that benefited the export-orientated production
(fruits, olive oil, wine) but dismantled a good deal of the protective
tariffs for industrial interests.[75] But what really incensed them was that
with the restoration of constitutional guarantees, on 30 March 1922,
Madrid embraced again the road of social conciliation.

A clash was bound to happen between the central administration
bent on abiding by the rule of law and Martínez Anido, who was behav-
ing as if Barcelona was his own satrapy. Aware of the staunch support
amongst the Catalan industrialists whose eulogies for the 'city saviour'
never ceased,[76] the prime minister was wary of the potential backlash
that would result if he acted against the general. The wounding of
one of the most charismatic CNT leaders, Angel Pestaña, in Manresa
(Barcelona), on 25 August 1922, followed by revelations that gunmen
were camping outside the hospital to finish him off with the connivance of the authorities, stretched Sánchez Guerra's patience to breaking
point.[77] He finally took the decision to dismiss Martínez Anido and his
chief of police in October after discovering that what initially appeared
as a thwarted attempt on the life of the civil governor was actually an
operation engineered at police headquarters to lure an Anarchist group
into a deadly trap.[78]

Catalan industrialists were livid at Madrid's 'treacherous' decision to
deprive them, yet again, of their champion against subversion. Their
displays of support for their heroes Martínez Anido and Arlegui culminated in a packed farewell reception, on 31 October, at the Hotel Ritz.[79]
Henceforth their exasperation continued to mount. To their chagrin,
the government appeared to accept reformist proposals suggested by

the Socialists. Employers perceived issues such as the regulation of the working day and compulsory social insurances as a challenge to their authority. In particular, they were incensed by suggestions of a new law for labour contracts that included giving the workforce a say in industrial management and a share of the profits. The FTN asserted, in a letter to the labour minister, that if any Socialist proposals were accepted, only God could save Spain. It also wondered why politicians were always keen on rewarding troublemakers and burdening the decent, hard-working creators of national wealth with unbearable taxation and regulations.[80]

Catalan employers could not contain their anger when, on 3 November, the government established by royal decree the workers' right of free association (*Sindicación Professional Libre*) that destroyed, in one stroke, their hopes for compulsory unionization.[81] To add insult to injury, Martínez Anido's departure cleared the path for the normal functioning of the CNT unions.[82]

The employers' nightmare was not alleviated with the return to office of a Liberal cabinet in December 1922. While the new government adhered scrupulously to state neutrality in labour conflicts, Barcelona gradually descended again into a new period of social violence. However, it was not so much the rise in the number of *atentados* they feared – after all, most victims were the result of tit for tat retaliations between the CNT and the Libres – but the threat presented by the reconstruction of union power. Their misgivings were confirmed with the outbreak of a massive transport strike in May 1923. It brought back memories of the dreaded Canadiense when, in a few days, the CNT paralysed Barcelona, while the authorities pursued a negotiated compromise instead of ordering a police crackdown.[83] Catalan employers reached the conclusion that the liberal regime was unwilling or unable to safeguard social discipline. Unlike 1919–20, they would not seek to overthrow particular administrations but the regime itself.

There were vested interests – employers, policemen, Libres – not prepared to relinquish the golden days of Martínez Anido's rule and therefore determined to prevent the reconstruction of the CNT. The murder in 1923 of many 'moderate' Anarcho-Syndicalists known for their opposition to terrorism appeared as a provocation aimed at strengthening the hands of the extremists eager to go down the road of violence.[84] In August 1923, the civil governor noted that there were agents provocateurs seeking, by all available means, to thwart any hopes of social peace in Barcelona.[85]

The international scene had also changed dramatically. The wave of political reaction gaining momentum in Europe, in particular the triumph of Italian Fascism in October 1922, provided a powerful model. Right-wing newspapers hailed Mussolini as Italy's saviour who had crushed the red subversion and done away with the redundant parliamentarian system.[86] Hard-line Catalan employers were enthused by the Fascist example. Some, like Tomás Benet, the CPE's secretary, contributed to the emergence of *La Camisa Negra* (The Black Shirt), a Madrid-based newspaper that appeared in December 1922 to broadcast the deeds of Fascism.[87]

Though encouraged by the Fascist example, employers were aware of its failure to take off in Spain. Unlike Italy, there was neither the 'revolutionary' elite to lead such a movement nor the thousands of post-war ex-combatants and officers to organize its cadres. The Mauristas were the closest street phenomenon to the Fascist *squadristi*. However, they were divided in their political approach, some embracing a reformist and Christian ideology while others, although authoritarian and nationalist, lacked the mobilizing, modernist and cross-class character of Fascism, and remained a Monarchist, Catholic and middle-class movement. Even the Sindicatos Libres, despite their plebeian character and open exaltation of violence, were overwhelmingly a Catalan phenomenon; their main international connections were with Catholic organizations in Europe, their ideological foundations came from counter-revolutionary Carlism and their activities remained in the labour arena and never ventured into the political field.[88]

However, industrialists could always turn to the military. Furthermore, following the debacle in Morocco in the summer of 1921 when some 9,000 Spanish troops were massacred, both the armed forces and the monarch were more receptive than ever to the idea of overthrowing the ruling order. In particular, they were incensed that both the Sánchez Guerra and the Liberal governments had placed the question of responsibilities for that disaster – in which king and officers were criticised – on the parliamentary agenda. Indeed, the military were furious that the politicians were shielding themselves behind traditional political manoeuvring and trying to pin the blame for the debacle on them. King Alfonso confided to Romanones that he considered it an affront to be investigated in parliament.[89]

Catalan industrialists now found a new champion in Miguel Primo de Rivera, captain general of Barcelona since March 1922. Previously in that post in Valencia, Primo de Rivera had experience of countering urban social violence and had not concealed his belief that only expeditious methods, which he doubted the constitutional regime could carry out, would crush the subversive threat. Once in Barcelona, he was furious when the government removed two *dignísimos* (very worthy) officers, Martínez Anido and Arlegui, whose philosophy he fully shared.[90]

As Canadiense had done in 1919, so the transport strike of May 1923 rallied the Catalan bourgeoisie behind Primo de Rivera. As the dispute progressed, employers contended that when the government tolerated and protected the CNT troublemakers, their only 'glimmer of hope' was the captain general.[91] On 8 June, at the funeral of Josep Franquesa, a murdered member of the Somatén, the civil governor was called the CNT representative and only escaped unhurt because none other than Primo de Rivera, loudly cheered by the crowds, ensured his safe passage to his car.[92]

Governmental impotence was revealed when it was the civil governor who lost his post after being summoned, together with the captain general, to Madrid for consultations. Delighted industrialists packed the train station to welcome Primo de Rivera back to Barcelona.[93] As in 1919, the seditious alliance between army and employers now went on the offensive. Vain and ambitious, Primo de Rivera was courted, fêted and encouraged by the powerful barons of Catalan capitalism to become Spain's 'iron surgeon'.

With troops and Somatén ensuring the return of a normal transport service on 12 July, a workers' delegation visited the new civil governor, Manuel Portela Valladares, to announce an end to a strike that had lasted over two months.[94] Still, the CNT's combative rhetoric remained and Spain, let alone Barcelona, was plagued by daring raids and hold-ups.[95] With momentum on their side, captain general and industrialists now sought to overthrow the existing regime as the prerequisite to crush the revolutionary threat once and for all. In Málaga, a mutiny of troops about to embark for Morocco in late August, and separatist incidents in Barcelona on 11 September, dispelled any lingering doubts.

Despite all the populist rhetoric, the *coup d'état* had a clear class component. It was hatched in Barcelona and fulfilled the Catalan employers' expectations after years of growing separation from – if not rejection of – the ruling order. On the key night of 12–13 September, leading Catalan tycoons (Count Guell, Alfonso Sala, Jaume Cussó, the Marquis of Comillas, Domingo Sert, Felix Graupera, etc.) stood side by side with the captain general. The next morning, when Primo de Rivera somehow found the time to attend the opening of a furniture exhibition, the cream of Catalan capitalism turned up to cheer. That day, the Somatén remained fully armed in the streets and the local chambers of industry and commerce and the Patronal expressed their enthusiastic support for the insurrection.[96] But none other than the FNT, the doyen of Catalan capitalism, best expressed the identification of the Catalan business elites with the praetorian revolt. Its board of directors endorsed unanimously its president's decision to remain with the captain general during the crucial night of the coup. They stated that the preservation of social order was worth the liquidation of civil liberties and stressed that Primo de Rivera should not make the mistake of restoring constitutional practices before undertaking the regeneration of Spain. But, of course, as they noted in their sycophantic letter of support for the coup, Primo de Rivera was not seen as a seditious general but as a God-given saviour:

> With our righteousness and our rights swamped by this stinking ocean of ruins, concupiscence and sarcasm, we come to purify ourselves and feed our souls in the magnificent light which emanates from the programme of government devised by Your Excellency [General Primo de Rivera]…which – by Divine Providence – coincides brilliantly with our patriotic feelings.[97]

Notes

I would like to thank Angel Smith for his comments on earlier drafts.

1. The manifesto can be found in *La Correspondencia de España* (13 September 1923). The coup's code is in Biblioteca de la Real Academia de la Historia (hereafter BRAH), *Archivo Santiago Alba* (hereafter ASA), Leg. 9/8077–13 (4/51–2), Colonel Agustín Robles's narrative.
2. Angel Ossorio, *Barcelona* (Madrid: Ricardo Rojas, 1910), pp. 13–14.
3. Ignacio Bernis, *Consecuencias económicas de la guerra* (Madrid: Estanislao Maestre, 1923), pp. 95–6.
4. Pedro Gual Villalbi, *Memorias de un industrial de nuestro tiempo* (Barcelona: Sociedad General de Publicaciones, 1923), pp. 104–21; Joaquín M. Nadal, *Memòries*, 2nd edn (Barcelona: Aedos, 1965), pp. 256–7; Antoni Jutglar, *Historia crítica de la burguesía en Cataluña* (Barcelona: Anthropos, 1984), pp. 365–82.
5. The average annual immigration for 1900–10, of 3,400 people, increased during the following decade to 20,000 per annum. Albert Balcells, *El Sindicalisme a Barcelona, 1916–23* (Barcelona: Nova Terra, 1965), p. 11; José Luis Martín Ramos, 'Anàlisi del movement vaguístic a Barcelona, 1914–23', *Recerques*, 20 (1988), pp. 94–7; Chris Ealham, 'Class and the City: Spatial Memories of Pleasure and Danger in Barcelona, 1914–23', *Oral History*, 29/1 (Spring 2001), pp. 39–40.
6. Pere Gabriel, 'Red Barcelona in the Europe of War and Revolution', in Angel Smith (ed.), *Red Barcelona: Social Protest and Labour Mobilization in the Twentieth*

Century (London: Routledge, 2002), pp. 46–53; Ealham, 'Class and the City', pp. 41–2.

7. Confederación Regional del Trabajo, *Memoria del Congreso celebrado en Barcelona los días 28, 29, 30 de Junio y el 1 de Julio de 1918* (Barcelona: CRT, 1918), pp. 17–20, 77–9. The Anarcho-Syndicalist mouthpiece, *Solidaridad Obrera* (2 July 1918), noted that the proletariat now possessed the instrument to succeed in the class struggle.

8. Contemporary authors noted that the first organized *atentado*, that is, one that was not the product of random or sporadic violence, was the killing of the foreman Lorenzo Casas on 3 August 1916. See Jose María Farré Moregó, *Los atentados sociales en España* (Madrid: Artes Gráficas, 1922), p. 111; Ramón Rucabado, *Entorn del sindicalisme* (Barcelona: Políglota, 1925), p. 181; and works by Angel Pestaña, *Lo que aprendí en la vida*, 2 vols. (Murcia: Zero, 1971), 1, p. 75 and 2, p. 64 and *Terrorismo en Barcelona* (*Memorias Inéditas*), in Javier Tusell and Genoveva Queipo de Llano (eds) (Barcelona: Planeta, 1979), p. 100. For recent analyses of terrorism see Eduardo González Calleja, *El Máuser y el sufragio: Orden público, subversion y violencia política en la crisis de la Restauración, 1917–1931* (Madrid: CSIC, 1999), pp. 116–22, 227–8; Angel Smith, *Anarchism, Revolution and Reaction: Catalan Labour and the Crisis of the Spanish State, 1898–1923* (Oxford: Berghahn, 2007), 250–3; Francisco J. Romero Salvadó, *Foundations of Civil War: Revolution, Social Conflict and Reaction in Liberal Spain, 1916–1923* (London: Routledge, 2008), pp. 139–43; Eduardo González Calleja and Fernando del Rey, 'Violència política i pistolerisme a la Catalunya de la primera postguerra mundial. Propostes d'anàlisi', *L'Avenç*, 192 (May 1995), pp. 34–41; Albert Balcells, 'Violencia y terrorismo en la lucha de clases en Barcelona de 1913 a 1923', *Estudios de Historia Social*, 42–3 (July–December 1987), pp. 37–79.

9. See, for instance, the attacks on enterprises partially or totally owned by French businesses in *Archivo del Ministerio de Asuntos Exteriores* (hereafter AMAE), H 2789. The collusion between Anarchists and the German spy network is recognized in Pestaña, *Terrorismo*, pp. 84–96; Emili Salut, *Vivers de Revolucionaris* (Barcelona: Catalònia, 1938), p. 149. For further discussion of the subject see Francisco J. Romero Salvadó, *Spain 1914–18: Between War and Revolution* (London: Routledge, 1999), pp. 166–7.

10. BRAH, *Archivo Conde de Romanones* (hereafter AR), Leg. 10, Exp. 6, Romanones believed that Catalan aspirations should not be met with stern opposition but brought within the framework of the law. The model he had in mind was the English Home Rule Bill for Ireland of March 1914. AR, Leg. 12, Exp. 31: the government urged the civil governor of Barcelona to avoid taking measures that could be interpreted as provocation in Catalanist quarters (December 1918–January 1919); Officers' anger is in AR, Leg. 20, Exp. 18 (January 1919).

11. Instructions to the civil governor to take measures against the CNT can be found in Archivo Histórico Nacional, *Serie A Gobernación* (hereafter AHN), Leg. 42 A, Exp. 3, (7 January 1919); and AR, Leg. 12, Exp. 31 (16 January 1919). For the CNT's neutrality in the autonomist issue see the editorial entitled *'Ni con unos ni otros'* (Neither one nor the other) in *Solidaridad Obrera* (16 December 1918).

12. The main events of the *Canadiense* strike can be followed in AHN, Leg. 57 A, Exp. 10. See also Balcells, *El sindicalisme*, pp. 73–82. The influential newspaper *El Sol* (18 March 1919) described the outcome as the victory of the only organized power in Spain. The CNT's victory is also underlined by the British ambassador (Sir Arthur Hardinge) in The National Archives, *Foreign Office Papers* (hereafter FO) 371–4120/35,476 (18 March 1919).
13. Gual Villalbi, *op.cit.*, pp. 165–70. *Memorias.*
14. Archivo del Foment del Treball Nacional (hereafter AFTN), *Memoria de la Junta Directiva del Foment del Treball Nacional correspondiente a 1919–1920* (Barcelona: Hijos de Domingo Casanova, 1920), p. 19.
15. AFTN, *Memoria 1919–1920*, p. 22; AFTN, *Actas*, 13 (9 April 1919), p. 299. Local conservative newspapers such as *El Correo Catalán* (22–3 February 1919) and *La Veu de Catalunya* (11 and 13 March 1919) also argued that the Catalans had been abandoned by the government. The Catholic mouthpiece, *El Debate* (8 and 12 March 1919), called it an unprecedented capitulation of power.
16. AFTN, *Federación Patronal de Cataluña: Memoria de los trabajos realizados en su primer periodo activo* (hereafter *Patronal*), p. 28.
17. Ibid., pp. 4–5.
18. Archivo del Gobierno Civil de Barcelona (hereafter AGCB), *Asociaciones*, no. 366, Exp. 9722, Statutes of the Federación Patronal de Barcelona registered in the Civil Government (14 March 1919) and of the Federación Patronal de Cataluña (31 July 1920). AFTN, *Patronal*, pp. 6–7. See also Fernando del Rey, *Propietarios y patronos: la política de las organizaciones económicas en la España de la Restauración, 1914–23* (Madrid: Ministerio del Trabajo y Seguridad Social, 1992), pp. 107, 110–31; Magda Sellés i Quintana, *El Foment del Treball Nacional, 1914–1923* (Barcelona: Publicacions de l'Abadia de Montserrat, 2000), pp. 285–9; Soledad Bengoechea, *Organització Patronal i conflictivitat social a Catalunya* (Barcelona: l'Abadia de Montserrat, 1994), pp. 154–65, 192–5. Briefer analyses are in works by Bengoechea: 'Los sindicatos patronales en Catalunya: dispersión y unidad', *Historia Social*, 32 (1998), pp. 41–8 and 'Los hombres de la Patronal a principios del Siglo XX: Luis Ferrer-Vidal, José Sabadell y Félix Graupera', *Historia Social*, 48 (2004), pp. 76–82.
19. Sellés (*El Foment*, pp. 273, 279–80, 312–3) emphasizes the competition between the Patronal and the FTN for hegemony amongst Catalan employers. Rey (*Propietarios*, pp. 137, 163–5) suggests there was a certain rivalry between the Patronal and a less intransigent FTN. Rey also argues that the FTN had to accept the leadership of the Patronal in the class struggle as a necessary fait accompli. Bengoechea (*Organització*, pp. 27, 98–101, 212–13, 238, 243; and 'Los hombres', p. 73) puts forward a different view: the FTN and the Patronal complemented each other rather than competed. The FTN focused more on high politics and commercial objectives, while the Patronal constituted the shock troops of the employers' resistance. Evidence in FTN's archives appears to bear out Bengoechea's views: for instance, FTN's support for the Patronal's hard-line strategy and its description of the Patronal can be seen in AFTN, *Memoria 1919–20*, pp. 44–6. Bengoechea's ideas are sustained in Angel Smith, 'The Catalan Counter-Revolutionary Coalition and the Primo de Rivera Coup, 1917–23', in *European History Quarterly*, 37/1, 2007, pp. 14–15 and Romero Salvadó, *Foundations of Civil War*, p. 194.

20. Soledad Bengoechea, *El Locaut de Barcelona* (Barcelona: Curial, 1998), pp. 40–1, 65. On *sindicación forzosa* see Smith, 'The Catalan Counter-Revolutionary', pp. 15–16; and Fidel Gómez Ochoa, 'El partido conservador y el problema social durante la crisis final de la Restauración: la sindicación profesional y obligatoria', in Javier Tusell, Julio Gil Pecharromán and Feliciano Montero (eds), *Estudios sobre la derecha española* (Madrid: UNED, 1993), pp. 274–5.
21. See works by Bengoechea, *El Locaut*, pp. 52–3 and '1919: La Barcelona colpista; L'aliança de patrons i militars contra el sistema liberal', *Afers*, 23–4 (1996), p. 311.
22. For the birth of the Somatén of Barcelona see *El Debate* (16 January 1919). Examples of the establishment of the Somatén in other cities are in AHN, Leg. 59 A, Exp. 9.
23. A thorough analysis of the Somatén as a bourgeois militia in the context of Europe's post-war social polarization is in Eduardo González Calleja and Fernando del Rey, *La defensa armada contra la revolución* (Madrid: CSIC, 1995), pp. 16–21, 71–9, 91–6. See also Charles S. Maier, *Recasting Bourgeois Europe: Stabilization in France, Germany and Italy in the Decade after World War I* (Princeton, NJ: Princeton University Press, 1988), p. 8; and Romero Salvadó, *Foundations of Civil War*, pp. 187–8.
24. For the farcical trial and then release of Bravo Portillo see Benito Márquez and José M. Capó, *Las juntas militares de defensa* (La Habana: Porvenir, 1923), pp. 255–68; AHN, Leg. 41 A, Exp. 19 (16 December 1918); *El Sol* (7–8 December 1918); *El País* (10 December 1918); *Solidaridad Obrera* (10–11 December 1918). On links between Bravo Portillo and the employers see Manuel Burgos y Mazo, *El verano de 1919 en Gobernación* (Cuenca: Tipos, 1921), pp. 595–6; and Bengoechea, *Organització*, pp. 208–11. On the delinquent character of Bravo Portillo's parallel police see González Calleja, *El Máuser y el sufragio*, pp. 126–7, 146; Francisco Madrid, *Ocho meses y un día en el Gobierno Civil de Barcelona* (Barcelona: La Flecha, 1932), pp. 58–60.
25. Pere Foix, *Los archivos del terrorismo blanco* (Madrid: La Piqueta, 1978), pp. 31, 49–53, 57, 82. For FTN's involvement in the *Fichero Lasarte* see AFTN, *Actas*, 15 (14 September and 6 October 1922), pp. 77–9.
26. There were, naturally, radically different obituaries. For the Republican newspaper *España Nueva* (19 September 1919) acting as the CNT's mouthpiece while *Solidaridad Obrera* was closed down, Bravo Portillo, a thug who maintained several lovers out of the fortune he had made from his spying activities and the persecution of workers, had been 'executed' by the collective hatred of the proletariat. By contrast, conservative newspapers such as *La Acción* (7 September 1919) and *El Debate* (7–8 September 1919) considered him to be a martyr who had been risking his life daily in order to bring peace back to Barcelona. The satisfaction produced by his death in proletarian quarters can be found, for instance, in Mauro Bajatierra, *¿Quiénes mataron a Dato?* (Barcelona: Jasón, 1931), pp. 144–6; Manuel Buenacasa, *El movimiento obrero español, 1886–1926* (Gijón: Júcar, 1977), p. 55; and Adolfo Bueso, *Recuerdos de un cenetista* (Barcelona: Seix i Barral, 1976), pp. 126–8.
27. The official account of the shady activities of Koening and his expulsion from Spain can be found in AHN, Leg. 34 A, Exp. 3, no. 19. The gang's deeds were exposed in *España Nueva* (14–15, 24 May 1920); and *El Heraldo de Madrid* (1 June 1920). See also González Calleja, *El Máuser y el sufragio*,

pp. 146–7, 152–9, 165; Jordi Ventura, 'La personalitat veritable del Baró de König', *Serra D'or* (September 1970), pp. 82–4; León Ignacio, *Los años del pistolerismo* (Madrid: Planeta, 1981), pp. 86–8; Madrid, *Ocho meses*, pp. 53–6, 60–7; and Burgos y Mazo, *El verano de 1919*, pp. 591–2, 597, 600–13.

28. For the registry of the statutes of the Sindicato Libre in the Civil Government see AGCB, *Asociaciones*, no. 380, Exp. 10,323 (11 December 1919). For the military input in the creation of the Libres see Bengoechea, *El Locaut*, pp. 47–8; and Soledad Bengoechea and Fernando del Rey, 'Militars, patrons i Sindicalistes Lliures', *L'Avenç*, 166 (January 1993), p. 12. See also Feliciano Baratech Alfaro, *Los Sindicatos Libres de España* (Barcelona: Cortel, 1927), pp. 65–73; Antonio Elorza, 'Los Sindicatos Libres en España: teorías y programas', *Revista de Trabajo*, 35–6 (1971), pp. 154–8; Colin M. Winston, *Workers and the Right in Spain, 1900–1936* (Princeton, NJ: Princeton University Press, 1985), pp. 111–12.

29. Antonio Gramsci, 'On Fascism, 1921', in David Beetham (ed.), *Marxists in the Face of Fascism* (Manchester: Manchester University Press, 1983), pp. 82–3.

30. According to Fernando Soldevilla, *El año político 1919* (Madrid: Julio Cosano, 1920), p. 96, there were 11 workers held by the military. See also Conde Romanones, *Notas de una vida, 1912–1931* (Madrid: Marcial Pons, 1999 [1947]), p. 434.

31. AFTN, *Actas*, 13 (1 April 1919), pp. 278–9.

32. Bernardo Pla y Armengol, *Impresiones de la Huelga General de Barcelona del 24 marzo-7 abril 1919* (Barcelona: n.p., 1930), pp. 13–96.

33. AFTN, *Actas*, 13 (9 April 1919), pp. 293–5.

34. Industrialists noted that private enterprises already had systems to look after the welfare of their employees. Besides, if workers could afford to pay their union dues, they should also contribute more to their own pensions. Opposition to the government initiatives and accusations of the latter's 'partiality' can be seen in AFTN, *Memoria 1919–20*, pp. 22–3, 34–6.

35. *La Correspondencia Militar* (17 April 1919) called the accusation that the army had expelled the civil governor of Barcelona slanderous. Yet, evidence that the local garrison was bent on crushing the CNT and in the process overthrowing the government in Madrid is overwhelming. See Doval's interview in *El Sol* (1 August 1919); Fundación Antonio Maura, *Archivo Antonio Maura* (hereafter AAM), Leg. 219, Carp. 16: account of the forced departure of Montañés and Doval by Count Figols (15 April 1919); BRAH, *Archivo Eduardo Dato* (hereafter AED), Leg. 83: Milans del Bosch's first resignation due to his opposition to the government's lenient strategy (19 March 1919); Montañés's critical radiogram of the repressive measures endorsed by the captain general (8 April 1919); Milans del Bosch's second resignation in which he stressed his total support for Bravo Portillo (9 April 1919); Milans del Bosch's version of the 'courtesy visit' paid by Martínez Anido to find out when the civil governor was leaving (undated); AR: Leg. 20, Exp. 5, Transcripts of telephonic conferences between Milans del Bosch and the war minister (8, 9 and 14 April 1919); Leg. 96, Exp. 38, Letter from secretary of the Patronal, José Palleja, backing wholeheartedly the continuity of Bravo Portillo (April 1919); Exp. 60, Doval's report of his incompatibility with the methods carried out by Bravo Portillo (8 April 1919).

36. AFTN, *Actas*, 13 (29 April 1919), pp. 312–13. Other industrialists' greetings, including from the Patronal, can be seen in AAM, Leg. 221, Carp. 4 (15–16 April 1919).
37. The faction led by Maura doubled its representation but its remaining in office was dependent on the goodwill of the Conservatives. When the latter withdrew their support, they were accused of treason by right-wing newspapers such as *El Debate* (19–20 July 1919) and *La Acción* (19–20 July 1919). The FTN (*Memoria 1919–20*, p. 37) described the fall of Maura as being blown by a parliamentarian hurricane. Similar reaction by other industrialists and members of the Somatén can be found in AAM, Leg. 219, Carp. 11 (22–3 July 1919).
38. *La Correspondencia Militar* (9 October 1920).
39. Burgos y Mazo, *El verano de 1919*, p. 467.
40. Amado's negotiations with imprisoned union leaders were reported in *El Diluvio* (27 August 1919). He explained his plans in an interview in *La Publicidad* (13 September 1919).
41. *La Publicidad* (3 and 11 September, 12 October 1919).
42. Confederación Patronal Española, *Memoria General del II Congreso del 20 al 26 de Octubre de 1919* (Barcelona: Elzeviriana, 1919). Graupera's recognition that the objective of the lockout was to force the workers to abandon their unions is in AHN, Leg. 45 A (13 December 1919). *El Imparcial* (28 October 1919) noted that the manoeuvre that brought down the Romanones administration was being tried again. *Cenetistas* such as Simó Piera suggested that the Patronal's real objective was to overthrow the government: Joaquim Ferrer, *Simó Piera: Perfil d'un sindicalista. Records i experiencies d'un dirigent de la CNT* (Barcelona: Portic, 1975), p. 168. See also Rey, *Propietarios*, pp. 136–7; and Bengoechea, *El Locaut*, pp. 19, 68–9, 103–5. The employers' visit to Milans del Bosch is in *El Socialista* (30 October 1919).
43. AHN, Leg. 45 A, Exp. 13, Amado's impressions (3 November 1919); Burgos y Mazo, *El verano de 1919*, pp. 451–2.
44. For ample evidence of the employers' stance see AHN Leg. 45 A, Exp. 13 (titled *Federación Patronal*, October–December 1919). *Solidaridad Obrera* (22 November 1919) wondered why workers were arrested during social conflicts and not the industrialists when engaged in a lockout. See also Burgos y Mazo, *El verano de 1919*, pp. 516–23; and Sellés, *El Foment*, pp. 291–4.
45. AHN, Leg. 45 A, Exp. 13, Graupera's position (22–3 November 1920). See also Burgos y Mazo, *El verano de 1919*, pp. 526–41.
46. The FTN's support for the lockout is in AFTN, *Memoria 1919–20*, pp. 44–5; and *Actas*, 14 (6 December 1919), p. 25. *Archivo del Palacio Real*, Sec. 15,601, Exp. 6, Milans del Bosch to the king's secretary (29 November and 7 December 1919); ASA, Leg. 9/8082, 9/115–2, King's sympathy for the Patronal's hardline approach (21 October 1919). AGCB, Arch. 269, Reports on unemployment (November 1919–January 1920). See also Bengoechea, *El Locaut*, pp. 104–5, 112–13 and '1919', pp. 320–1.
47. AFTN, *Boletín de la Federación Patronal de Barcelona* (23 and 29 December 1919).
48. The final blow came with further army defiance: court-martialling and expelling some students of the Military School despite the government's instructions.

49. Pestaña (*Lo que aprendí*, 2, pp. 82–3) recognized the increased power of the diehards following the lockout.
50. AGCB, Arch. 269, Police reports of incidents in Barcelona during the lockout (December 1919–January 1920). For reactions to the *atentado* on Graupera see *El ABC* (6–7 January 1920); *El Correo Catalán* (7–9 January 1920). On the Koening gang see Manel Aisa i Pampols, *L'efervescència social dels anys 20* (Barcelona: AEP, 1999), pp. 20–2; Madrid, *Ocho meses*, pp. 74–7.
51. A master of the political game, Romanones saw his chance to get even when, on 5 February 1920, a right-wing senator, Count Limpias, in order to defend Milans del Bosch revealed some private letters. Romanones who had a minister in the cabinet asked the government to oust Milans del Bosch or he would withdraw his parliamentary support. On 10 February, Milans del Bosch announced his resignation on the grounds of ill-health.
52. The rebellious mood of employers and officers can be found in AR, Leg. 96, Exp. 38 (14 February 1920). For the industrialists' anger see AGCB, Arch. 269 (6 February 1920). The letter to the monarch is in AFTN, *Actas*, 14 (11 February 1920), pp. 77–81 See also FO 371–4121/20, Report from British Consul in Barcelona Arthur L. Rowley (12 February 1920). *El Debate* (11–12 February 1920) called it a sad day when an honourable officer was sacrificed to satisfy the rancour of a failed politician like Romanones.
53. For the tense situation and royal hesitations see the diaries of Natalio Rivas, then minister of education in the government: BRAH, *Archivo Natalio Rivas* (hereafter ANR), Leg. 11–8910 (February 1920). For Weyler's assurances see AFTN, *Actas*, 14 (3 March 1920), pp. 106–7.
54. AMAE, *Manuel Allendesalazar's Papers*, mail from Milans del Bosch (December 1919–January 1920); AGCB, Arch. 269–70, Reports of arrests including the Republican lawyers (José Puig de Asprer, Rafael Guerra del Río and José Ulled) and conditions aboard the warships (January 1920).
55. AGCB, *Asociaciones*, no. 366, Exp. 9722 (25 January 1920).
56. To the dismay of the Catalan industrial elites, Bas sought to create the right atmosphere for workers and employers to engage in negotiations. He ordered the release of jailed militants and allowed the unions to return to their normal activities.
57. For examples of clashes between *Cenetistas* and Libres see *La Publicidad* (8, 11, 17, 19 October 1920); and *El Correo Catalán* (27 October, 5–6 November 1920). See also the Consul's Rowley Report in FO 371–5493/44 (23 September 1920).
58. After his open carriage was ambushed by a group of assailants, Salvatierra and his sister-in-law were killed and his wife was gravely wounded. For a detailed narrative see *El Mercantil Valenciano* (4 September 1920). Regarding demands for repressive measures see *El ABC* (5 August 1920); and *La Epoca* (6 and 10 August 1920). For mail from the FTN to Dato demanding harsh measures see AFTN, *Actas*, 14 (5 and 8 August 1920), pp. 206–9; and for the prime minister's reply promising to carry these out see AFTN, *Correspondencia* (13 August 1920).
59. For the industrialists' opposition to Bas see AFTN, *Patronal*, p. 5; and *Correspondencia* (2 and 6 November 1920). See also *La Veu de Catalunya* (30 October, 2–6 November 1920); and *El Correo Catalán* (4–7 November 1920). Dato's close friend Piedad Iturbe, the Princess of Hohenlohe – whose famil-

iarity extended to her calling him *tío Eduardo* (uncle Eduardo) –, acted as go-between with Francesc Cambó, the leader of the Lliga Regionalista, a party that championed the interests of the Catalan industrial bourgeoisie. She urged him – 'for God, Spain and the lives of many Spaniards!' – to act promptly and appoint a new civil governor. When Dato enquired whom he should nominate, she replied that Cambó had put forward the name of Martínez Anido. See Pilar Iturbe, *Erase una vez* (Madrid: Industrias Gráficas y Seix Barral, 1954), pp. 263–4; AED, Iturbe to Dato (mail undated but probably written in October and November 1920). They were first cited in Carlos Seco Serrano, 'El último gobierno de Eduardo Dato', in Carlos Seco Serrano (ed.), *Estudios sobre el reinado de Alfonso XIII* (Madrid: Real Academia de la Historia, 1998), pp. 204–6.

60. AFTN, *Patronal*, p. 22; *Correspondencia*, the FTN to Martínez Anido (10 November 1920); and *Actas*, 14 (22 December 1920), p. 265.

61. An account of the bloodbath that followed the appointment of Martínez Anido as civil governor of Barcelona can be found in Romero Salvadó, *Foundations of Civil War*, pp. 225–32.

62. *El Sol* (1 December 1920).

63. In August 1919, Layret denounced the impotence of past administrations to prevent Milans del Bosch and his industrialist allies from subverting constitutional legality. Henceforth he became a vociferous critic of the role played by the military in Barcelona. See Joaquim Ferrer, *Layret, 1880–1920* (Barcelona: Nova Terra, 1971), pp. 189–92, 208–10.

64. On 14 April 1921, one Republican lawyer, José Lastra, was shot dead at his home, while a further *atentado* the same day left another lawyer, José Ulled, injured and his assistant dead. See *España Nueva* (16 April 1921).

65. AGCB, Arch. 269, Report of incidents (November 1920–June 1921).

66. Dato was shot dead while travelling home by car after a session in parliament. The killers had arrived from Barcelona and belonged to an action group linked to the Catalan metallurgical sector. Pedro Mateu was arrested a few days later. The other two members of the hit squad, Ramón Casanellas and Luis Nicolau, managed to flee the capital. Casanellas eventually reached the Soviet Union and became an officer in its air force. Traced to Berlin, Nicolau was captured together with his girlfriend, Lucía Joaquina Concepción, by the German police. See Juan Jaime Montón de Lama, 'Los asesinos de Dato', *Historia* 16/178 (February 1991), pp. 31–8.

67. In fact the *Ley de Fugas* was used for the first time in June 1920 in Valencia when three prisoners were 'executed' by the Civil Guards escorting them. In AHN, Leg. 39 A, Exp. 3 (Valencia), the civil governor backed the version given by the Civil Guards, even though the third prisoner had not been shot but beaten to death by rifle butts (22 June 1920).

68. *La Publicidad* (11–12 February 1921).

69. The Libres were not exactly a creation of the industrialists but their links with the military (and since November 1920, the police) were very close. Martínez Anido himself became the honorary chairman of one of the strongest Libres' unions, that of the cooks and waiters, and the official biography of the organization written by Feliciano Baratech was dedicated to him. The press attaché at the British Embassy, Mr Deakin, categorized the Libres as a police organization, see FO 371–7119/180, Weekly Report

(19 January 1921). For the expansion of the Libres see AGCB, *Asociaciones*, nos. 401–2, 404–8, 414–16 (1921–2).

70. AHN, Leg. 37 A, Exp. 1, amongst others, one can find letters from the Chamber of Industry and Commerce of Barcelona and neighbouring towns, Asociación Textil de Gracia, Asociación de Industriales Textiles de Hospitalet, Círculo Nacional de Industria, Federación Textil de Cataluña, etc. (March–April 1921).

71. *La Correspondencia Militar* (25 April 1921).

72. AFTN, *Actas*, 14 (11 May 1921), p. 283; and *El Trabajo Nacional* (May 1921).

73. AFTN, *Actas*, 14 (3 June 1921), p. 294.

74. Following Dato's murder, Spain was ruled first by a Monarchist coalition led by Allendesalazar (March–August 1921) and then by Maura (August 1921–March 1922).

75. AFTN, *Memoria de la junta directiva del Foment del Treball Nacional correspondiente al ejercicio de 1922* (Barcelona: Tipografía Hijos Domingo Casanova, 1923), pp. 9–13; Rey, *Propietarios*, p. 245; Sellés, *El Foment*, pp. 174–8.

76. AFTN, *Actas*, 15 (11 August and 14 September 1922), pp. 63–6, 76; *El Trabajo Nacional* (August 1922).

77. *El Liberal de Bilbao* (28 August 1922). Martínez Anido was incensed when told by the interior minister, Vicente Piniés, that he had to report daily on Pestaña's state of health. See Juan Oller Piñol, *Martínez Anido* (Madrid: Victoriano Suárez, 1943), pp. 131–3.

78. The police operation degenerated into a battle through the streets of Barcelona. Three Anarchists as well as one policeman who had acted as agent provocateur were killed. The police then seized from his house a remaining member of the Anarchist group, Amalio Cerdeño, shot him and left him for dead. However, he survived a few hours and while dying in hospital gave a statement of the facts to a judge who promptly informed Madrid. Furious at this blatant case of *Ley de Fugas*, Sánchez Guerra dismissed over the phone Martínez Anido and Arlegui. See Joan Manent i Pesas, *Records d'un Sindicalista Llibertari Catalá, 1916–1943* (Paris: Catalanes de París, 1976), pp. 72, 75, 79–99; Ignacio, *Los años*, pp. 238–45.

79. Oller Piñol, *Martínez Anido*, p. 166.

80. For opposition to reforms see AFTN, *Memoria 1922*, pp. 33, 37–9, 55–6; and *Memoria de la Junta Directiva del Foment del Treball Nacional correspondiente a 1923–24* (Barcelona: Tipografía Hijos Domingo Casanova, 1924), pp. 10–17. The FTN's letter can be found in AFTN, *Actas*, 15 (24 November 1922), pp. 94–9. See also Angeles Barrio Alonso, 'El sueño de la democracia industrial', in Manuel Suárez Cortina (ed.), *La Restauración, entre el liberalismo y la democracia* (Madrid: Alianza, 1997), pp. 313–14.

81. AFTN, *Memoria 1922*, pp. 49–50; Gómez Ochoa, 'El partido conservador', pp. 286–7.

82. The legalisation of several unions is in AGCB, *Asociaciones*, nos. 420–2 (November 1922).

83. Bengoechea, *Organització*, p. 270.

84. *Solidaridad Obrera* (6 March 1923) condemned terrorism but added that the *Cenetistas* would not remain passive while they were being hunted down. Four days later, the most charismatic Catalan labour leader, Salvador Seguí, was assassinated. Newspapers close to the regime, such as *La Libertad*

(11 March 1923) and *El Heraldo de Madrid* (12 March 1923), suggested that the idea was to provoke the CNT into retaliation. See also Pestaña, *Terrorismo*, pp. 148–51.

85. AHN, Leg. 58 A, Exp. 13 (24 August 1923).
86. See for instance *El Correo Catalán* (31 October 1922); *El Debate* (26 November 1922, 20 July 1923); *El ABC* (16 March 1923); *La Acción* (30 October 1922, 12 January, 13 June and 29 July 1923).
87. Soledad Bengoechea and Fernando del Rey, 'En vísperas de un golpe de estado. Radicalización patronal e imagen del fascismo en España', in Tusell et al., *Estudios*, pp. 301–23.
88. For the failure of Fascism to take off in Spain see Javier Tusell, *La política y los politicos en los tiempos de Alfonso XIII* (Barcelona: Planeta, 1976), pp. 93–4; Stanley Payne, *Fascism in Spain, 1923–1977* (Madison: University of Wisconsin Press, 1999), pp. 19–23. For the Libres, see Winston, *Workers*, pp. 157–61.
89. For royal frustration revealed in cabinet councils see ANR, Leg. 11–8909 (5–7, 12 February and 11–12 March 1923). According to Romanones (*Notas de una vida*, p. 465), the king described it as an 'affront'.
90. Primo de Rivera's support for the *Ley de Fugas* can be seen in AED, Primo de Rivera to Dato (22 and 26 January 1921). For his sorrow at losing two *dignísimos* officers see *El Correo Catalán* (28 October 1922); and Oller Piñol, *Martínez Anido*, pp. 164–6.
91. AFTN, *Memoria 1923–24*, p. 54.
92. AHN, Leg. 58 A, Exp. 13 (9 June 1923); *El Correo Catalán* (10 June 1923).
93. AFTN, *Actas*, . 15 (22 June 1923), pp. 187–8. Javier Tusell, *Radiografía de un golpe de estado: El ascenso al poder del General Primo de Rivera* (Madrid: Alianza, 1987), pp. 80–1.
94. *La Veu de Catalunya* (13 July 1923).
95. *Solidaridad Obrera* (14 July 1923) told employers to enjoy their victory since the transport strike had only been the first battle in a long war. Pestaña (*Lo que aprendí*, 1, pp. 88–90 and *Terrorismo*, pp. 183–95) recognized that some activists resorted to stealing to raise funds quickly. Examples of armed robberies in the summer of 1923: hold-ups at the Hotel Ritz (1 July), the Bank Padrós in Manresa (19 July), a tax collection agency (9 August), the Bank of Gijón (1 September), etc.
96. A succinct but very thorough analysis of the links between industrialists and the coup can be found in Fernando del Rey, 'El Capitalismo Catalán y Primo de Rivera: En torno a un golpe de estado', *Hispania*, XLVIII/168 (January–April 1988), pp. 294–307. See also Rey, *Propietarios*, pp. 848–50; González Calleja and Rey, *La defensa armada*, pp. 160–3. Bengoechea, *Organització*, pp. 266, 279–83; Sellés, *El Foment*, pp. 360–2.
97. For the FTN's stance see AFTN, *Memoria 1923–24*, pp. 63–7; *El Trabajo Nacional* (14 September 1923); *Actas*, 15 (26 October 1923), p. 200; and *Correspondencia* (15 September and 1 October 1923).

8
Nation and Reaction: Spanish Conservative Nationalism and the Restoration Crisis

Alejandro Quiroga

On 11 September 1923, Catalan, Basque and Galician nationalists gathered in Barcelona to commemorate Catalonia's national day and demand home rule for their regions. During the course of the demonstration some chanted slogans against Spain and in favour of the Rifean rebels in Morocco, which led to violent clashes with Spanish nationalists and police forces. The street battle ended with 30 people injured. The events left the military officers of the Barcelona garrison fuming. For most of them this was the last straw of an escalating provocative offensive by separatists determined to destroy the Spanish nation. Noticing the high level of indignation among his colleagues, Captain General Miguel Primo de Rivera, who had been plotting against the constitutional government for months, decided to bring forward the date of the coup (originally scheduled for 15 September). On the night of 12–13 September Primo de Rivera declared martial law in Catalonia, told the king about the insurrection, asked other captain generals for support and launched his manifesto. In Madrid, a group of generals who had also been plotting against the government formed a provisional junta. On 14 September, Alfonso XIII returned from his holidays in San Sebastian, stated his support for the coup, dismissed the constitutional government and invited the Captain General of Catalonia to come to the Spanish capital. The following morning Primo de Rivera arrived in Madrid. After a brief meeting, the king named him head of a Military Directory with executive and legislative powers and dissolved parliament. The coup had succeeded.[1]

In his manifesto to the nation, the Captain General of Catalonia justified his action against the constitutional government as the only way to save 'the Fatherland from a dishonourable end'.[2] In his view, trade unionists, Catalan and Basque nationalists and incompetent civilian politicians had constantly threatened the *patria* since Spain had lost the remnants of its empire to the USA in 1898. After a quarter of a century of continuous disasters and decadence, Primo de Rivera stated, the army had to intervene to avoid national disintegration. The unmistakable nationalist nature of the manifesto reflected the growing importance that Spanish patriotism had gained in the discourse of a variety of groups of the Right during the last years of the Restoration. Since the beginning of the 20th century, such groups had elaborated a new nationalist discourse, as a response to the rapid and accelerating process of modernization that Spain was undergoing. As the political crisis of the Restoration deepened after the end of the First World War, the nationalist and apocalyptic tones of the Right increased and many of its jingoist ideas found a fertile ground among military officers.

Contrary to the view of some scholars, this chapter argues that the last years of the Restoration were the key period in the ideological construction and social propagation of a modern conservative nationalism that would eventually constitute the basis of the *primorriverista* dictatorship.[3] It is true that, unlike Italy with first the Nationalist Association and later the Fascists, Spanish nationalism was not centred around a single party. Yet, as was the case in France, Spanish nationalism permeated a wide range of elites, political movements, institutions and the media from the beginning of the 20th century. This conservative nationalism was prominent in the discourse of political groups such as the Mauristas, the Liga Patriótica Española and the Asociación Católica Nacional de Propagandistas. These groups sought to regenerate conservative thought, became increasingly authoritarian in the years after the First World War and attempted to transform the Restoration political system from the inside. But a renovated Spanish nationalism was not exclusive of those groups of an emerging 'New Right'. A growing and renewed patriotic rhetoric is also to be found during those years among the Traditionalists, who openly opposed the Restoration regime and remained on the fringes of the liberal regime.[4] Additionally, the pages of conservative newspapers, like *El ABC* and *La Vanguardia*, and large sectors of the army, were also to embrace ultranationalist concepts of Spain. This new patriotic agenda presented some variations from one group to another, but by the 1910s it certainly emphasized the three major components of Spanish conservative nationalism in the 20th century, namely militarism, anti-Catalan and Basque nationalism, and the concept of Catholicism as the spiritual essence of the nation.

The role of Catholicism is central to this chapter. Traditional historiography has argued that Catholicism hindered the development of a modern nationalism in the 20th century. According to this line of interpretation, in Spain, the strong presence of religious postulates in the conservatives' discourse necessarily hampered the development of a modern and solid nationalism.[5] A stout allegiance to Rome, the argument goes, did not allow for the emergence of full-blown patriotism linked to the Spanish nation-state among the various conservative groups. Furthermore, during the Restoration era the Vatican was at times reluctant to support the Spanish political regime. The Holy See had a history of confrontation with different Spanish governments throughout the 19th century and considered the Restoration settlement too liberal for its taste. Thus traditional historiography has claimed that the Vatican did not promote the identification of Spanish Catholics with the Restoration state, for it saw the parliamentary monarchy as a danger to ecclesiastical interests. The following pages show the compatibility of religion and nationalism in the discourse of the Spanish Right. Moreover, the chapter demonstrates the full co-operation of the Catholic Church with the Spanish governments in the promotion of the nation. In the last years of the Restoration, ecclesiastical leaders participated together with civil authorities in parades, the opening of monuments, patriotic celebrations and all kinds of commemorations of the nation, in an attempt publicly to endow the *patria* with sacred connotations opposed to those seeking to challenge the political system. Nation and reaction went hand in hand.

The chapter is divided into two parts. The first section analyses the discourse of the main groups that were to regenerate the message of the Right, namely the Mauristas, Social Catholics, the Liga Patriótica Española and the monarchist leagues of Bilbao and Barcelona. It also focuses on the Traditionalists (Carlists and Catholic Integrists), groups on the fringes of the political system, which developed a highly nationalist discourse during the last years of the Restoration. The second part explores the official policies of mass nationalization implemented by the Conservative Party when in power. This section concentrates on the policies of education, the celebration of national holidays and the monuments built to incorporate the masses into the conservative nationalist project. Unlike the Carlists, this project did not aim at transforming the political establishment, but rather sought to keep the status quo while preventing any further democratization of the Restoration regime.

The reformulation of conservative Spanish nationalism

During the month of April 1898, a wave of jingoism was felt throughout most of Spanish society. As the war with the United States approached, newspapers speculated on the possibility of a rapid Spanish victory, the urban masses patriotically gathered to support the struggle and political parties united in their defence of the military.[6] By early July, the fleet lay at the bottom of the sea and Spain had lost the remains of her once great empire to the United States. 'The Disaster' of 1898, as it came to be known, signalled a turning point in the development of modern Spanish nationalism. As in Italy after the defeat at the hands of the Ethiopians at Adowa (1896), the loss led to a crisis of national identity. An entire generation of intellectuals, the so-called 'Generation of 1898', devoted its work to solving the 'problem of Spain'. Political groups presented diverse alternatives to 'regenerate' the 'sick' nation. Disaffection with the nation-state became paramount. The lower classes radicalized and demanded deep social and political transformations, while Catalan regionalism and Basque nationalism increased their social support. Different groups on the Right reacted to these changes and embarked on a mission of national regeneration.

To be sure, it was Maurismo, the movement formed around the Conservative leader Antonio Maura, that represented the first real attempt to organize a modern political party and regenerate the country 'from above'. In a speech in parliament in 1899, Maura had already warned of the need to undertake a 'revolution from above', in order to avoid a revolution 'made in the streets'.[7] From then on, Maura's discourse would be one of national regeneration and active counter-revolution. Deeply influenced by his friend Charles Maurras, Maura's idea of Spain was essentially based on the conservative canon of the nation elaborated in the 19th century. In this canon, monarchy and Catholicism were much emphasized as the keystones of the fatherland. To preclude revolution from below, the Maurista movement took to the streets in the second decade of the 20th century. The aim was to mobilize what was seen as the apolitical middle classes, the so-called 'neutral mass', and to create an educated 'citizenry' to change the system from within. In other words, Maurismo intended to attract the middle classes hitherto not involved in the oligarchic system, in order to transform the Restoration and ultimately combat the Left. Achieving these goals involved the creation of modern propaganda machinery, the organization of mass rallies, the formation of a Maurista Youth and the creation of Maurista Centres all around Spain, something until then unknown to the monarchist parties. With a propaganda machine ready, a nationalist rhetoric and a paternalistic approach to the 'social question', Maurismo felt confident to fight the working-class parties on their home ground. Since early 1915, Mauristas had opened 'social centres' in working-class neighbourhoods to compete with Socialist, Anarchist and Republican educational and cultural centres. The aim was to 'educate' the lower classes in patriotic, Catholic, corporative and monarchist values, and separate the proletariat from the left-wing parties.[8]

The fact that the first Spanish attempts to form fascist-type groups emerged around the Mauristas should come as no surprise. Since the First World War, an important sector of Maurismo, and particularly the Maurista Youth, was convinced that parliamentary politics had failed and advocated a strong government to save the nation. For many Mauristas the only way to stop the Left was by physical confrontation, either via bourgeois militias or military-led repression. As early as March 1919, the Maurista daily *La Acción* had called for a military dictatorship.[9] When Mussolini gained power in Italy in October 1922, *La Acción* enthusiastically welcomed Fascism as the solution to sweep away the political parties, and called Spaniards to follow the Italian example and form a national legion. Two months later, in December 1922, *La Palabra*, an ultranationalist paper was launched in Barcelona. It called for the middle classes to save the Spanish nation and claimed it was time to 'smash the separatist slugs' in Catalonia.[10] At the same time, the Maurista Joaquín Santos Ecay, the director of *La Acción*, Manuel Delgado Barreto, and the president of the Spanish Employers' Confederation (an extension of the Barcelona Employers' Federation), Tomás Benet, attempted to form the first Fascist organization around the newspaper *La Camisa Negra* in Madrid.[11] In the summer of 1923, another pro-Fascist organization, La Traza, was founded by a group of army officers in Barcelona. The new party blamed politicians for the loss of the colonies, the Moroccan disaster of 1921 and the *caciques'* destruction of the 'popular will', which was leading the fatherland to internal disintegration. Their foundational manifesto, La Traza, called for a 'sacred union of Spaniards', beyond their 'monarchic or republican, aristocratic or democratic' ideas, to save the nation, and suggested violence against the internal enemies of the fatherland was a valid option to redeem Spain.[12] Although the lives of *La Camisa Negra*, *La Palabra* and La Traza were ephemeral, their appearance proves that the ground was fertile for the growth of authoritarian nationalist alternatives to the Restoration. If they did not develop further it was because the military dictatorship, an option much favoured by the Mauristas, although not by Maura himself, was to integrate all these extreme-right groups into the regime of Primo de Rivera.

The growth of Spanish nationalism can also be detected in the formation of new coalitions of members of the governmental parties, the Liberals and Conservatives, to confront regional nationalism in Catalonia and the Basque Country. In Catalonia, the offensive was led by the former Liberal Alfonso Sala. Early in 1919, he founded the Unión Monárquica Nacional (UMN), a coalition that attracted some important members of Catalan high society, with the specific aim of combating the Lliga Regionalista. This reaction of the monarchist parties was not accidental. First, the increasing pressure of the democratic forces and the reorganization of the trade union movement after the First World War hardened the discourse of the dynastic parties. Second, the international recognition of the right of self-determination of national minorities after the First World War fuelled the emergence of more radical Catalanist opinions which pushed for full 'home rule'. The moderate Lliga also launched a campaign to gain political autonomy for Catalonia. On 20 November 1918, just nine days after the armistice, a group of delegates of the Mancomunitat (the regional institution controlled by the Lliga), handed a proposal to the Spanish prime minister, Manuel García Prieto, demanding Catalan home rule. Against home rule, the UMN proposed monarchism, corporatism and regionalism – the latter understood in the Maurista sense of local and regional regeneration of the whole of Spain.[13] The anti-Catalanism of the UMN initially did the trick. The new group galvanized *españolista* Liberals and Conservatives, gathered support from some sectors of the middle classes and improved the electoral results of the monarchists in Catalonia.[14]

In November 1918, just a couple of months before the formation of the UMN, Barcelona also witnessed the emergence of the Liga Patriótica Española (LPE). This league was formed by a conglomerate of Mauristas, Republican *lerrouxistas*, Carlists and military officers. The LPE embodied the most populist branch of Spanish nationalism and specialized in street fighting and shootings of radical Catalanists. It acted as the *españolista* 'shock troops' against the 'separatists' and tried to gain mass support of the lower classes through meetings, public lectures and a series of publications characterized by a highly demagogic rhetoric. Interestingly, the leadership of the LPE recommended its members vote indistinctively for the UMN and for Republican candidates, which demonstrates that the Right–Left split was much less significant than the *españolista–catalanista* one. By the spring of 1919 the LPE claimed it had thousands of members, and even if the exact figure is very difficult to reckon, the fact remains that Spanish nationalism in Barcelona was a cross-class phenomenon that went far beyond the small clique formed by the monarchist elites.[15]

The situation was no different in the Basque Country. In January 1919, Conservatives, Liberals and Mauristas met in the Maurista Circle of Bilbao and formed the Liga de Acción Monárquica to fight 'separatism'. In the same year, the readership of the Bilbao daily *El Pueblo Vasco* included an important number of intellectuals, who formulated a first ultranationalist concept of Spain. Among these writers and politicians were Ramiro de Maeztu, Víctor Pradera, José Calvo Sotelo, Eduardo Aunós, Rafael Sánchez Mazas and Count Rodezno.[16] With the exception of Sánchez Mazas, all of them were later to collaborate, in one way or the other, with the dictatorship of General Primo de Rivera. Although regional nationalism was not as strong as in Catalonia, the logic behind the Liga de Acción Monárquica was the same as in the UMN: a defensive reaction of Spanish nationalism to fight the challenges from regional nationalists. In the case of the Basque Country, the Liga de Acción Monárquica formed an electoral alliance with the Socialists and agreed to present a series of candidates in the working-class areas of Vizcaya.[17] As in Catalonia, the alliance meant breaching the gap between the Right and the moderate Left, in the name of protecting the Spanish nation from the regional nationalists' threat. The immediate outcome was the consolidation of Spanish nationalism in Barcelona and Bilbao, with the monarchist parties increasing their votes in both cities.

While Maurismo and the unions of dynastic parties were born in the big cities, another conservative movement proposing national regeneration that was to have a key influence in the ideological and political organization of Primo de Rivera's dictatorship found its strength in the towns and villages of Old Castile and the northern provinces. Since the publication in 1891 of Pope Leo XIII's *Rerum Novarum*, the interest of the Catholic hierarchy in the social situation of the lower classes had increased.[18] The intense diffusion of Social Catholic doctrines in the press, congresses and collective pilgrimages was complemented in *fin de siècle* Spain with the opening of Catholic centres and, eventually, with the creation of Catholic trade unions in order to deal with the 'social question'. As left-wing ideas spread throughout rural Spain, the Catholic Church launched a multiple-front offensive seeking a complete 're-clericalization of society'.[19]

This process of 're-clericalization of society' was a European phenomenon. As secularization advanced in the last years of the 19th century and the beginning of the 20th century, French, Austrian, Belgian and Italian Catholics fostered the principles of Social Catholicism to attract the lower classes to the Church's agenda.[20] In Spain, clericalism grew intensively at the beginning of the 20th century, too. Partially as a reaction to the anti-clericalism showed by the popular classes and liberal intellectuals during the Tragic Week, the Church encouraged the creation of a series of new Catholic agencies.[21] Acción Católica subsequently grew under the umbrella of the ecclesiastical authorities and developed as a modern association with different sections, including women, youth, trade unions and education.[22] Fully aware of the importance of the media and up-to-date propaganda, the Jesuit Ángel Ayala founded the Asociación Católica Nacional de Propagandistas (National Catholic Association of Propagandists – ACNP) in 1909. The Propagandists' views were heavily indebted to the historic Romanticism and Neo-Thomist thought that had framed the 19th-century conservative canon of Spain. Following the ideas of Antonio Cánovas del Castillo and Marcelino Menéndez Pelayo, Ángel Herrera, the Propagandists' leader, considered nations to be the work of God in history. In his view, Spain was a 'moral unity' historically framed by the monarchy and the Church under providential supervision. Equally, Herrera considered liberal democracy not suitable to Spain. First, because sovereignty was believed to lie ultimately in God, and, second, due to the fact that Spain's social and territorial disparities were thought too great to implement a real universal suffrage without dangers. As an alternative, the Propagandists defended an 'organic democracy' based on the family, municipalities and corporations that would eventually rejuvenate 'the people's sap'.[23] In other words, Catholicism, a hierarchical notion of society and populism infused the Propagandists' biological concept of the Spanish nation.

From the beginning, the ACNP realized the importance of propaganda to obtain Catholics' social and doctrinal cohesion. The famous 'Propaganda Campaigns' orchestrated by the ACNP mouthpiece, *El Debate*, sought to indoctrinate and mobilize followers in a militant Social Catholicism in an unprecedented manner. In addition, Social Catholics created trade unions and Centres of Social Defence to compete with the Left, though with very limited success.[24] In fact it was in the rural areas of Old Castile, Navarre and Aragon where Catholic propaganda paid off. The diverse agrarian unions created during the first years of the Great War finally came together in 1917 and formed the Confederación Nacional Católico-Agraria (National Catholic Agrarian Confederation – CNCA). A genuine interclass organization, the CNCA was made up of smallholders, directed by big landowners and focused on halting the advance of leftist ideas in the countryside.[25] It was no coincidence that one of the first groups to promote the creation of an official *primor-riverista* party, what eventually became the Unión Patriótica (Patriotic Union) in 1924, emerged from this social basis of Castilian militant Catholics.

In fact, by 1924 many members of the ACNP had previous experience in organizing a political party. As the demands for a democratization of the Restoration grew dramatically from 1917 onwards, the Social Catholics became increasingly aware of the need to change the system. In Zaragoza, Valencia and Sevilla, the so-called Catholic Leagues were formed to run in the elections against the dynastic parties. These leagues obtained fairly decent electoral results and, backed by the ACNP, became the kernel of the Partido Social Popular (Popular Social Party – PSP) in December 1922. Seeking to unite the different factions of the Spanish Right, the PSP managed to attract not only many Propagandists, such as José María Gil Robles, but also Traditionalists like Víctor Pradera and Mauristas like Ángel Ossorio y Gallardo. Together with an increasing state intervention to regulate the economy, the party proclaimed the need for radical change, including the creation of a corporatist state, the reform of the 1876 Constitution and the end of *caciquismo*.[26] During its short life, the PSP distinguished itself for its anti-liberal rhetoric, its message of national regeneration and its attacks on a parliamentary system which was depicted as obsolete and corrupt.[27] Not surprisingly, most of the PSP leaders joined the Unión Patriótica in 1924.[28]

Changes also occurred in those reactionary groups that openly opposed the Restoration political establishment. After 1898, Carlists and Catholic Integrists tried to retain their customary influence in the areas of Navarre, the Basque Country and Catalonia. However, political unity amongst the Traditionalist groups was never achieved during the Restoration. Quite the contrary, in 1919 a major split in the Carlist ranks occurred, when the party's main ideologue, Juan Vázquez de Mella, walked out to form the Traditionalist Party. Despite the schism, or perhaps because of it, ideologues such as Vázquez de Mella, Salvador Minguijón and Víctor Pradera sought to revitalize Carlist doctrine during the first decades of the 20th century, by incorporating ideas from thinkers outside Spanish Traditionalism such as Charles Maurras and Joaquín Costa. This new Traditionalism focused on social questions in an attempt to gain mass political support and simultaneously sought to attract the most conservative political and ecclesiastical forces of the Alfonsine regime. Thus Traditionalists intensified their propaganda campaigns, participated in mass pilgrimages and even opened social centres for workers in Barcelona and Bilbao.[29]

At the turn of the century, Traditionalists accentuated the patriotic tones of their political discourse in response to the emergence of Basque nationalism and Catalan regionalism. These movements competed with Traditionalism for a similar political market and seriously eroded Carlist popular support in Catalonia and the Basque provinces.[30] Like Basque nationalists, Traditionalists fiercely defended the *fueros* (the medieval regional and local charters and statutes) and proposed a decentralized Spain based on pre-liberal laws. However, it is also important to note that this conception of the nation, for all its emphasis on regional liberties, did not preclude an imperial idea of Spain. After all, the Carlists argued that Spain had created her world empire in the 16th century, while maintaining the internal division of her various component parts. Since the 1890s, all Traditionalist factions ardently supported the Spanish struggle in the colonies. The military humiliation of 1898 was no discouragement: just three months after the defeat in Cuba, the Catholic Integrist daily *El Siglo Futuro* demanded the creation of a Spanish colony in Morocco.[31] Soon after the intervention in Northern Africa was accomplished, in 1911 Vázquez de Mella called for the revocation of the international agreements with France and Great Britain in order to strengthen the Spanish position in the Moroccan protectorate. According to this logic, if Spain was to have a 'moral empire' over the Hispanic American countries, as Vázquez de Mella wished, she needed to expand further into Morocco.[32] Territorial gains were thus linked to 'spiritual expansion' in the imperial destiny Traditionalists foresaw for Spain. The beginning of the First World War did nothing to placate Vázquez de Mella's imperial desires. In his book *El ideal de España* (1915), he explicitly declared himself an imperialist and insisted on the need to claim Spanish total sovereignty over the Straits of Gibraltar, a federation with Portugal (the Spanish *irredenta*), and a loose union with the Spanish American republics which would adopt a common foreign policy under Spanish direction.[33]

This Pan-*Hispanismo*, which Vázquez de Mella confessed should imitate aggressive Pan-Germanism, was not without roots in the Spanish Right. *Hispanismo*, the belief that Spaniards and Spanish Americans are members of the same 'race', had been an essential element in the discourse of Spanish politicians since the late 19th century.[34] Both the Right and the Left had used the idea of a transatlantic spiritual community as an external projection of the Spanish nation. On the Right, Menéndez Pelayo had framed the intellectual bases of *Hispanismo* during the 1890s, stressing the Catholic, linguistic and cultural ties between Spain and its former colonies. After the loss of Cuba and Puerto Rico, this conservative *Hispanismo* gained a new impulse and a wider audience with the writings of Julián Juderías and José María Salaverría, who emphasized the Spanish concept of mission in America. The most popular work of these writers was Juderías's *La Leyenda Negra*, a book acclaimed by both press and public. A disciple of Menéndez Pelayo, Juderías denounced foreign powers for inventing the 'Black Legend' to diminish Spanish influence in the world and complained of the positive reception this interpretation of history had had amongst Spaniards themselves.[35]

This new drive towards conservative *Hispanismo* has to be understood, first of all, as an optimistic nationalist response against the pessimism that invaded regenerationist writers of the generation of 1898. A good example of this patriotic optimism can be found in the writings of Salaverría, which constantly attacked the negative image of Spain portrayed by the artists of the generation of 1898 and those foreigners who had invented the Black Legend. To overcome this 'masochism' that in Salaverría's view many Spaniards were suffering from, the Basque journalist proposed the creation of 'a new Spaniard' proud of the nation's imperial history, advocated a rapprochement with the Spanish American countries and supported the occupation of the Rif in Northern Africa.[36] Second, the imperial rhetoric and the promotion of *Hispanismo* have to be considered as a reaction against regional nationalism. Conservative newspapers like *El ABC*, *El Debate* and *La Vanguardia* developed a deep anti-regional nationalist discourse in which the imperial past played the positive role versus the 'mutilated' Spain desired by Catalan and Basque nationalists.[37] The growth of regional nationalism at the beginning of the 20th century encouraged Spanish nationalists to deploy the concept of *Hispanismo*, which increased the sense of unity of the 'Spanish race' and implied the negation of Catalan and Basque nationalists' claims.[38]

There can be no doubt that in the last years of the Restoration a new authoritarian Right emerged in the political arena, which modernized conservatism by turning nationalism into a key element of its discourse. It strengthened conservatism's Catholic, imperial, corporative and anti-democratic characteristics and incorporated new features such as radical militarism and anti-regional nationalism. As in other European countries, the New Right showed a genuine will to gain mass support, but in Spain, despite all its organizational and propagandist efforts, it failed both to reform the Restoration regime and to attract great popular backing. The regime simply proved too resilient to the challenges of the New Right and the Traditionalists, and the Restoration was able to keep the *caciquil* system going. By 1923 the authoritarian route of the military dictatorship was welcomed by all the New Right groups. They hoped the army would impose on the masses their authoritarian view of Spain and implement their political agendas. It was something of an acknowledgement of their own failure to rally mass support.

A new Spanish nationalism in a state of siege

The emergence of the New Right and the incorporation of nationalism as one way of coping politically with mass mobilization was the reflection of a changing society. During the first two decades of the 20th century, social and economic transformations accelerated and the state was partially modernized. These changes were to have a direct impact on the process of nation-building, to the extent that during this period important steps towards the complete nationalization of Spanish political and cultural life were taken. In other words, these were the years when the nation, and not the region or the town, became dominant in the field of social and political preoccupations.[39]

To begin with, the loss of the colonies had the effect of increasing the integration of the national market. The Catalan textile industry lost its profitable market in Cuba and soon sought to gain new customers inside Spain. The political pressures of the Catalan bourgeoisie in Madrid proved fruitful and Spain significantly raised its already high tariffs to protect its products, which in turn led to the growth of national markets. Second, during the two decades that followed 1898, a system of national education developed, urbanization proceeded and the transport system was enlarged, increasing the mobility of the population within Spain. On top of this, illiteracy was severely reduced, although it still remained high by Western European standards, and the mass press expanded creating a national market and invigorating the idea of an imagined national community.

Some of the state institutions also improved their performance as agents in the process of nation-building. Newly regulated, the public administration grew significantly in the first two decades of the 20th century, and civil servants, such as magistrates and functionaries, became more influential in provincial towns and villages. More to the point, the liberal state attempted to develop a competent national education system, which would include the entire population. Led by proposals of educational and social regeneration, the Ministry of Public Instruction was created in 1900, and a series of official institutions, such as the Escuela de Estudios Superiores de Magisterio (1909), the Centro de Estudios Históricos (1910) and the Instituto-Escuela (1918), followed. In addition, a massive corpus of legislation regulated state educational intervention, which led to serious improvements, especially in primary education, and confirmed public instruction as the agent of controlled social modernization.[40]

This state intervention has to be understood not only as an attempt to improve the appalling illiteracy rates, but also as a conscious means of nationalizing the masses in bourgeois values. As a royal decree put it plainly in October 1911, the curricula for adult education sought to put 'even more emphasis [than in primary education] on the formation of Fatherland loving citizens [...] respectful of the Law, Property, and other citizens'.[41] It is worth observing here that in this role of nationalization via education, both Conservative and Liberal governments played a key part. For all their rhetoric on the right of the Church to educate without state interference, the Conservatives under Maura promoted the role of state-controlled education and imposed compulsory universal primary schooling in 1909. Moreover, they were fully aware of the need to 'produce' a new patriotic youth who would 'place love for the Fatherland beyond all interest and conveniences'.[42] To achieve a complete 'national pedagogy', the Maurista Minister of Education César Silió argued, it was necessary to fight all those 'humanitarian, pacifist, anti-militarist, and anti-patriotic' doctrines taught in schools. He claimed these ideas were merely a 'hypocritical cover' of the Left that sought to 'destroy those armed organizations that impeded the triumph of revolution'.[43] Nationalization went hand in hand with counter-revolution. No wonder that when the Mauristas were in power several of their governmental initiatives aimed to transmit nationalist values. In September 1921, for instance, Silió created a patriotic prize awarded to the children's book that most inspired love for the nation. The following month, a royal order stated that there must be a portrait of Alfonso XIII, 'as the head of the power that represented the unity of the Fatherland', in a visible place in all state schools.[44]

Not all state agencies were to improve their role in the process of mass nationalization. The army proved unable to achieve this with any competency in the first decades of the 20th century. As shown above, the mounting military intervention in politics and the steady use of the army in social repression did nothing but increase popular anti-militarism throughout the period 1898–1923. Neither did the continuity of the unfair conscription system improve matters. In spite of the legislation reducing monetary redemptions introduced by the Liberal

Prime Minister José Canalejas in 1911, the system remained basically unchanged until 1921, and so did the understandable alienation of the popular classes from the army. Furthermore, in some areas of the countryside, the lower classes' contempt for the armed forces was emphasized by the actions of the Civil Guard, a militarized force created to defend proprietors' interests in rural districts.[45]

Nevertheless, the army was to play a crucial role in the regeneration of Spanish nationalism. A new version of Spanish nationalism came out of the military barracks at the turn of the century. This nationalism aimed at transforming the nation-state and combined the requirement of modernization with conservative beliefs.[46] After 1898, professional officers openly advocated modernizing the nation via an authoritarian state.[47] In their view, Spain needed a strong economy, a regimented society and an up-to-date army ready for new imperialist expansions to solve the post-colonial crisis. To achieve these aims the military demanded internal state reforms, including gearing industry towards arms production, a better educational system, an honest public administration and restructuring of the state-Catholic Church relationship.[48] For the military, these transformations could not be carried out by the inefficient two-party system of the Restoration. They required a strong government led by a general and not subordinated to parliamentary control.

The army not only felt it was the guarantor of the nation-state but, moreover, saw itself as the interpreter of the popular will.[49] In a corrupt political system in which male universal suffrage was little more than a charade, army officers often presented themselves as the real voice of the masses. Despite the decline of left-wing Republican officers and a clear move to the Right in the army since 1898, the rhetoric of populism remained well into the 20th century.[50] However, this populism should not lead us to consider the military as the champions of democratic reforms. Almost invariably, the army sided with the Restoration civilian elites and was regularly used for internal repression. In reality, there was nothing democratic in this populist rhetoric. Scorn for the working classes was manifest in the military press and most officers feared the inclusion of the masses in the political arena. When using the populist discourse the army was indeed appealing to certain sectors of the population, but mostly the middle classes or, to put it in military terms, 'the healthy segments' of society.[51] Moreover, this new military nationalism shared many of the myths of the New Right. It saw in the martial spirit of the *reconquista*, the colonization of America, the fight against Protestants and the 'War of Independence', the real 'soul' of the nation.[52]

Ideologically, military nationalism gained momentum after 1898 due to the growing strength of Catalan regionalism and, to a lesser extent, Basque nationalism, as well as the latent anti-militarism of the working class. In defining itself as the repository of the quintessential qualities of the fatherland, the army considered criticism of the military as an attack on the *patria* and regional nationalism as mere treason to the nation. According to this logic, political violence to punish enemies of national unity became a patriotic duty.[53] In 1902, on three different occasions, officers attacked Catalan and Basque nationalist demonstrators.[54] On the evening of 25 November 1905, after a satirical cartoon mocking the army appeared in the magazine *Cu-Cut!*, junior officers assaulted the editorial offices of the publication and then moved on to destroy the presses of the Catalanist newspaper *La Veu de Catalunya*.

The reactions to the assault showed how deep anti-Catalanist sentiments were in many sectors of the establishment. The action was applauded almost unanimously in garrisons throughout Spain; crowds of officers gathered at stations to greet military delegates sent to Catalonia, while junior officers in Madrid and Barcelona prepared an ultimatum for the king requiring action against the Catalanists and the closure of the Cortes. The officers also formed commissions and demanded that all crimes against the army, the nation and the state be tried by military tribunals. As had been the norm in the past, the government took no action against the aggressors. On the contrary, on 29 November 1905, it declared martial law in Barcelona, enforced the closure of newspapers and arrested Catalanist sympathizers.[55] In March 1906, the bill for the Repression of Crimes against the Fatherland and the Army (popularly known as the Law of Jurisdictions) was passed in parliament with the support of Liberals and Conservatives. The new law was drafted by the Liberal government of Segismundo Moret and, although it retained offences against the nation and the state under civilian jurisdiction, it allowed military jurisdiction over verbal and written offences against the army.[56] The message to the military officers was clear: political violence and insubordination paid off in the short term.

If the Law of Jurisdictions confirmed the military's belief that the army was the only genuine guardian of the fatherland and made official the military concept of Spain, the consequences in the long term proved to be disastrous. Republicans, Socialists and Carlists opposed the new legislation and its repeal became central to the political debate. In Catalonia, Solidaritat Catalana gathered Carlists, Republicans and Catalanists in a political alliance whose main goals were the abolition of the Law of Jurisdictions and the creation of Catalan regional institutions. The action–reaction spiral set off by the *Cu-cut!* affair seems clear: the military gained even more control of the state apparatus and regionalism gained more social support.

Subsequent crises only widened the gap between the military and the popular classes. When in 1909 an anti-war demonstration sparked off the events of Tragic Week in Barcelona, another episode of the action–reaction spiral was set in motion.[57] The working-class challenge to the imperial adventure 'confirmed' to the military that leftist ideologies worked against 'national grandeur'. In turn, the brutal repression ordered by the Maura government and executed by the army logically amplified the bitterness and mistrust of the working class towards the military. During the period 1917–20 this very same pattern was to be repeated on a regular basis. What began as a military revolt to defend the army's privileges in 1917 with the formation of the *Juntas Militares de Defensa* of junior officers, ended up as harsh repression of the working class, military control of public services and continual declarations of martial law between 1919 and 1922. Obviously, these actions only radicalized popular anti-militarism even more, while contributing to the strengthening of conservative military mentality. Moreover, after the 'Disaster of Annual' (1921) and the abolition of the *Juntas* (1922), the army adopted a unified stand in the face of social tensions and peripheral nationalism, which was to crystallize in Primo de Rivera's coup in September 1923.[58] It is hardly surprising that the day after the united demonstration of Catalan, Basque and Galician nationalists in Barcelona on 11 September 1923, the military press complained of the 'separatist riff-raff' and demanded the strict enforcement of the laws of crimes against the fatherland. 'If impunity continued, good Spaniards should intervene to correct such grievances', the military threatened.[59] The following day, the captain general of Catalonia launched a coup. In his manifesto, Primo de Rivera justified his action by claiming the nation had to be saved from the 'shameless separatist propaganda' and from the 'impunity of Communist propaganda'. The military press unanimously welcomed the coup.[60]

One of the reasons why military officers felt alienated from the constitutional system was because they deemed the dynastic parties unable to generate a cohesive Spanish national identity. For all the rhetoric of 'revolution from above' and national regeneration that followed the 'Disaster', electoral falsification and patronage continued to be the rule, hence hampering popular identification with the political system. Moreover, as the economy and society modernized, the system proved too rigid to absorb political opposition. True, Liberals were able to integrate into their party some members of Alejandro Lerroux's Partido Republicano Radical (Radical Republican Party) and Mequiades Álvarez's Partido Reformista (Reformist Party), while the Conservatives were happy to incorporate Catalan regionalists in their cabinets. Yet, on many occasions, the best alternative that the Restoration politicians found to confront political challenges from below was to increase the already intense military intervention in social repression, which, in turn, led to a greater alienation of the populace from the political system. Crucially, the steady growth of a Socialist and Anarchist proletariat and Republican-leaning middle classes meant not only an increasing challenge to the political system but also the social expansion of alternative identities to the official concept of Spain promoted by the Restoration elites.

On the counter-revolutionary side, the idea of order was linked to the Spanish nation. In January 1919, Catalan regionalists of the Lliga, Spanish nationalists of the UMN and the Carlists joined forces and, with the support of the local business elite, created the Barcelona Somatén, a civic guard (*guardia cívica*) under military supervision integrated in the general framework of the Catalan Somatén. Its declared aims were protecting property, fighting the alleged 'Bolshevik' menace, keeping order and maintaining factories and public services working during strikes. In effect, the setting up of the Barcelona Somatén meant the establishment of a bourgeois armed force funded by industrialists and organized by the military. Among the employers linked to this group, the Second Marquis of Comillas was to play the most relevant role. A staunch Catholic obsessed with endowing the counter-revolutionary citizens' militias with a modern character according to the spirit of the times, the Marquis was a founding member of the Barcelona Somatén in January 1919. Nine months later he sponsored the creation of the militia, Defensa Ciudadana, in Madrid. By the end of 1919, employers' organizations and other conservative groups had created civic guards in Madrid, Zaragoza, Valencia, Granada and Alicante following the Barcelona Somatén model. In the next two years, Palma de Mallorca, Sevilla and San Sebastian followed suit.[61]

Counter-revolutionary violence, however, had its limitations as a tool of national integration. The dynastic parties seem to have realized the importance of the symbolic order in the formation of a popular national identity. During the decades that preceded Primo de Rivera's dictatorship, the creation of national symbols was completed. It was then that the Maura governments promoted the *Marcha Real* to the rank of national anthem (1908) and the national flag was made compulsory in every public building (1908). Again under Maura in 1918, 12 October, the 'Day of the Race' (*Día de la Raza*), was officially declared a national holiday in commemoration of the Discovery of America by Christopher Columbus. On this Day of the Race, local authorities organized many ceremonies all over Spain to pay homage to Columbus and the conquistadors.[62] In Madrid, dozens of children paraded in front of the statue of Columbus, where they left bouquets of flowers. The king also attended the celebrations, during which politicians and South American ambassadors gave rather pompous speeches before the customary mass sanctified the Spanish nation and its glorious past.[63] Additionally, the Spanish Right, the government and the media began a campaign to prove that Christopher Columbus was Spanish in an attempt to use him as a figure of Spanish national regeneration.[64] The creation of the Day of the Race as an official national holiday precisely in 1918 has to be understood not only as a step further in the state's endorsement of *Hispanismo*, but also as an attempt to promote political patriotism and nationalist exaltation in the context of the dramatic institutional crisis that Spain had been suffering since 1917.[65] In other words, stirring nationalist feelings among the population was thought to be the internal panacea for a seriously sick political system.

The Restoration also witnessed an upsurge of nationalist commemorations. Since the late 19th century celebrations of anniversaries of patriotic figures and deeds had led to what has been called a 'centenary craze'.[66] The centenaries of the deaths of Pedro Calderón de la Barca (1881), Bartolomé Murillo (1882), the conversion to Christianity of the Visigoth king Recadero (1889), the Discovery of America (1892), the publication of the first part of *Don Quixote* (1905), the popular uprising against the Napoleonic troops (1908), different battles of the War of Independence, the Cádiz constitution (1912), the death of El Greco, the death of Miguel de Cervantes and the battle of Covadonga (1918), to mention the most significant, were commemorated in many Spanish cities.[67] It is important to note that both Conservatives and Liberals equally fostered these patriotic celebrations when in government, seeking to unite the population in nationalist values.[68] At times, this led to the confrontation between liberal and conservative models of the Spanish nation at a symbolic level. For example, the commemoration of the 100th anniversary of the 1808 and 1809 Napoleonic capture of Zaragoza led to serious clashes between the liberal and the conservative versions of the Spanish nation and, consequently, to the celebration of multiple and competing patriotic events.[69] During the construction of the Covadonga Sanctuary in Asturias, liberals and conservatives also fought to control the symbolic meaning of the site and, hence, its collective identity.[70] However, from 1914 liberal nationalism lost ground to its conservative counterpart in the field of official commemorations. Those who described Spain as conterminous to Catholicism and talked about discipline and order steadily gained the support of the authorities. In the field of commemorations, conservative Spanish nationalism became hegemonic in a clear reaction to what were perceived as revolutionary and separatist threats.[71]

Additionally, as in the case of the United Kingdom, Belgium, Germany and Italy, the king played an incredibly active role in patriotic commemorations and ceremonies. Alfonso XIII was particularly keen to associate the crown with the *patria* and during his reign Spanish nationalism was often displayed in monarchical terms.[72] Thus the king repeatedly took part in the celebrations of anniversaries of patriotic figures and events and granted money for the building of national monuments. For instance, only six years into his reign, Alfonso XIII bestowed 20,000 pesetas to the construction of the Covadonga Sanctuary.[73] Other examples of the monarch's involvement in nationalist ceremonies reached tragic-comic proportions. In 1921, he was presiding over the transportation of the remains of Rodrigo Díaz de Vivar, El Cid, in front of the relics of Saint Fernando, the medieval monarch who conquered vast areas of Andalusia from the Muslims, when the first news of the Annual Disaster in Morocco broke.[74] The monarch's celebration of the Christian nation forged during the *reconquista* had taken place literally hours after Moroccan rebels had slaughtered thousands of Spanish soldiers, who had followed Alfonso XIII's military strategy in the African protectorate.

Like many members of the Restoration elites, Alfonso XIII became increasingly conservative and counter-revolutionary. Crucially, from the First World War onwards, it is possible to talk about an authoritarian turn in the behaviour and discourses of the king.[75] Extremely mindful of the tsar's fate in Russia, Alfonso XIII presented monarchy, nation, order and religion in the same ideological package. At a symbolic level, this nationalist and authoritarian turn was epitomized on Saint Fernando's Day 1919. On 30 November that year, Alfonso XIII personally consecrated the Spanish nation to the Sacred Heart of Jesus, at the Cerro de los Ángeles (Getafe), in an impressive and lavish ceremony.[76] Many of the New Right's ideas, that explosive cocktail of religion, nationalism and anti-parliamentarianism mixed with important doses of revolutionary fear, were embraced by the monarch too.

As in France and Germany, the 'monumentalist fever' of the 1880s and 1890s was to take off in Spain from the beginning of the 20th century onwards.[77] It was then that a group of artists connected to the Royal Academy of San Fernando built the monuments celebrating the nation's dead heroes and portraying the crown as the symbolic personification of the fatherland, the best examples of which were the sculpture of Eloy Gonzalo García, the so-called 'hero of Cascorro' (Madrid, 1902), and the monumental complex to Alfonso XII in El Retiro Park (Madrid, 1902). By an official directive, the same artists were active in the provinces, where all sorts of 'national' fighters were commemorated, from the Celt-Iberian resistance against the Romans (Numancia, 1905), through to the 16th-century imperial commander-in-chief El Gran Capitán (Córdoba, 1909) and the heroine of the 'War of Independence' Agustina de Aragón (Zaragoza, 1908). All of them were manifestations of the process of creating from above a historical national identity that was gaining momentum in particular after the loss of the last colonies. These monuments, together with the ever-increasing construction of 'national' museums, libraries, theatres and archives, created 'sacred places' in which the national history and culture were venerated. After the beginning of the 20th century, the whole process of 'inventing traditions' was set in full motion in Spain. By 1923, an official image of the nation, as perceived by the state-elites, had been consolidated.[78] More importantly, the very fact that on numerous occasions the commemoration of national deeds and the money to build monuments to the patriotic heroes came from public subscriptions demonstrates the existence of a widespread, inter-class, popular Spanish nationalism in the years that preceded the dictatorship of Primo de Rivera.

It is worth emphasizing here that the creation of a national 'civic religion' from above, with its symbols, holidays and shrines, usually developed from associations with Catholic symbols, rites and traditions. As mentioned above, religion was a pivotal element in the conservative canon of the nation and many rightists maintained a strong identification between Catholicism and Spain. The 1876 Constitution declared Catholicism to be the official religion of Spain and Antonio Cánovas soon accommodated the Church within the Restoration establishment, which meant ecclesiastical representation at almost every single public event. Thus it was no coincidence that one of the most notorious public ceremonies during the reign of Alfonso XIII was the king's consecration of the *patria* to the Sacred Heart of Jesus at El Cerro de los Ángeles. Neither was it by chance that some memorials commemorating the 'War of Independence' were considered monuments 'to the martyrs of Religion and the Fatherland' at the same time, such as the one inaugurated at Zaragoza in 1904.[79] This overlapping of national and Catholic symbolism became even more evident with the creation of the Fiesta de la Raza, because 12 October coincided with the popular religious celebration of the Virgin Pilar, which had already gained a strong nationalist sentiment during the 19th century.[80] The Restoration establishment seems to have realized that representing and celebrating the nation intermingled with religion in a Catholic country was a good way to obtain popular support for the official patriotic ideal, without having to pay the toll of a real democratization of the political system.

Not that the Church's co-operation with the Restoration's political elites came out of any charitable spirit. In the last decades of the 19th century, the Church agreed to provide its authority to the 'civil religion' that sanctified the social and political order of the Restoration, in exchange for the constitutional and legal protection of its ideological monopoly. In the early 20th century, as the democratic threat to the system grew, the ecclesiastical authorities became fully aware of the fact that they shared the goal of protecting the established social and political order with the Restoration political elites.[81] When the Church felt the heat of secularization increasing then it reacted by orchestrating a vast mobilization using modern means. The Church organized a new series of Catholic leagues, press campaigns and street demonstrations to face the challenge posed by secular liberals, anti-clerical Republicans, Socialists and Anarchists, especially after 1909.[82]

Again, there was no Spanish 'exceptionalism' in this phenomenon. Established Churches lent their sacred authority to governments in order to promote patriotic feelings all over Europe.[83] This 'sacralization' of politics was in fact one of the by-products of secularization, which dramatically accelerated at the beginning of the 20th century.[84] In France, the secular policies of the Third Republic led to virulent reaction by a New Right, which thought its clerical view of the nation was the real *patria* and its reactionary agenda the only hope for regeneration.[85] Likewise, in Spain, the increasing secularization of society went together with the process of the sacralization of politics. Amid this struggle between clericals and anticlericals, the former increasingly appealed to the nation, an entity that had been sanctified and had now become the epitome of social order.

The Church's hierarchy realized the utility of embracing the myth of the nation and saw how it could be brought into play to ensure Catholic social mobilization. Thus Pope Leo XIII and the Spanish Church supported from its inception the celebration of the Day of the Race, which they interpreted as the remembrance of the successful Christianization of America.[86] Another example of interwoven Catholic and nationalist sentiments were the popular pilgrimages to Rome, where the participants combined appeals to Catholic unity with prayers for the 'salvation of Spain'.[87] After all, in the last quarter of the 19th century schools, congresses and associations under ecclesiastical control had been stressing imperial Spanish history as the hallmark of national grandeur, following the works of Manuel Merri y Colón and Marcelino Menéndez Pelayo.[88] This endeavour of popular indoctrination ultimately proves the Church found no contradiction in promoting simultaneously nationalist and Christian doctrines. In this sense, the process of 're-clericalization' of Spanish society carried out by the Church in the early 20th century was equivalent to the nationalization of Spaniards in Catholic values.

The two decades that followed the Disaster of 1898 definitively changed Spanish nationalism in terms of discourse and social scope. Ideologically, the conservative canon of Spain was reformulated. This new Spanish nationalism became increasingly martial, clerical, Panpan-Hispanic and anti-liberal, and developed a deep hostility towards regional nationalisms and the organized working class. Political groups, intellectuals, the armed forces, conservative newspapers and a plethora of organizations generally related to the Church constructed a new Spanish nationalism in a siege situation. The fact that these groups were unable to come together into a single party should not lead us to assume the absence of a Spanish political nationalism in the years that preceded Primo de Rivera's dictatorship. Indeed, most of the ideas that would eventually constitute the official ultra-nationalist discourse of the *primorriverista* regime were first formulated during the last years of the Restoration.

The endurance and centrality of Catholicism as a key factor in the Right's concept of nation and as an element of social and political mobilization during the crisis of the Restoration debunks the assumption that Catholicism was a handicap for the development of a modern nationalism. All the groups of the New Right emphasized Catholicism as a constituent element of Spanish nationality and gained popular support in those areas where the social influence of the Church was strongest. Furthermore, in the process of mass nationalization, the state overlapped civic and religious symbols, holidays and ceremonies to create collective memories and loyalties, with the active collaboration of a Catholic Church integrated into the establishment. Catholicism, far from being incompatible with the development of a modern nationalism, was rather an appropriate ideological, discursive and symbolic element for the creation of a national identity and the mobilization of social support. Miguel Primo de Rivera, first, and Francisco Franco, later, would use this bond of nation and religion to reformulate the National–Catholic rhetoric that portrayed Spain as the antithesis of democracy. In both instances, the Catholic Church backed the military coups and the ensuing dictatorships.

Notes

All translations from Spanish are by me.

1. The events of the coup are described in great detail in Javier Tusell, *Radiografía de un golpe de Estado: el ascenso al poder del general Primo de Rivera* (Madrid: Alianza, 1987).
2. The manifesto is in Jordi Casassas Ymbert, *La Dictadura de Primo de Rivera (1923–1930). Textos.* (Barcelona: Anthropos, 1983), pp. 81–5.
3. For the theory of Spain as lacking a modern nationalism at the beginning of the 20th century see Stanley Payne, 'Los nacionalismos', in *Historia general de España y América* (Madrid: Rialp, 1981), pp. 109–30; Payne, *Fascism in Spain, 1923–1977* (Madison: University of Wisconsin Press, 1999), pp. 3–23; and Pedro Carlos González Cuevas, *Historia de las derechas españolas* (Madrid: Biblioteca Nueva, 2000), p. 264.
4. For the relationship between the different far-right Catholic tendencies – the Carlists, Traditionalists and Integrists – see the Introduction to this volume, pp. 1–31.
5. For example, Payne, *Fascism in Spain*, p. 14.
6. Gregorio Alonso, 'La mirada de la izquierda. Las guerras coloniales de 1898 desde la prensa socialista y federal', in Rafael Sánchez (ed.), *En torno al 98*, (Huelva: Universidad de Huelva, 2000), 2, pp. 261–9.
7. Cited in Sebastian Balfour, *The End of the Spanish Empire, 1898–1923* (Oxford: Oxford University Press, 1997), p. 188.
8. María Jesús González Hernández, *Ciudadanía y acción. El conservadurismo maurista* (Madrid: Siglo XXI, 1990), pp. 149–61.
9. Francisco J. Romero Salvadó, 'The Failure of the Liberal Project of the Spanish Nation-State, 1909–1923', in Clare Mar-Molinero and Angel Smith (eds), *Nationalism and the Nation in the Iberian Peninsula* (Washington and Oxford: Berg, 1996), p. 130.
10. *La Palabra* (17 December 1922 and 6 January 1923).
11. Antonio Elorza Domínguez, 'Las variantes del fascismo (1931–1936)', in Joan Antón and Miquel Caminal (eds), *Pensamiento político en la España contemporánea, 1800–1950* (Barcelona: Teide, 1992), pp. 989–1006.
12. La Traza manifesto is in Eduardo González and Fernando del Rey, *La defensa armada contra la revolución* (Madrid: Consejo Superior de Investigaciones Científicas, 1995), pp. 326–7.
13. Josep Puy i Juanico, 'La Unión Monárquica Nacional frente al catalanismo de la Lliga, 1918–1923', *Estudios de Historia Social*, 28–9/1–4 (1984), pp. 471–2.
14. Javier Moreno Luzón, 'De agravios, pactos y símbolos. El nacionalismo español ante la autonomía de Cataluña (1918–1919)', *Ayer*, 63/3 (2006), p. 146.

15. Ibid., pp. 146–7; Enric Ucelay-Da Cal, 'Entre el ejemplo italiano y el irlandés: la escisión generalizada de los nacionalismos hispanos 1919–1922', *Ayer*, 63/3 (2006), pp. 84–5, 108.

16. Juan Pablo Fusi, 'Centre and Periphery 1900–1936: National Integration and Regional Nationalism Reconsidered', in Frances Lannon and Paul Preston (eds), *Elites and Power in Twentieth-Century Spain* (Oxford: Clarendon Press, 1990), pp. 38–9.

17. Ignacio de Loyola Arana Pérez, *El monarquismo en Vizcaya durante la crisis del reinado de Alfonso XIII* (Pamplona: EUNSA, 1982), pp. 37–40.

18. Domingo Benavides, *Democracia y cristianismo en la España de la Restauración, 1875–1931* (Madrid: Nacional, 1978); Feliciano Montero García, *El primer catolicismo social y la 'Rerum Novarum' en España* (Madrid: Consejo Superior de Investigaciones Científicas, 1983).

19. Manuel Revuelta González, 'La recuperación eclesiástica y el rechazo anti-clerical', in José Luis García Delgado (ed.), *España entre dos siglos, 1875–1931* (Madrid: Siglo XXI, 1991), p. 213; Carlos Serrano, 'Crisis e ideología en la Restauración' in García Delgado (ed.), *España entre dos siglos*, p. 187.

20. Michael Burleigh, *Earthly Powers: Religion and Politics in Europe from the Enlightenment to the Great War* (London: HarperCollins, 2005), pp. 388–403 and 408–14.

21. For more details on Tragic Week see the chapters by Javier Moreno Luzón and Angel Smith in this volume, pp. 32–61 and 145–74.

22. Feliciano Montero, 'Del movimiento católico a la Acción Católica. Continuidad y cambio, 1900–1930', in Julio de la Cueva and Feliciano Montero (eds), *La secularización conflictiva. España, 1898–1931* (Madrid: Biblioteca Nueva, 2007), pp. 169–86.

23. Pedro Carlos González Cuevas, *Acción Española. Teología política y nacionalismo autoritario en España, 1913–1936* (Madrid: Tecnos, 1998), pp. 47–8.

24. Juan José Castillo, *El sindicalismo amarillo. Aportación al estudio del catolicismo social español, 1912–1923* (Madrid: Cuadernos para el diálogo, 1977), p. 278.

25. Juan José Castillo, *Propietarios muy pobres: sobre la subordinación política del pequeño campesinado (la Confederación Nacional Católico-Agraria), 1917–1942* (Madrid: Servicio de Publicaciones Agrarias, 1979), pp. 340–4.

26. Julio Gil Pecharromán, *Conservadores subversivos. La derecha autoritaria alfonsina, 1913–1936* (Madrid: Eudema, 1994), pp. 36–7.

27. Miguel Martorell and Fernando del Rey, 'El parlamentarismo liberal y sus impugnadores', *Ayer*, 63/3, (2006), p. 43. For a different but debunked view of the PSP, as an embryonic Christian Democrat Party, see Javier Tusell and Juan Avilés, *La Derecha Española Contemporánea: Sus Orígenes, El Maurismo* (Madrid: Espasa Calpe, 1986).

28. Among those former militants of the PSP in the executive committee of Primo de Rivera's official party were José Gabilán, Vice President of the Unión Patriótica, and Gabriel de Aristizábal, General Secretary of the Unión Patriótica and brother of the president of the Confederación Nacional Católico-Agraria. The great exception of the massive integration of the members of the PSP into the Unión Patriótica was Ángel Ossorio, who opposed the dictatorship. José Luís Gómez-Navarro Navarrete, 'La Unión Patriótica: análisis de un partido del poder', *Estudios de Historia Social*, 32–3, (January–June, 1985), pp. 93–163.

29. As early as 1894, Vázquez de Mella and Count Cerralbo participated in per-egrinations to Rome. See Montero García, *El primer catolicismo'*, pp. 120–1. For the workers' centres see Colin M. Winston, 'Carlist Worker Groups in Catalonia, 1900–1923', in Stanley Payne (ed.), *El Carlismo, 1833–1975* (Madrid: Actas, 1996), pp. 85–101.

30. Martin Blinkhorn, *Carlism and Crisis in Spain, 1931–1939* (Cambridge: Cambridge University Press, 1975), pp. 33–5.

31. *El Siglo Futuro* (4–5 November 1898).

32. Juan Ramón de Andrés Martín, *El cisma mellista* (Madrid: Actas, 2000), p. 58.

33. Juan Vázquez de Mella, *El ideal de España* (Madrid: Imprenta Alemana, 1915), pp. 73–5, 85–95.

34. This concept of race was a cultural one. Race was understood as being shaped more by common culture, historical experiences, tradition and lan-guage, than by blood. See Fredrick B. Pike, *Hispanismo, 1898–1936* (Notre Dame, Indiana: University of Notre Dame Press, 1971), pp. 1–2.

35. Juderías defined the Black Legend as 'the legend of the inquisitorial, ignor-ant and fanatic Spain, a nation unable to stand among the cultured ones, today as in the past, always ready for violent repressions; enemy of progress and innovations; or, in other words, the legend that began to spread in the sixteenth century, with the Reformation, and since then has continuously been used against us, especially in critical moments of our national life'. The book was first published in 1914 and a new enlarged edition, dedicated to Alfonso XIII, came out in 1917. The quotation is in Julián Juderías Loyot, *La leyenda negra* (Salamanca: Junta de Castilla y León, 1997), p. 24.

36. José María Salaverría, *La afirmación española. Estudios sobre el pesimismo y los nuevos tiempos* (Barcelona: Gustavo Gili, 1917), pp. 14–19, 21, 30–41, 48, 123–32, 136–7. See also his articles in *El ABC*, 'El masoquismo español. Viendo un cuadro de Zuloaga' (20 August 1914); 'Aspectos españoles. Historicismo y patriotería' (18 October 1917); 'Si España quiere ir a America' (15 August 1922).

37. See, for example, the articles by José María Salaverría, 'Cuadros estivales. Los ricos de Bilbao', *El ABC* (7 October 1916); 'En memoria del carlismo', *El ABC* (28 August 1923). See also Salaverría, *La afirmación española*, pp. 52–7, 62, 65, 81–92.

38. Isidro Sepúlveda Muñoz, 'Nacionalismo español y proyección americana: el pan-hispanismo', in Justo Beramendi, Ramón Máiz and Xosé M. Núñez (eds), *Nationalism in Europe* (Santiago de Compostela: Universidad de Santiago de Compostela, 1994), pp. 317–36.

39. Juan Pablo Fusi, 'Los nacionalismos y el Estado español: el siglo XX', *Cuadernos de Historia Contemporánea*, 22 (2000), pp. 21–52. For an analysis of the pro-cess of nationalization in the 19th century see José Álvarez Junco, *Mater Dolorosa. La idea de España en el siglo XIX* (Madrid: Taurus, 2001). A critique of the views of Álvarez Junco is in F. Archilés and M. Cruz, 'Un país extraño como cualquier otro. La construcción de la identidad nacional española contemporánea', in M. C. Romero and I. Saz (ed.), *El siglo XX. Historiografía e historia* (Valencia: Universitat de València, 2002), pp. 245–78.

40. Alfonso Capitán Díaz, *Historia de la Educación en España* (Madrid: Dykinson, 1994), 2, pp. 385–92; Manuel de Puelles Benítez, *Educación e ideología en la España contemporánea* (Madrid: Tecnos, 1999); Carolyn P. Boyd, *Historia*

Patria: Politics, History and National Identity in Spain, 1875–1975 (Princeton, NJ: Princeton University Press, 1997).
41. Capitán Díaz, *Historia*, pp. 394–5.
42. César Silió, *La educación nacional* (Madrid: Francisco Beltrán, 1914), pp. 224–5.
43. Ibid., pp. 181–2.
44. María del Mar del Pozo Andrés and Jacques F. A. Braster, 'The Rebirth of the "Spanish Race": The State, Nationalism, and Education in Spain, 1875–1931', *European History Quarterly*, 29/1 (1999), pp. 82, 89.
45. Xosé Manoel Núñez Seixas, *Los nacionalismos en la España contemporánea, siglos XIX y XX* (Barcelona: Hipótesi, 1999), pp. 24–5.
46. Geoffrey Jensen, 'Military Nationalism and the State: The case of Fin-de-Siècle Spain', *Nations and Nationalism*, 2/6 (2000), pp. 257–74.
47. Sebastian Balfour, 'The Lion and the Pig: Nationalism and National Identity in Fin-de-Siècle Spain', in Mar-Molinero and Smith (eds), *Nationalism and the Nation*, p. 116.
48. Balfour, *The End*, p. 171.
49. María Teresa González Calbet, *La Dictadura de Primo de Rivera. El Directorio Militar* (Madrid: El Arquero, 1987), p. 49.
50. José Alvarez Junco, 'Leftist Militarism and Anti-Militarism, 1875–1936' in Rafael Bañón and Thomas M. Barker (eds), *Armed Forces and Society in Spain* (New York: Columbia University Press, 1988), pp. 149–75.
51. Francisco Clocha, 'Military Press of the Restoration', in Bañón and Barker (eds.), *Armed Forces*, p. 199.
52. Sebastian Balfour and Pablo La Porte, 'Spanish Military Cultures and the Moroccan Wars', *European History Quarterly*, 30/3 (2000), p. 314.
53. Carolyn P. Boyd, 'Violencia pretoriana: del *Cu-cut!* al 23-F', in Santos Juliá (ed.) *Violencia política en la España del siglo XX* (Madrid: Taurus, 2000), pp. 300–1.
54. Carolyn P. Boyd, *Praetorian Politics in Liberal Spain* (Chapel Hill, NC: University of North Carolina Press, 1979), p. 12.
55. Balfour, *The End*, pp. 179–81.
56. The Law of Jurisdictions can be found in *La Correspondencia Militar* (21 March 1906).
57. Joan Connelly Ullman, *The Tragic Week: A Study of Anticlericalism in Spain, 1875–1912* (Cambridge, MA: Harvard University Press, 1968).
58. Fernando Fernández Bastarreche, 'The Spanish Military from the Age of Disasters to the Civil War', in Bañón and Barker (eds), *Armed Forces*, p. 233. For more information on these *Juntas Militares de Defensa* see also the chapters by Javier Moreno Luzón, Francisco J. Romero Salvadó and Sebastian Balfour in this volume, pp. 32–61, 62–91 and 255–74. The 'Disaster of Annual' is dealt with in depth by Pablo La Porte. See especially, this volume, pp. 230–54.
59. *El Ejército Español* (12 September 1923).
60. For the response of the military press to the coup see *El Ejército Español* (14 September 1923); *Ejército y Armada* (14 September 1923); *Revista Hispano Africana* (September–October 1923); *La Correspondencia Militar* (14 September 1923).
61. For the nationalist rhetoric and the actions of the Unión Cívica and Defensa Ciudadana in Madrid see, for example, *La Acción* (7 November 1919, 15,

19–20, 23 December 1919), and *El Debate* (16–17 November, 14 December 1919, 27 January 1920). For the formation of militias in Barcelona, Madrid and Zaragoza in 1919 and 1920 see Fernando del Rey Reguillo, *Propietarios y Patronos. La política de las organizaciones económicas en la España de la Restauración, 1914–1923* (Madrid: Ministerio de Trabajo y Seguridad Social, 1992), pp. 626–82. On the *guardias cívicas* and the repressive side of the Restoration regime see Eduardo González Calleja, *El Máuser y el sufragio. Orden público y violencia política en la crisis de la Restauración, 1917–1931* (Madrid: Consejo Superior de Investigaciones Científicas, 1999), pp. 19–246; and Eduardo González Calleja and Fernando del Rey Reguillo, *La defensa armada contra la revolución* (Madrid: Consejo Superior de Investigaciones Científicas, 1995), pp. 15–141.

62. Some examples in *La Vanguardia* (13–14 October 1920).

63. *El ABC* (13 October 1920 and 13 October 1921).

64. On the dispute about the nationality of Christopher Columbus, the transformation of the Admiral into a symbol of Spanish regeneration and the celebration of the Fiesta de la Raza see David Marcilhacy, 'Cristobal Colón, un héroe hispanizado. Controversia en torno a su patria de origen y homenajes monumentales', in Javier Moreno Luzón (ed.), *Construir España. Nacionalismo español y procesos de nacionalización* (Madrid: CEPC, 2007), pp. 153–81.

65. Carlos Serrano, *El nacimiento de Cármen. Símbolos, mitos y nación* (Madrid: Taurus, 1999), pp. 318–21.

66. Javier Moreno Luzón, 'Mitos de la España inmortal. Conmemoraciones y nacionalismo español en el siglo XX', *Claves de Razón Práctica*, 174, (2007), pp. 29–32.

67. Eric Storm, 'El tercer centenario del *Don Quijote* en 1905 y el nacionalismo español', *Hispania*, 58 (1998), pp. 625–54; Storm, 'Conmemoración de los héroes nacionales en la España de la Restauración. El centenario de El Greco de 1914', *Historia y Política*, 12/2 (2004), pp. 79–104; Javier Moreno Luzón, 'Memoria de la nación liberal. El primer centenario de las Cortes de Cádiz', *Ayer*, 52 (2003), pp. 207–35; Javier Moreno Luzón, 'Entre el progreso y la virgen del Pilar. La pugna por la memoria en el centenario de la Guerra de la Independencia', *Historia y Política*, 12/2 (2004), pp. 41–78; Javier Moreno Luzón, 'Fighting for the National Memory: The Commemoration of the Spanish "War of Independence" in 1908–1912', *History and Memory*, 19/1 (2007), pp. 68–94; Carolyn P. Boyd, 'The Second Battle of Covadonga: The Politics of Commemoration in Modern Spain', *History and Memory*, 14 (2002), pp. 37–65; Jordi Canal, 'Recadero contra la revolución: el carlismo y la conmemoración del XIII centenario de la Unidad Católica', in Carolyn P. Boyd (ed.), *Religión y política en la España contemporánea* (Madrid: Centro de Estudios Políticos y Constitucionales, 2007), pp. 249–70.

68. For the different versions of Liberal and Conservative nationalisms in the 19th and 20th centuries see D. Muro and A. Quiroga, 'Spanish Nationalism: Ethnic or Civic?', *Ethnicities*, 5/1 (2005), pp. 9–29.

69. Moreno, 'Entre el progreso', pp. 43–72.

70. Carolyn P. Boyd, 'Paisajes míticos y la construcción de las identidades regionales y nacionales: el caso del Santuario de Covadonga', in Carolyn P. Boyd (ed.), *Religión y política*, pp. 275, 285–93.

71. Moreno, 'Mitos', p. 32.
72. Javier Moreno Luzón, 'El rey patriota. Alfonso XIII y el nacionalismo español', in María Ángeles Lario (ed.), *Monarquía y República en la España contemporánea* (Madrid: Biblioteca Nueva, 2007), pp. 269–94.
73. Boyd, 'Paisajes míticos', p. 283.
74. Moreno, 'Mitos', p. 32.
75. Francisco J. Romero Salvadó, *The Foundations of Civil War: Revolution, Social Conflict and Reaction in Liberal Spain* (London: Routledge, 2008), pp. 190 and 192.
76. Moreno, 'El rey patriota', pp. 270–7.
77. Carlos Reyero, *La escultura conmemorativa en España. La edad de oro del monumento público, 1820–1914* (Madrid: Cátedra, 1999); María del Cármen Lacarra Ducay and Cristina Jiménez Navarro, *Historia y política a través de la escultural pública, 1820–1920* (Zaragoza: Instituto Fernando el Católico, 2003). For the French case see Pierre Nora (ed.), *Les lieux de mémoire*, 3 vols (Paris: Gallimard, 1984–1992). For the German case see Rudy Koshar, *From Monuments to Traces: Artifacts of German Memory, 1870–1990* (Berkeley, CA and Los Angeles, CA: University of California Press, 2000).
78. José Álvarez Junco, 'El nacionalismo español y las insuficiencias de la acción estatal', *Historia Social*, 40, (2001), p. 50.
79. Serrano, *El nacimiento*, p. 199.
80. Moreno, 'Mitos', p. 32.
81. Carolyn P. Boyd 'Introducción', in Carolyn P. Boyd (ed.), *Religión y política*, p. 8.
82. William J. Callahan, 'Los privilegios de la Iglesia bajo la Restauración, 1875–1923' in Carolyn P. Boyd (ed.), *Religión y política*, pp. 30–2.
83. Michael Burleigh, *Earthly Powers: Religion and Politics in Europe from the Enlightenment to the Great War* (HarperCollins: London, 2005).
84. Renato Moro, 'Religion and Politics in the Time of Secularization: The Sacralization of Politics and Politicization of Religion', *Totalitarian Movements and Political Religions*, 6/1 (June 2005), pp. 71–86.
85. Herman Lebovics, *True France: The Wars over Cultural Identity, 1900–1945* (Ithaca, NY and London: Cornell University Press, 1992), pp. x, 7.
86. Pozo and Braster, Rebirth of the 'Spanish Race', p. 85.
87. María Victoria López-Cordón Cortezo, 'La mentalidad conservadora durante la Restauración', in José Luis García Delgado (ed.), *La España de la Restauración. Política, economía, legislación y cultura* (Siglo XXI: Madrid, 1985), p. 92.
88. Ibid., pp. 81–91.

9
The Moroccan Quagmire and the Crisis of Spain's Liberal System, 1917–23

Pablo La Porte

Most historians agree that the crisis of Spanish Liberalism in the 1920s should be considered as part of the general collapse of Europe's parliamentary regimes during the interwar period, especially given the similarities between Spain's situation and that of other southern and Eastern European countries.[1] Just like other European nations, Spain suffered the economic consequences of the post-war depression and the social repercussions of the Russian Revolution, but was furthermore weakened because parties under the Restoration Settlement (1874–923) were unable to open up the parliamentary monarchy to new economic and social forces. The increasing strength of organized labour came into conflict with the regime's inertia and reluctance to assimilate or channel the new social demands which resulted from the industrialization process, and this led to greater social instability and a gradual weakening of civilian rule over the course of the first few decades of the 20th century. Just as in other European countries, the Spanish army intervened to face down the threat of revolution.

However, in this general crisis of European parliamentary regimes, there are some features which are specific to the Spanish case. First, Spain was one of the nations which took a neutral stance during the First World War. Furthermore, the influence of working-class radicalism was greater and the regional question remained unresolved, in addition to the general economic backwardness of the country.[2] Another aspect of the crisis of Spain's Liberal order was the colonial problem of Morocco, which began as a 'regenerationist' venture at the beginning of the century and later became a living nightmare for the regime. In short, even if the crisis of Spanish Liberalism followed the same trends seen in other European countries, this chapter argues that it had some special features, the most prominent being the Moroccan problem.[3]

The most important consequences of colonialism in Morocco have already been discussed in great detail elsewhere and it is not necessary to examine them in depth again. Today, the widely accepted conclusion is that the Moroccan problem played a crucial part in the final disintegration of the Restoration regime. The military campaigns undertaken between 1917 and 1923, it is usually argued, had a long-lasting, profound impact. Morocco became a burden for the Spanish Treasury and caused anxiety amongst the Spanish people, who were always distrustful of news from the other side of the Straits of Gibraltar. In the last few years of the regime, the colonial problem accentuated divisions between the different political factions in a setting which was already highly fragmented since the crisis of 1917. The rewards and promotions awarded following the African military campaigns caused deep rivalries within the army. At the same time, the war in Morocco increased the tensions between civilians and the military; tensions which had intensified since the beginning of the century, and which concluded to the detriment of the former.

The disaster of Annual (21 July 1921), when – in a matter of days – the Army of Africa lost all of the territory conquered in the eastern part of Morocco since 1912, as well as 9,000 soldiers and enormous amounts of material and equipment, merely made the situation worse. Calls were made for politicians and army officers to be held responsible for the defeat, and as a result the existing fragile political consensus that sustained the regime was weakened. It is widely argued that divisions between the different Monarchist factions became more intense, and anti-dynastic forces gained renewed drive. In the military arena, the defeat fuelled the army's growing inclination to intervene in public matters. In the eyes of the general public, the disaster was irrefutable proof that parliament was losing its prestige and that the regime was chronically inefficient. In the end, the events which took place in Morocco helped justify the *coup d'état* which took place in September 1923, and were an important factor in Alfonso XIII's acceptance of that coup.[4]

This chapter develops a somewhat different perspective. It argues that although the Moroccan disaster was clearly a decisive factor in the eventual disintegration of the regime, it provided an opportunity, albeit a slim one, to democratize its structures and start moving the public administration in a different direction. The Moroccan disaster of 1921 shook Spain's public opinion out of its deep lethargy and also made it easier to attempt quite extensive reforms, spurred on by the catalysing role of the crisis. The defeat triggered a series of initiatives, both within the regime and in the ranks of the anti-dynastic parties – especially, but not only, by the Partido Socialista Obrero Español (Spanish Socialist Workers' Party – PSOE) –, which aimed to transform the existing political structures. In the first case, these new initiatives aimed to improve the functioning of the political order. In the second, they directly questioned how representative the regime was, giving anti-dynastic forces the chance to become more visible and to play a more important role in denouncing the ruling system's shortcomings.

This chapter focuses on the four most significant areas affected by the impact of the Moroccan debacle: political parties, the military, state finances and public reaction. It will conclude that Primo de Rivera's coup was not an inevitable consequence of the colonial rout, but that it became an almost unavoidable outcome once the aspirations which had emerged from that defeat had disappeared or had been discredited.[5]

Morocco and the political framework

In the last six years of the regime, the colonial question weakened Spain's political stability. To some extent, one could argue that the Moroccan problem, which had provoked a certain level of political consensus amongst Spain's dynastic forces in the early 20th century, became the element which caused the greatest divisions between them in the 1920s. The international agreements signed by Liberals and Conservatives from the beginning of the century onwards, and which were approved by parliament with relatively little conflict (such as the 1904 Franco-Spanish Agreement, the Algeciras Conference in 1906 and the Protectorate Treaty signed in 1912) provided a comparatively stable framework and a certain degree of harmony with regard to the colonial enterprise. However, this was to change following the unexpected political earthquake that gained momentum, with the disaster of Annual at its epicentre.

First, the disaster of Annual radicalized the stances of the various political forces and eroded the precarious political stability on which the regime rested. The scale of the debacle and its massive public repercussions forced all of the dynastic (and non-dynastic) factions firmly to express their views on the action that Spain should take in Morocco in the future.[6] Amongst the Conservatives, the group most affected by the disaster (given that the latter occurred while they were in power), the defeat at Annual polarized the opinions of the three main factions (headed by Antonio Maura, Juan de la Cierva and José Sánchez Guerra, respectively). The first group believed that Spain's presence in Morocco should be reduced to positions along the Moroccan coast, the second that the entire territory should be conquered, and the third that military action should gradually be replaced with civil action in order to achieve stability in the region. These differences in opinion, which were initially silenced under Maura's national government in the summer of 1921, later caused a series of difficulties during the last few months of that administration in early 1922. Amongst the Liberals, who were also divided into three main factions under the leadership of Santiago Alba, Count Romanones and Manuel García Prieto (Marquis of Alhucemas), opinions were much less varied, and focused on reducing military contingents in the area, formalizing pacts with the rebels and insisting on the need for the civilian authorities rather than the military to take the lead in the Protectorate. However, it was not just the Liberals and Conservatives who came under closer scrutiny over the Moroccan problem. Other sectors of the political spectrum were also forced to outline their stance with regard to the colonial question as a result of events in Annual. In some cases, this led to new divisions amongst these groups. The Republicans, for example, split into a colonialist faction, led by Alejandro Lerroux, who favoured the total conquest of Morocco, and an *abandonista* faction, led by Diego Martínez Barrio, who argued for a gradual retreat from the Protectorate. Martínez Barrio's view was shared by the Spanish Socialists (led in parliament by Julián Besteiro and Indalecio Prieto), who took what some have considered to be the most coherent political stance at the time.[7]

Differences in opinion between political groups were not limited to future strategy. They were also apparent in other, more thorny aspects of the defeat and, especially, in the issue of 'responsibilities', which became a real bone of contention after the disaster. Three different options were presented in parliament once the *Expediente Picasso* (the report commissioned to clarify what had happened in Annual) was finalized in the summer of 1922.[8] The Conservatives believed that no responsibility lay with politicians. For their part, the Liberals agreed that the responsibility lay with the head of the Conservative government at the time of the disaster (Manuel Allendesalazar), his Foreign Minister (Marquis of Lerma) and Minister of War (Marquis of Eza). The Socialists, in turn, argued that responsibility for the disaster lay both with the members of Allendesalazar's cabinet and with those of Antonio Maura's government which came into power in August 1921, and which, according to them, had merely reproduced past colonial errors. The suggested punishments were also quite different. While the Liberals believed that an admonition should be issued by the lower chamber of parliament (Congress) and that the accused parties should be banned from holding public office, the Socialists went further, demanding that after Congress had issued a direct formal accusation of corrupt practices those responsible should be brought before the upper house (Senate), which, acting as a court, would impose the corresponding punishments.[9]

These conflicting opinions led to increased political instability in Spain and to contradictory colonial policies in Morocco. The three different governments which followed in the final two years of the regime – Antonio Maura (August 1921–March 1922), José Sánchez Guerra (April–December 1922) and Manuel García Prieto (December 1922–September 1923) – owed their existence to a large extent to the repercussions of the Moroccan problem. Likewise, most cabinet reshuffles which took place during those years shared one common denominator: the evolution of the Moroccan campaign.[10] Inevitably, the continuity and coherence of colonial policies also suffered as a result of the volatile political situation. Three high commissioners (Dámaso Berenguer, Ricardo Burguete and Manuel Silvela) were appointed in quick succession in a period of less than three years to run the Spanish High Command in Morocco, each with their own strategy and method, some of which were polar opposites, and none of which had the time to become established and give results. The lack of continuity in Spanish colonial policy also affected relations with France, which were crucial for the colonial undertaking, as the success of the Spanish initiatives depended, to a great extent, on a good understanding with France.[11] In short, the Moroccan problem, which worsened after the defeat at Annual, increased the fragmentation amongst dynastic forces and made it difficult for stable governments to form. This, in turn, decreased the effectiveness and coherence of colonial policy, and hindered the resolution of the crisis.

However, these were not the only effects of the African venture. The disaster also had a particular impact on the touchstone of the regime, the king, who had backed the colonization of Morocco from the outset. Indeed, from the beginning of his reign, Alfonso XIII had distinguished himself as an enthusiastic supporter of the colonial enterprise. He hoped that Africa would restore Spain's imperial glory and would help regenerate the national spirit. In fact, the monarch (who was to become known as 'el Africano') probably wanted the colonization of Morocco to become the success story which set his reign apart from the regency of his mother, María Cristina, which had been marred by the Cuban crisis.[12] Alfonso's personal support for the conduct of the

Moroccan campaign, however, contradicted the discretion required for his duties as a monarch. The investigation into events in Africa in 1921 revealed the king's special relationship with General Manuel Silvestre (commander-in-chief of the Spanish troops routed at Annual) and convinced large sectors of the political and public spheres that he was implicitly responsible for what had happened.[13] Accusations against the monarch were first made when parliament reopened following the disaster of Annual. In Congress, the Socialist minority and some Catalan regionalists blamed the king for the events in Africa. In the Senate, several generals who had held office as Spanish High Commissioners in Morocco hinted at the fact that Alfonso had suggested and encouraged operations without their knowledge.[14]

However, the king's popularity was not only affected by the parliamentary discussions of events in Annual. In December 1922, not long after calls of 'death to the monarchy!' had been heard during a turbulent session of Congress, the monarch confided in Sánchez Guerra and García Prieto his intention to announce a national referendum to ascertain whether or not he had the support of the Spanish people. If the results of that plebiscite showed that he did not have it, he was ready to abdicate in favour of his heir, Prince Alfonso, who would turn 16 on the day of the proposed referendum, in May 1923.[15] It is difficult to know whether Alfonso was truly willing to step down or if it was merely a ploy to show the politicians that, despite the political problems, he still had popular support. In any case, it seems obvious that the Moroccan problem confirmed the king's belief that the throne was in danger and that the ineptitude of dynastic politicians might lead to the overthrow of the monarchy in Spain. This belief is probably what made him tacitly accept Miguel Primo de Rivera's *coup d'état*.[16]

The Moroccan problem also had a parliamentary dimension, becoming the almost exclusive topic of debate in numerous sessions in both chambers. Debates took place in two stages. In the first phase (November–December 1921 and April–June 1922), they focused on the causes and consequences of the disaster. In the second (November–December 1922 and May–July 1923), the debate centred on the *Expediente Picasso*. No clear conclusions were reached in either phase. In fact, the debates were exceedingly long and boring affairs, replete with mutual accusations and lacking in effective suggestions. When it came to determining political responsibilities, the discussions degenerated into confrontations between parties.[17] Furthermore, bringing the African problem to parliament also had a number of other negative repercussions. First, it blocked other parliamentary bills which urgently needed to be approved and which could not be given a slot in the overbooked session calendar. In addition to this, it helped discredit the parliament more than any other matter. Over the course of these debates, some truly embarrassing scenes took place. The resignation of Sánchez Guerra's government, for example, occurred in the middle of a parliamentary session in December 1922, amidst fights between ministers and cries of death to the monarchy.[18] In the summer of 1923, the incident between General Francisco Aguilera and Senator Joaquín Sánchez de Toca, when threats against civil power were heard in the Senate, seemed to be the final straw for parliament. Ultimately, neither the debate on the causes and consequences of the disaster nor the discussion about responsibilities enhanced parliament's reputation. Instead, they confirmed that the Spanish Cortes were falling into a state of chronic disrepute.[19]

However, not all of the consequences of the defeat were negative. In fact, some effects of the disaster actually provided opportunities to renew and transform the regime's political structures. For example, the crisis led to the formation of the last national government of the constitutional monarchy headed by Antonio Maura (August 1921–March 1922). Despite the fragmentation of the parliamentary map in 1921, the defeat convinced the king and the leaders of the most important dynastic groups that they needed to present a united front in the face of adversity. Under Maura's leadership, and with the support of Liberals, Conservatives and Republicans (including the tacit approval of the Spanish Socialist Party), the new cabinet obtained a great deal of respect and included representatives from the most important political forces. Certainly, it is true that its political calibre was not as high as that of 1918 (when another national government had brought together – again under Maura – leading political figures such as Frances Cambó, Count Romanones, Eduardo Dato and Santiago Alba) but it still enjoyed considerable respect. However, the national government of 1921, like its predecessor three years earlier, proved eventually unable to contain internal rivalries between ministers. The military deadlock in Morocco and the increasingly obvious disagreements between the war minister (Juan de la Cierva), the Treasury minister (Francesc Cambó) and the foreign minister (Manuel González Hontoria) made this impossible. After the fall of the cabinet in March 1922, one journalist claimed that no other government had ever enjoyed more public support than Maura's.[20] This opportunity, however, was missed and collective support was not enough to restore the prestige of the Spanish governing class.

Despite the negative aspects pointed out above, parliamentary sessions acquired a resonance hitherto unknown. In fact, as a number of journalists pointed out at the time, one could say that, thanks to Morocco, parliament turned into the 'sounding board' for national problems from 1921 onwards.[21] The debate surrounding the Moroccan question, which took place throughout autumn 1921 and was the central focus of parliamentary sessions in autumn 1922, was not restricted to the finer points of colonial policy but covered the regime's structures in their entirety.[22] The eradication of corrupt political practices, the solution to the social problem, the need for tax reforms and Spain's economic backwardness were some of the topics discussed at length. Some sessions were attended by large numbers and followed in detail by several newspapers. However, most of these proposals did not result in any concrete initiatives and suffered setbacks as a result of other, more pressing questions. In fact, from the summer of 1923 onwards, the parliamentary debate came to a halt because of new arguments over political 'responsibilities' and the seriousness of the social problem in Barcelona, which became the country's greatest concern. Despite all this, it could be said that the parliamentary sessions of 1922 and 1923 showed that the deputies and senators had a highly insightful awareness of the flaws of the Spanish constitutional system, a factor that created optimum conditions for its reform.[23]

In the political arena, the defeat also gave rise to radical proposals. The Liberal government, which came to power in December 1922, introduced measures which it hoped would limit the military's role in the Protectorate and thus reaffirm civil authority on the other side of the Straits of Gibraltar. The appointment of a civilian as high commissioner for the first time since the Protectorate came into being (Luis Silvela, May 1923), the rescue of prisoners captured in Annual (January 1923) and the creation of a voluntary colonial army (May 1923), were all initiatives which aimed to reduce Spanish military presence in Morocco. They represented a major u-turn from previous colonial strategies and were speedily implemented (April–August 1923).

In addition to these governmental plans, some minority political forces also found that the repercussions of the disaster gave them an opportunity to present proposals for radical reform, which helped them gain a higher profile in the national political spectrum. None more so than the PSOE which, during the elections of April 1923, campaigned on a platform of seeking 'responsibilities' for the colonial disaster. The Socialists increased their representation at national level (from four MPs to seven) thanks to votes won in areas – especially Madrid – where the campaign had been most intense. Other, smaller political groups also became more prominent as a result of events in Morocco: for example, the Partido Comunista de España (Communist Party of Spain, PCE), formed in 1920, used the Moroccan problem as its political baptism of fire. In addition to demanding that Spanish troops withdraw from Morocco, the PCE also carried out demonstrations against the call-up, and in some cases these led to violence, such as the mutiny of troops in Málaga in August 1923.[24] Subsequent rallies reaffirmed the PCE's anti-colonial stance, gaining support from some working-class sectors, especially in Asturias and Bilbao. The position of other radical forces, like the traditional political abstentionism of the Anarcho-Syndicalist Confederación Nacional del Trabajo (National Labour Confederation – CNT), was also affected, to a degree, by the aftermath of events in Morocco. Shortly before the April 1923 elections, Salvador Seguí, one of the CNT's most charismatic leaders, declared that the anarcho-syndicalists were going to 'bring the whole of Spain together against the War in Morocco ... and fight against the regime using the call for responsibilities as ammunition'.[25] Just as controversial, although somewhat more limited, were the aspirations of the more radical sectors of the Catalan nationalist movement, which made the Moroccan problem a key part of their separatist strategy. When the Lliga Regionalista split in 1923, the new nationalist formation, Acció Catalana, used the Moroccan campaign as a platform to reaffirm its separatist proposals and to tighten links with other separatist groups (from the Basque Country and Galicia), as seen in the rallies which took place in Barcelona during the National Day of Catalonia (*Diada*) on 11 September 1923.[26]

Morocco and the army

The Moroccan quagmire (i.e., the impasse in which the Spanish army found itself in the Protectorate) aggravated a number of long-term issues within Spain's army, especially the deep-rooted problem of the overloaded officer corps. In addition, Morocco intensified tensions between the military and civilians which had begun to re-emerge from the beginning of the century and which would end up weakening the foundations of the regime. Ultimately, Morocco did not just fail to regenerate the spirit and military virtues of the Spanish army but was also responsible for the latter's massive decline in reputation.[27]

The African campaigns gave young, ambitious officers the chance to try their fortune in Africa, hoping for a promotion which would allow them to scale rapidly up the overloaded rungs of the peninsular army's hierarchical ladder. Given the high prices which characterized the Spanish economy during the First World War, the hopes of these officers, known as *africanistas*, were bound to create difficulties. Indeed, the abundance of rewards during the African campaigns soon led to accusations of favouritism from mainland-based military personnel who did not receive them, and who found themselves in an exceedingly precarious position. A clear manifestation of this discontent was the creation during the war of 'unions' or *juntas* by junior officers to defend their corporate interests, the *Juntas Militares de Defensa*.[28] As the *junteros* took on a dominant role in the army from 1917 onwards, they fought hard to defend the closed hierarchical system and the tradition of promotion through seniority as maxims to avoid favouritism and corruption. From then on, Morocco, and above all the promotions and rewards given as a result of the African campaigns, became a controversial issue.[29]

The disaster of Annual merely exacerbated these tensions. Four years after the establishment of the *Juntas* (known as *Comisiones Informativas* from 1918), the defeat in Africa revealed a series of deep flaws in the way in which the army worked. These flaws included far-reaching corruption in units of the Army of Africa, serious failures to fulfil duties, as well as the lack of equipment, material and training of peninsular battalions sent to Morocco after the defeat. Furthermore, the question of military 'responsibilities' fuelled animosity between the *junteros* and the *africanistas*. While the *junteros* believed that the defeat was due to the overweening ambitions of commanding generals in Morocco such as Manuel Silvestre and Dámaso Berenguer, the *africanistas* felt that the lack of military spirit of many officers in Africa (which was, according to them, due to the compulsory rota system imposed by the *Juntas* in Morocco from 1918 onwards) was the real cause of the disaster. The bitterness between the two branches of the army had negative repercussions in Africa, where it provoked disagreements between officers and, on occasion, compromised the success of military operations. It also extended to mainland Spain where it led to a never-ending series of incidents which hindered the army and increased rivalry between its different units. In the first case, a number of military campaigns and troop movements in Morocco were made more difficult as a result of tensions and rivalries between those in charge (as occurred, for example, in Tizzi Azza in November 1921). In the second, the recriminations between both army groups were settled by replacements, suspensions or resignations of important military personnel who were playing a major role in the African campaigns – Miguel Cabanellas (November 1921), Dámaso Berenguer (June 1922) and José Millán Astray (November 1922) – which endangered their continuity and future success.

Tensions were not limited to the military sphere, but also affected the struggle between civil and military power which had resurfaced at the beginning of the century. These rivalries were apparent in a number of different ways. First, the *junteros* launched a public campaign via their press organizations to express their viewpoint with regard to colonial policy. They disagreed with government policies put in place after the disaster, opposed new rewards in Morocco, and sought to protect those *junteros* brought to trial as a result of the disaster.[30] This attitude led to a crucial confrontation between the *junteros* and Maura's war minister, Juan de la Cierva, which resulted in the cabinet stepping down in January 1922. During this crisis, sparked off by the presentation of a bill which aimed to make these bodies adhere more strictly to the Ministry's orders, the *junteros* physically threatened the war minister, demanding that he resign from the cabinet.[31]

Africanistas also used their influence on civil power. The expeditionary units of the Army of Africa which were most sympathetic to *africanista* principles, the *Legión* and the *Regulares*, showed their explicit support for Maura's government during the January 1922 conflict by sending letters in which they expressed their backing for Cierva's reorganization project.[32] In addition, a number of *africanista* circles put pressure on the government so that military operations which they deemed crucial in order to maintain control over territory would be carried out.[33] In some cases, the motivation behind this pressure was nothing more than the desire to repair the damage done to military honour by what they perceived as shameful episodes (such as the payment of 4 million pesetas as ransom for the liberation of 346 Spanish prisoners from the hands of Abd el Krim on 27 January 1923). In addition, the new measures imposed by the Liberal government in 1923 in Morocco were met with firm resistance from *africanista* commanders in the territory, directed especially against bills drawn up by the Foreign Minister Santiago Alba.[34]

Despite tensions between the civil and military authorities, some effects of the defeat could be seen as positive. First, one exceedingly important factor was the backing that public opinion gave to the Maura government during the conflict with representatives of the *Comisiones Informativas* in January 1922. As a number of journalists noted at the time, the numerous demonstrations of support were, to some extent, a rejection of the interference of the army in politics.[35]

It seems clear that Maura, aware that he could count on widespread popular backing, decided to provoke an open conflict with the *junteros*, refusing to remain in office until they had been subjected to the strict control of the Ministry of War. His strategy was successful. Public support as well as that of other political leaders became decisive factors in the resolution of the dispute. Finally, the king sanctioned the bill for the reorganization of the *Comisiones Informativas* (16 January 1922) and civil power emerged strengthened from the conflict. Hence, following the disaster of Annual, the *Juntas de Defensa,* which five years before had been seen as pioneers of military regeneration, lost their legitimacy and *raison d'être.* This did not lead to their immediate disappearance, but it did result in their influence being severely curtailed. When the Sánchez Guerra government decided to dismantle them in November 1922, it was doing nothing more than confirming their now minor role within the Spanish army.[36]

Also positive for the army were the actions of the Supreme Council of War (Consejo Supremo de Guerra y Marina), the military high court in charge of the judicial inquiry into the military responsibilities for the disaster. The investigations carried out by this institution meant that its president, General Aguilera, became a hugely popular figure. The Council's actions were significant because they showed the determination of certain sectors of the army to punish all the military groups which held some responsibility for the disaster, and because its resolutions became an incentive to call for civil responsibilities. Its decisions were certainly very severe, to the point that some were deemed to be overly zealous.[37] The 22 prosecutions recommended in the *Expediente Picasso* rose to 37 as a result of the Council's decisions, and the majority of the punishments outlined in the *Picasso* report were increased, in some cases to include sanctions for members of the original military tribunals in Melilla, which were accused of leniency in the fulfilment of their duties. Military authorities exempted from the enquiries of the *Picasso* report came under investigation by the Council, and some were accused of playing a role in the disaster. Between January and May 1923, the Council passed 11 guilty verdicts. In addition, it put an end to military promotions, even those which dated back to before 1921. These measures combined to cause a double effect. On the one hand, they exposed the irregularities and numerous failures of colonial commanders to fulfil their duties. On the other hand, the sanctions of the Supreme Council of War had a cathartic effect which enhanced the military's reputation in the eyes of society. The war minister of the Liberal government, Niceto Alcalá Zamora, recognized this, and believed that the series of guilty verdicts had resulted for the army in 'an effect similar to a successful war, in terms of respect and admiration from the public'.[38]

This was also the view of the military newspaper *Ejército y Armada* that stated, in its editorial of 23 March 1923, that, thanks to the work of the Supreme Council, the army was recovering its self-esteem, and that this was giving it the moral authority to demand the greatest severity when it came to investigating political responsibilities.[39] Most politicians were also aware of this point, as shown in the speeches made in the Congress throughout the summer of 1923.[40] In fact, the popularity that General Aguilera enjoyed at first was due to the fact that the decisions taken by his institution sparked some hope that the governing class would be forced to accept the need for political responsibilities.[41]

Indeed, the cathartic work carried out within the army itself during the investigation into military responsibilities (symbolized in the rulings of the Supreme Council) gave certain prestige back to the corps and, above all, was an excellent opportunity for dynastic forces to show a similar severity when it came to calling for political responsibilities, which could have gained a certain measure of popularity for the regime. Once again, these hopes were dashed. Political responsibilities for the disaster were never sought, and this had a crucial effect on the growing hostility of the armed forces towards politicians, which would prove crucial in explaining the stance of the army in September 1923.[42]

The financial implications

The colonial venture also had deleterious consequences for the Spanish Treasury. First, because the financial benefits of colonial action were very limited, and second, because Spain's spending in Morocco increased constantly, especially after the Protectorate Treaty was signed in 1912. The financial deficit meant that the colonization of Morocco became a costly enterprise. The situation grew worse following the defeat at Annual. The economic repercussions of the disaster therefore joined a long list of military and political concerns, forcing successive governments to draw up hasty plans but nonetheless failing to reduce costs substantially in the Protectorate.

First of all, it is important to highlight that Spain's zone of influence in Morocco was marked by few resources and poor prospects. Apart from a few mining concerns around Melilla there were no large areas where Spanish capital could be invested with guaranteed returns. The region was unsafe and split by the Rif Mountains which were inhabited by tribes which had traditionally been hostile to foreign advances. In addition to the lack of main roads and railways, there was some conflict with the natives when it came to property and land exploitation rights, which had been ongoing since 1907. Understandably, Spain invested a relatively small amount in the region.[43]

The means through which the Spanish government could obtain any direct benefits from the Protectorate (taxes, exploitation rights) were not very promising either, as a result of the low numbers of Spanish residents in the territory (as against the situation in the French zone) and the limited investments made by mining companies in prospection and exploitation permits. The Spanish colonial economy centred on the Protectorate's large cities (Ceuta, Melilla, Tetuán, Larache) which, because they were not linked by any large transport networks, depended more than anything on the presence of the army and developed in isolation from one another, in closed, parallel circuits. Taxes collected by the sultan, a share of which the Spanish state was authorized to receive because of its *protective* mission, were also not a significant help, and the total collected was very small.[44]

In addition to this, from 1912 onwards Spain's spending in the Protectorate began to increase. This was due mainly to the need to create an administrative structure to respond to the international commitments which were taken on at that time. Effective control of the territory meant the extension of colonial action and thus military campaigns which placed Spain's Treasury under relentless strain. Between 1912 and 1921 the Moroccan budget jumped from 100 to 170 million pesetas.[45] These funds were not, however, distributed in an effective manner. First, most of them were used to pay the salaries and wages of the colonial army, and not, as the new mission required, to improve equipment. The war minister normally administered up to 90 per cent of the Moroccan budget, and the remaining 10 per cent was administered by other ministries to finance the scant civilian services set up during this period.[46] In addition to this unequal distribution of spending, there were a number of other problems associated with the presence of the army in Morocco – in particular, extensive corruption in a number of units and expeditionary corps, which compromised their effectiveness to an even greater extent. In short, the growing economic deficit of the colonial enterprise was not just the result of the scarce resources available in the Protectorate but was also due to the inefficient way in which the Moroccan budget was spent.

The disaster of Annual took spending in Morocco to another level. The loss of equipment and arms (129 canons, 10,000 rifles, livestock and other supplies) meant that Spain had to make a considerable economic effort in order to replace the units destroyed and finance new military campaigns. Furthermore, following the discovery that many of the troops sent to Melilla lacked some of the most basic material requirements, the government was also forced to allocate additional funds, reaching a value of 600 million pesetas during Maura's administration alone.[47] In addition to this, the means through which the government was able to collect taxes in the Protectorate were further reduced. Most Spaniards with farms in Morocco were forced to migrate to Algeria after they lost their land, while others waited in vain for the government to provide them with compensation. Levels of investment in the territory, especially in Melilla's mines, fell dramatically in the years that followed.[48]

Two different, almost complementary strategies were designed to respond to these new needs. First, the Maura government agreed to issue new public debt bonds under particularly advantageous conditions in order to attract the large amount of private capital which had accumulated during the war boom and thus meet the needs of the Treasury. This strategy, which simply prolonged a practice which had become common to Spanish governments since the First World War, offered immediate dividends – the first debt bonds were issued on 4 November 1921 and were covered in less than 24 hours – with the result that Maura's government was able to respond to the most urgent requirements.[49] However, this method also led to considerable pressure to meet interest payments. In the long term, it accentuated Spain's negative financial context: the gradual withdrawal of private capital from productive areas and its growing fondness for state public debt, practices which became an obstacle to Spain's industrial growth.[50]

The Conservative government of Sánchez Guerra (1922) and the Liberal government of the Marquis of Alhucemas (1923) opted for a different strategy; one centred on the reduction of the Protectorate's budget. In colonial terms, this helped prepare for the gradual repatriation of troops, the progressive reduction of military operations and the parallel expansion of political action. For the 1922–3 budgetary year, for example, Sánchez Guerra's government reduced spending in Morocco by 500 million pesetas, which it hoped to use to respond to these new priorities.[51] The Liberal government also planned significant reductions in spending in Morocco, as well as a redistribution of resources. Unfortunately, the assumptions on which these reductions in spending were based did not materialize. The worsening situation in the Protectorate throughout autumn 1922 and, especially, in summer 1923, meant that Spain had to suspend all troop repatriation, readjust spending and even send new reinforcements to the other side of the Straits.

Despite these problems, events in Morocco also gave rise to a number of reform bills which aimed to balance Spanish finances. Of these, the most notable was that drawn up by the Treasury minister of Maura's government, Francesc Cambó. With the unabated support of Maura, Cambó was convinced of the need to implement far-reaching reforms in the budget and, especially, in the Spanish tax system.[52] In the aftermath of the disaster, the minister saw the perfect opportunity to put forward measures which aimed to remove the traditional tax privileges of Spain's upper classes.

Cambó's tax reform bill outlined a series of significant changes for the country's tax structure. As he explained, his ultimate goal was to balance the budget. His plan centred around the need for the upper classes to pay more taxes by increasing their direct contributions (creating up to 22 new taxes) and making changes to existing taxes. The government would also collect some taxes which used to be collected by local corporations.[53] Cambó also took advantage of the opportunity to make a drastic reduction in wasteful bureaucracy. He was forced to accept that his measures were radical ones, but believed that they were essential in order to improve the financial situation:

> I admit that the sacrifice which must be asked for in the interest of the community as a whole demands that the government provides an example of supreme authority... putting an end to the uncontrolled increase in spending, especially in terms of personnel, which we have suffered over recent years, and severely cutting back on those services which we believe to be inefficient.[54]

Although some ministers believed that several of Cambó's proposed measures were good, they criticized the plan saying that it was unfeasible. For example, shortly after finding out the contents of the bill, the Marquis of Cortina, the Minister of the Navy, said to Maura: 'what we need is one thing and what we are in a position to do is another'.[55] In the end, the bill was not presented in parliament because Maura's government stepped down in March 1922. Cambó's proposals were later taken up by Sánchez Guerra's new Conservative administration, but the more controversial articles were removed in order to facilitate its approval by parliament.

Another consequence of the Moroccan campaigns which could be thought of as positive, especially once Spanish troops had recovered some of the territory lost in 1921, was that they led to a more equal distribution of spending in the Protectorate. Most reforms, which aimed to create a more balanced colonial budget, were drawn up by the Liberal government of 1923, and they focused on the need for civil authorities to take on a more important role in Morocco.[56]

The new colonial budget for 1923–4 tripled the funds available for the Foreign Office (75 million pesetas) within the total budget for Morocco, doubling the proportion allocated the previous year (18 per cent as against 9 per cent). In parallel to this, the budget assigned to the Ministry of War in Morocco was reduced. Although this reduction was not drastic (it was between 4 and 5 per cent of the previous budget), it reflected a certain change in direction of Moroccan finances.[57] In this way, the Liberal government tried to strike a balance between the importance of the new projects and the amount of money assigned to them. This was the work, above all, of the foreign minister, Santiago Alba, who was determined to give new direction to the Protectorate's finances as well as to the way in which it was administered. However, Alba's initiatives were thwarted by the growing difficulties of the military campaigns in summer 1923, which altered the fragile budgetary balance and, in the end, led to new troops being sent to Morocco.

In short, the colonization of Morocco turned into a huge burden for the Restoration regime, becoming a venture which brought little profit and led to increasing demands on the Treasury. However, the defeat also acted as an incentive to overhaul public finances and, in particular, to reorganize the Moroccan budget once and for all. These plans were hindered by the volatility of the political situation, and the direction that the situation in Morocco took. In the end, these two factors meant that the plans were doomed to fail.

Public opinion

The Moroccan undertaking had four main effects on Spanish public opinion during the last years of the regime. First, it widened the gap between people and the institutions of the Restoration. Second, it became a catalyst for other social tensions which erupted in the context of the hostility towards the Moroccan campaigns. Third, it discredited the regime more than any other issue in its last turbulent years. Ultimately, the impact of the African venture deprived the Spanish Liberal monarchy of any remnants of social support at a time when it was absolutely essential for its survival.

The colonization of Morocco enjoyed little popular support from the outset. The Cuban disaster in 1898 and the loss of the last overseas territories meant that most Spaniards were no longer interested in colonial enterprises, and instead were filled with a growing pessimism with regard to the country's imperial abilities. A crucial aspect of the problem was the inability of the dynastic politicians to keep public opinion informed about the agreements reached in relation to Morocco at the beginning of the 20th century: the presence in Morocco was mainly due to British interests in keeping the status quo of the region, thereby preventing France from occupying the coast facing Gibraltar, as well as Spain's need to recover some of its status in the European international order. However, these reasons were not properly explained, mainly due to the fact that the government feared that public opinion would react negatively.[58]

The African venture was also unpopular for a number of more practical reasons: the scarce resources available in the Spanish zone; the fact that the colonial army was made up primarily of peninsular battalions which had been sent to serve in difficult, dangerous conditions; and the unfair system of military recruitment in place at the beginning of the century, by which the period of compulsory military service (three years) could be shortened by paying a fee (*cuota*). In short, the reasons for Spain's presence in Morocco were never completely understood by a large part of the Spanish population, who viewed the enterprise with utter mistrust.

The debacle of 1921 also led to more discontent, which manifested itself in criticism of the Moroccan campaign, thus increasing social unrest during the last few years of the regime. The military defeat stirred up traditional popular animosity towards the Moroccan venture whilst simultaneously becoming the clearest piece of evidence that the ruling order had become ineffective. A large number of issues linked to the colonial rout emerged from 1921 onwards as the public expressed its discontent with the dynastic governments. They included the unfinished military campaigns, which were always meant to reach a conclusion but which were continuously renewed, and the poor, late and incomplete repatriation of military contingents. There were also a number of smaller-scale questions, such as the release of the prisoners captured after the disaster and the repatriation of *soldados de cuota*. The cry for political 'responsibilities', perhaps the most pressing issue for Spanish public opinion, was consistently delayed by the different cabinets which came to power. Finally, in July 1923, the matter was referred to a new parliamentary committee, but even the members of this committee admitted that there was little hope of resolving the matter.[59] The crisis of Annual, in conclusion, widened and deepened the gap between public opinion and the regime. Crucially, the crisis ultimately convinced large sectors of society that the ruling Liberal order was chronically and irremediably inefficient. When Primo de Rivera finally overthrew it, nobody jumped to its defence.[60]

Despite the negative outcome of events in Morocco, public opinion also reacted positively at certain stages of the military campaigns. During the months following the disaster, for example, and especially between June and December 1921, patriotism flourished, and the public was stalwart in its support of the government's determination to recover the territory lost in the disaster. To the surprise of most dynastic parties and the disbelief of those who wanted to mobilize public opinion against the Moroccan campaign, the farewell ceremonies for soldiers who were sent to Morocco became popular tributes where the public gave shows of support to the soldiers and displayed a truly patriotic spirit.[61] A number of factors combined to explain these events. First, troops were sent urgently before the public was completely aware of the magnitude of the defeat. Second, soldiers who were close to finishing their period of service were not sent to Morocco. Finally, the *soldados de cuota* were dispatched along with the rest of the contingent. Other factors should also be mentioned here such as the strict press censorship, accepted with little resistance by the main national newspapers, the efforts of local institutions such as municipal corporations and town councils to channel public reaction, the important role played by the Catholic Church in the farewells for soldiers and, finally, the inability of the anti-dynastic forces (CNT, PCE, etc.), to react to events.

Throughout the country, people gave donations and engaged in the collection of financial or material support. There seemed to be some degree of consensus between public opinion and dynastic rulers regarding Morocco, something which had probably not occurred since 1912.[62] Although this enthusiasm gradually waned from December 1921 onwards, when the military advances stopped, it provided undeniable support for the national government which came to power after the disaster and fortuitously allowed the regime's position to coincide with Spanish public opinion.[63]

The public response to the Annual disaster also materialized in campaigns which mobilized wider sections of Spanish society.[64] Of these, none was more pre-eminent than the call for political 'responsibilities', which provoked a general reaction, attracting public interest and galvanizing a wide-ranging response. Demonstrations, numerous public acts and petitions took place in various parts of the country, promoted by associations from a variety of backgrounds, which repeatedly stated that they were not motivated by partisan interests but by national ones.[65] Even before the new Liberal government summoned general elections to be held in 1923, the call for political responsibilities had become a popular, civic movement, which made even those who viewed the passivity of Spanish society most critically harbour a little hope. In December 1922, *El Socialista*, a newspaper which did not tend to exaggerate the public's enthusiasm, declared that the Spanish people had started to wake up, 'to shake off the drowsiness which had turned them into a conformist, lazy beast'.[66] In short, one could say that the call for 'responsibilities' channelled the public's desire for reforms and changes to be made to the regime's modus vivendi, reflecting a popular, widely felt longing for a greater democratization of the regime's structures.

The 1923 elections seemed to offer a timely opportunity for public opinion to express its concern about the African crisis. These elections were called by the new Liberal government in order to achieve a parliamentary majority with which to work more effectively. Traditionally, the elections have been thought of as some of the most fraudulent of the regime, although some aspects of them should perhaps be examined in more detail.[67] The number of members of parliament voted in as a result of article 29 (those elected automatically for lack of opposition in their constituencies) was very high: 146. The wide-scale application of this article actually brought to light one of the most recurrent practices of the old regime: the tacit sharing out of districts amongst the different political groups in order to avoid direct confrontations and make sure that a minimum number of their respective members were returned. Nevertheless, if we take into account the general turnout, not counting the percentage of voters who did not exercise their right to vote as a result of the application of article 29 (35 per cent of the total), we can conclude that 41 per cent of the electorate did exercise their right to vote, and only 23 per cent of voters abstained. These percentages show that, in the districts where votes could be cast, the electoral turnout was much higher than it had been on previous occasions, especially the last elections held in 1920. As the colonial problem had become a central part of the electoral campaign (repatriation of troops, political 'responsibilities'), it could be concluded that the increased turnout in the districts where votes could be cast was a result of the Spanish electorate's growing interest in and concern for the issue.[68]

Another aspect of these elections which should be highlighted is the victory of the Socialist Party in the Spanish capital. The Socialists won a majority in Madrid, increasing their representatives from the province from three to five members. The press put the PSOE's success down to its campaign calling for political responsibilities, which it used as the crux of its electoral strategy. For some political commentators, the elections in Madrid had actually become a plebiscite regarding the question of political responsibilities, which the Socialist Party had known how to use to its advantage.[69] In short, the April 1923 elections reflected the growing concerns of some sectors of society for the Moroccan question and, in some constituencies (Madrid was one of the few places where the old political practices did not have much influence), a demonstration in favour of radical measures in response to the disaster of Annual.[70]

Conclusions

It seems logical to conclude that the problem of Morocco was of decisive importance during the final years of Spain's Liberal regime. After the disaster of Annual in particular, a number of conflictive aspects of the colonization of Morocco took on a central role in Spanish politics, making it even more difficult for both parliament and for the dynastic parties to function effectively. In this way, Morocco intensified the fragmentation of the Spanish political arena, exacerbated tensions within the army and accentuated rivalries in civil–military relations. The costly military campaigns also had a destabilizing effect on the Treasury and, ultimately, on the development of the economy. In addition, the accumulated loss of reputation of institutions and political parties as a result of the Moroccan problem (political responsibilities, stagnation of military campaigns) was a crucial factor in explaining the public's apathy and restraint when the survival of those institutions came under threat in September 1923. In short, at the beginning of the 1920s the Moroccan problem became a quagmire in which the successive dynastic governments became stuck and which brought about the end of the Restoration regime founded by Cánovas in December 1874.

However, as we have seen throughout this chapter, the defeat also gave rise to a series of political and civil initiatives (reform bills, public demonstrations) which bore witness to a certain desire for change and provided opportunities for the democratization of public life and, above all, the eradication of corrupt practices which had become ingrained in the regime's foundations. In this sense, one could say that Morocco was a terrible burden for the ruling order, but that it also acted as a catalyst for definitive reform. The public's passionate call for political 'responsibilities', the tax reform bills of Maura's government, the lively parliamentary debates under Sánchez Guerra's government, the Liberal government's change in stance in terms of colonial policy or the relevance acquired by political forces which claimed that the disaster was an example of the lack of democratization of the regime (PSOE) are just some examples of this. Some of these aspirations did materialize, as can be seen in their political repercussions (resignation of ministers, cabinet changes, public demonstrations) and speeches made by the most relevant politicians at the time. Ultimately, however, they were short-lived and their relevance was fleeting. In fact, some of these reactions had barely begun to emerge and others were discredited months before the *coup d'état* took place. By September 1923, the focus of attention had shifted to Barcelona's social struggle, which had become the most pressing problem facing the country: an extra-parliamentary solution was seen by many as an inevitable alternative to the deadlock which had been reached. Together with delivering the *coup de grâce* to an ailing body, it could be argued that Primo also buried a premature child.

Notes

* Research for this chapter was made possible by a grant from the Carnegie Trust for the Universities of Scotland. I would also like to thank Ann McFall and Becky Hendry for their help in the preparation of this chapter.

1. Dirk Berg-Schlosser and Jeremy Mitchell (eds), *Authoritarianism and Democracy in Europe, 1918–1939* (London: Macmillan, 2002), pp.1–10.
2. Juan J. Linz, 'L'effondrement de la démocratie. Autoritarisme et totalitarisme dans l'Europe de l'entre-deux-guerres', *Revue International de Politique Comparée*, 2/4 (2004), pp. 531–84.
3. This point has been highlighted recently by Douglas Porch, 'Spain's African Nightmare', *Quarterly Journal of Military History*, 18/2 (2006), pp. 28–37.
4. Ángeles Barrio Alonso, *La Modernización de España (1917–1939). Política y Sociedad* (Madrid: Síntesis, 2004), pp. 54–63.
5. There are two historical interpretations of the crisis of the Restoration settlement. Some authors believe that the regime was irreparably damaged by events in the late 1910s and early 1920s (Seco Serrano, Esdaile), while others maintain that it was showing stirrings of vitality (Carr, Malerbe, Malefakis). In general, the argument presented in this article backs the first interpretation, while aiming to highlight the most relevant aspects of the second.
6. Morgan C. Hall, *Alfonso XIII and the Failure of the Liberal Monarchy in Spain, 1902–1923* (Columbia: Columbia University Press, 2003), pp. 454–566.
7. Diego Sevilla Andrés, 'Los partidos políticos y el Protectorado', *Archivos del Instituto de Estudios Africanos*, 65/1 (1963), pp. 61–86. Speeches made by representatives of different groups can be seen in the *Diario de Sesiones de Cortes* (hereafter DSC), *Congreso* (Madrid, 1922), pp. 3948–4080, 4108–16 and 4448–60.
8. The report has recently been reprinted: Various authors, *El Expediente Picasso: las Sombras de Annual* (Madrid: Almena, 2003).
9. Conde de Romanones, *Las Responsabilidades políticas del Antiguo Régimen* (Madrid: Renacimiento, 1924). Rulings can be seen in DSC, *Congreso*

252 Pablo La Porte

(15 November 1922), appendices 1, 2 to 102 and DSC, *Congreso* (16 November 1922), appendix 1 to 103.

10. Including the resignations of the foreign minister in the Maura administration, Manuel González Hontoria (8 February 1922), the ministers Joaquín Fernández Prida and Mariano Ordóñez in the Sánchez Guerra government (5 December 1922), and the Minister of War Niceto Alcalá Zamora in the Liberal Concentration government (24 May 1923).

11. As noted by Daniel Rivet, *Lyautey et l'institution du Protectorat Français au Maroc, 1912–1925* (Paris: L'Harmattan, 1988), 3, pp. 269ff.

12. Javier Tusell, *Alfonso XIII. El Rey polémico* (Madrid: Taurus, 2001), p. 56.

13. Beatriz Frieyro de Lara, 'La cuestión militar en la revista *España*', *Historia Actual On-line*, 5, (2004), pp. 39–53.

14. For the first case, see the speeches made by Indalecio Prieto on 27 and 28 October 1921 (DSC, *Congreso, 1921*, Madrid, 1922, pp. 3820ff) and by Julián Besteiro on 3 and 10 November 1921 (DSC, *Congreso, 1921*, Madrid, 1922, pp. 3938ff). For the second, see Public Record Office (hereafter PRO), Foreign Office (FO) 371/7069, doc. 241, report by Charles Wingfield, chargé d'affaires at the British Embassy in Madrid (10 December 1921).

15. Biblioteca de la Real Academia de la Historia (hereafter BRAH), Archivo Natalio Rivas (hereafter ANR), doc. 11/8909 (December 1922).

16. This is the impression given by the famous letter written by Gabriel Maura to his father following a conversation with King Alfonso in August 1923. Archivo Antonio Maura (hereafter AAM), file 259, folder 8 (6 August 1923).

17. For a summary, see Mercedes Vázquez de Prada Tiffe, *La Conquista de la Democracia. España, 1900–2000* (Pamplona: Eunate, 2001), pp. 46–55.

18. ANR, doc. 11–8908 (5 December 1922).

19. Carlos Seco Serrano (ed.), *Alfonso XIII en el Centenario de su reinado* (Madrid: Real Academia de la Historia, 2002), pp. 89ff.

20. Francisco Hernández Mir, *Del Desastre al fracaso. Un mando funesto* (Madrid: Pueyo, 1922), p. 19.

21. *ABC* (3 December 1922).

22. See, for example, the records of the sessions held at the end of November and beginning of December 1922, DSC, *Congreso, 1922* (Madrid, 1923), pp. 4290–398.

23. Miguel Martorell Linares and Fernando Del Rey Reguillo, 'El parlamentarismo liberal y sus impugnadores', *Ayer* 63/3 (2006), pp. 23–52.

24. Manuel Gómez, *El largo viaje. Política y cultura en la evolución del Partido Comunista de España, 1920–1939* (Madrid: Ediciones de la Torre, 2005), pp. 62–86.

25. *La Libertad* (23 January 1923). Seguí was assassinated in Barcelona two months later (10 March 1923) (all translations are mine unless otherwise stated).

26. Historians' opinions with regard to the significance of these demonstrations vary greatly. While some authors feel that the success of this strategy was relative, others believe it was highly significant. For the former, see Eloy Martín Corrales, *Marruecos y el colonialismo español* (Barcelona: Bellaterra, 2002), pp. 202–4; for the latter, see José Luis de la Granja Sainz, 'Las alianzas estratégicas entre los nacionalismos periféricos en la España del siglo XX', *Studia Historica, Historia Contemporánea*, 18 (2000), pp. 149–75.

27. Fernando Ramos, 'Razones de la imagen del ejército ante la sociedad española', *Ámbitos*, 7–8 (2002), pp. 197–214.
28. For further analysis of the *Juntas Militares de Defensa*, see the chapter on the revolutionary crisis of 1917 by Francisco J. Romero Salvadó and the chapter by Sebastian Balfour, this volume, 62–91 and 255–74.
29. Geoffrey Jensen, *Irrational Triumph: Cultural Despair, Military Nationalism and the Ideological Origins of Franco's Spain* (Nevada: University of Nevada Press, 2002), pp. 140–56.
30. *La Correspondencia Militar* (November and December 1921).
31. Archives Diplomatiques du Ministère des Affaires Étrangères (hereafter ADMAE), Maroc, 1917–1940, file 589, report by Mr Defrance, French Ambassador in Madrid (28 December 1921).
32. *ABC* (14 January 1922).
33. This was seen in the requests made by several captain generals to the Liberal government of 1923 that the operation to Alhucemas was not to be delayed (ANR, 11/8909, 5 February 1923).
34. Andrés Mas Chao, *La formación de la conciencia africanista en el ejército español, 1909–1926* (Madrid, Servicio Geográfico del Ejército, 1988), pp. 51ff.
35. *España* (14 January 1922).
36. Alberto Bru Sánchez-Fortún, 'Padrino y Patrón. Alfonso XIII y sus oficiales', *Hispania Nova*, 6 (2006), pp. 14ff.
37. BRAH, Archivo Romanones, file 58, no. 32 (notes, July 1922).
38. Servicio Histórico Militar (hereafter SHM), r. 535, file 373, folder 9, letter to General Vives, Commanding General of Melilla (10 April 1923).
39. *Ejército y Armada* (23 March 1923).
40. The Catalan MP Felipe Rodés stated on 5 July 1923 that 'the only way to regain this prestige, perhaps to save Spain's parliamentary regime, is by taking on and resolving the problem of responsibilities without delay': DSC, *Congreso, 1923* (Madrid, 1924), p. 749.
41. Francisco Alia Miranda, *Duelo de sables: el general Aguilera, de ministro a conspirador contra Primo de Rivera, 1917–1931* (Madrid: Biblioteca Nueva, 2006), pp. 120–30.
42. Carlos Seco Serrano, *Militarismo y civilismo en la España Contemporánea* (Madrid: Instituto de Estudios Económicos, 1984), p. 298.
43. As such, between 1913 and 1921, only 34 companies were set up, with an estimated capital of 114 million pesetas. Around the same time, and although the two territories are difficult to compare due to differences in size and conditions, there were 268 European companies in the French zone with a total capital of 174 million francs. See Víctor Morales Lezcano, 'Las Minas Del Rif y el Capital financiero peninsular (1906–1930)', *Moneda y Crédito*, 135 (1975) pp. 61–79.
44. José Fermín Bonmatí, *Españoles en el Maghreb, siglos XIX y XX* (Madrid: Mapfre, 1992), pp. 93ff.
45. AAM, file 382, Spending in Morocco since 1909.
46. An interesting examination of this conflict can be seen in José L. Villanova, 'La pugna entre militares y civiles por el control de la actividad interventora en el Protectorado español en Marruecos (1912–1936)', *Hispania*, 65/2 (2005), pp. 683–715.

254   *Pablo La Porte*

47. AMM, file 276, folder 1 (February 1922).
48. Ministerio de Trabajo, *Anuario Financiero de Sociedades Anónimas de España* (Madrid, 1923), pp. 112–14.
49. *El Diario Universal* (5 November 1921).
50. José Luis García Delgado and Juan Carlos Jiménez, 'El reinado de Alfonso XIII', in VV. AA., *Historia de España* (Madrid: Marcial Pons, 2003), pp. 314–17.
51. DSC, *Congreso* (Madrid, 1923), session 9 May 1922, appendix 2 to 33, pp. 1–309.
52. AMM, file 441, folder 10, Maura to Cambó (3 February 1922).
53. The importance of these measures has been highlighted by Gabriel Tortella, *The Development of Modern Spain* (Cambridge, MA: Harvard University Press, 2000), p. 413.
54. AMM, file 276, folder 1, Cambó to Maura (16 February 1922).
55. AMM, file 278, folder 8, Cortina to Maura (16 February 1922).
56. Despite reforms introduced by Sánchez Guerra's government, the Ministry of War continued to be assigned almost 85 per cent of the budget in Morocco in 1922–3.
57. *Liquidación provisional del Presupuesto de 1923–1924*, (Madrid, 1924), p. 51.
58. Tim Rees, 'Between the Rock and a Hard Place: Spain's International Relations in the 20th and 21st centuries', *Journal of Contemporary History*, 38/4 (2003), pp. 633–46.
59. Indalecio Prieto in *El Pueblo Vasco* (22 August 1923).
60. Teresa Carnero, 'El lento avance de la democracia', in María Cruz Romeo and Ismael Saz (eds), *El siglo XX. Historiografía e Historia* (Valencia: Publicacions de la Universitat de València, 2002), pp. 167ff.
61. Celso Almunia, 'El desastre de Annual y su proyección sobre la opinión pública española', *Investigaciones Históricas. Época Moderna y Contemporánea*, 8 (1988), pp. 183–245.
62. AMM, file 18, folder 8, reports for July 1922.
63. Almunia, 'El desastre de Annual', p. 244
64. Arturo Osuna Servent, *Frente a Abd el Krim* (Madrid: Felipe Samarán, 1922), p. 8.
65. *ABC* (21 December 1922).
66. *El Socialista* (13 December 1922).
67. See, for example, Santos Juliá, 'Política y sociedad', in VV. AA., *La España del siglo XX* (Madrid: Marcial Pons, 2003), pp. 60–1.
68. This has been highlighted by Mercedes Cabrera, 'Elecciones y cultura política en la crisis de la monarquía de la Restauración', in Rosa Ana Gutiérrez, Rafael Zurita and Renato Camurri (eds), *Elecciones y cultura política en España e Italia, 1890–1923* (Valencia: Publicacions de la Universitat de València, 2003), pp. 190ff.
69. *El Sol* (2 May 1923).
70. Pere Gabriel believes that 'it put the Socialists in the sphere of real politics, in that of government politics': Pere Gabriel, 'Sociedad, Gobierno y Política (1902–1931)', in Ángel Bahamonde (ed.), *Historia de España, siglo XX, 1875–1931* (Madrid: Cátedra, 2000), p. 427.

10
The Making of an Interventionist Army, 1898–1923

Sebastian Balfour

In the light of the repeated intervention in politics of the Spanish military over two centuries, the title of this chapter might seem somewhat inappropriate. In a sense, the army was already interventionist in the early 19th century. But the term is used here in a much more restricted sense to denote government by the military, that is, the intervention of the military to replace democratic regimes, or at least civilian regimes such as that of the Restoration of 1876–1923, by a state controlled by the military or by a bureaucratic coalition in which the military play a hegemonic role.[1] In the case of Spain, the term refers therefore to those considerable sections of the Spanish military that supported the 1923 coup and the dictatorship of General Miguel Primo de Rivera, and those that rose in revolt in 1936 against the Second Republic and supported the Franco Dictatorship. In making a qualification about different elements within the military, what is being stressed is the fact that there were progressive minority tendencies within the military in the first quarter of the 20th century and, in particular, the fact that in 1936, many sections of the military supported the Popular Front government against the military revolt eventually led by General Francisco Franco. But the main purpose of this chapter is to argue that within the authoritarian coalition of the Primo de Rivera Dictatorship (and indeed among the Nationalists under Franco) a key role was played by colonial officers, whose sense of identity and relationship with the peninsular Spain was very different to those of their peninsular counterparts. This is a distinction largely ignored in the literature.[2]

Across Western Europe, colonial wars during most of the 20th century had a similar though varying effect on metropolitan politics. One of the most striking examples of the political repercussions of colonial war at the domestic level was the French *coup d'état* of 1958, in which the colonial troops in Algeria under the command of Generals Salan and Massu brought down the Fourth Republic and installed General de Gaulle in power. Another equally salient model was the military revolt of Portuguese officers, many of whom had served in the Portuguese colonial wars in Africa, who toppled the Caetano regime in 1974. The Italian colonial wars in Libya and Ethiopia in the 1920s and 1930s were a means whereby Mussolini hoped to mobilize Italians for the greater task of establishing a new empire. The Italian air force's use of chemical weapons in all these colonial wars served further to brutalize the colonial army as a whole.[3] Similarly, Britain's use of extensive bombing, incendiary and probably chemical as well as conventional arms, destroyed resistance against colonial penetration in Iraq, Kurdistan and the North-West Frontier in the early 1920s but it also transformed British colonial policy. The tactic of blunt air power undermined the strategic and peaceful use of local intermediaries as sources of authority.[4] It also created a precedent for the bombing raids on civilians in the Second World War, though of course it did not lead to any form of interventionism. With the exception of Britain's secretive and little-known deployment of weapons of mass destruction in Iraq in 1919–20, the Spanish colonial experience is the least known despite the fact that its offensives against indigenous resistance in northern Morocco had an even greater impact on domestic politics and military culture than any of the other examples given.

In all these cases, colonial officers developed different strategies, identities and values to those of their metropolitan counterparts. The multipolarity of the officer class was especially true of the 19th-century Spanish army. In the first half of that century, the military contained officers who were radical Liberals and Freemasons, and many had risen from the lower ranks as a result of the opportunities for promotion provided by the civil wars between Liberals and absolutists and then between progressive Liberals and Conservatives. Indeed, it is possible that a majority of officers had been opposed to the *ancien régime* and some had even embraced Republicanism, though most Republican supporters in the military were non-commissioned officers or rank-and-file soldiers.[5] In those civil wars, regimes were made and unmade by generals and officers from across the spectrum of 19th-century Spanish politics through the praetorian mechanism of the *pronunciamiento*. However, the purpose of this military intervention was to replace one civilian government with another, not to replace civilian government altogether.

The Restoration settlement of 1876 ensured, for a while at least, the withdrawal of the army from the political arena which it had dominated for more than half a century. This was in exchange for a tacit agreement that the state would give the army considerable latitude in defining its professional interests and running its own affairs. These included the benefits that it derived from control of Spain's remaining colonies overseas. The top layer of officers was integrated into the regime by selective promotions, ennoblement and the award of lucrative political appointments. The continued threat of Carlist uprisings, which the army had been employed to suppress for decades on behalf of the Bourbon monarchy, further helped to ensure its loyalty.[6] According to the new legislation of the Restoration regime, the military remained the guarantor of the state and the nation against not just external but, more significantly, internal enemies. In the last quarter of the century, two new internal threats beyond that of Carlism helped to cement the consensus between the regime and the military: the rise of organized labour protest and the emergence of regional movements for autonomy. Both of these movements represented a challenge to the role of the military as the principal gatekeeper of law and order and national unity. Both therefore helped to consolidate the rightward drift of officers.[7]

The shift in values among sections of the military in the 20th century was the result of a range of interactions between the internal dynamics of military institutions and the wider processes of socio-economic modernization, political change and international pressure. This chapter will examine in particular the effects on the military of colonial war, that is, the aftermath of 'the Disaster' of 1898 and the campaigns in Morocco between 1908 and 1927. The consequences of the wars and the wider processes to which I refer cannot easily be disentangled. It would make sense therefore to adopt a narrative structure. However, a very brief reference to the existing literature would help to anchor the discussion within a theoretical framework. The two political scientists whose theories about the causes and dynamics of military intervention have sparked most debate are Samuel P. Huntington and Guillermo O'Donnell. Both identify a range of independent variables to explain military interventionism, one of which is the effects of socio-economic modernization. For O'Donnell, whose historical focus is Latin America above all, the latter has been the most important cause of the military recourse to authoritarian government. Huntington, on the other hand, argues that during this process of modernization military interventionism was more likely to occur in countries with high levels of mobilization and low levels of institutionalization.[8] While Huntington's paradigm provides a more useful explanatory framework than O'Donnell's, I will argue that, like that of O'Donnell, it doesn't sufficiently take into account value-based variables, in particular questions of ideology and identity. And it is these I will be focusing on in particular in this chapter.

The paradox of the 1898 Disaster is that in its aftermath, and indeed for almost two decades, there was no significant institutional crisis in Spain. The regime that had presided over such a national catastrophe remained in place and survived for the next 25 years. Elsewhere, disasters of a similar magnitude provoked radical political change. The historical model that most troubled the Spanish political elites was the defeat of Napoleon III's army by the Germans at Sedan in 1870. The resulting loss of Alsace-Lorraine led to the collapse of the Napoleonic regime and the proclamation of the Third Republic. The name of Sedan resonated in political speeches and articles in Spain in the aftermath of the Disaster with gloomy foreboding.[9] Yet no general rose up in revolt and the Liberal government that had overseen the national humiliation was back in power two years later under the man most identified with the Disaster, Mateo Sagasta, whose cabinet was made up of many ministers closely associated with the defeat.

Perhaps the most important reason for the stability of the regime was the absence of any alternative. The traditional arbiters of political change, the military, had been the direct agents of the defeat. They were also divided, and uncertain about their role in a post-imperial Spain. Only the conservative general Camilo García de Polavieja, who had been governor-general in the Philippines colony during the war against Spain, contemplated seizing power temporarily but was dissuaded by the Queen Regent, who, unlike her son 25 years later, understood the danger to the monarchy of any wilful disregard of the Constitution.[10] Moreover, the military were on the back foot after the Disaster. Endorsing a widespread feeling throughout the country, the Conde de las Almenas had launched a bitter attack in the Senate on the generals, demanding that 'medals should be torn from chests and sashes raised from waists to necks'.[11] The right-wing paper *El Nacional* defended the armed forces against the Conde de las Almenas and his supporters, on the grounds that any army was only as good as the society from which it sprang. Shrewdly manipulating the Socialists' wartime slogan against the evasion of conscription by the better-off families, 'Everybody or nobody', the editor argued that all of Spain was responsible for the Disaster.[12] During the months that followed the end of the war, several prominent military and naval commanders were put on trial but those few who were found guilty were simply struck off the active list and received full salary entitlements.

Yet beyond institutional immobility, the effects of the Disaster were profound.[13] The defeat exposed as a hollow delusion the belief that Spain was, at the least, a middle-ranking world power, a conviction embedded in the national culture. The loss of the remnants of the Empire provoked a post-imperial crisis of identity among sections of Spanish society, a crisis that had been delayed since the loss of the mainland Spanish American Empire in the early 19th century. Spain's political system, its national character and the concept of the nation itself now began to be questioned. This crisis was all the more acute because it occurred at the apogee of modern European empires when the possession of colonies was seen as the benchmark of a nation's fitness to survive. Lord Salisbury's speech on 4 May 1898, in which Spain was implicitly referred to as a 'dying nation', reverberated throughout the Spanish press.[14]

It comes as no surprise that the military was the institution most traumatized by the defeat. Military opinion became suffused with indignation and self-justification. There was a widespread belief among officers that the army and the navy had been sacrificed by the politicians. Some rather scant evidence from Spanish sources suggests that Spain had been offered the choice of selling Cuba to the United States or going to war and had chosen the latter course. The Liberal politician Count Romanones described a meeting he attended in the Royal Palace between the Queen Regent and leading politicians after she had received the offer of a purchase from the US President. He claimed that the unanimous feeling amongst all present at that meeting, and in further unofficial talks held by the Queen Regent with opposition politicians, was that selling Cuba was the more dangerous option for the regime and that war was the unavoidable price of maintaining peace at home. War, Romanones insisted, 'was the only honourable means whereby Spain could lose what little was left of her immense colonial empire'.[15] For his part, the Minister of Overseas Colonies, Segismundo Moret, was supposed to have said in confidence to a friend that war with the United States would be lunacy because Spain was no match for the military power of that country. However, he went on, airing his opinion in public would threaten not just the government but the monarchy itself.[16] It could thus be deduced that the regime went to war with the United States knowing Spain would be overcome but believing defeat and the loss of the overseas colonies were a lesser evil for the regime than capitulation.

However, officers were too much on the defensive and too absorbed in the problems of demobilization to contemplate a military takeover.

The military press devoted much space to the critical professional problems that arose as a result of the sudden end of war. Once the poorly organized repatriation of the army was completed, the military and the government faced the conundrum of how to deal with the excess of officers in a peacetime army. The number of soldiers still in service at the end of 1898 amounted to around 80,000. The officer corps was made up of 499 generals, almost 600 colonels and 24,000 or more officers of lower rank. In other words, there was one general for every 160 soldiers and approximately one officer for every three men. The contrast with the French army could not be greater. With a standing army of around 180,000, France had six times fewer officers than Spain. The disproportion in the navy was even more striking: after the destruction of two out of Spain's three squadrons, there were 142 admirals left for 2 warships.[17] To add to the problems, the wars had given rise to a flurry of promotions and decorations, creating a sense of injustice among those who had not served abroad. Some 17,000 citations and military crosses had been awarded to officers on duty in the colonies (as well as 341,000 similar decorations to soldiers out of a total of 350,000 rank-and-file troops).

There was agreement on all sides that the officer corps needed to be restructured. By 1908, some 10,000 officers, a large majority from the Reserve List, had been retired or were made redundant under the generous terms offered by the government, with the result that only around 14,000 officers remained on active service.[18] However, the real problems in the aftermath of the wars concerned the distribution of redundancy payments, for example whether officers on the Reserve List were to receive as much as those on the Active List, the lack of mobility for those remaining on the Reserve, and the substantial cut in officers' pay, which amounted to up to half of their salary, that took place as a result of the termination of the war, exacerbating what they claimed to be an already low income.[19] There were other questions that were equally difficult to resolve, such as the imbroglio of professional scales inherited from the policy of easy promotions during the wars and the placing of redundant military personnel into civilian jobs.

For at least two years after the Disaster, the military were as engrossed in these professional matters as they were with the political situation.[20] Moreover, they were acutely conscious of the weaknesses of army organization exposed by the war. Successive ministers of war – Polavieja, Linares, Weyler and Luque – drew up reform projects to tackle both the problem of promotions and that of internal structures embracing territorial organization, administrative overmanning and overcentralization. Although these plans were welcomed by the military press,[21] little came of them, largely because of the vulnerability of governments to conflicting military pressure. Between 1897 and 1909, there were 15 different cabinets, whilst the post of minister of war was reshuffled 20 times. Liberal and Conservative cabinets were also more concerned with cutting military expenditure, as part of a compulsive effort to reduce the state deficit, than reorganizing the armed forces. They failed, for example, to make military service compulsory until 1911 (until then the better-off could buy exemption from full military service), despite widespread support for such a measure, especially amongst officers themselves.[22]

Military bitterness as a result of the defeat and the state handling of demobilization was reflected in the rightward shift of the two most moderate military papers of the time, *La Correspondencia Militar* and *El Ejército Español*.[23] Of course, military criticism of the Restoration regime had been an almost daily fare and there had been frequent calls for praetorian intervention of some sort. Despite the tacit agreement of mutual non-interference between government and military, officers had repeatedly browbeaten the cabinet over questions of budget and military honour and, at moments of heightened tension, had issued veiled threats to impose military government.[24] In any case, the Restoration consensus whereby the army withdrew to the barracks had always been fragile. Even before the Disaster the military had shown signs of restiveness. The Liberals had weakened the traditional ties bounding them to the officer class through their political and social reforms, while the rise of anarchism and regionalism had strengthened the conservative drift of the military. In other words, the defeat of 1898 and the loss of the residue of the Empire intensified an ongoing process of transformation of military values.

As a result of their humiliation, Spanish officers began to turn increasingly towards an anti-democratic ideology, shedding the populist and Republican tendencies of the 19th century. One of the factors encouraging the growth of authoritarian values was the wave of anti-military feeling amongst the people after the Disaster. Officers found themselves being mocked by sections of the public. Left-wing and Catalanist papers questioned their military competence and bravery. In these circumstances it was difficult for them to pose as the champions of the people against a corrupt class of politicians. Instead, with increasing stridency, the military began to threaten to intervene in politics unilaterally. The main focus of their grievances was regional nationalism and in particular the anti-military press in Catalonia. Their action against two newspapers in 1905 sparked off a political crisis which led the Liberal government to promulgate the Law of Jurisdictions giving the military courts wide-ranging powers to try civilians. Thus the military emerged from the Disaster as one of the institutions least affected by the reforms that followed. The new law, backed by the King in defiance of the government, helped to destroy the fiction of civil supremacy cultivated by the regime and marked the return of the military as the ultimate arbiter of politics in the country.[25]

Deep though the trauma of the defeat was, however, it was not the sole cause of the rightward drift of the military. The provincial inertia of military life before the wars of 1895–8, and the low level of culture and technology that characterized its training, had left the officer caste virtually untouched by modernizing currents. In addition, the Restoration governments made little effort to invest in the professionalization of the military. On the contrary, the armed forces were being drawn increasingly into a dual role of policeman and judge by their deployment in the repression of social protest and the use of military courts to rule on labour disputes. What further pushed the military towards the Right was their perception that the expanding Catalan and Basque movements threatened the national unity of Spain, of which they saw themselves traditionally as the incarnation, having resisted the dissolvent tendencies of Carlism and Federalism in the 19th century.[26] Lastly, their conviction that the Disaster of 1898 was the fault of politicians and that they had been sacrificed, led them to question not just the Restoration system but civilian government itself.

The combined effect of the loss of empire and the growth of new social forces as a result of the accelerating process of modernization buried the residual progressive tendencies of the previous century and swung the military towards a range of traditional conservative and new rightist ideologies. Amongst the latter was a new right-wing regenerationism, which attributed the Disaster not just to Restoration politicians but also to parliamentary democracy itself.[27] Another belief was that Spain could only be redeemed by the action of a providential *Caudillo*. It should be stressed that this shift in military thinking in Spain was part of a European-wide reaction against 19th-century liberal positivism. One of its features was the adoption of new vitalist currents influenced by Friedrich Nietzsche. The French model of the citizen army, so important in 19th-century Spain, was giving way in some military circles to the Prussian model of an elitist professional army whose strength lay in moral and spiritual values allied to military science.[28] Thus longer-term sociological and cultural change interacted with the effects of the

Disaster to foster the development of a conservative officer class imbued with deep grievances and interventionist inclinations.

Military history in Spain during the first two decades of the new century is particularly complex because of the cleavages between the different units of the armed forces. These were professional and political as well as ideological. The corporatist military *Juntas Militares de Defensa*, for example, were the expression of the comparative grievances of more technical units, such as the artillery, the medics, the engineering corps and the General Staff, against other units of the army also engaged in the colonial war in Morocco, above all the infantry and cavalry. The *Juntas* arose in 1916, partly in response to the effects in Spain of the inflationary pressures of the First World War.[29] Their demands were couched in a vaguely articulated and traditional praetorianism seeking national regeneration, but within their ranks there were considerable divisions over the political direction the movement should take, whether towards an authoritarian solution or a government of national unity.[30] Their immediate objective, however, was to halt the growing inequality of pay between officers in the metropolitan garrisons and those serving in Morocco as a result of monetary rewards for officers on active duty and the extraordinary inflationary pressures in the metropolis to which the colonial officers were less exposed.

Another grievance articulated by the *Juntas* was the promotion system. Promotion through merit had been a long-standing source of division within the Spanish army since the mid-19th century. The system had fostered nepotism and favouritism and, before the 20th-century Moroccan campaigns, had also benefited the careers of officers of the technical corps because they enjoyed special status. From 1909, however, merit promotions and bonuses had become the reward for those, in particular in the infantry and cavalry, who were engaged in direct action in the battlefields of Morocco. Such rewards were often abused. Promotions and decorations were often awarded for heroism as computed by wounds rather than military competence. Officers of the Artillery and Engineering Corps, the General Staff and those involved in the interface with the local Moroccans saw the system as deeply unjust because they had few opportunities to display the heroism in military action that so favoured their colleagues in other corps.[31] The least acknowledged of these officers were the medics and military doctors. In the aftermath of the 1921 Annual Disaster, for example, a young medical lieutenant called Manuel Miranda Vidal was entrusted, with his team of six soldiers, with collecting 5,000 bodies, sometimes at the risk of their own lives. Alongside other medical teams, they were also expected to clean up the military posts recaptured during the counter-offensive or carry out surgery near the front line. Such people received none of the adulation or the rewards enjoyed by their embattled colleagues in the infantry and cavalry but they did much to maintain morale and restore the health of the soldiers.[32]

It should be stressed that contrary to much of the literature on the military, such as Stanley Payne's *Politics and the Military* (though not Carolyn Boyd's *Praetorian Politics in Liberal Spain*), the *Juntas* were active in the colonial army. Indeed, membership of the *Juntas* was obligatory for all officers in Morocco. It is true that most of the *Junta* supporters in the Army of Africa were normally based in the metropolis and were doing a compulsory term of service in Morocco. Yet there were professional officers serving in Morocco who were *Junta* activists or sympathizers and saw themselves as colonial officers at the same time.[33] The tension between the colonial officers and *junteros* was not, initially at least, so much a question of politics but of professional grievances. The revolt of the *junteros* in Spain in 1917 brought down one government and forced the next to introduce a closed scale whereby promotion and pay were largely determined by seniority and length of service. Promotion on the basis of merit displayed in war was now subject to a rigorous procedure whose final stage was a parliamentary ballot. The measure dismayed and angered many of the colonial officers. Governments of both Liberals and Conservatives sought to placate or support one or other of the military factions and, increasingly, the divided army became the pivot of Restoration politics. In other words, military factionalism became politicized, encouraging the tendency among officers of both factions to see themselves as arbiters of national politics.[34]

The increasing fault-line in the military between the metropolitan professional corps and the front-line units of the colonial army became a problem for the emerging military interventionist tendency in the post-First World War period led eventually by General Primo de Rivera. The colonial war was giving rise to a new elite within the army, estranged from its metropolitan counterparts. Among those officers who had been pursuing a career in Morocco, some of whom had served in the colonial wars in the overseas colonies, what could be termed a military *africanista* culture emerged in opposition to the culture of the Spanish garrisons, which they viewed as corrupt and unprofessional. The term 'military culture' is employed here to distinguish the ideology, aspirations, practices and strategies of different tendencies within the Spanish military in the period under discussion. Sociological studies of the army usually employ terms such as military generations or elites to differentiate models of military officers.[35] Unlike generational distinctions, the term military culture cuts across the age of its participants. It also allows for a more complex description of the values and practices than the term 'elite', which tends to define differences on the basis of social fissures.

Many of these so-called *africanistas* had chosen to serve in Morocco because colonial service there offered them the opportunity for rapid promotion and better pay. But many also justified their involvement in ideological terms. Official discourse encouraged the belief that the colonial army was in Morocco to enable the penetration into North Africa of Western civilization, embodied not only by capitalist modernity but also by traditional Spanish values, which were buttressed by Christianity. Underpinning this sense of mission was the belief that of all the European powers, Spain was the best suited for this task because of its historic links with the Arab world. Beyond this rationalization lay a further conviction. Through military and civil penetration into the area, Spain could once again grow into a colonial power with a status among nations that it had lost in Spanish America. This could only be achieved, according to the *africanista* discourse, through the forging of a highly disciplined and professional army, properly trained and equipped and led by officers hardened by war and strengthened by the esprit de corps created by battle.[36]

Indeed, the military *africanistas* were united by a sense of mission in Morocco to restore the prestige of the army and the nation. 'The African campaign', Francisco Franco wrote in 1921, 'is the best training-school, if not the only one, for our Army, and in it positive values and qualities are put to the test, and this officer corps on combat duty in Africa, with its high morale and self-esteem, must become the heart and soul of the mainland army.'[37] The camaraderie of war in Morocco, together with the commitment to this mission, helped to erode the divisions between the different corps of the military that set them apart as castes in the mainland army. The more technical artillery and engineering corps and the small but prestigious group of pilots mixed socially with infantry and cavalry officers in camp and garrison life. Their collaboration on the fields of battle, especially after the Disaster of Annual in 1921, imbued many officers of the different corps with a shared hatred of the enemy and a common purpose of retribution. Nevertheless, because the military campaigns in Morocco were largely fought by infantry and cavalry, that new esprit de corps was most developed in their ranks.

The *africanistas* shared an unqualified contempt for garrison life in Spain and, in particular, for the conduct of the peninsular *junteros*, whom they felt were impeding a reform of the army that could release the resources necessary for a victorious conclusion of the campaigns in Morocco. They also distrusted the politicians of the Restoration system and deeply resented those civilian elites who failed to recognize the sacrifices endured by the Army of Africa. Civil society in Spain was seen as tainted, and full of compromises. These attitudes eroded any residual faith in the efficacy of the Restoration regime or indeed of any civilian regime. Africanism united officers who had fought in the 1895–8 colonial wars and had felt betrayed by the regime, and a new generation,[38] who experienced war for the first time in Morocco and felt increasingly bitter towards the same regime for its apparent failure to support them. The colonial campaigns were seen as the forge shaping a new military elite that would regenerate Spain. A leading *africanista* officer, Gonzalo Queipo de Llano, in the editorial of the first edition of the *africanista* journal, *Revista de Tropas Coloniales*, written a few months after the military coup of General Miguel Primo de Rivera de Rivera in 1923, wrote that Spain's progressive fall into an abyss of anarchy under the Restoration regime was halted by 'a few men of heart, who, risking everything, confronted the arduous task of resurrecting the spirit of Spain dulled by Muslim fatalism ... to guide it onto the path worthy of its glorious history'.[39]

Similar principles also set the *africanistas* against some other officers serving in Morocco, not all of whom could be described as *junteros*. These officers continued to behave according to the traditional practices of the military in Spain. Among them were those who had not volunteered to fight but had been posted to Morocco and for whom military intervention there had little ideological or political appeal. Rather than undergo the harsh conditions of campaign life, some sought to spend as much time as possible in the more relaxed context of the garrisons in the main towns of Ceuta, Tetuan and Melilla. As is evident in the report of General Picasso, the military magistrate in charge of investigations into the Disaster of 1921, several officers (including a leading *juntero*) were in these towns rather than with their units when the military rout took place.[40]

Indeed, what evoked scorn from the *africanistas* and greater division among officers serving in the colonial army was the reproduction of the culture of peninsular military life in the Moroccan garrisons. Though womanizing was acceptable to the *africanistas*, other common practices such as nepotism, bureaucracy, corruption and gambling were deeply despised as typical vices of Restoration society and obstacles not just to the military campaign but also to the regeneration of Spain.

Traditional military tactics, such as the deployment of large numbers of troops over a vast area, linked by isolated defensive posts difficult to supply, were also frowned on. Instead, the *africanistas* sought modern models of military tactics amongst the German and French armies. Thus some pushed for the use of planes, tanks and toxic gas (see below) in the Moroccan campaigns, although the use of tanks had few positive consequences. For the military *africanistas*, the two major disasters of 1909 and 1921 had at least provided the opportunity for the regeneration of the army. The Annual Disaster, in particular, turned the deeply felt professional disputes between the military *africanistas* and the *junteros* into profound antipathy. So tense were their relations that a pro-*Junta* military paper saw in them 'the germs of a fearful civil war'.[41] The particular focus of the renewed factionalism was the issue of responsibility for the Disaster, which the *junteros* above all were seeking to impose.

The Annual Disaster itself had triggered a fierce military reaction in the army and jingoist demonstrations in Spain. It undermined the already cracked cement of the Restoration state and provided a further self-justification for the military coup of General Primo de Rivera in 1923. It had been an open secret that the army in Spain was about to seize power. Of the four main co-ordinators of the coup, two were veterans of the colonial war. The support of the majority of colonial officers for Primo de Rivera's coup might seem paradoxical. The general had been the most decided supporter in the army of withdrawing from Morocco altogether. The latter part of his career had been based exclusively in Spain so he did not form part of the *africanista* coterie. Unpardonably for many colonial officers, he had backed the *Juntas Militares de Defensa*, the corporatist movement among officers in Spain. Yet the *africanistas* shared his determination to end what they saw as the civilian government's persecution of the military for the Disaster of Annual. The second board of inquiry over the Disaster set up by the government, the Responsibilities Committee, was due shortly to pronounce its verdict. Primo de Rivera's coup brought the whole juridical process to a halt, and among his first initiatives was an attempt to confiscate the board's report from the parliamentary archive.[42]

Since 1917 in particular, social and political polarization had deepened to such a degree that the consensus underpinning an unreformed Restoration state had dissolved. The coup was backed by most of the military and conservative forces, including Catalan right-wing political and business circles, which furnished some of the money to launch the action.[43] For a brief while, *junteros* and *africanistas* buried their differences to support government by the military. The new dictator's declaration on assuming power asserted a continuity of military grievance and a military vocation to regenerate Spain stretching back to 1898. Yet the coup was the first military intervention in Spain to sweep aside civilian government. Even though the political Right had consented to a military takeover and was awarded ministries in a later reshuffled regime, this was a decidedly praetorian government. Moreover, alongside the adoption of the regenerationist discourse of post-1898, Primo de Rivera and his ideologues sought to build a new corporatist and centralist state following the counter-revolutionary currents that had burgeoned in Europe in the post-war period, especially fascism.[44] In other words, the coup brought into being not just a largely military government but also a new value-based interventionism.

Primo de Rivera, however, had to reconcile the two broad factions of his army. The most important issue dividing them was the colonial war. Primo de Rivera had come to power to bury the issue of an inquiry into the causes of the Disaster. But he was also committed to a military withdrawal from Morocco with the avowed purpose of focusing efforts on the regeneration of Spain. This initial policy of pulling out from the colonial war would give way, under angry pressure from his colonial officers, to a massive injection of troops and weapons, including mustard-gas projectiles, into a fresh offensive in 1925. It should be stressed that Primo de Rivera's decision was also conditioned by a number of factors: the costly operations of retreat to a new defensive line, the failure of efforts to reach a deal with the leader of the Rifian resistance, and the offer of the French, firmly opposed to Spanish military withdrawal, to stage a joint offensive.[45] This radical shift of policy signalled the emergence of the colonial army, and in particular its military *africanista* elite, as the dominant wing within the regime (as it would be later within the Nationalist coalition that rose in revolt against the Second Republic in 1936).

In what ways was this military elite in Morocco distinct from its metropolitan counterparts? First, the experience of colonial war brought about a revolution in the norms of war amongst officers stationed for long periods in Morocco. This began, above all, with the escalation of atrocities sparked off by the 1921 Disaster. The violence of the Moroccan enemy unleashed a reaction–repression logic, which, after Annual in particular, swept away all reserve about methods of war, even amongst relatively progressive officers. The atrocities committed by the enemy were considered as validating a response in kind. In a confidential report, one of these supposedly progressive officers argued that the new strategy of chemical warfare might soon bring the war to an end and thereby save lives. Taking rationalization to an extreme degree, he suggested that the use of chemical weapons would be 'the best pacifist propaganda'.[46]

Yet for most officers atrocities were rationalized on the grounds of both victimhood and the denial of an equal human status for the enemy. The emnification of the Moroccan foe had been a problem in the colonial war because the Spanish were able to mobilize Moroccan against Moroccan. Who the enemy was had not always been clear because Spain's policy of divide and rule had encouraged tribes to change allegiance. Moroccan mercenaries fighting for Spain some-times went over to the enemy of Spain, their fellow Moroccans. This, of course, created problems because the construction of the Other is vital to military effectiveness in war. The invention of the enemy entails a considerable degree of self-dehumanization and a denial of the human-ity of other people.[47] The Annual Disaster destroyed any ambivalence about who the enemy was, helping to legitimize the use of brutal force both against enemy troops and against civilians who could be identi-fied as the Other.

The war also helped to transform other components of the colonial officers' identity. Especially after 1921 this identity had begun to be recast in the light of the traditionalist canon. An irregular and scrappy war was turned into a conflict with the epic proportions of historical myth. The military *africanista* began to conceive of himself as the per-sonification of traditional Spanish values. This tendency would be rein-forced in the 1930s by the perception of the threat of foreign influences in Spain itself, such as communism. The colonial officers felt estrange-ment from Spanish politics, an alienation that extended even to their military colleagues in the metropolitan garrisons. This estrangement derived also from a separate imagined identity. Their self-image was permeated with a colonial exoticism derived from years of contact with North African culture. The harsh environment, the relatively tough conditions of the campaigns and the frequent engagements with the guerrillas reinforced this sense of uniqueness. For many years after the Civil War, Franco expressed this otherness by surrounding himself with his Moorish guard, the Guardia Mora. He himself wrote during the Civil War: 'My years in Africa live within me with indescribable force...without Africa, I can scarcely explain myself to myself, nor can I explain myself to my comrades in arms.'[48]

The colonial war thus forged a new kind of colonialism and national-ism amongst the professional colonial military that set them apart from peninsular culture. It differed from traditional conservative nationalism, which tended to be utopian, rural and clerical, in that it was modernizing and expansionist. It was also impregnated with the culture of war in North Africa. The brutality of that war and the extreme conditions in which it was fought widened the sense of alienation from the broader dominant cultures of Spain among many colonial officers. Life in metropolitan Spain, both in the military garrisons and in the cities, was seen as flaccid. Unless they came from wealthy families, officers lived in genteel poverty and ritual domesticity in provincial cities. Their careers were subject to slow progression up the scale of promotion through length of service. Routine and bureaucracy dominated their professional lives. Service in the Moroccan War, on the other hand, provided opportunities for the excitement of war, for promotion, good pay, celebrity, drink and extra-marital sex or sometimes rape, male bonding and the reaffirmation of manliness or machismo. This was set against the slackness of metropolitan military life. All of this amounted to an elite identity superior to any in the peninsula. Spanish civil society was also viewed with disdain. Civilian life was feminine. The Spanish race needed resuscitating by war to compensate for the racial decline brought about by liberalism and other supposedly alien political cultures.[49] This notion was legitimated by the social Darwinism that had been widespread among European empires since the 19th century. In a conceptual transposition of the Moroccan Other to a Spanish internal Other, *africanistas* began to see their fellow citizens as imbued with Muslim fatalism and indolence.[50]

José Ortega y Gasset's famous phrase, 'Morocco turned the scattered soul of our Army into a closed fist', is untrue of the metropolitan army.[51] As I have already mentioned, a large number of its officers would remain loyal to the Republic in 1936, especially those who had supported the *Juntas* in 1917. But even if applied to the colonial army the statement is only partly true. By the mid-1920s most *africanista* colonial officers would unite around a core of authoritarian and nationalist values, a shared ideology of authoritarian regenerationism whose vehicle was the colonial army. What they lacked, however, was a common strategy of intervention. Politics among the elite of *africanista* officers ranged from fascism to monarchism to authoritarian Republicanism. The declaration of the Republic in 1931, therefore, would find them disunited. Nevertheless, they would begin to draw on a shared stock of myths about the colonial war, a common hatred of the Left and a redemptionist mission to cleanse Spain that were more important than their political and professional differences.[52] Five years later the vast majority of them would unite to overthrow the Republic.

Notes

1. This chapter takes into account the debate around the issue of praetorianism whose most prominent and classical exponents include Samuel P. Huntington, *Political Order in Changing Societies* (New Haven, CT and London: Yale University Press, 2006 [1968]); Samuel Finer, *The Man on Horseback: The Role of the Military in Politics* (London: Pall Mall, 1962); Eric A. Nordlinger, *Soldiers in Politics: Military Coups and Governments* (Upper Saddle River, NJ: Prentice-Hall, 1977); and Amos Perlmutter, *The Military and Politics in Modern Times* (New Haven, CT and London: Yale University Press, 1977).
2. Notable exceptions are María Rosa de Madariaga's *España y el Rif. Crónica de una historia casi olvidada* (Melilla: La Biblioteca de Melilla, 2000) and her *Los moros que trajo Franco: la intervención de tropas coloniales en la guerra civil española* (Barcelona: Martínez Roca, 2002).
3. See Angelo Del Boca, *I gas di Mussolini. Il fascismo e la guerra d'Etiopia* (Rome: Editori riuniti, 1996), pp. 17–18, 33–44, 53–4; by the same author, *Gli italiani in Africa Orientale. La conquista dell'Impero* (Rome-Bari: Editori Laterza, 1979), pp. 490–1, and *L'Africa nella coscienza degli italiani Miti, memorie, errori, sconfitte* (Rome-Bari: Editori Laterza, 1992), pp. 71–2; Christopher Hollis, *Italy in Africa* (London: Hamilton, 1941), pp. 225–6; and Ludwig Fritz Haber, *The Poisonous Cloud: Chemical Warfare in the First World War* (Oxford: Oxford University Press, 1986), pp. 307–8.
4. See Timothy R. Moreman, ' "Small Wars" and "Imperial Policing": The British Army and the Theory and Practice of Colonial Warfare in the British Empire, 1919–1939', *Journal of Strategic Studies*, 19/4 (1996,) pp. 105–31; Toby Dodge, *Inventing Iraq: The Failure of Nation Building and a History Denied* (London: Columbia University Press, 2003).
5. Between 1878 and 1911, there were at least six Republican uprisings in Spanish garrisons. The organization responsible for the uprisings in the early 1880s was the Unión Republicana Militar, an offshoot of Manuel Ruiz Zorrilla's Republicans. It was formed in 1880 and had members in 22 garrisons: Gabriel Cardona, *El poder militar en la España contemporánea hasta la guerra civil* (Madrid: Siglo XX1, 1983); see also José Alvarez Junco, *El Emperador del Paralelo. Lerroux y la demagogia populista* (Madrid: Alianza, 1990), ch. 3. For details of the different currents within the military see Manuel Espadas Burgos, 'La Institución Libre de Enseñanza y la formación del militar español durante la Restauración', in *Temas de Historia Militar (ponencias del Primer Congreso de Historia Militar)*, 1 (1983), pp. 493–514; and for an analysis of the military in the 19th century, see Stanley G. Payne, *Politics and the Military in Modern Spain* (Stanford, CA: Stanford University Press, 1967) and Carolyn Boyd, *Praetorian Politics in Liberal Spain* (Chapel Hill: University of North Carolina Press, 1979).
6. For Carlism see the introduction and the chapter by Alejandro Quiroga in this volume, pp. 1–31 and 202–29.
7. Sebastian Balfour, *The End of the Spanish Empire, 1898–1923* (Oxford: Oxford University Press, 1997), p. 172.
8. Huntington, *Political Order*; Guillermo O'Donnell, *Bureaucratic Authoritarianism: Argentina 1966–1973 in Comparative Perspective* (Berkeley, CA: University of California, 1988).

9. For example, 'Sedan', *La Campana de Gracia* (23 September 1898).
10. Joaquín Romero-Maura, *'La rosa de fuego'*. *El obrerismo barcelonés de 1899 a 1909* (Madrid: Alianza, 1989 [1974]), pp. 17–18.
11. *El Imparcial* (8 September 1898); according to *El Cardo* ('Al Conde de las Almenas', 19 September 1898), anti-military sentiments were widespread after the Disaster. Other newspapers that attacked the military and the navy included *La Época* (e.g., 11 May 1899) and *El Heraldo* ('Los verdaderos culpables', 11 August 1899).
12. 'Ejército y Pueblo' (8 September) and 'Todos o ninguno' (13 September 1898). For a lengthy discussion of the contemporary search for responsibility for the Disaster, see Rafael Nuñez Florencio, *Militarismo y antimilitarismo en España* (Madrid: Consejo Superior de Investigaciones Científicas, 1990), pp. 269–329.
13. For a more extensive treatment see Balfour, *The End of the Spanish Empire*, and 'Riot, Regeneration and Reaction: Spain in the Aftermath of the 1898 Disaster', *The Historical Journal*, 38/2 (June 1995), pp. 405–23; Juan Pan-Montojo (ed.), *Más se perdió en Cuba. España, 1898 y la crisis de fin de siglo* (Madrid: Alianza, 1998).
14. Rosario de la Torre del Río, 'La prensa madrileña y el discurso de Lord Salisbury sobre "las naciones moribundas" (Londres, Albert Hall, 4 mayo 1898)', *Cuadernos de Historia Moderna y Contemporánea*, 6 (1985), pp. 163–80.
15. Álvaro de Figueroa y Torres (Conde de Romanones), *Las responsabilidades políticas del antiguo régimen de 1875 a 1923* (Madrid: Renacimiento, 1925), p. 33 (all translations are mine unless otherwise stated); also Gabriel Maura Gamazo, *Historia crítica del reinado de don Alfonso X111 bajo le regencia de Doña María Cristina de Austria* (Barcelona: Montaner y Simón, 1919), 1, pp. 359–60.
16. E. Gutiérrez-Gamero, *Mis primeros ochenta años (memorias)* (Barcelona: n.p., 1934), pp. 34–5.
17. Figures from José Ramón Alonso, *Historia política del ejército español* (Madrid: Editora Nacional, 1974), pp. 439–42 and Julio Busquets Bragulat, *El militar de carrera en España. Estudio de sociología militar*, 2nd edn (Barcelona: Ariel, 1971), p. 25.
18. Alonso, *Political Order*, p. 449.
19. Jorge Cachinero, 'Intervencionismo y reforma militares en España a comienzos del siglo XX', *Cuadernos de Historia Contemporánea*, 10 (1988), pp. 155–84.
20. For examples of this preoccupation see 'Problemas militares pendientes', *El Correo Militar* (28 February 1900), and 'Hay que hacer algo', *El Progreso Militar* (9 October 1900).
21. Looking back on the year 1901, for example, *La Correspondencia Militar* warmly approved the performance of successive Ministers of War: '1901–2' (1 January 1902).
22. Cachinero, 'Intervencionismo', pp. 155–84. In any case, the imposition of compulsory military service would have alienated many powerful supporters of the dynastic parties who were able to buy exemption for their sons under existing legislation.
23. Josep Solé i Sabaté and Joan Villaroya i Font, *L'exercit i Catalunya (1898–1936): La premsa militar espanyola i el fet militar* (Barcelona: Llibres de l'Index, 1990), p. 24.

24. Nuñez Florencio, *Militarismo*.
25. Carolyn P. Boyd, *Praetorian Politics*, p. 14. See also Alejandro Quiroga in this volume, pp. 202–29.
26. See for example *La Correspondencia Militar* (25 July 1899).
27. For a brief but incisive analysis of right-wing regenerationism see Manuel Vázquez Montalbán, *Los demonios familiares de Franco* (Barcelona: Planeta, 1987), pp. 32–40.
28. Robert Geoffrey Jensen, 'Intellectual Foundations of Dictatorship: Spanish Military Writers and their Quest for Cultural Regeneration, 1898–1923' (PhD dissertation, Yale University, 1995).
29. For more details on the *Juntas Militares de Defensa*, see also Romero Salvadó, 'Spain's Revolutionary Crisis of 1917', and Alejandro Quiroga, in this volume, pp. 62–91 and 202–29.
30. Ex-Coronel Márquez and J. M. Capó, *Las Juntas Militares de Defensa* (Barcelona: Librería Sintes, 1923); for an analysis of the broader crisis of the period see Francisco J. Romero Salvadó, *Spain, 1914–18: Between War and Revolution* (London: Routledge, 1999), and by the same author, *Revolution, Social Conflict and Reaction in Spain, 1916–1923* (London: Routledge, 2008).
31. Sebastian Balfour, *Deadly Embrace: Morocco and the Road to the Spanish Civil War* (Oxford: Clarendon Press, 2002), pp. 164–8.
32. Xosé Ramón Fernández Oxea, *Crónicas de Marruecos. Tras la ruta de Annual* (Santiago de Compostela: Sotela Blanco, 1985), pp. 62–3. For other anecdotal evidence of the bravery and skill of the medical teams see Manuel Bastos Ansart, *De las guerras coloniales a la Guerra Civil. Memorias de un cirujano* (Barcelona, Ariel, 1969), pp. 92 and 162–4.
33. For details of the *Juntas* in the colonial army in Morocco in July 1917, see Servicio Histórico Militar, *Archivo de la documentación de la Guerra de Liberación Nacional*, R271, leg. 72, carp. 13.
34. Boyd, *Praetorian Politics*, ch. 6.
35. As in the classic studies of Julio Busquets Bragulat, *El militar de carrera en España*, and Miguel Alonso Baquer, 'La selección de la élite militar española', in Mario Hernández Sánchez-Barba (co-ord.), *Historia social de las fuerzas armadas españolas*, 5 (Madrid: Alhambra, 1986), ch. 18.
36. For more on tendencies within the colonial army see Balfour, *Deadly Embrace*, chapter 6 and Sebastian Balfour and Pablo La Porte, 'Military Cultures and the Moroccan Wars, 1909–36', *European History Quarterly*, 30/3 (2000), pp. 307–32.
37. Francisco Franco Bahamonde, *Papeles de la guerra de Marruecos, Diario de una bandera* (Madrid: Fundación Francisco Franco, 1986 [1922]), pp. 85–6.
38. Defined by Busquets as the generation of 1915 in *El militar de carrera*.
39. 'Nuestro propósito', *Revista de Tropas Coloniales* (January 1924), Año 1, Número 1. The French colonial military, usually scornful of their Spanish counterparts in Morocco, were unimpressed with both *africanistas* and *junteros*. They found the generals of all stripes 'ignorant of their métier', without 'tactical sense or offensive spirit' and with a 'feeble culture': 'Rapport établi par les officiers de liason du Maréchal Pétain auprès du Générale Primo de Rivera de Rivera', 30 October 1925, *Service Historique de l'Armée de Terre*, SHAT3 H100.
40. Juan Picasso González, *El expediente Picasso* (Mexico: 1976, facsimile edition), pp. 137, 402, 417, 421, 427, 459, 534.

41. 'En defensa de la verdad. Sobre las Juntas de Defensa', *La Correspondencia Militar* (21 October 1921). For a more extensive treatment of the effects of the Annual Disaster on the military see Pablo La Porte in this volume (pp. 230–54), along with, *La atracción del Imán. El desastre de Annual y sus repercusiones en la política europea, 1921–1923* (Madrid: Biblioteca Nueva, 2001).
42. Juan Pando, *Historia Secreta de Annual* (Madrid: Temas de Hoy, 1999), pp. 312–13.
43. For more on the relation between Catalan employers and the Spanish Right see Angel Smith, 'The Catalan Counter-revolutionary Coalition and the Primo de Rivera de Rivera Coup, 1917–1923', *European History Quarterly*, 37/1 (2007), pp. 7–34.
44. Alejandro Quiroga, *Making Spaniards: Primo de Rivera de Rivera and the Nationalization of the Masses, 1923–1930* (London: Palgrave MacMillan, 2007).
45. For details see Balfour, *Deadly Embrace*, pp. 93–108.
46. Coronel Ignacio Despujols, Estado Mayor, Informe del 28 de julio de 1923, in Real Academia de la Historia, *Archivo Romanones*, Leg. 58, Carp. 37.
47. Robert W. Reiber and Robert J. Kelly, 'Substance and Shadow: Images of the Enemy' in Robert W. Reiber (ed.), *The Psychology of War and Peace: The Image of the Enemy* (New York, London: Plenum Press, 1991), pp. 3–39.
48. From F. Franco, *Palabras del Caudillo 19 abril 1937–31 diciembre 1938* (Barcelona: Ediciones FE, 1939), p. 314.
49. Narciso Gibert, *España y Africa* (Madrid, n.p., 1912).
50. Queipo de Llano, 'Nuestro propósito' and 'El problema de Marruecos' in *Revista de Tropas Coloniales* no. 1 (January 1924) and no. 2 (February 1924).
51. José Ortega y Gasset, *La España invertebrada*, 15th edn (Madrid: Revista de Occidente, 1967), p. 82.
52. Balfour, *Deadly Embrace*, p. 183.

Index